EARLY JEWISH AND CHRISTIAN EXEGESIS

Scholars Press
Homage Series

Israelite Wisdom: Theological and Literary Essays in Honor of Samuel Terrien
> John G. Gammie, editor

Selected Papers of Lionel Pearson
> Donald Lateiner and Susan A. Stephens, editors

Mnemai: Clasical Studies in Memory of Karl K. Hulley
> Harold D. Evjen, editor

Classical Texts and Their Traditions: Studies in Honor of C. R. Trahman
> David F. Bright and Edwin S. Ramage, editors

Hearing and Speaking the Word: Selections from the Works of James Muilenburg
> Thomas F. Best, editor

Greek Poetry and Philosophy: Studies in Honour of Leonard Woodbury
> Douglas E. Gerber, editor

Nourished with Peace: Studies in Hellenistic Judaism in Memory of Samuel Sandmel
> Frederick E. Greenspahn, Earle Hilgert, and Burton L. Mack, editors

EARLY JEWISH AND CHRISTIAN EXEGESIS

Studies in Memory of William Hugh Brownlee

edited by
Craig A. Evans
and
William F. Stinespring

Scholars Press
Atlanta, Georgia

EARLY JEWISH AND CHRISTIAN EXEGESIS
Studies in Memory of William Hugh Brownlee

edited by
Craig A. Evans
and
William F. Stinespring

Library of Congress Cataloging in Publication Data

Early Jewish and Christian exegesis.

(Homage series ; no. 10)
Bibliography: p.
1. Bible—Criticism, interpretation, etc.,
2. Bible. O.T.—Criticism, interpretation, etc.,
Jewish. 3. Bible—Criticism, interpretation, etc.,
History—Early church, ca. 30-600. 4. Brownlee,
William Hugh. I. Brownlee, William Hugh.
II. Evans, Craig A. III. Stinespring, William F.
IV. Series. III. Series.
BS511.2.E26 1987 220.6'09'015   86-31394
ISBN 1-55540-108-2 (alk. paper)

Printed in the United States of America
on acid-free paper

TABLE OF CONTENTS

Early Jewish and Christian Exegesis:
Studies in Memory of William Hugh Brownlee

FOREWORD

WILLIAM HUGH BROWNLEE (1917–1983)

This volume of essays in honor of William Brownlee takes the place of a *Festschrift* his unexpected death did not provide time to produce. His colleagues and pupils wish in this way to honor a scholar whom they learned to admire professionally and love personally, and who is very much missed among us.

Prof. Brownlee did his doctorate at Duke University under William Stinespring. It is itself a poignant indication of the untimeliness of his death that his doctoral father functions as co-editor of this memorial volume.

Brownlee had the good fortune at the beginning of his academic career to spend just the right year at the American School of Oriental Research in Jerusalem, the year in which the Dead Sea Scrolls surfaced. Indeed he had the added good fortune that the Director was away on a field trip when the first scrolls were brought to the School, and thus Brownlee (together with another beginning scholar at the School that year, John Trever) was the first to examine, identify and recognize the importance of the manuscripts that they were shown.

Brownlee's scholarly career was decisively altered by this experience. His dissertation on Ezekiel did not in fact point the direction of his work to come, but Ezekiel had to wait its turn. He ultimately published his interpretation of Ezekiel in an encyclopaedia-length article for the new edition of *The International Standard Bible Encyclopedia.* And it was as a labor of love for his retirement years that he was working on a two-volume commentary on Ezekiel for Word Books at the time of his death. The typescript was sufficiently complete for the first volume, containing Chapters 1–19, to have been edited by Leslie Allen and Gerald Keown and published posthumously in 1986.

Thus Brownlee's professional career was largely devoted to translating and interpreting the Dead Sea Scrolls. He prepared the *editio princeps* of the Habbakuk Commentary, *The Dead Sea Scrolls of St. Mark's Monastery, 1: The Isaiah Manuscript and the Habakkuk Commentary,* 1950, followed by a monograph on the text, *The Text of Habakkuk in the Ancient Commentary from Qumran,* 1959, reprinted 1978, and finally a commentary on that commentary as the first volume in his Dead Sea Scrolls Project of the Institute for Antiquity and Christianity,

The Midrash Pesher of Habakkuk: Text, Translation, Exposition with an Introduction, 1979. His general introduction to the Dead Sea Scrolls, *The Meaning of the Qumran Scrolls for the Bible,* 1964, provided his overall assessment of the discovery. A large part of his teaching throughout his career was devoted to the minutiae of the Dead Sea Scrolls, as his voluminous file of notes on practically every text eloquently documents.

After a brief pastorate in Newton, Kansas and a beginning professorship at the Divinity School of Duke University, Brownlee had become in 1959 the first Professor of Religion at Claremont Graduate School, which, with this appointment, launched its doctoral program in Religion. Brownlee served that institution the rest of his professional career.

Brownlee's year in Jerusalem was at the time when the British were releasing their control over Palestine and the state of Israel was coming into existence. The tender sensibilities of the divinity student from Sylvia, Kansas were hardly prepared for the hard realities of the street battles, terrorism, sniping and casualties that were all too common in Jerusalem at that time. With the American School of Oriental Research on the Arab side of the Mandelbaum Gate, he had first-hand experience of the Arab experience of that period of crisis, and for the rest of his life devoted a considerable amount of his time, emotion, and writing to the Arab cause in Palestine.

JAMES M. ROBINSON
CLAREMONT GRADUATE SCHOOL, AND
THE INSTITUTE FOR ANTIQUITY AND CHRISTIANITY

PREFACE

The sudden illness and death of Professor William H. Brownlee came as a shock to us all. It seemed appropriate to me and to others who knew him that a collection of scholarly papers should be published in his honor and memory. His Claremont colleagues Professors James A. Sanders, Rolf P. Knierim, John C. Trever, and James M. Robinson responded with immediate interest and support, without which this volume could never have been realized.

Most of the contributors to this volume are either former colleagues or former students of the late Professor Brownlee, while those who are not were long-time friends or scholars with common interest. To all of them I owe a debt of gratitude. I also wish to record a special word of thanks to Professor William F. Stinespring for agreeing, early on in the project, to be co-editor with me. His support, suggestions, and contacts were very helpful. George J. Brooke is to be commended for compiling Professor Brownlee's bibliography, and Richard A. Wiebe, Research Librarian at Trinity Western University, for preparing the indices to this volume.

A word of appreciation is also due Conrad Cherry and Dennis Ford of Scholars Press for their encouragement and support. Naturally, apart from many generous financial contributions such a volume as this could not be published. With this in mind I would like to express special thanks to Louise Brownlee and family, to the Claremont Presbyterian Church, to James A. Sanders and the Ancient Biblical Manuscript Center, to John C. Trever and the Dead Sea Scrolls Project, to George J. Brooke and the University of Manchester, to James R. Butts and Le Moyne College, to Scholars Press, to A. S. Barker, and to many of my students. I would also wish to record my thanks to my academic dean, Dr. Kenneth R. Davis, who provided me with both funds and encouragement.

Langley
August 1986

C. A. EVANS

IN MEMORIAM: WILLIAM H. BROWNLEE

W. F. STINESPRING
PROFESSOR EMERITUS
Duke University

It was good to learn that there will be a memorial volume for Bill Brownlee. He was among the very first of my approximately twenty-five Ph.D. products and certainly one of the best. I was studying at Yale under C. C. Torrey when Torrey published his very controversial book, *Pseudo-Ezekiel and the Original Prophecy* (1930). After receiving the Ph.D. in 1932, spending three years at the American School of Oriental Research in Jerusalem in archaeological study and field work, and teaching Bible courses at Smith College for one year, I was called to Duke University in 1936.

In a little less than a decade, Brownlee appeared at Duke for further graduate study, having received his theological degree at Pittsburgh-Xenia Theological Seminary. He said that he had become interested in the manifold problems of the book of Ezekiel and would like to do a master's thesis on that subject to present to his seminary. I asked him if he had seen Torrey's book. He said that he had read it, was much impressed by it, but felt that he could make a further contribution to the subject. I agreed to let him try his hand. In due time he wrote the thesis, presented it in Pittsburgh, and received a Th.M. degree.

He remained at Duke and asked me to guide him in a doctoral dissertation that would continue his study of Ezekiel, which he was thinking of making the main interest in the scholarly career which he hoped would lie ahead. I agreed, and the result was a success for both of us. Even the members of the examining committee who were not biblical scholars were impressed. This was in 1947. Dr. Brownlee then followed my own pattern and went for a year's post-doctoral study at the American School of Oriental Research in Jerusalem, where he became involved with the newly-discovered Dead Sea Scrolls, as Professor Robinson has said in his Foreword to this volume.[1]

With my new responsibility for directing doctoral study I needed assistance. Dr. Brownlee was invited to return to Duke as an assistant professor, my assistant particularly. One of my favorite courses was in

[1] For numerous details see Millar Burrows, *The Dead Sea Scrolls* (New York: Viking Press, 1955) chapter 1.

advanced Hebrew that included the reading and exegesis of Deutero-Isaiah. Of course I immediately turned over this course to Professor Brownlee, since he had come to us bearing one of the only two existing photographic copies of the Great Isaiah Scroll.[2] So Brownlee told the students that they could keep their Masoretic texts for comparison, but could also read from an older and probably better version. Thus Duke in 1948 may inadvertently have become the first university to have a class reading Dead Sea Scrolls material.[3]

The next thing that I recall in this connection was Bill's concern with translating and interpreting the Habakkuk scroll. Sometimes he would call me on the telephone, even rather late at night, to get my opinion on a new interpretation at which he had arrived after many hours of struggle with a difficult passage. Soon he had put so much effort on the scrolls that he regretfully postponed his cherished plan to devote all of his spare time to the Ezekiel problem. He now felt that it was his duty to biblical scholarship to help to elucidate the meaning of these "new" old documents. The result is known. In the next eleven years at Duke he became one of the outstanding authorities in this field.[4]

But he became also a good teacher, much honored by his students, and very helpful to me in building up Old Testament study at Duke University. Bill spent eleven very fruitful years of teaching and scholarship at Duke. All five of his children were born at Durham. In all of his endeavors he was ably supported by his good wife, Louise, and he was very proud of his family.

Then came the call to Claremont. This meant a major decision for Bill and Louise. We agonized over it together. I insisted that he and Louise must make the decision alone, because I was not a disinterested party. I was very happy in having him as a helper and colleague in the work that I was trying to build up at Duke, yet I realized the advantage to him of an opportunity to help build a new program at Claremont and to stand as an independent scholar in his own right. After many hours of soul-searching at home and in my office, he decided to go. This book is one of the numerous testimonies to his success in the new work.

He always remained loyal to me and was concerned to send me from time to time copies of his articles and books, as well as news about the

---

[2] See *The Dead Sea Scrolls of St. Mark's Monastery, Volume I: The Isaiah Manuscript and the Habakkuk Commentary* (ed. Millar Burrows with John C. Trever and William H. Brownlee; New Haven: American Schools of Oriental Research, 1950).

[3] The bulk of Brownlee's researches on 1QIsaiah[a] may be found in his *The Meaning of the Qumrân Scolls for the Bible with Special Attention to the Book of Isaiah* (The James W. Richard Lectures in Christian Religion, University of Virginia, February, 1958; New York: Oxford University Press, 1964) esp. 155–259.

[4] See the bibliography provided in this volume, especially from 1948 on.

growth and careers of his children—all of which I gladly received. His last letter to me, in 1981, told of his prospective retirement in 1982 at the age of 65, which should give him the time to complete and publish his long-delayed commentary on Ezekiel,[5] and in addition, he hoped, another book on the Qumran Scrolls, a book on Daniel, and still another on Isaiah, provided of course, as he said, "if the Lord gives me health and a sound mind." He mentioned that he had already completed a long article on Ezekiel,[6] a copy of which he later sent me, as well as a typescript of his forthcoming study on Ezekiel's idiom, "Son of Man Set Your Face."[7] It was fitting that our final communication, like our first many years ago, concerned the prophet Ezekiel. That was my last word on him until the fateful announcement of July, 1983, from Claremont Graduate School that Bill had passed away.

I believe that Bill's influence will be a lasting one, both in terms of his fine scholarship, and in terms of the lasting memories of all who knew him.

---

[5] *Ezekiel 1–19* (Word Biblical Commentary 28; Waco: Word Books, 1986). This volume contains that part of the commentary finished by Dr. Brownlee.

[6] "Ezekiel," *The International Standard Bible Encyclopedia* (volume 2; ed. Geoffrey W. Bromiley; Grand Rapids: Eerdmans, 1982) 250–261.

[7] " 'Son of Man Set your Face,' Ezekiel the Refugee Prophet," *HUCA* 54 (1983) 83–110.

BIBLIOGRAPHY OF THE WRITINGS OF WILLIAM HUGH BROWNLEE

Compiled by GEORGE J. BROOKE*

1945

"The Minister's Use of the Original Languages," *Christian Horizons* 8 (1945–46) 7–10.

1946

The Major Critical Problems in the Book of Ezekiel, Th.M. Thesis, Pittsburgh-Xenia Theological Seminary, 1946, v + 181 pp.

1947

The Book of Ezekiel: The Original Prophet and the Editors, Ph.D. Thesis, Duke University, 1947, vi + 455 pp.

1948

"The Jerusalem Habakkuk Scroll," *BASOR* 112 (1948) 8–18.

1949

"Further Light on Habakkuk," *BASOR* 114 (1949) 9–10.
"Further Connections on the Translation of the Habakkuk Scroll," *BASOR* 116 (1949) 14–16.

1950

The Dead Sea Scrolls of St. Mark's Monastery, Volume 1: The Isaiah Manuscript and the Habakkuk Commentary, edited by Millar Burrows with the assistance of John C. Trever and William H. Brownlee, New Haven: American Schools of Oriental Research, 1950, xxiii pp. + 61 plates.
Program for the Exhibition of the Ancient Hebrew Scrolls at Duke University, Durham, N.C.: Duke University Library, 1950, 8 pp.
"The Original Height of the Dead Sea Habakkuk Scroll," *BASOR* 118 (1950) 7–9.
"A Comparison of the Covenanters of the Dead Sea Scrolls with Pre-Christian Jewish Sects," *BA* 13 (1950) 49–72.
"Exorcising the Souls from Ezekiel 13:17–23," *JBL* 69 (1950) 367–73.

1951

The Dead Sea Manual of Discipline: Translation and Notes, BASOR Supplementary Studies 10–12, New Haven: American Schools of Oriental Research, 1951, 57 pp.
The Dead Sea Scrolls of St. Mark's Monastery, Volume 2, Fascicle 2: Plates and

---

*I am most grateful to Donn Michael Farris, Librarian of Duke University Divinity School, for help in locating several items in *The Duke Divinity School Bulletin*.

Transcription of the Manual of Discipline, edited by Millar Burrows with the assistance of John C. Trever and William H. Brownless, New Haven: American Schools of Oriental Research, 1951, 11 plates.

"Excerpts from the Translation of the Dead Sea Manual of Discipline," *BASOR* 121 (1951) 8–13.

"Biblical Interpretation among the Sectaries of the Dead Sea Scrolls," *BA* 14 (1951) 54–76.

"Light on the Manual of Discipline (DSD) from the Book of Jubilees," *BASOR* 123 (1951) 30–32.

"The Text of Isaiah VI 13 in the Light of DSIa," *VT* 1 (1951) 296–98.

Review: J. Patterson, *The Praises of Israel* (New York: Charles Scribner's Sons, 1950), *DDSB* 16 (1951–52) 60–61.

1952

"The Historical Allusions of the Dead Sea Habakkuk Midrash," *BASOR* 126 (1952) 10–20.

"The Manuscripts of Isaiah from which DSIa was Copied," *BASOR* 127 (1952) 16–21.

"Benediction from the Dead Sea Manual of Discipline," *DDSB* 17 (1952–53) 2–3.

"The 'New' Bible," *DDSB* 17 (1952–53) 69–71.

1953

The Dead Sea Habakkuk Midrash and the Targum of Jonathan, Durham, NC.: Duke Divinity School, 1953, 12 pp.

"The Servant of the Lord in the Qumran Scrolls I," *BASOR* 132 (1953) 8–15.

"The Cross of Christ in the Light of Ancient Scrolls," *The United Presbyterian* 111/48 (1953) 6–7, 11; 111/49 (1953) 11; 111/50 (1953) 7–8; 111/51 (1953) 12–13; 111/52 (1953) 10–11.

1954

"Certainly Mašaḥti!" *BASOR* 134 (1954) 27–28.

"The Servant of the Lord in the Qumran Scrolls II," *BASOR* 135 (1954) 33–38.

"Emendations of the Dead Sea Manual of Discipline and Some Notes concerning the Habakkuk Midrash," *JQR* 45 (1954–55) 141–58.

"Discoveries in the Judean Wilderness," *Land Reborn* 5/5 (1954) 8–10.

"The Christ as 'Salvation' in the Light of Ancient Scrolls," *The United Presbyterian* 112/46 (1954) 6–7; 112/47 (1954) 12–13.

"The Christ as the 'New Law' in the Light of Ancient Scrolls," *The United Presbyterian* 112/48 (1954) 10–11.

"The Christ as 'Our Righteousness' in the Light of Ancient Scrolls," *The United Presbyterian* 112/49 (1954) 12; 112/50 (1954) 10, 13.

Review: H. H. Rowley, *The Zadokite Fragments and the Dead Sea Scrolls* (New York: Macmillan, 1952), *JR* 34 (1954) 309–10.

Review: K. Elliger, *Studien zum Habakuk-Kommentar vom Toten Meer* (BHT 15; Tübingen: J. C. B. Mohr, 1953), *JBL* 73 (1954) 255–56.

Review: F. A. W. van't Land and A. S. van der Woude, *De Habakuk-rol van ʿAin Fašḥa, tekst en vertaling* Semietische teksten met vertaling I; Assen: Van Gorcum, 1954), *JBL* 73 (1954) 256.

Review: J. T. Cleland, *The True and Lively Word* (New York: Scribner, 1954), *DDSB* 19 (1954–55) 45–48.

Review: J. Bright, *The Kingdom of God* (Nashville: Abingdon, 1953), *DDSB* 19 (1954–55) 49.
Review: L. Wallis, *Young People's Hebrew History* (New York: Philosophical Library, 1953), *DDSB* 19 (1954–55) 49–50.

1955
"Emendations of the Dead Sea Manual of Discipline and Some Notes concerning the Habakkuk Midrash," *JQR* 45 (1954–55) 198–218.
"John the Baptist in the New Light of Ancient Scrolls," *Int* 9 (1955) 71–90.
"The Incarnation in the Light of Ancient Scrolls," *The United Presbyterian* 113/5 (1955) 12–13, 15.
Review: J. Klausner, *The Messianic Idea in Israel* (New York: Macmillan, 1955), *DDSB* 20 (1955–56) 49–50.
Review: Ed. G. A. Buttrick and others, *The Interpreter's Bible Volume 4* (Nashville: Abingdon, 1955), *DDSB* 20 (1955–56) 80.

1956
"The Habakkuk Midrash and the Targum of Jonathan," *JJS* 7 (1956) 169–86.
"Importance of the Dead Sea Scrolls," *The Duke Chronicle* 51/37 (1956) 2–3.
"Scrolls and New Testament Interpretation," *The Duke Chronicle* 51/38 (1956) 2, 7.
"The Scrolls Solve Many Enigmas," *The New Republic* 134/15 (1956) 21–22.
"My Eight Years of Scroll Research," *DDSB* 21 (1956–57) 68–81.
"Messianic Motifs of Qumran and the New Testament I," *NTS* 3 (1956–57) 12–30.
Review: G. Vermes, *Les Manuscrits du Désert de Juda* (Tournai: Desclée, 1953), *JBL* 75 (1956) 157–59.
Review: A. Parrot, *The Flood and Noah's Ark, The Tower of Babel* (Studies in Biblical Archaeology 1 & 2; New York: Philosophical Library, 1955), *DDSB* 21 (1956–57) 28.
Review: R. E. Hough, *The Ministry of the Glory Cloud* (New York: Philosophical Library, 1955), DDSB 21 (1956–57) 54.
Review: H. Wheeler Robinson, *The Cross in the Old Testament* (Philadelphia: Westminster, 1955), *DDSB* 21 (1956–57) 54.
Review: R. S. Cripps, *A Critical and Exegetical Commentary on the Book of Amos* (London: SPCK, 1955[2]), *DDSB* 21 (1956–57) 55.

1957
"John the Baptist in the New Light of Ancient Scrolls," *The Scrolls and the New Testament* (ed. K. Stendahl; New York: Harper & Brothers, 1957; London: SCM, 1958; reprinted Westport, Conn.: Greenwood, 1975), 33–53, 252–56.
"Messianic Motifs of Qumran and the New Testament II," *NTS* 3 (1956–57) 195–210.
"Muhammad ed-Deeb's Own Story of His Scroll Discovery," *JNES* 16 (1957) 236–39.
Review: Ed. G. A. Buttrick and others, *The Interpreter's Bible Volumes 5 and 6* (Nashville: Abingdon, 1956), *DDSB* 22 (1957–58) 18–19.
Review: H. A. Bosley, *Sermons on the Psalms* (New York: Harper Brothers, 1956), *DDSB* 22 (1957–58) 30–31.
Review: A. Parrot, *Nineveh and the Old Testament, St. Paul's Journeys in the*

Greek Orient (Studies in Biblical Archaeology 3 & 4; New York: Philosophical Library, 1955), *DDSB* 22 (1957–58) 54.

Review: G. E. Wright, *Biblical Archaeology* (Philadelphia: Westminster, 1957), *DDSB* 22 (1957–58) 86.

Review: E. Würthwein, *The Text of the Old Testament* (New York: Macmillan, 1957), *DDSB* 22 (1957–58) 87.

Review: A. Parrot, *The Temple of Jerusalem* (Studies in Biblical Archaeology 5; New York: Philosophical Library, 1955), *DDSB* 22 (1957–58) 89.

1958

"Ezekiel's Poetic Indictment of the Shepherds," *HTR* 51 (1958) 191–203.

Review: T. H. Gaster, *The Dead Sea Scriptures in English Translation with Introduction and Notes* (Garden City, N.T.: Doubleday Anchor, 1956), *JBL* 77 (1958) 383–86.

Review: Ed. G. A. Buttrick and others, *The Interpreter's Bible Volume 12* (Nashville: Abingdon, 1957), *DDSB* 23 (1958–59) 61–62.

1959

The Text of Habakkuk in the Ancient Commentary from Qumran, Journal of Biblical Literature Monograph Series 11, Philadelphia: Society of Biblical Literature and Exegesis, 1959, viii + 130 pp.; reprinted with minor corrections and revisions, 1978.

"The Priestly Character of the Church in the Apocalypse," *NTS* 5 (1958–59) 224–25.

Review: G. Vermes, *Discovery in the Judean Desert* (New York: Desclée, 1956), *JNES* 18 (1959) 102–103.

Review: P. Wernberg-Møller, *The Manual of Discipline Translated and Annotated with an Introduction* (STDJ 1; Leiden: E. J. Brill, 1957), *JBL* 78 (1959) 175–76.

1960

Review: P. Wernberg-Møller, *The Manual of Discipline Translated and Annotated with an Introduction* (STDJ 1; Leiden: E. J. Brill, 1957), *JNES* 19 (1960) 56–57.

1961

Review: K. Schubert, *The Dead Sea Community: Its Origins and Teachings* (New York: Harper, 1959), E. F. Sutcliffe, *The Monks of Qumran as Depicted in the Dead Sea Scrolls* (Westminster, Md.: Newman, 1960), *JBL* 80 (1961) 278–80.

1962

"Maccabees, Books of," *The Interpreter's Dictionary of the Bible* (Volume 3, K–Q; ed. G. A. Buttrick and others; Nashville: Abingdon, 1962), 201–15.

"The Literary Significance of the Bisection of Isaiah in the Ancient Scroll of Isaiah from Qumran," *Trudy Dvardtsat Pyatogo Mezhdunarodnogo Kongressa Vostokokovedov* (Tome 1; Moscow: Tzolatel'stvo Vostochnoi Literatary, 1962), 431–37.

"Edh-Dheeb's Story of His Scroll Discovery," *RevQ* 3 (1961–62) 483–94.

Review: J. van der Ploeg and others, *La Secte de Qumrân et les Origines du*

Christianisme (RechBib 4; Brussels: Desclée de Brouwer, 1959), *JBL* 81 (1962) 190–94.

1963
"Cave," "Dead Sea," "Habakkuk," "Mourning Customs," *Dictionary of the Bible* (ed. J. Hastings; revised by F. C. Grant and H. H. Rowley; New York: Charles Scribner's Sons; Edinburgh: T. & T. Clark, 1963), 129b, 204b, 355–56, 679–80.

"The Placarded Revelation of Habakkuk," *JBL* 82 (1963) 319–25.

"The Scroll of Ezekiel from the Eleventh Qumran Cave," *RevQ* 4 (1963–64) 11–28.

"The 11Q Counterpart to Psalm 151, 1–5," *RevQ* 4 (1963–64) 379–87.

"Some New Facts Concerning the Discovery of the Scrolls of 1Q," *RevQ* 4 (1963–64) 417–20.

Review: M. Mansoor, *The Thanksgiving Hymns Translated and Annotated with an Introduction* (STDJ 3; Leiden: E. J. Brill, 1961), *JBL* 82 (1963) 461–62.

1964
The Meaning of the Qumrân Scrolls for the Bible with Special Attention to the Book of Isaiah, The James W. Richard Lectures in Christian Religion, University of Virginia, 1958, New York: Oxford, 1964, xxi + 309 pp.

1965
Reader's Guide for the Song of Solomon, Bible Readers' Service Guide OT 22, Nashville: Abingdon, 1965, 5 pp.

Reader's Guide for Ruth, Bible Readers' Service Guide OT 23, Nashville: Abingdon, 1965, 5 pp.

1966
"Foreword," *Treasure of Qumran: My Story of the Dead Sea Scrolls* (by A. Y. Samuel; Philadelphia: Westminster, 1966) 9–21.

"Le Livre grec d'Esther et la Royauté Divine," *RB* 73 (1966) 161–85.

"A Light to the Nations," *Adult Teacher* 19/9 (1965–66) 9–19.

"The Significance of 'David's Compositions'," *RevQ* 5 (1964–66) 569–74.

1967
"Excavation at Shechem; manuscript discoveries in Jordan and Israel," *Year Book of the American Philosophical Society*, 1967, 472–76.

"Letter to the Editor," *Christian Century* 83/36 (1967) 1130.

1968
"Jesus and Qumran," *Jesus and the Historian* (ed. F. F. Trotter; Philadelphia: Westminster, 1968) 52–81.

1970
"The Dead Sea Scrolls," in J. M. Robinson and others, "The Institute for Antiquity and Christianity," *NTS* 16 (1969–70) 193–94.

"The Aftermath of the Fall of Judah according to Ezekiel," *JBL* 89 (1970) 393–404.

"An Announcement Published by the Department of Antiquities of Jordan and the archaeologists Dr. William H. Brownlee and Dr. George E. Mendenhall regarding the decipherment of Carian Leather Manuscripts found in 1966 in the Hebron area, the Hashemite Kingdom of Jordan," *Annual of the Department of Antiquities* 15 (Amman: Department of Antiquities, 1970) 39–40, plates 1–3.

1971

"The Book of Ezekiel," *The Interpreter's One-Volume Commentary on the Bible* (ed. C. M. Laymon; Nashville: Abingdon, 1971) 411–35; reprinted in an edited form in *The Major Prophets* (Interpreter's Concise Commentary 4; Nashville: Abingdon, 1983) 233–306.

"The Composition of Habakkuk," *Hommages à André Dupont-Sommer* (ed. A. Caquot et M. Philonenko; Paris: Librairie d'Amérique et d'Orient Adrien-Maisonneuve, 1971), 255–75.

"Why do you think there is little mention of Jesus' life from the time he was born until the time he was baptized?" *What did the Bible mean?* (ed. C. A. Frazier; Nashville: Broadman, 1971) 34–37.

"Philistine Manuscripts from Palestine?" *Kadmos* 10 (1971) 102–104 (with George E. Mendenhall and Yacoub Oweis).

"Philistine Manuscripts from Palestine? A Supplementary Note," *Kadmos* 10 (1971) 173.

"Psalms 1–2 as a Coronation Liturgy," *Bib* 52 (1971) 321–36.

1972

"Anthropology and Soteriology in the Dead Sea Scrolls and in the New Testament," *The Use of the Old Testament in the New and Other Essays: Studies in Honor of William Franklin Stinespring* (ed. J. M. Efird; Durham, N.C.: Duke University, 1972) 210–40.

"Whence the Gospel According to John?" *John and Qumran* (ed. J. H. Charlesworth; London: Geoffrey Chapman, 1972) 166–94.

"Two Elegies on the Fall of Judah (Ezekiel 19)," *Ex Orbe Religionum: Studia Geo Widengren* (Vol. 1; ed. J. Berman, K. Drynjeff, H. Ringgren; Studies in the History of Religions [Supplements to *Numen*] 21; Leiden: E. J. Brill, 1972) 93–103.

"Ezekiel's Copper Cauldron and Blood on the Rock," *For Me to Live: Essays in Honor of James Leon Kelso* (ed. R. A. Coughenour; Cleveland: Dillon/Liederbach, 1972) 21–43, 3 photographs.

"The Dead Sea Scrolls," *Annual Report 1969–70 and 1970–71: Bulletin of the Institute for Antiquity and Christianity* 3 (1972) 20–21.

1973

Rights and Wrongs in Palestine: The Theological Significance of the Gift of the Land, Beirut: The Near East Ecumenical Bureau for Information and Interpretation, 1973, 53 pp.

"Personal Opinion Versus Biblical Authority," *Should Preachers Play God?* (ed. C. A. Frazier; Independence, Mo.: Independence, 1973) 166–88.

Review: W. S. LaSor, *The Dead Sea Scrolls and the New Testament* (Grand Rapids: W. B. Eerdmans, 1972), *Int* 27 (1973) 484–86.

1974
Rights and Wrongs in Palestine, Simi Valley, Ca.: Middle East Fellowship, 1974, 21 pp.

1975
"Faith and Criticism are Allies," *What Faith Has Meant to Me* (ed. C. A. Frazier; Philadelphia: Westminster, 1975) 20–27.

1976
"Twenty-Five Years Ago," *BA* 39 (1976) 118–19; abbreviated form of "Biblical Interpretation among the Sectaries of the Dead Sea Scrolls," *BA* 14 (1951) 54–76.

1977
"The Cosmic Role of Angels in the 11Q Targum of Job," *JSJ* 8 (1977) 83–84.
"The Ineffable Name of God," *BASOR* 226 (1977) 39–46.

1978
"The Background of Biblical Interpretation at Qumrân," *Qumrân: Sa piété, sa théologie et son milieu* (BETL 46; ed. M. Delcor; Paris: Duculot; Leuven: University Press, 1978) 183–93.
"Ezekiel's parable of the watchman and the editing of Ezekiel," *VT* 28 (1978) 392–408.

1979
The Midrash Pesher of Habakkuk: Text, Translation, Exposition with an Intro-duction, Society of Biblical Literature Monograph Series 24, Missoula: Scholars, 1979, ix + 220 pp.; in the review by J. H. Charlesworth in *RelSRev* 7 (1981) 83 there are numerous corrections supplied by Brownlee himself.

1981
"The Dead Sea Scrolls," *The Institute for Antiquity and Christianity Report 1972–80* (ed. M. W. Meyer; Claremont, Ca.: The Institute for Antiquity and Christianity, 1981) 13–14.

1982
"Ezekiel," "Gilgal," *The International Standard Bible Encyclopedia* (Volume 2, E–J; ed. G. W. Bromiley and others; Grand Rapids: W. B. Eerdmans, 1982) 250–61, 470–72.
"The Ceremony of Crossing the Jordan in the Annual Covenanting at Qumran," *Von Kanaan bis Kerala: Festschrift für Prof. Mag. Dr. J. P. M. van der Ploeg O. P.* (AOAT 211; ed. W. C. Delsman, J. T. Nelis, J. R. T. M. Peters, W. H. Ph. Römer, A. S. van der Woude; Neukirchen-Vluyn: Neukirchener, 1982) 295–302.
"The Wicked Priest, the Man of Lies, and the Righteous Teacher—the Problem of Identity," *JQR* 73 (1982–83) 1–37.

1983
The Rights of the Palestinians, Public Affairs Series 22, Moral Appeals Con-cerning Palestine 1, New York: Americans for Middle East Understanding,

1983, iv + 50 pp. including an introductory In Memoriam by J. C. Trever and D. Meyers.

The Lion that Ravages Palestine, Public Affairs Series 23, Moral Appeals Concerning Palestine 2, New York: Americans for Middle East Understanding, 1983, iv + 38 pp. including an editorial foreword by J. C. Trever and D. Meyers.

"From Holy War to Holy Martyrdom," *The Quest for the Kingdom of God: Studies in Honor of George E. Mendenhall* (ed. H. B. Huffmon, F. A. Spina, A. R. W. Green; Winona Lake: Eisenbrauns, 1983) 281–92.

"'Son of Man Set Your Face,' Ezekiel the Refugee Prophet," *HUCA* 54 (1983) 83–110.

Review: M. P. Horgan, *Pesharim: Qumran Interpretations of Biblical Books* (CBQMS 8; Washington: The Catholic Biblical Association of America, 1979), *JBL* 102 (1983) 323–27.

1984

Israel and The Ten Commandments: An Appeal to the Conscience Based Upon The Modern History of Palestine, Public Affairs Series 24, New York: Americans for Middle East Understanding, 1984, 77 pp. including an introductory In Memoriam by J. C. Trever.

1985

"'The Anointed Ones of Aaron and Israel,'—Thesis, Antithesis, Synthesis," *Mélanges bibliques et orientaux en l'honneur de M. Mathias Delcor* (AOAT 215; ed. A. Caquot, S. Légasse, M. Tardieu; Neukirchen-Vluyn: Neukirchener, 1985) 37–44.

1986

Ezekiel 1–19, Word Biblical Commentary 28, Waco: Word Books, 1986.

To appear:

"Kittim," *The International Standard Bible Encyclopedia* (Volume 3; ed. G. W. Bromiley and others; Grand Rapids: W. B. Eerdmans).

Abbreviations used in Brownlee Bibliography

AOAT   Alter Orient und Altes Testament
BA   *Biblical Archaeologist*
BASOR   *Bulletin of the American Schools of Oriental Research*
BETL   Bibliotheca ephemeridum theologicarum lovaniensum
BHT   Beiträge zur historischen Theologie
Bib   *Biblica*
CBQMS   Catholic Biblical Quarterly—Monograph Series
DDSB   *Duke Divinity School Bulletin*
HTR   *Harvard Theological Review*
HUCA   *Hebrew Union College Annual*
Int   *Interpretation*
JBL   *Journal of Biblical Literature*
JJS   *Journal of Jewish Studies*
JQR   *Jewish Quarterly Review*
JNES   *Journal of Near Eastern Studies*
JR   *Journal of Religion*
JSJ   *Journal for the Study of Judaism*
NTS   *New Testament Studies*
RB   *Revue biblique*
RechBib   Recherches bibliques
RelSRev   *Religious Studies Review*
RevQ   *Revue de Qumrân*
STDJ   Studies on the Texts of the Desert of Judah
VT   *Vetus Testamentum*

PART ONE

THE FUNCTION OF SCRIPTURE
IN THE OLD TESTAMENT

Customs, Judges, and Legislators in Ancient Israel[1]

ROLF P. KNIERIM

School of Theology at Claremont, and
Claremont Graduate School
Claremont, California

Introduction

The important role which the subject of law plays in virtually all the parts of the OT literature seems to be known only among the experts but not generally—save for the Jewish community. The fact of that role indicates that ancient Israel ranks prominently in the genealogy of human societies for which public law was a major mechanism to becoming and remaining orderly and civilized. It is important that we recognize this place of ancient Israel in the history of civilization, not only because we understand ourselves as a civilized society based on law, but also because we read the Bible. The Bible is a theologically oriented book. But any understanding of the Bible that ignores the OT's attention to societal realities, public life, and certainly public law, faces major problems with the Bible's and our own theology.

In the following, I cannot afford to discuss all the aspects of each reference to law in the OT. Instead I want to focus with selected examples on some of the major aspects concerning our topic and on some of the major problems in interpretation. These aspects and the related problems concern above all the areas of legislation, adjudication, ethical instruction, and societal custom in as much as they affect these areas and their relationship among one another.

The entire subject is loaded with problems, and I cannot avoid laying out some of those problems before you even as I shall attempt to put some of the pieces of the puzzle together. Of the greatest urgency is the question of how the various areas of Israel's legal, ethical, and customary life are interrelated. Because of that open question any approach to the

[1] In memory of William H. Brownlee, a meticulous scholar and gracious person, with whom I had the distinct privilege to be closely associated for almost two decades in the OT division at the Claremont Graduate School and the School of Theology at Claremont, and whose premature death I shall forever deplore.

With only minor changes, this paper reflects the style of the oral presentation given on April 2, 1985 as the second William H. Brownlee memorial lecture at Claremont under the sponsorship of the Institute for Antiquity and Christianity.

subject, be it anthropological, sociological, or historical, is possible and at the same time relative. It is for this reason that my approach is pragmatic. I shall begin with what we may say with a higher degree of certainty, and move on to what is more and more difficult to interpret.[2]

I. *The Courts and the Judges*.[3]

A. In Ancient Israel, legal cases were adjudicated in courts and by judges. This fact is in many ways and frequently documented. The terminology, the legal, historical, and prophetic literature, and even the Psalms and the Wisdom literature mention judges and their activities; and they narrate or portray legal disputes and trials in courts as well.

B. We have quite a number of narratives about trials and legal disputes and negotiations. Most prominent among them are the stories about Jacob and Laban in Gen 31:25–54, Shechem and Dinah in Genesis 34, Judah and Tamar in Genesis 38, Moses, Jethro, and the Israelites in Exod 18:13–27, the Israelite who committed blasphemy in Lev 24:10–23, the daughters of Zelophehad in Num 27:1–11, Achan in Joshua 7, the concubine of a Levite in Judges 19f., Boaz and Ruth in Ruth 4, Saul and Jonathan in 1 Samuel 13f., Saul and Samuel in 1 Samuel 15, Saul and David in 1 Samuel 24 and 26, David and Nathan in 2 Samuel 12, Ammon-Tamar and David-Absalom in 2 Samuel 13f., Solomon and the two women in 1 Kgs 3:16–28, Rehoboam and the northern tribes in 1 Kings 12, Naboth's vineyard in 1 Kings 21, the trial of Jeremiah in Jeremiah 26, and others.[4]

To be sure, none of these stories was written in the form or for the sake of a trial-protocol. They all were written under different and varying intentions. They reflect the court proceedings only in part and indirectly.[5] Nevertheless, they reveal that their writers presupposed the

---

[2] In view of the fact that this paper is more problem- than history of research-oriented, bibliographical notes are kept to a minimum. My bibliographical catalogue on the subject approaches the four thousand plateau.

[3] For convenient introductions, see the articles in lexica on the subject, and especially: R. De Vaux, *Ancient Israel* (2 vols.; New York: McGraw-Hill, 1965); H. J. Boecker, *Redeformen des Rechtslebens im Alten Testament* (WMANT 14; 2. Aufl.; Neukirchen-Vluyn: Neukirchener, 1970); D. Patrick, *OT Law* (Atlanta: John Knox, 1985); W. Malcolm Clark, "Law," *OT Form Criticism* (ed. J. Hayes; TUSMR 2; San Antonio: Trinity University, 1977) 99–139.

[4] Many more texts show a legal background, e.g. the Joseph novella in Genesis 37–45, and from the primeval history of Genesis 3–11 on, the entire OT is pervaded in language and perception by the legal dispute or trial between God and humans, especially God's people.

[5] Cp. on this problem now C. Mabee, "The Problem of Setting in Hebrew Royal Judicial Narratives" (Claremont: Claremont Graduate School, 1977) and B. Long, *1 Kings: with an Introduction to Historical Literature* (FOTL 9; Grand Rapids: Wm. B. Eerdmans, 1984).

existence of such judicial proceedings and a corresponding understanding on the part of their readers.

C.   The picture of the judicial events unfolding before our eyes is very diverse. This diversity results on the one hand from the changes throughout a millennium of Israel's court-institutions, and on the other hand from the variety of typical court-settings or -forms.[6]

1.   The most pervading court-forum was the *family* or *clan* in which the *pater familias* was the legal head endowed with the right and obligation to adjudicate intra-family disputes and violations, including the execution of punishment such as, e.g., the chastisement of a disobedient son (Deut 21:18), and in early times possibly even the death-penalty as in the Judah-Tamar story (Genesis 38).[7] When Sarai was treated contemptuously by her maid Hagar and appealed to Abram to rectify the injustice done to her, just read Gen 16:1–6 to see how fast Abram restored justice.

2.   Another court-setting was the *village-* or *town-* forum. Its location was the "gate in the city" and the judiciary consisted of the elders of the place.[8] These elders functioned as witnesses in negotiations as in the marriage of Ruth to Boaz. They arbitrated disputes between litigants, as is indicated by one of the meanings of the Hebrew word for "to judge," namely "to arbitrate," and by much additional evidence. And they proclaimed judgments in criminal cases including at times the death-penalty (which is documented in Deut 21:18–21), the Naboth story, and the story of Jeremiah's trial.

3.   The individual *tribes* do not seem to have been a regular judicial forum. We still know too little that is definitive about the tribal organization of Israel before the monarchy. It is not impossible, however, that the minor and major judges in the book of Judges who are said to have judged Israel were in fact judges who administered justice in their respective tribes on behalf of the Israelite confederacy. We may likewise assume that on occasion several tribes or their representatives functioned as a judicial forum in a case of pan-Israelite interest, as in the case of the rape of the concubine of a Levite by the Benjaminites, and certainly in the cases of the elections of Saul and David as king (1 Samuel 11; 2 Samuel 5).

4.   There can be no doubt that once the monarchy was established, the

---

[6]That history can to some extent be reconstructed. The major difficulty in this regard lies in the historical distance of many texts from the conditions which they describe, and in the possibility that they reflect a picture of their past from the ideas or conditions of their own time just as much, if not more, as from that past itself.

[7]In later times, the right to execution was obviously taken away from the *pater familias*, as Deut 21:19–21, among others, shows.

[8]Cp. H. J. Boecker, *Law and the Administration of Justice in the Old Testament and Ancient East* (Minneapolis: Augsburg, 1980) 31.

royal court itself became a judicial setting presided over by the king as
the supreme judge. This fact is so well known that it need not be
belabored at this point.

5.   In the discussion of Israel's jurisdictional authorities, one institution
often falls by the wayside: the sanctuary and the priests. The neglect of
this institution is far-reaching and unwarranted. Not only does it ignore
an additional jurisdictional setting; it suggests on our part a picture of the
structure of the Israelite society as a whole which is based—as we would
say—on the separation of church and state. It portrays a structure in
which the cultic sector either had nothing at all to do with jurisdiction or
in which jurisdictional competences were a strictly intramural affair,
subject to but not part of the law of the land.

Such an understanding is indefensible. Indeed, our texts precisely
portray the opposite picture for all the periods of Israel's history. The
sacred realms of the sanctuaries, certainly of the two temples in Jerusalem, were subject to laws and regulations and their supervision, enforcement, and treatment in cases of violation. This jurisdiction was in the
hands of the priests, and lastly in cases of royal sancturies such as Bethel
(Amos 7:10–17) and the first temple in the hands of the kings. Josiah's so-
called cultic reform (2 Kings 23) is a vivid example. But the role of the
priests by far exceeded their jurisdictional authority over the realm of the
sanctuaries. It reached deeply into the lives of the people. They decided
about clean and unclean, i.e., the realms of taboo in daily life. They
administered the ordeal concerning adultery (Numbers 5) and presided
together with others over trials of complaint-petitioners, i.e., individuals
who under prosecution or threat to life had to submit their cases to cultic
adjudication.[9] They administered the temple entrance liturgies, which
dealt with the adjudication of the ethical conditions for admission to the
sanctuary as we learn especially from Psalms 15 and 24. They adjudicated
litigations at the sanctuary that otherwise could not be solved (Exod
22:9), played a role in trials for blasphemy (as in Jeremiah's trial) and,
together with other judges, in trials against persons accused of any sort of
crime. This list is by no means complete or fine-tuned. It only demonstrates that Israel's Yahweh religion was institutionally an intrinsic and
even a controlling part of the theocratic intentionality of Israel's societal
life. The jurisdictional authority of the sanctuaries and the priests, who
were primarily concerned with the affairs of that religion, made up a
prominent element of Israel's *overall* public legal institutions. This authority was part of and not a religious administration separate from and

---

[9]Cp. E. Gerstenberger, *Der bittende Mensch: Bittritual und Klagelied des
Einzelnen im Alten Testament* (WMANT 51; Neukirchen-Vluyn: Neukirchener,
1980).

under the law of the land. Law and justice were not invented by the prophets.

6.   I could go on speaking about the institutions of asylum, of lower and higher courts, courts of appeal, etc. Instead, I need to refer summarily to the judges associated with the types of courts just mentioned, and to the basic elements of court-proceedings.

D.   We should assume that the variety of identifiable court-systems reflects the complexity of the Israelite society virtually throughout its history. Accordingly, we can see that the competences of the different *kinds* of *judges* were essentially determined by the settings in which they functioned. The *patres familias* acting alone were confined to their families and properties. The *elders* of clans and local communities dealt with their communal affairs. There were *supra-local* and *circuit*-judges, such as Deborah (Judg 4:5) and Samuel (1 Sam 7:15–17), and perhaps judges functioning on behalf of the early confederacy (Judg 10:1–5; 12:8–15). There was in due time the king assisted by the princes and his advisors. There were the priests. We may also have to account for jurisdictional functions of military officers, civil leaders of the militia, and last but not least judges appointed by higher courts for lower courts (Exod 18:21–26; Deut 16:18–20; 2 Chr 19:4–11).

E.   The *proceedings* themselves vary, depending on the nature and setting of the occasion.

1.   In the cultic realm the ordeal of a woman suspected of adultery consisted of a specific procedure which is reported in Numbers 5 (for men, no such ordeal was "necessary"). The ritual for complaint-petitioners was very different. It can be reconstructed hypothetically.[10] The same is true for the temple entrance liturgy.

2.   As we come to the non-cultic judicial processes we see a difference between what we call civil and criminal cases. As long as no criminal acts were involved, all sorts of legal decisions were basically made directly through the agreement of the involved parties, sometimes in the presence of witnesses as the story of Ruth's marriage shows very nicely.[11] Where direct agreement could not be reached, which led to the call on a court in the first place, a judge or the court of elders arbitrated by proposing a settlement which was not enforced but had to be implemented by the parties themselves.[12]

---

[10] Cp. E. Gerstenberger, *Der bittende Mensch*, 147–151.

[11] Cp. still the classic by L. Köhler. "Justice in the Gate" in *Hebrew Man* (Nashville: Abingdon, 1956) 127–50. It must be noted, however, that the involvement of the elders in the gate changed when crimes had to be adjudicated.

[12] Cp. G. Liedke, *Gestalt und Bezeichnung alttestamentlicher Rechtssätze: Eine formgeschichtlich-terminologische Studie* (WMANT 39; Neukirchen-Vluyn: Neukirchener. 1971).

F.   The question of *enforcement* of judgments becomes more problematic when, in cases e.g. of theft, embezzlement, damage caused by negligence, rape, murder, not only compensation but also fine or penalty were stipulated. The execution of such judgments was by and large also left to the winner of a judgment; but it is unlikely that the community would not have been interested in the compliance with its judgments, or not accessible to protests against non-compliance.

In cases of murder, it was primarily the blood-avenger backed by the elders of a city who had the task of punishing a murderer (Deut 19:11–13). Manslayers had the chance to be protected in cities of refuge. In other types of capital crimes at least the major local communities, and possibly the clans before them, and certainly the royal administration executed their judgments themselves (Deut 19:15–21). This type of execution of a judgment is probably true for someone's expulsion from the community or the expulsion from the cultic congregation, the ban, and above all for the death-penalty (cp. Lev 24:10–23; Joshua 7; 1 Kgs 2:13–25; 1 Kings 21; Deut 21:18–21; 17:2–6; and others).

Important is the judicial function of the curse. The curse was most likely pronounced in cases where a crime had been committed which polluted the land and its community, and the criminal was either unknown or out of reach.[13]

G.   Finally, our texts know of pre-trial disputes, accusation, defense, investigation of evidence, witnesses, confession of guilt or plea of innocence, verdicts either as acquittal or conviction, and sentences following verdicts.[14]

II.   *The Legislators*

A.   To speak of legislators and legislation is problematic. In our modern context, these words refer to people and institutions that enact laws, new laws. Compared with this context, it is often pointed out that ancient Israel, and by and large the Ancient Near East, had no such legislative bodies; and that the ancient law is customary law. More specifically: the ancient Israelite laws are not legislation but descriptions or reports of decisions rooted in the customary judiciaries.[15]

---

[13] Cp., however, the interpretation by W. Schottroff, *Der Altisraelitische Fluchspruch* (WMANT 30; Neukirchen-Vluyn: Neukirchener, 1968).

[14] Cp. H. J. Boecker. *Redeformen;* H. Schulz. *Das Todesrecht im Alten Testament. Studien zur Rechtsform der MOT-JUMAT Sätze* (BZAW 114; Berlin: Alfred Töpelmann, 1969); G. Liedke, *Gestalt und Bezeichnung;* M. Clark, "Law" in Hayes, *OT Form Criticism;* R. Hutton, "Declaratory Formulae: Forms of Authoritative Pronouncement in Ancient Israel" (Claremont: Claremont Graduate School, 1983).

[15] Typical for this understanding is G. Liedke's interpretation of the casuistic laws, *Gestalt und Bezeichnung,* 19–100.

1.   I must confess that I have difficulties with this configuration of the ancient situation. There is certainly enough evidence that Israel's kings, the highest legal authorities in the land, proclaimed and enacted new laws, often prompted by and referring to a momentary situation.[16] King Jehu commands the Baal prophets to attend a sacrificial offering and says: "whoever is missing shall not live" (2 Kgs 10:19). Similar pronouncements are recorded for military commanders (1 Sam 11:7; 30:24), heads of clans (Gen 31:32; 44:9), and the tribal league (Judg 21:5).

2.   Most important, however, is the following: The well known fact that the Israelite and Ancient Near Eastern laws are rooted in customary decisions does not mean that such decisions could not be enacted legislatively, i.e., prescriptively, as laws. Such enactment does not constitute *new* law. It only represents the legislative *expression* of a *tradition* of adjudicated cases. And both the promulgation of laws as well as the pronouncements of judgments in courts are rooted in the legal custom. Both represent customary law. We should not assume that the practice of legislation was in ancient times confined to the enactment of *new* laws.

3.   The need for recognizing legislation as a specific legal activity emerges above all from the stylistic form in which a large number of the OT laws is expressed. I am referring to the so-called case law, as, e.g., "When a man strikes his slave, male or female, with a rod, and the slave dies under his hand—he shall be punished" (Exod 21:20). This case law consists of two parts: the statement of the case, and the statement of the consequence.

In the history of research, interpretation has created a problem when saying that these laws *are* customary decisions. In fact, they are *based* on customary decisions. They *reflect* judicial custom. However, that fact does not mean that they are *formulated* in the actual form of judgments pronounced at the end of the trials. I am speaking of two different forms of legal expression. Both state, or at least presuppose, the correspondence of case and consequence. However, one of them reports a case that has already happened, and stipulates the consequence to be implemented in the future, even though the *sequence* of the two statements may alternate. It says, as in the trial against Jeremiah: "This man does not deserve the sentence of death, for he *has spoken* to us in the name of Yahweh our God" (Jer 26:16).[17] This type of expression is spoken *after* a *past* action and *before* the consequence stipulated for the future. Its

---

[16] Cp. the material listed by Liedke, *Gestalt und Bezeichnung*, 120–138. The picture is probably broader than the evidence based on the limited texts shows.

[17] Both statements of this type may be made by the accusing party at the beginning or by the judges at the end of the trial, as in Jer 26:11. Also, the sequence in which both statements are made can be reversed. Decisive is the difference between the *report* of an actual case under accusation in court, and a possible case assumed for the future.

principal form of language is: *Because* you/he/she *have/has done*/not done this, the following *shall/shall* not happen.

By contrast, the other type of expression says: If you do this, the following shall happen. This type is—in variable forms—spoken or written not only before the stipulated consequence but also before the described action. This type of expression is clearly prescriptive, or legislative, in nature; whereas the other is clearly adjudicatory. Once we recognize this basic difference, we will find ample evidence for both legislative and adjudicatory language in the OT. And it should be clear that case law is not non-legislative because it rests on the customary adjudication of cases. Both types of expression, the adjudicatory and the legislative, are parts of case law which in turn rests for the most part on customary law.

4.   This distinction means that we must take a more specific look at the OT laws as legislation and the legislators behind it.[18] These laws are frequently documented and cover a wide range of substantive aspects. On occasion they also represent procedural law as in Deut 17:2–6 in the case of suspected apostasy. Here the rumor must be diligently investigated, the truth beyond doubt ascertained on the basis of at least two or three witnesses; and if proof is established, the convicted person must be taken to the city-gate and there executed by stoning which must be started by the witnesses themselves (cp. also Deut 13:12–18; 19:15–20; 21:18–21). Numbers 5 represents procedural law concerning the ordeal of the suspected adulteress. We should also consider the prescriptions for the procedure of the sacrificial rituals in Leviticus 1–7 as procedural law pertaining to the realm of the cult and dealing with the forensically understood elimination of guilt.

5.   It is also well known that these laws cover the areas of what one may call primary and remedial law. In primary law the statement of the *case* describes legal relationship, whereas the statement of the consequences prescribes the terms of that relationship, i.e., the rights and duties *before* violation.[19] E.g., Exod 21:2 says: "When you buy a Hebrew slave (legal relationship), he shall serve six years, and in the seventh he shall go out free, for nothing (in terms of that relationship)." In remedial law a hypothetically stated violation is followed by the definition of a remedy.

6.   Finally, the forms in which these laws are expressed greatly vary syntactically. Third person statements alternate with second person address forms. Conditional formulations such as "if, or when, a person does so and so," "a person who does so and so," etc., alternate with participial formulations such as "One striking a man so that he dies shall be put to

---

[18] Cp. my forthcoming paper, "The Problem of Ancient Israel's Prescriptive Legal Traditions."

[19] Cp. D. Patrick, *OT Law*, 23.

death" (Exod 21:12). These syntactical and stylistic variations occur in statements of both cases and consequences. The basic reason for this phenomenon lies in the different origins of individual laws or smaller groups of laws before they were combined in the larger corpora. But the difference, e.g. between the introductions "if a person . . ." and "when a person . . . ," also indicates a *logical* relationship of two juxtaposed laws, namely the subordination of one law under the preceding law. The Covenant Book is well known for this type of organization of the material.

7.   Now, however, we must directly address the question of *legislators* and the setting of legislation. And this is the area in which our knowledge is embarrassingly minimal. Part of the problem is methodological. Our texts give us very few, if any, direct clues about legislative settings. They tell us neither who the people were who gave us the legislative formulations that are contained in the Covenant Book, the laws in Deuteronomy, and the Holiness Code; nor even who gave us these law books themselves; nor in which settings these people operated. Yet we cannot avoid postulating such persons and their settings.

We are on relatively firm ground when referring to royal and priestly legislation. Clans may have been another setting. The oldest part of the Covenant Book in Exod 21:2–22:16 reflects, in my opinion, a tribal setting, most probably that of the tribe of Ephraim in the twelfth century. Specific data can throw a bit more light on the question, and a number of theories have been advanced.

8.   The one question, however, that needs urgent clarification concerns the *relationship* between the judges and the legislators, and between the judicial and legislative institutions. About this relationship we know virtually nothing. All that can be developed for the moment is a hypothetical scenario which lays out the options. The legal function of the *king* gives us a first clue. The king was both judge and legislator in personal union. Accordingly, the place where he acted in either function was the same: in principle the royal palace. However, the king acted in different *functions* when he pronounced either judgments or laws.

A similar scenario may be assumed for the priests at the sanctuary, even though the king's authority over a royal sanctuary must not be ignored.

If one draws analogy from these settings for the other legal settings, one would have to assume a legal system, or legal systems, in which the adjudicating and the legislative bodies were not separate but the same. In such a legal system the same body, while representing the authority of the respective community, alternated between its adjudicating and legislative functions, and that on the basis of its legal customs; and where necessary created new legal conditions through either judgment or law. Such a scenario would help us to understand better the interpenetration of judgments and laws in the case-laws, and also of new developments,

which include *changes* in decisions as well as in laws throughout the
process of ancient Israel's legal history.

The comparison of the laws in Deuteronomy with those in the
Covenant Book shows that such new laws, if only as updatings of older
ones, were indeed formulated.[20] And while it is true that the legislative
formulations originally evolved from decisions, we may have to account
for the possibility in principle that once legislative formulations were in
existence, adjudicating decisions could evolve from such legislation. We
may have to account for a two-way street process, a process in which
adjudication and legislation alternately influenced each other.

B.   Another basically unresolved problem associated with legislation
concerns our understanding of the so-called commandments. The ten
commandments are only the outstanding paradigm: you shall not commit
murder, etc. These commandments occur as individual statements, and
in smaller and larger series as well. Mostly formulated as prohibitions,
they are clearly not judicial pronouncements. Nor are they case laws.
They stipulate no consequences for their violation.

1.   The fact that for a long time they were called laws does not help
because that label reveals neither their original generic nature, nor their
function, nor their setting. And the assumption held for some time that
they represent the specific nature of *Israelite* law in contrast to the
Ancient Near Eastern case law has been discarded, too. The interpretation prevalent more recently says that they were originally *clan*-ethos,
and not law at all. But this assumption, too, is subject to scrutiny. And
again, we do not yet know the answer to our questions.

2.   In as much as these imperatives represent ethos we must admit that
one genuine matrix was the family or clan. The series of prohibitions that
forbids the sexual abuse of women-in-laws in Lev 18:6–18 is the clearest
example. In this matrix such prohibitions reflect the ethos of the *tradition* or the *customs* of clans and families, or of the primary groups. By
expressing what is forbidden these prohibitions *e silentio* presuppose the
traditional or customary ethos which respects the integrity of women.
"You shall not commit adultery" presupposes that according to the tradition you respect and honor marriage.

3.   However, imperatives were not only given in clans and families.[21]
They could originate in any societal setting in which an authority could
impose its will on invdiduals or groups or the entire society. In Exod

---

[20]Already M. Weber has given a vivid portrayal of this phenomenon in: *Ancient
    Judaism* (New York: Free Press, 1952; London: Collier McMillan, 1952) 61–89;
    reprinted from: *Archiv für Sozialwissenschaft und Sozialforschung*, 1917–1919.
[21]Cp. G. Fohrer, "Das sogenannte apodiktisch formulierte Recht und der Dekalog,"
    Studien zur alttestamentlichen Theologie und Geschichte (BZAW 115; Berlin:
    Walter de Gruyter & Co., 1969) 120–148.

23:1–9 we have a series of prohibitions that forbids corrupt behavior of jurors in the courts—in the city gate. And the series of ten commandments in Deuteronomy 5 par. Exodus 20 and Exod 34:11–26 originated most probably in the cult, and neither in the clan nor in the city gate.

Nor did imperatives always have to reflect *customary* ethos. They could reflect new situations. It is therefore important that we establish specific evidence from case to case about the specific setting of specific imperatives or jussives, a somewhat weaker form;[22] and also whether they reflect traditional ethos or new situations.

4.   The other question concerns the relationship between ethos and law. Is a command or prohibition only an *ethical* and not a legal instruction because its formulation contains no statement of sanctions for the case of violation? Is our definition of law exclusively based on a certain type of formulation? Or can commands or prohibitions also be *laws* the violation of which can be prosecuted? To be sure, not every commandment can be understood as law. It is difficult to prosecute the breach of a prohibition such as "You shall not hate your brother in your heart" (Lev 19:17). For such a prosecution, one would have to assume a psychoanalytically trained secret state police force which keeps constant checks on the mindsets of individuals.

5.   But what about a prohibition such as "You shall not commit murder" (Exod 20:13) and the parallel law that says: "One striking a man so that he dies shall be put to death" (Exod 21:12) let alone the rest of the legislation concerning the consequences for murder and manslaughter?[23] Do we have to assume that one statement is law and the other is not because of their different forms? And do we have to assume separate authorities and institutions, one instructing ethically and the other acting legislatively? The answer to these questions can scarcely be an unqualified yes. It is clear that in quite a number of instances, a substantive correlation exists between imperatives on the one hand and laws on the other.

This means that violations of some imperatives were prosecutable even though their formulations do not threaten prosecution. We have to assume that what is prosecutable and what is not, or what is legislative or merely ethical in nature, depends not so much on the *form* of *expression* as on the *content* of what is said in either expression, and furthermore on the authority of the promulgating bodies and on their resolve to exercise control over what they promulgate.[24]

6.   The problem can also be demonstrated by another telling example.

---

[22] Cp. W. Richter, *Recht und Ethos* (SANT 15; München: Kozusel, 1966), esp. Richter's reference to the place of the jussives in professional education.

[23] Cp. the discussion on this question by Schulz, *Das Todesrecht*, 5–84.

[24] One has to ask whether there was prosecution for violations of the prohibitions in the series Lev 18:6–18.

Jacob has an agreement with Laban that after seven years of service he could marry Laban's younger daughter Rachel. After the seven years there is a feast, and in the evening Jacob goes to his bride in the chamber only to discover the next morning that he had slept with Laban's *older* daughter Leah. When he confronts Laban over what he calls a deception, Laban answers: "It is not done thus at our place to give the younger before the firstborn" (Gen 29:26). This statement is, if anything, first of all an explicit reference to a custom, a marriage custom. Secondly, the formulation "It is not done thus . . ." is a parallel in the passive form to the active form of direct address: do not do it. It expresses binding ethos, even though impersonally. And thirdly, it expresses the binding custom- ary ethos of a local community, "at our place". This last point is interest- ing because it clarifies the difference between local and clan ethos. Jacob belonged to Laban's clan. *De facto*, Laban says to him: At your place of our clan, one may marry the younger daughter before the older, but not at our place of our clan. We have to realize that not only clans but also *local* communities were matrices for customary ethos.

7.   Is this ethos also legally binding? Laban may have tricked Jacob by not informing him at the outset about the local custom. But it is unlikely that he deceived him about the custom itself. It is more likely that he had no alternative because the custom was binding, and its violation would have had adverse consequences for him.

The case is even clearer in Gen 34:7 and 2 Sam 13:12 where we have the same formulation "Thus it is not done"—now—"in Israel". What is not done is the seduction or rape of a woman. In each of the two cases, the Shechem-Dinah and the Amnon-Tamar story, the violator of this ethos pays for his act with his life. Another case in which the legislative nature of an impersonal passive (Niphal) is quite evident from the context is the passage Exod 35:2 which reads "Six days shall work be done, but on the seventh day you shall have a holy Sabbath of solemn rest to the LORD; whoever does any work on it shall be put to death." Does this not mean that we must understand such a statement of customary ethos as a prohibition in a legislative sense?

Such an understanding of the problem means that we have to study *from case to case* what is ethos only in the imperatives, and where they are related to or actually represent legislation. Such study will inevitably involve intensive sociological and anthropological research in the fabric of ancient Israel's society, a large task ahead.

Conclusion

We have been concerned with the institutions of adjudication, legis- lation, ethos, and custom, and with the persons representing these institutions. How are these institutions related? This question involves a conceptualization of the societal reality of ancient Israel as a whole without which the individual institutions themselves can scarcely be understood adequately.

Should we assume that these institutions existed separately side by side, and that their representatives consisted of bodies of different persons? The discussion presented in this paper does not support such an assumption. Instead, we should assume a model according to which in each of the various societal entities—such as clan, city, supra-local districts, perhaps tribes, the realm of sanctuaries and the realm of the monarchy or later of the hierocratic administration (Ezra)—the adjudicatory, the legislative, the customary, and the ethical competences were integrally united and related, and they supported and influenced one another. Such a model does not so much suggest a strict unilinear evolution from imperative to judgment in court to legislation. But instead, it suggests a dynamic circle in which adjudication triggered legislation which in turn triggered adjudication, and in which ethos alternately triggered adjudication and legislation which in turn triggered ethical instruction and parenesis (as in Deuteronomy), and in which the societal entities themselves influenced each other.

As for people involved in the various communal entities, we would have to assume a *primary* model in which the same representatives of the communal authorities participated equally in instruction, adjudication, and legislation. Their various functions were expressions of the unity, integrity, and indivisible authority of their respective communities. Last but not least, this model implies the historical movement of Israel's institutions throughout the centuries. In this movement customs, courts, legislation, and ethical and legal instruction were changing. And while it is basically true that ethos, adjudication, and legislation reflected and were together rooted in the authority of custom, it is also true that in times of societal changes, *new* law, jurisdiction, ethos, and new customs emerged.

I have not attempted to portray the history of that movement. But there can be no doubt that the foundational assumption in any interpretation of Israel's legal and ethical institutions has to be this: that together with Israel's history, these institutions were constantly on the way from the old to the new, from the authority of the tradition to the significance of the new, even as in each new situation, the old and the new were critically merged. And thus, ancient Israel remained in the living interaction of customs, ethos, the courts, and law on the way from justice to justice.[25]

[25] I am indebted to Stephen Reed and Henry T. C. Sun, my research associates and senior OT Ph.D. students at Claremont Graduate School, for editorial assistance.

JUDICIAL INSTRUMENTALITY IN THE AHIMELECH STORY

CHARLES MABEE
Marshall University
Huntington, West Virginia

Law does not appear in the OT in isolation from its primarily religious interests and concerns.[1] Even so, one should not be led to the false conclusion that the legal sphere of ancient Israel's life had little or no impact on her religious thought and writings. In fact, the legal life of this society can be located close to the surface of the theological perceptions recorded in the OT. Far from being a completely artificial creation, it becomes increasingly obvious under careful exegesis, that the legal material found embedded in the OT was generated by the actual life of legal institutions,[2] even as this law was reshaped by later hands under theological suppositions.

The definition of the precise way that law and religion interrelate in the OT represents the central problem of OT legal research. Much of the problem has centered on the inability of the interpreters to find a methodology which adequately tackles the problem of the confluence of religious and legal conceptuality in OT texts.[3] Furthermore, it becomes

---

[1] "The authors of the Bible were theologians, and it is not surprising that they treated the law somewhat cavalierly," David Daube, "Law in the Narratives," in his *Studies in Biblical Law* (New York: Ktav, 1969) 25.

[2] For example, Bernard Jackson argues convincingly for the essentially literary tradition of the legal corpus of OT law. Nevertheless, he, correctly in my opinion, acknowledges the real legal world as a major source of this material. Cf. Bernard Jackson, "Reflections on Biblical Criminal Law," *JJS* 24 (1973) 11.

[3] For example, the potential for understanding the relationship revolved around the Hebrew conception of "covenant," widely discussed in recent years, has proven problematic methodologically. Aside from the difficulties inherent to the procedure of relating formal parallels (or near parallels) of ANE treaties to the OT, the age and complexity of the varied covenantal forms *within* the OT itself obstructs the construction of any paradigm of the relation of law and religion. Similarly, a second programmatic attempt of this century to mold an approach to the study of religion and law, found in the influential essay of Albrecht Alt entitled "Die Ursprunge des israelitischen Rechts," has proven ill-founded. Although a number of recent scholars have begun their separate investigations of OT law at the point of Alt's conclusions, none have found it satisfactory. Cf. Volker Wagner, *Rechtssätze in gebundener Sprache und Rechssatzungen im israelitischen Recht* (BZAW 127;

increasingly obvious to one who worries with such matters, that *meth-odology* is the key to the problem. The symbiosis of the two areas of concern penetrates to such a deep level that shoddy exegetical methodology cannot be passed off as an adequate tool for interpretation. As such, this paper will attempt to clarify programmatically how legal conceptuality is used in the service of the religion of the OT, by selecting the trial of Ahimelech (1 Sam 22:6–23) as a referential point.

In the analysis of the trial of Ahimelech one finds the aforementioned symbiosis of law and religion. Of course, in the case of a story such as this, these two components are wedded together by an unnamed narrator.[4] Therefore, with the establishment of the formal definition of the text to be discussed, we no longer can be satisfied with the general categories of "law" and "religion." We now reach the specific units of "judiciary" (legal operation) and "narrative" (religious stories). In this way, from the standpoint of form criticism, it may be said that one is confronted with the problem of setting in life *(Sitz im Leben)* at the heart of the exegetical process—namely, the setting of the legal sphere in which the text is grounded, and the setting of the narrator from which the text emerges. Because of the importance of this key component of OT form-critical research for our paper, it is instructive to pause and briefly review the current discussion with regard to it.

Since the work of Hermann Gunkel, the determination of the sociological or institutional setting in which a text is conceived and nurtured has played a constituent part in form-critical research.[5] Klaus Koch writes:

Berlin: de Gruyter, 1972); Erhard Gerstenberger, *Wesen und Herkunft des "apodiktischen Rechts"* (WMANT 20; Neukirchen-Vluyn: Neukirchener, 1965); Hermann Schulz, *Das Todesrecht im Alten Testament* (BZAW 114; Berlin: Topelmann, 1969); Willy Schottroff, *Der altisraelitische Fluchspruch* (WMANT 30; Neukirchen-Vluyn: Neukirchener, 1969). I have briefly reviewed these works from the standpoint of the question under consideration in Mabee, "The Problem of Setting in Hebrew Royal Judicial Narratives" (Ph.D. dissertation, Claremont Graduate School, 1977) 5–6, n. 1.

[4] Examples of such narratives are widely known from the ancient world. For a prime example of this kind of literature, see the so-called "Protests of the Eloquent Peasant" (ANET, 407–10).

[5] The best contemporary discussion of the role setting in OT exegesis, with paradigmatic illustrations, is given by Klaus Koch, *The Growth of the Biblical Tradition* (2d ed; New York: Charles Scribner's Sons, 1969) 26–38. Cf. also Gene Tucker, *Form Criticism of the Old Testament* (Philadelphia: Fortress Press, 1971) 15f. Jay Wilcoxen ("Narrative," in *Old Testament Form Criticism* [ed. by John H. Hayes; San Antonio, TX: Trinity University, 1974] 62f.) notes that the technical term *Sitz im Leben* was first used by Gunkel in his 1906 article, "Die israelitische Literatur." Cf. Wilcoxen's bibliography.

It was Gunkel who had the genius to perceive that one cannot usefully study a particular literary type without at the same time taking account of its proper setting in life. Apparently this realization came to him solely as the result of his study of the biblical material, and quite independent of general literary criticism. So it is not surprising that the *complete* involvement of a type with a setting in life became clear to him only gradually, and that the term 'setting in life' *(Sitz im Leben)* was a relatively late creation.[6]

However, the exact role of setting in form-critical methodology has yet to be completely defined and resolved. At the most elementary level, one notes that although the discipline of form criticism presupposes that every form does operate in a certain setting(s), the input that this setting has in the creation of the form itself varies considerably. For example, a form may be conceived strictly on the basis of setting (e.g., sermon); but far more frequently, the setting is only one of several considerations (e.g., the multiplicity of narrative forms).

Even more problematic than the above, is the fact that a piece of literature may comprise more than one so-called "pure" literary form.[7] Koch distinguishes between "component" and "complex" types of literature as follows:

> Therefore, whether in speech or in writing, there are *component literary types*, which build up into *complex literary types*. . . . The relation between a component type and a complex type may change over a period of time. Types can become merged, only later to divide again. . . . *Each exegesis must therefore not only define the literary type, but also discover whether this literary type is associated with other, perhaps complex, literary types.*[8]

He then adds, "The problem which arises out of this more complicated theory of literary types has not yet been thoroughly studied."[9] We may add to Koch's observations that when "complex" forms are studied, the additional question of setting is not far removed. Mixed literary forms *de facto* reflect the frequently divergent settings which stand behind them. In addition to Koch's "complex literary types", Wolfgang Richter has alluded to the phenomenon of so-called "nachahmende Gattungen" (imitative forms). These are forms which are secondarily constructed on

---

[6] Koch, 37.

[7] Cf. Gunkel, "Fundamental Problems of Hebrew Literary History," in his *What Remains of the Old Testament* (London: Allen & Unwin, 1928) 65f. Also see Wilcoxen, 95.

[8] Koch, 23f.

[9] Koch, 25.

earlier and more simple ones.[10] Implied here, also, is the idea that new settings may be involved in such a process. Finally, we may note that Rolf Knierim has conveniently summarized additional troublesome areas in the understanding and appropriation of setting as a critical tool of form criticism.[11] He calls attention to the fact that "setting" may be used as a single term to designate three different types of reality,[12] that there are different categories related to setting, and that "text-types"[13] can be used in various settings.[14] As such, Knierim rightly calls for an avoidance of a monolithic approach to the question of setting: "In sum, we should be able to apply the category of setting under the dictate of the manifold situations of texts, and not under a dogmatic concept of setting to which the interpretation of texts is subjected."[15]

We may conclude from this sketch of OT form-critical research, that the exact definition of the role of the sociological setting of a text in the creation of that text, has remained elusive. Most importantly, we must reckon with the phenomenon of a plurality of settings in some literary forms found in the OT. Narrative literature, of which our text is an example, by its very nature is particularly subject to this occurrence, and one should take this into account to complete the exegetical process. When the narrator relates his story, more than one setting *must* be involved (unless he tells a story set in the sociological setting of story-telling itself). The two settings are: (1) The setting(s) in which the story takes place, and (2) the setting of the narrator himself. The first of these settings may be designated the *depicted* setting, while the second refers to the *generative* setting in which the story is developed and nurtured (and, perhaps, created). It is the problem of the interaction between these two settings (depicted and generative) that gives rise to the primary exegetical problems relating to the trial of Ahimelech. When one reads the story of the trial carefully, one cannot simply presuppose its fac-tuality. Why? Not because one has a "liberal" view of biblical inspiration, or the like—but for a more fundamental reason. Because the text does

---

[10] Wolfgang Richter, *Exegese als Literaturwissenschaft* (Göttingen: Vandenhoeck & Ruprecht, 1971) 148.

[11] Rolf Knierim, "Old Testament Form Criticism Reconsidered," *Int* 27 (1973) 464ff.

[12] At this point Knierim elaborates the categorization of Richter (*Exegese als Liter-aturwissenschaft*, esp. pp. 145ff.). Knierim observes that settings may be institutional, a general "style of an age," or language itself.

[13] Cf. Knierim, 462f.

[14] Therefore, we find the phenomenon that one form may *reflect* more than one setting (complex forms), as well as the fact that one form may be *used* in more than one setting. It is, of course, the case that one setting can generate a number of forms. In general, see Richter, 148.

[15] Knierim, 462.

not have the earmarks of a *court report* (a verbatim account of the
proceedings with no narrative tendencies). In short, this story quite
readily yields a view of the two settings to which we have pointed. Here
we see that the basic task of the court reporter to relate a simple,
objective transcript of the judicial proceeding (to whatever degree we
may speak of such interests in ancient Israel) has been subsumed and
transcended by a schema born in the setting of the story-teller.

To gain an insight into the modus operandi of OT story-tellers, we
have analyzed the story of the trial of Ahimelech according to four basic
steps: (1) The delimitation of the narrative unit; (2) the narrative structure; (3) an expanded description of the judicial proceedings depicted in
the narrative; and (4) a concluding statement centered in the question of
narrative instrumentality, i.e., an evaluation of how the story is used by
the narrator *viewed from the standpoint of its judicial character.*

1. *The narrative context and unit.* Within the "narrative of the rise of
David" (1 Samuel 16–2 Samuel 1), the story of the trial of Ahimelech
stands as a major event in the ever-widening breach in the relationships
between Saul and Yahweh and Saul and David. The over-arching
story tells of the rapid rise to fame among the people of David which
follows upon the heels of the Goliath incident (chap. 17) and the subsequent intermittent notations of military success against the Philistines.
As a result of this success, Saul tragically begins to fall victim to jealousy
and suspicion with regard to David's political motives (beginning with
18:9). It is in the midst of the description of this deteriorating relationship
that the trial of Ahimelech takes place. David is now a fugitive from the
outstretched arm of royal might which seeks his elimination (19:1). Saul
himself is in charge of a bitter campaign to kill David (beginning at 19:22
with Saul's arrival at Ramah), in an attempt to remove the threat to the
throne which he perceives that David represents to himself and his son
Jonathan (20:31). Finally, chap. 21 tells of the aid David received from
Ahimelech the priest at Nob during this period of outlawry,[16] thereby
setting the backdrop for our own passage.

Chap. 22 opens with a terse, albeit graphic, description of what it
means to live on the run from Saul's forces. Verses 1–5 oscillate rapidly
between various locals where David and his family engage themselves in
their desperate attempt to remain outside the reach of Saul. The scene
and concerns switch quite abruptly at v 6. Now the reader is brought
back into the realm of Saul's activity and his interest in weeding out those

---

[16] For a detailed discussion, see H. Stoebe, "Erwägungen zu Psalm 100 auf dem
Hintergrund von 1 Sam. 21," in *Festschrift Friedrich Baumgärtel* (ed. J. Herr-
mann; Erlanger Forschungen 10; Erlangen: Universitätsbund Erlangen, 1959)
175–91.

in his midst who are in secret complicity with David.[17] The unit of vv 6–23 is itself divided into two major parts: vv 6–19 and vv 20–23. The setting and events with Saul at Gibeah is constitutive for the first part, while the escape of Abiathar to David is the focus on the latter. These two scenes are intimately related in that the second flows directly out of the first. Indeed, the establishment of Abiathar with David is central to the intention of the entire unit.[18] It is the narration of the first scene (vv 6–19) that uses judicial instrumentality, thereby becoming a fitting subject for a study of the problem of setting described above.[19]

2. *The Structure of the Text.*
    Episode of the Priests of Nob Before
    Saul and Its Consequence   1 Sam. 22:6–23

I. Before Saul	6–19
A. Setting the Scene	6
1. General	6a
2. Specific	6b
B. Before Saul	7–19
1. The Inquest	7–10
a. Saul's Complaint	7–8
1) Introductory Formula	7aα
2) Complaint Proper	7aβ–8
a) Sarcastic Reference	7aβ + b
b) Terms of Complaint	8
b. Doeg's Charges Against Ahimelech	9–10
1) Introduction	9a
2) Charges Proper	9b–10
a) Witness Report	9b
b) Allegations	10
(1) "he consulted Yahweh for him"	10aα
(2) "he gave him provisions"	10aβ
(3) "he gave him the sword of Goliath the Philistine"	10b

[17] This is in agreement with most commentators: Cf. H. Stoebe, *Das erste Buch Samuelis* (KAT: Gütersloh: Mohn, 1975) 407–16; H. Hertzberg, *I & II Samuel* (Philadelphia: Westminster Press, 1964) 185–9. However, it is not uncommon for vv 1–5 to be included with the priests of Nob pericope, e.g., G. Caird, "The First and Second Books of Samuel," in *IB* 2.1000–4; the drastic shift at v 6 which is essentially unconnected with vv 1–5 seems quite clearly to rule out this position.
[18] Cf. below in our concluding remarks.
[19] We may conclude our opening remarks by observing that the succeeding unit, 23:1–13, is a new episode centering on events of David and his men (including now Abiathar) at Keilah. This material stands as an independent unit and, thereby, falls outside the scope of our immediate interests.

As our structure indicates, v 6a is to be distinguished from v 6b in terms of the way these half-verses function in our unit. Verse 6a provides a

general introduction to the scene in that it relates that Saul heard *(šmᶜ)*
that the whereabouts of David and his men were known *(ydᶜ)*. Implied
here is the thought that this information was being withheld from the
King in a conspiracy of silence by those around him. On the other hand,
v 6b gives us the explicit setting for those events that transpire before
Saul. It is the departure of Abiathar from this setting that brings into
being the second major division of our pericope (vv 20–23).[20] Finally, we
may note that Abiathar's escape to David may carry out what is stated in v
6a. His immediate arrival on the scene before David seems to indicate
that David's whereabouts were known by those on friendly terms with
him.

3. *The Depicted Proceedings*

3.1   The Inquest (vv 7–10).

3.11   We have termed this section an inquest, for Saul's gathering
of his ᶜ*bdym* ("servants/advisers/ministers of state") begins an investigation into a matter that directly affects the interests and well-being of his
own office. Addressed in a general way to all of the aides gathered before
him, Saul initiates the proceedings by means of a complaint, censuring
them for "conspiring" *(qšr)* against him in his efforts to deal with the
threat which David poses to his administration (vv 7–8).[21] The first part of
the complaint is a sarcastic or ironical reference to the supposed power of
David (v 7aβ + b).[22] This accusing question in rhetorical style is followed
by the specific *terms* of the complaint of the inquest (v 8). This is
composed of two parts, each of which is centered on an alleged conspiracy of silence with regard to Jonathan's alliance with David. The corresponding structure of the two parts can be easily illustrated as follows:

---

[20] Saul's position under the Tamarisk with spear in hand undoubtedly denotes some
preunderstanding of official function on his part. H. Smith (*A Critical and Exegetical Commentary on the Books of Samuel* [ICC; New York: Scribner's Sons,
1904]205) draws a parallel to Deborah sitting under the palm to administer justice
in Judg 4:5. However, it is virtually impossible to separate entirely a political/
military role from a judicial one on the part of the king *at this point*. Hertzberg is
probably correct when he designates the setting with the neutral term
"assembly"; see Hertzberg, 186. A. F. Kirkpatrick (*The First Book of Samuel*
[Cambridge: University Press, 1984] 187) is a bit more graphic as he describes the
setting in terms of ". . . a solemn conclave met to deliberate on affairs of state or to
administer justice." Although it is impossible to treat v 6b strictly in terms of a
judicial setting, we conclude that judicial action may (and does) naturally grow out
of it.

[21] This is the only example in OT royal judicial narratives in which the judicial setting
is called into existence by this means.

[22] This seems to function as a narrative complement to the saying of the women at
18:7b; "Saul has killed his thousands, and David his tens of thousands."

First part—

> 1. *ky qšrtm klkm ᶜly*
> "that all of you have conspired against me
> *wᵓyn glh ᵓt ᵓzny bkrt*
> and not told me of the pact . . .

Second part—

> *wᵓyn ḥlh (ḥml) mkm*[23] *ᶜly*
> and none of you were sorry for me
> *wglh ᵓt ᵓzny ky hqym*
> and told me that my son has stirred
> up . . ."

The explicit wrong-doing of the *ᶜbdym* lies in the fact that they have not stepped forward to inform ("reveal to his ear") the king of the plotting of his son and David against him. Jonathan has covenanted with David, and aided him in setting an ambush against the king. All this without a word reaching Saul.[24] Such silence *must* denote conspiracy and corroboration. There is nothing in the complaint to indicate that Saul has any *proof* of specific acts against the *ᶜbdym*. Therefore, we are closer to the legal category of *allegation* or *complaint*, than *accusation*.

3.12 The second part of the inquest involves the response of the community to Saul's complaint, in this case represented by the person of Doeg (vv 9–10). Importantly, the form of this response takes the shape of further allegations, this time directed toward Ahimelech.

First, we should note that the narrative is quite careful to note that these allegations are brought by an Edomite,[25] a foreigner who "stood

---

[23] Stoebe decides against *ḥml*, which carries the meaning "to bear, become responsible" (BDB) or, "have compassion on" (K-B). Most, however, accept it, as Stoebe himself notes (Stoebe, *Samuelis*, 409). Hertzberg (*I & II Samuel*, 185) adopts *ḥml* with the English translation "support". Based on the generally parallel language and structure between the two parts, *ḥml* perhaps fits better with *qšr* than does *ḥlh*. In support of the former, note 1 Sam 23:21.

[24] J. H. Grønbaek (*Die Geschichte vom Aufstieg Davids* [Copenhagen: Munksgaard, 1971] 136) has an interesting discussion of this verse in terms of "eavesdropper motif." Hertzberg is off target with his observation that "Saul's brief speech chiefly contains accusations against Jonathan, . . ." (p. 187). The complaint is directed towards the servants, and not Jonathan.

[25] It is fitting that the allegations raised against one who aided the eventual heir to the Israelite throne be brought by a foreigner. Stoebe (*Samuelis*, 413) writes, "Für das Ganze ist es wichtig, dass es ein verhasster Edomiter ist, dessen Skrupellosigkeit Saul benützt und der das tut, was selbst die רצים verweigern; . . ." We first meet Doeg in 1 Sam 21:7(8) during David's initial visit to

by" (. . . *nzb ʿl*) the servants of Saul. The background of Doeg's allegations is narrated in the previous chapter. The allegations themselves are
introduced by a witness report: . . . . *rʾyty* ("I saw . . ."). Here Doeg
claims first hand knowledge of what he is about to speak, a fact
corroborated by 21:8. Subsequently (v 13), Saul simply assumes the
factuality of the allegations.[26] The three allegations stipulate that
Ahimelech aided David in the following ways: (1) Inquired of Yahweh,
(2) gave him provisions, and (3) gave him the sword of Goliath.[27] It is
obvious that the acts, in and of themselves, are not criminal in
nature. It is only when they are taken in the context of the antagonism
between the king and David which exists at this point in the narrative,
that they assume the criminal connotation of high treason. Saul's view is
that one who befriends or helps David is *de facto* an enemy of the crown
(and, hence, the state). This has already been seen in the previous
complaint with regard to Jonathan's alliance with David (v 8).

Doeg's allegations propel the course of judicial events in the direction
of the trial of Ahimelech. From this time onward the affair is strictly that
of the king himself (who acts as both prosecutor and judge) and the
defendant.[28] The king is determined to maintain the viability of the
existing royal order among his people. This is all the more true among
the priests of his realm.[29] It remains to be determined whether this

---

Nob. Here he is described as *ʿbyr hiʿym ʾšr lšʾwl*, "chief of Saul's guardsmen."
This is one of the ways that the narrative of 21:2–10 is joined to our pericope.
Compare Doeg's allegations (v 10) with the same narrative block. For an excellent
review of the literary-critical problems involved in the relationship between these
two pericopes see Grønbaek, *Geschichte*, 129–31. Cf. also Stoebe, *Samuelis*, 413–
14.

[26] Cf. 21:7(8). Doeg's position as "chief of the   " lends more weight to his
allegations. *rṣym* literally means "runners." In Deuteronomy they have the function of an elite guard attached to the person of the king or to the temple: 1 Kgs
14:27–28 (2 Chr 12:10–11); 2 Kgs 10:25; 11:4 (2 Chr 23:12), 6, 11, 13, 19. They
appear as executioners for the king against priests in 2 Kgs 10:25. For the
remainder of these texts, we may summarize by saying that they performed
individual tasks assigned to them either by the king or the chief priest (2 Kings
11). In 2 Chr 30:6, 10, they perform the function of couriers. The rendering of
Cross "henchmen" in the NAB does not seem etymologically appropriate.

[27] For the correspondence with Saul's accusation, note our discussion of the latter
below. Interestingly, of the three allegations, the first one is not mentioned in
chap. 21. Thus, the reader has no certain means of determining whether or not
Ahimelech should be viewed as having "consulted Yahweh" for David. Caird is
correct when he notes that the sole means of making a determination on this issue
lies with Ahimelech's subsequent reply (Caird, *IB*, 2.1001).

[28] Until we come to the final matter of implementing the judgment which is reached
in the trial.

[29] Our passage, of course, is a significant one for the task of determining the nature of
the priesthood in the OT. The major issues are raised in A. Cody, *A History of Old
Testament Priesthood* (AnBib 35; Rome: Pontifical Biblical Institute, 1969) 83–86.

order is maintained by an impartial arbitration of the allegations against Ahimelech, or by the despotic will of the sovereign.

3.2   The Trial: Prosecution of the Case (vv 12–16).

Verse 11 marks the transition from the inquest to the actual trial of Ahimelech. The trial commences upon the summons by the king of Ahimelech and "all the house of his father, the priests who were in Nob" (v 11). The first stage of the proceedings themselves we have termed the "call to attention" (v 12). Set within the judicial context, this brief element appears to have two functions. First, it alerts the defendant that charges have been made against him which will presently be made explicit in the accusation, and declares that the defendant is to stand before the supreme authority and face these charges. Secondly, the identity of the defendant is established for the formal proceedings to be brought against him.[30] Ahimelech's response *hnny 'dny* ("Here I am, my lord") marks his readiness to stand trial.

3.3   Accusation (v 13).

The accusation by the judge-prosecutor is composed of three parts. First, the legal significance of Ahimelech's aid to David is now made explicit by the king *within* the context of the trial setting. Ahimelech

---

Cody rejects Möhlenbrink's thesis of an underlying conflict existing between the priesthood of the "Shiloh-confederacy" and those of the "Gilgal-confederacy," i.e., Samuel vs. Saul, as a way to interpret the hostility reflected in our text. Cf. K. Möhlenbrink, "Sauls Ammoniterfeldzug und Samuels Beitrag zum Königtum des Saul," ZAW 58 (1940/41) 57–70. Such an interpretation presupposes that the Nob priesthood represents a continuation of the Elide priesthood established at Shiloh. Although this connection is normally accepted by scholars (including Stoebe, *Samuelis*, 416), recently Gunneweg has taken the position that the genealogy (1 Sam 14:3) is a later construction designed to bind the Zadokites with the Elides, and not of historical reliability. See A. H. J. Gunneweg, *Leviten und Priester* (FRLANT 89; Göttingen: Vandenhoeck & Ruprecht, 1965) 104–116, esp. p. 116. For an excellent recent discussion of the overall problem, viewed particularly from the perspective of David's choice of Abiathar and Zadok for the central sanctuary in Jerusalem, see F. Cross, *Canaanite Myth and Hebrew Epic* (Cambridge: Harvard University Press, 1973) 195–215. Regardless of the position which one assumes with regard to this question, the theme and intention of the narrative in its own right is unaffected. For it, the reason for the slaying of the priests of Nob is due to Ahimelech's crime against the state, as determined by Saul, as our analysis will indicate.

[30] This aspect of the call to attention seems to conform to 2 Sam 1:13, where the defendant is also executed. Hertzberg (*I & II Samuel*, 187) writes: "The very form of address, 'son of Ahitub', shows the seriousness of the situation." This is correct as far as it goes.

(along with David) is guilty of conspiring (*qšr*) against the king (v 13aβ). This is a statement which declares the criminality of the defendant's act.[31] We may say that Doeg's earlier allegations are "reinstituted."[32] Whereas Doeg had simply enumerated the things which he had seen Ahimelech do as a witness, Saul makes explicit the criminal result of these actions—high treason.[33]

The second part of the accusation delineates in specific terms those acts of the defendant which have been charged as criminal. These are given in the form of a paraphrase of Doeg's earlier allegations. A comparison of Doeg's allegations with Saul's accusation reveals the similarity between them, with only the order of the catena being at variance—

Doeg's allegations (v 10)	*Saul's accusation* (v 13)
"he consulted Yahweh for him	"Why have you conspired
he gave him provisions	. . . in giving him bread and a sword
he gave him the sword of Goliath the Philistine."	and consulting God for him. . . ?"

This coherence clearly unites the trial proceedings with the inquest which precedes it. Nothing new is added in the accusation by Saul. It is only the reinstitutionalization of the allegations that is new.

The accusation concludes with a statement that ties the allegations back to the initial statement of legal significance with which it opens. Specifically, the result of the defendant's actions is that David is able "to rise up against me (Saul) to lie in wait as this day." David is a threat to the existence of the king, and Ahimelech has aided and abetted him. The language here is nearly identical to the conclusion of Saul's opening

---

[31] This aspect of the proceedings is very similar to the declaration of crime which we find, for example, in 2 Sam 1:14 and 2 Sam 4:11a. The difference between them is that the facts are not positively known or proven in the present text, while they are (by means of the self-admission of the defendants) in the 2 Samuel texts. This is an extremely important distinction. One cannot *declare* crime or guilt until complicity is *established* by means of accepted judicial procedure.

[32] Cf., Mabee, "The Problem of Setting," 61, a discussion generated from a reading of Paul Bohnnan, "The Differing Realms of the Law," in his *Law and Warfare: Studies in the Anthropology of Conflict* (Garden City, NY: Natural History Press, 1967) esp. p. 48.

[33] Also noted by G. Macholz, "Die Stellung des Königs in der israelitischen Gerichtsverfassung," ZAW 84 (1972) 162. He designates the crime as *Hochverrat* or *Beihilfe zum Hochverrat*. Henry Black (*Black's Law Dictionary* [4th ed; St. Paul: West, 1968] 1672) defines treason as follows: "The offense of attempting by overt acts to overthrow the government of the state to which the offender owes allegiance; . . . ." *High* treason is "treason against the *king* or *sovereign*, ..."

complaint (v 8b). In both cases we find opening references to criminality qšr), followed by certain allegations, and concluded by the statement of the threat to the king's existence. This provides us with an excellent example of how *setting* alters the meaning of language, in this case *within the context of the depicted setting itself.* The initial complaint of Saul establishes the material constitution for the inquest. It evokes the allegations which Doeg levels against Ahimelech. But now, within the context of the trial setting, the accusation carries legal implications of the highest gravity. Whereas before, no single member of Saul's company stands specifically accused, now there exists one who is. The shift from inquest to trial, all under the umbrella of the judicial setting, reconstitutes the field of meaning for nearly the same words.

We may conclude our discussion of the accusation by again calling attention to the fact that it is rendered by Saul, the judge-prosecutor, rather than Doeg, from whom emanates the pretrial charge. OT royal judicial narratives are not uniform at this point. Plaintiffs or prosecutors may appear before the royal judge (e.g., 2 Sam 19:21), or the latter may assume this role himself. In the case of the present text, by the bare fact that it is Saul (rather than Doeg) that is the author of the "official" (i.e., within the context of the trial setting) accusation against Ahimelech, responsibility for the proceedings against him is all the more placed before him. This has increased importance in light of the overall bias against Saul present in the Saul/David complex.

3.4   Plea of Innocence (vv 14–15).

Ahimelech's defense is composed of two parts. First, he ascribes highest praise to David by pointing to his singular faithfulness among the king's servants (v 14b). In light of Saul's immediately preceding accusation, particularly the conspiracy with which the king sees David involved, this does not appear to be an expedient statement.[34] From a judicial standpoint, however, it is a well-conceived attack upon the heart of Saul's case. The crime of conspiracy (high treason) is explicitly denied by Ahimelech at this point, although he does not materially deny the allegations. Why should he have suspected David? How could he be accused of conscious criminality? Whatever help that Ahimelech might have afforded David would have been done with the most honorable of

[34] Of course, from the previous chapter, the reader knows that Ahimelech cannot deny the facts of the accusation. It is the intention of the narrative of David's rise to repeatedly manifest the righteousness of David. A confirmation of his innocence with regard to ill-will toward Saul by a priest of Yahweh accords itself very well with this perspective.

intentions. Why? Simply because David was known as the most trusted of Saul's servants. Therefore, it is the assumption behind the acts (treason), rather than the acts themselves that are denied.[35]

The second part of the plea of innocence complements the preceding general denial of the crime of conspiracy with a specific denial of the alleged act of "consulting God" on behalf of David (v 15).[36] Ahimelech's position is summed up at the conclusion of v 15b: . . . *l' yd' 'bdk bkl z't dbr* (". . . your servant knew nothing of this whole matter"). The first two allegations made by Saul (giving of *lḥm* and *ḥrb* to David) cannot be denied in light of chapt. 21, but the *criminality* of these actions is hereby implicitly denied. Of the three allegations, it is this "inquiring God" that is the most serious. Only here is the employment of the function of the priesthood at stake. This is not true of the other two allegations. It is for this reason that all the priests of Nob are implicated in the allegation, and that the question of high treason centers on the placing of their services at the disposal of David.

3.5   Judgment (v 16).

The pronouncement of judgment is made by the judge in the ancient judicial formula *mwt tmwt* "you shall surely die",[37] followed immediately by the identification of the party for whom it is intended (Ahimelech and "all your father's house"). Most importantly, from the standpoint of judicial instrumentality, the judgment is *not* substantiated. The only basis for this declaration of Ahimelech's death is the latter's own declaration of loyalty of David, given in v 14. His denial of the grounds for the accusation has *not been proven false,* because prior to that he would have to prove David's criminality. This is not a possibility in light of the pro-

---

[35] The general view of the commentators with regard to this part of the plea of innocence is not adequate from the judicial perspective. The plea is normally viewed in terms of Ahimelech's defense of his action in terms of good faith (Caird, *IB* 2.1002), denial of evil intent (Smith, *Commentary on the Books of Samuel,* 205), or compelling arguments (Hertzberg, *I & II Samuel* 187–8. While these characterizations are true, they fail to detect the more profound attack made upon the heart of Saul's accusation. That is, that the alleged acts are not denied, but rather the criminal intentionality with which they took place.

[36] The translation of *hywm hhlty lš'wl lw b'lhym* has proven problematic to scholars. Smith (*Commentary on the Books of Samuel,* 208) proposes the following sense for the phrase: "I have been accustomed to consult the oracle for David on his other expeditions, with your knowledge and consent; . . . ." A study of the word *hll* by P. P. Saydon ("The Inceptive Imperfect in Hebrew and the Verb *hll* 'To begin'," *Bib* 35 [1954] 47) shows that the verb may be used with the understanding "to do something for the first time." Saydon himself translates the phrase, "Is this the first time that I have consulted?"

[37] Cf. Schulz, *Das Todesrecht im Alten Testament.*

David tendency of the narrative of the rise of David. As a result, the case against Ahimelech does not stand up, but is supported solely by the iron will of the royal sovereign who has determined *in his own mind* (but not judicially) that David (and, hence, Ahimelech) is a criminal of the state. Stated more precisely, the narrative actually imputes *criminality* to Saul because of this unfounded judgment. In this way from this point on in the story of David's rise, Saul no longer has any *legal* claim to the throne. How could an unjust judge be king over Israel? The judicial narrative has provided the instrument by which this breach between Saul and his office can be dramatized most effectively.

3.6   Death Order (vv 17–19).

The death order which is initially addressed to the *rṣym* is not acceptable to them (v 17). Certainly this magnifies the inherent *illegality* of Saul's judgment. The refusal of the *rṣym* is a testimony that Saul has not allowed due process of law to run its course. We can only suppose that these functionaries would have complied with the death order *if* Ahimelech's criminality had been substantiated in the judicial setting.[38] It is the foreigner Doeg who accedes to the order. The slaying of the Nob priesthood becomes essentially a massacre of innocents, but with the spilled blood now washed from the hands of the Israelite Officials.[39]

4.   *Judicial Instrumentality in the narrative.* The judicial encounter of Saul with the priests of Nob marks the prominent event in the former's demise as an effectual ruler among his people, as narrated in the story of David's rise. The result of this savage massacre with the sword which takes place here is ostracism, not only from the Elide priesthood (as traced in the overall story), but also from his closest circle of functionaires *(rṣym)*. The spilling of innocent blood by Saul will eventuate in his own violent death by sword (1 Samuel 31, 2 Samuel 1). His only ally in the account (the one who brings the charges and performs the execution) is a

---

[38] Of course, this is a speculative statement as we cannot know what the text does not tell us. Yet, one is left with this distinct impression. For an opposing view see Smith, *Commentary on the Books of Samuel*, 208. He writes: "The soldiers refuse to carry out the command, owing to the sacred character of the accused." This is the natural interpretation if one does not see implications of judicial process involved.

[39] Numerous commentators have drawn attention to the quality of the *ḥrm* ("ban") at work in Doeg's destruction. A. F. Kirkpatrick (*First Book of Samuel* [Cambridge: University Press, 1984] 189) particularly, has pointed to the interesting contrast to 1 Samuel 15, where Saul *fails* to execute the *ḥrm* against the Amalekites. That is to say, Saul is portrayed as more vengeful against his own people than against foreigners. This is a preliminary stage in the narration of Saul's demise, of which our text is the culmination.

foreigner. The clear implications are that an irreparable rupture has occurred between Saul and the subjects of his kingdom.[40] Similarly, Saul's mindless pursuit of David has resulted in an irreconcilable split between these two which has now penetrated to the level of Saul's abuse of the judicial powers inherent in his office. We may conclude with this concise statement of the basic intention of the passage: The story relates how the priests of Yahweh at Nob were illegally slain (murdered!) by Saul; and how, as a result, the remnant of that priesthood came to be united with David. As such, the judicial instrumentality reflected in the story functions to indict *legally* Saul of the abuse of his royal power.

The interaction between the depicted setting (judicial) and the generative setting (narrative) has resulted in what we may term "narrative spill." By this we mean that the position of the king in the overarching narrative (story of the rise of David) has been severely altered, *just as conviction in a court of law alters one's position vis-a-vis society in real life*. That is to say, the mentality of the depicted setting has "spilled over" and has been utilized by the narrator for his own intentions and purposes. This is an art form of the highest order. Whereas a transcript of judicial proceedings would necessarily treat each of the parties in even-handed fashion, it is the king who stands in the center of the story we have discussed in some detail. In this latter instance, it is the role of the litigants (Ahimelech and the priests of Nob) to serve as props or supporting characters. For our narrator to have simply stated that "the king was guilty of murder in the instance of his slaying of the priests of Nob," or the like, would have been pale and ineffectual when compared with the telling of a story in which the reader "participates" in such a verdict. Now the reader is drawn into the story in such a way that he "must" be convinced of Saul's guilt, because he has "witnessed" it with his own eyes.

The conclusion is obvious that this story is a more faithful representation of the narrator's craft, than it is of the trial which it depicts. But, it is equally true that the narrator has remained faithful to the broad features of the judicial setting, because it is his desire to impute the mentality of this setting upon his own creation. Therefore, the "reliability" of the passage is grounded more in the narrator's desire to create "judicial reality" in his story, than it is in his interest for historicity.

---

[40] Caird, *IB*, 2.1003: "From this point it is but a short step to his downfall."

NARRATIVE PARALLELISM AND MESSAGE IN JEREMIAH 34-38

ELMER A. MARTENS
Mennonite Brethren Biblical Seminary
Fresno, California

The stylistic technique of narrative parallelism could be one of the keys to understanding the present arrangement of materials in the book of Jeremiah. The book is obviously not arranged chronologically. Even a topical grid is problematic. A typical sentiment is expressed by John Bright, who refers to a reader's difficulty with the book's arrangement or "apparent lack of arrangement . . . all seems confusion."[1] One could set aside the challenge of the book's organization as unimportant except that one cannot easily escape the notion that the message of the book is related to its structure. Besides, one is motivated to "break the code" if indeed there is a rationale to the book's ordering.

Helpful cues, such as "tradition complexes,"[2] inclusio and chiasmus,[3] and word and idea associations to form "cycles"[4] have been part of the recent scholarly discussion. Chiasmus, a form of parallelism has been advanced as a way of understanding the pre-history of certain parts of the narrative portion of Jeremiah.[5]

Given the penchant for parallelism in Hebrew poetry and prose, it is quite possible that larger narrative blocks of material in Jeremiah were intentionally arranged in parallel format. James Kugel observes that,

---

[1] John Bright, *Jeremiah* (AB; Garden City: Doubleday, 1965) lvi. His remarks about a topical arrangement for the book are found on lix. A. Weiser notes that chaps. 26–29 are partly chronological and that chaps. 30–33 are partly arranged by subject matter, but that there is no transparent principle of ordering discernible for chaps. 34–35; cf. *Das Buch Jeremia* (ATD; Göttingen, Vandenhoek & Ruprecht, 1969) xlii.

[2] T. R. Hobbs, "Some Remarks on the Composition and Structure of the Book of Jeremiah," *CBQ* 34 (1972) 257–275.

[3] Jack Lundbom, *Jeremiah: A Study in Ancient Hebrew Rhetoric* (SBLDS 18; Missoula: Scholars, 1975).

[4] W. L. Holladay, *The Architecture of Jeremiah 1–20* (Lewisburg: Bucknell University, 1976). The departure from a solely atomistic approach is to be applauded.

[5] A chiastic arrangement for a Jehoiakim cluster (chaps. 25, 26, 35, 36) is proposed by Lundbom, 107–109.

"Biblical parallelism—and still more so the 'seconding sequence' which is at its heart—appears in a great variety of contexts. While it is concentrated in the so-called 'poetic' books, it is to be found almost everywhere."[6] This essay investigates Jeremiah 34–38 for its organizing pattern and proposes that parallelism is the stylistic technique that accounts for the present arrangement of this one segment of the book.

Towards a Sensitivity to Parallel Patterns

W. H. Brownlee, to whose memory this essay is gratefully dedicated, alerted his students to the frequently unrecognized, yet pervasive role of parallelism. He suggested that entire books such as Isaiah could be helpfully understood as bifid compositions with parallel features. He elaborated his view in conjunction with the Isaiah Qumran scrolls in seeking an explanation for the gap between chapters 33 and 34 of the Isaiah scroll. "These two books of Isaiah [1–33; 34–66] are amazingly parallel in their overall structure and outline. . . ."[7] He also called attention to the parallel structuring in Ezekiel, 2 Maccabees, Mark, Revelation, and noted the pairing of some of Jesus' parables. Brownlee wrote, "I believe the love of parallelism to be characteristic of Hebrew literature, not merely in poetic verse structure, but also in larger units."[8] His provocative statement along with recent literature on parallelism gives impetus to the present investigation into Jeremiah.[9]

William Holladay, in a provocative essay on stylistic techniques, eschews the word "parallelism" since it has come to refer in restricted fashion to "semantic balance." He prefers the word "balance" to "parallelism." The term "balance" indicates "a correspondence or identification, of whatever sort, between any given components of poetry, whether they be units, cola, lines, or stanzas."[10] Balance, symbolized by A, A_1, or AB, A_1, B_1, differs from sequentiality A B C D. For our purpose balance and parallelism can be used interchangeably; neither term is limited to semantic considerations, or even to poetic components. Our concern is

[6] James L. Kugel, *The Idea of Biblical Poetry: Parallelism and Its History* (New Haven/London: Yale University, 1981) 59. Compare the reviews, e.g., Francis Landy, Wilfred C. E. Watson, and Patrick D. Miller Jr. in *JSOT* 28 (1984) 61–106.
[7] W. H. Brownlee, *The Meaning of the Qumrân Scrolls for the Bible With Special Attention to the Book of Isaiah* (New York: Oxford University, 1964) 247.
[8] Brownlee, 257.
[9] The probe into parallel structuring was more immediately occasioned for me by the preparation of a commentary on Jeremiah in the Believers Church Bible Commentary series: *Jeremiah* (Scottdale: Herald Press, 1986). Pa.
[10] William Holladay, "The Recovery of Poetic Passages of Jeremiah," *JBL* 85 (1966) 407.

not with parallelism of poetic lines but with a stylistic device, specifically the paralleling of prose units.[11]

Examples of parallel patterning, other than in lines of poetry, are more and more being identified. Moshe Greenberg writes of the "halving pattern," which he explains as follows: "A theme, A, is propounded in the first, usually longest, part of an oracle; it is followed by a second theme, B, which is somehow related to the first theme . . .; B characteristically ends, or is followed by a cola, with elements of A and B intermingled."[12] Robert Cohn has presented an illuminating example of parallelism in narrative. He develops the parallelism contained in I Kings 17–19 and shows how "parallel episodes build upon each other and thus generate a cumulative logic subliminally undergirding the narrative." He identifies a similar sequence of events, and points out the correspondences between the parallels. He concludes that from the carefully shaped story there emerges a powerfully nuanced theme, "the establishment of the reign of the God of Israel."[13]

Parallel patterning of larger blocks of material has been recognized in Jeremiah. Thomas Overholt observed a structure involving parallelism in 27–29. The first half, chapters 27–28, deals with the problem of false prophecy at home; the second half deals with the false prophecy in Babylon, chapter 29. Each of these parts describes the conflict of Jeremiah with the false prophets and in each the following sequences are discernible: message; negative response; resolution.[14] Larger poetic sections, such as the oracle against Babylon (chaps. 50–51), have both order and progression and exhibit a parallel format. Kenneth T. Aitken specifies the framework for these two oracles as follows.

A.	Introduction	50: 1–3
B.	Oracle Part I	50: 4–45
C.	Intermediate Conclusion	50:46
D.	Oracle Part II	51: 1–53
E.	Final Conclusion	51:54–58[15]

---

[11] "Stylistic analysis" is discussed relative to literary writing by H. G. Widdowson who comments, "What does seem crucial to the character of literature is that the language of a literary work should be fashioned into patterns over and above those required by the actual language system"; cf. *Stylistics and the Teaching of Literature* (London: Longman, 1975) 97.

[12] Moshe Greenberg, *Ezekiel 1–20* (AB; Garden City: Doubleday, 1983) 26. He notes that the halving pattern is the organizational principle in some of Ezekiel's oracles, such as chaps. 6, 7, 13, 16, 18, and 20 (See pp. 26–27).

[13] Robert Cohn, "The Literary Logic of I Kings 17–19," *JBL* 101 (1982) 334, 343, 350.

[14] Thomas W. Overholt, *The Threat of Falsehood: A Study in the Theology of the Book of Jeremiah* (SBT 2/16; Naperville: Allenson, 1970) 29–30.

[15] Kenneth T. Aitken, "The Oracles Against Babylon in Jer 50–51: Structures and Perspectives," *TynBul* 35 (1984) 25–63.

Structurally, as Aitken has shown, there are three major movements in each of the two parts. The parallel nature of the two parts is more implicit than explicit in Aitken's treatment. One example must suffice: there is a progression (using Aitken's structure and labels) in Part I from section A (50:4–20) to section C (50:33–46), just as there is a progression in the second half from section E (51:34–44) to section F (51:45–53). The progression, in Aitken's words, is from "Israel's return as a reversal of its fate at the hands of Babylon (Sections A and E) to Yahweh's ability to intervene, despite appearance to the contrary, as an encouragement to faith and hope (sections C and F)."[16] The two examples, one by Overholt in prose narrative and the other by Aitken in poetic material, signal parallel structuring as a fruitful field for investigation.

A striking example of narrative parallelism is found in Jeremiah 18–20. Both halves (chaps. 18 and 19–20) record symbolic action, the one of pottery-making and the other of pottery-smashing. The similar sequencing of the two parts has been identified by W. Thiel as follows: symbolic act and speech; scenic comment; persecution of the prophet; lament.[17]

In a summary formulation Thiel restates the parallel of composition between chaps. 18 and 19–20 as: occasion, judgment speech, persecution, lament. The messages in each part have a common core and share similar vocabulary. "Behold, I am shaping calamity" (yôṣēr rāʿâ, 18:11) and "Behold, I am bringing calamity" (mēbî . . . hārāʿâ, 19:15). Similarly the accusation about "stubborness of heart" (18:12) is matched by the phrase, "stiffening of necks" (19:15). The two laments each contain a prayer in which the prophet prays for vengeance on his enemies. The prayer for vengeance on the prophet's adversaries in chapter 18 is the longest and most biting of any of the laments (18:21–23).

The theme of the two parts is similar, if not identical. Both focus on the obstinacy of a people and the prophet's reaction. Each half describes how schemes were laid to silence the messenger (18:18; 20:1–2). Both stories highlight the prophet's reaction by concluding with a lament, as if to say, If Jeremiah the messenger is broken up and angry because of the people's non-listening and defiance, how much more must Yahweh be disconcerted with His people?[18] The unifying symbol, the potter's vessel, embraces the whole story of the people from the time of their

---

[16] Aitken, 61 and the diagram there.

[17] Winfried Thiel, *Die deuteronomistische Redaction von Jeremia 1–25* (WMANT 41; Neukirchen-Vluyn: Neukirchener, 1973) 219–229. Cf. Bright, 125; D. J. A. Clines and D. M. Gunn, "Form, Occasion and Redaction in Jeremiah 20" *ZAW* 88 (1976) 404; Timothy Polk, *The Prophetic Persona: Jeremiah and the Language of the Self* (JSOTSup 32; Sheffield: JSOT, 1984) 152–162.

[18] Cf. Polk (p. 154) who says, "Once again, the conflict between God and people in its manifold aspects is focused, crystalized, and held up to view in the life and person of the prophet."

shaping to the time of their smashing. Each narrative has a forceful message of its own, but the message is compounded in its impact by the juxtaposition of the two accounts and their parallelism. [19] Narrative parallelism in Jeremiah is not limited to chaps. 18–20. Two other examples are found in chaps. 34–35 and 36–38.

Narrative Parallelism in Jeremiah 34–35

There is at first glance little reason to place the story of a king's policies on slave-holding alongside a narrative about a clan which tenaciously observes a custom not to drink wine. Yet in these two chapters two narratives from disparate times are placed side by side. The first deals with King Zedekiah and his officials, who make a commitment to release their slaves, only to renege and to re-enslave them when the military danger has passed (34:8–22). The second incident, chronologically earlier, involves the semi-nomadic Recabite clan who refuse to drink wine (chap. 35). Closer examination discloses that these two stories have a similar structure and are built around an identical theme. They are paired deliberately with parallel patterned sequence and that for good effect. Conclusions such as these, however, beg for an exposition.

There is good reason for holding that these two chapters belong to a unit, which in turn is part of a larger unit that embraces Jeremiah 34–38. The break between chaps. 33 and 34 is quite distinct. Chap. 34 introduces a new historical context and a story line. Nebuchadnezzar king of Babylon and all his army were fighting against Jerusalem and all its surrounding towns. Such narrative material is easily differentiated from the preceding chapters (30–33) commonly known as the extended Book of Consolation and characterized by salvation oracles. Mention of Nebuchadnezzar's siege in 34:1 headlines a series of episodes, which, while chronologically disarranged, nevertheless are prelude to the succinct report of the catastrophe introduced in 39:1 with "This is how Jerusalem was taken."

Oracles of salvation for Judah are absent in chaps. 34–38, except that an isolated favorable promise is given to the Recabite clan (35:18–19). Accusations abound, followed by threats, as is characteristic of the prophetic judgment speech (e.g., 34:17; 35:15; 36:29). The five chapters are marked by narrative discourse. Names of people, dialogue, and action reports also distinguish these chapters from the immediately preceding material (chap. 33).

---

[19] Clines and Gunn (p. 404) have explored the significance of the juxtaposition of the lament and the Pashhur incident, even though, as they argue, the lament is not historically to be connected with the prose account which precedes it. The combination of 20:1–6 with 20:7–13 is redactional. Cf. also Polk, 157.

True, 39:1 continues with narrative. However, beginning with 39:1
the story is once again straightforward and chronological. It is not punctuated with prophetic exposés and tirades, at least not till the story line
moves beyond the catastrophe of Jerusalem's fall and the aftermath
(chaps. 39–41). Neither is the narrative in chaps. 39–45 punctuated by
flashbacks to earlier incidents from Jehoiakim's reign, as are chaps. 34–
38. In short, a distinct style of narrative sets chaps. 34–38 apart from the
preceding Book of Consolation and the subsequent newspaper-like report of Jerusalem's fall.

The proposal that chaps. 34–38 are an integral unit goes against
prevailing scholarly opinion.[20] It has become customary to speak of
"tradition complexes"; chap. 36 is said to conclude one such complex or,
according to others, to begin another.[21] Something new is said to begin
in chap. 37, where the story identifies Zedekiah as though for the first
time. The fresh introduction to Zedekiah and the information given about
him seem to signal a new section, and appear dislocated in the present
canonical arrangement, since Zedekiah has already featured prominently
in the preceding sections. If one is tracing the prehistory of the various
blocks of material in chaps. 34–38, then there is reason to distinguish new
headings, one of which is 37:1. Nevertheless, that chaps. 34–38 comprise
a unit *as the material now stands* is a position that is credible, not only
because of similar themes and the parallel structuring (to be explained
below), but also because of an *inclusio* feature.

The opening section (34:1–7) and the closing section (38:14–23) are
linked by the technique of inclusion.[22] The word to Jeremiah to be

[20] W. Rudolph can be representative of those who see disconnectedness in this block
of materials. He says (*Jeremia*, 3 Auflage, [HAT 12; Tübingen: Mohr, 1968] 220,
225), "Der Abschnitt [34:1–7] steht ganz für sich." "Auch dieser für sich stehende
Abschnitt [35:1–19]. . . ."

[21] Recent scholars follow Martin Kessler ("Form-critical Suggestions on Jer 36,"
CBQ 28 [1966] 389–401; "Jeremiah Chapters 26–45 Reconsidered," *JNES* 27
[1968] 81–88) who sees chap. 36 as climaxing and ending a "tradition complex"
begun in chap. 26. Cf. E. W. Nicholson, *Preaching to the Exiles: A Study of the
Prose Tradition in the Book of Jeremiah* (New York: Schocken, 1970) 105; Hobbs,
257–275. W. Thiel (*Die deuteronomistische Redaktion von Jeremia 26–45*
[WMANT 52; Neukirchen-Vluyn: Neukirchener, 1981] 38–61) links chap. 36 with
chaps. 34–35. He argues that the unit which then begins in chap. 37 extends
through chap. 41. Rudolph (p. 229), however, regards chap. 36 as beginning the
fourth and last part of the Baruch section.

[22] Theodore Hiebert ("God of My Victory: An Ancient Hymn of Triumph in Habakkuk 3" [Ph.D. Dissertation, Harvard University, 1984; Ann Arbor: University
Microfilms International, 8503536, 1985] 91), who demonstrates inclusion as the
defining structural technique for Habakkuk 3, explains: "Inclusion, also called
cyclic, envelope, or ring composition is a stylistic device with which the poet
effects closure by linking the beginning and end of a unit or sum unit of the
poem." N. Lohfink (*Lectures in Deuteronomy* [Rome: Pontifical Biblical Institute,
1968]) has discussed inclusion in the prose of Deuteronomy.

conveyed to King Zedekiah is a word given without specific context other than that Nebuchadnezzar is fighting against Jerusalem (34:1–7).[23]

These opening verses are set off from 34:8–22 where the word of God is addressed as a response to a specific incident, namely Zedekiah's action concerning the slaves. In the opening verses (34:1–7) Jeremiah addresses the king alone, so it appears. Jeremiah warns the king that Babylon will capture Jerusalem and will burn down the city, and that Zedekiah will not escape the Babylonians' grasp (34:2–3). Yet a promise is extended to the king; he is informed he will not die by the sword (34:4). This interview finds its *inclusio* or envelope feature in the concluding interview described in 38:14–23. There too Jeremiah is alone with Zedekiah, and there too, Zedekiah is faced with the possibility that "this city will be handed over to the Babylonians and they will burn it down" (38:18; cf. v 23). Moreover, Zedekiah will not escape from their hands (38:18). One finds here also a promise, though heavily qualified, that if Zedekiah follows directives, "then it will go well with you, and your life will be spared" (38:20).

In his last interview with the king Jeremiah further sketches a scenario of women taunting the king, should Zedekiah refuse to surrender to Babylon (38:21–23). Such a conclusion recalls the initial interview between king and prophet described in 34:1–7, in which Jeremiah, by contrast, sketches a scenario of a people making a funeral fire in honor of Zedekiah and lamenting, "Alas, O Master" (34:5). To bring these first and last scenarios into accord with a consistent message has its own problems, but the *inclusio* features of 34:1–7 and 38:14–23 argue at a minimum for an openness to the proposal that these five chapters (34–38) are intended to comprise a formal unit. Parallel patterning within this unit (34:8–38:28) would be additional evidence for treating chaps. 34–38 as a discrete unit of material.

From a review of the context of chaps. 34–35, we turn, to the ordering of the content within chaps. 34–35. A form-oriented outline shows that the two narratives have a symmetrical, indeed a parallel sequence.

---

[23] H. Migsch (*Gottes Wort über das Ende Jerusalems. Eine literar-, stil- und gattungskritische Untersuchung des Berichtes Jeremia 34:1–7; 32:2–5; 37:3–38:28* [Oesterreichische Biblische Studien 2; Klosterneuburg: Oesterreichisches Katholisches Bibelwerk, 1981], summarized in Peter R. Ackroyd, "The Book of Jeremiah—Some Recent Studies," *JSOT* 28 [1984] 50) has isolated 34:1–7 and by placing it with 32:2–5 and 37:2–5 and 37:3–38:28 attempts to show how closely these passages belong together and how they help in a reconstruction of the final day by day, hour by hour report of the occurrences prior to Jerusalem's fall. Migsch, like John Bright (*Jeremiah*), seems too intent on setting up a linear story line at the expense of the theology which the present arrangement is meant to convey.

38:8–22	SEQUENCE	35:1–19
34:8 "The word which came to Jeremiah from the Lord"	A. Prophetic Revelation Formula	35:1 "The word which came to Jeremiah from the Lord"
(haddābār 'ăšer hāyâ' el-yirmĕyāhu mē'et Yahweh)		(haddābār 'ăšer hāyâ'el-yirmĕyāhu mē'et Yahweh)
34:8b–11 Granting and rescinding of liberty	B. Description of Incident	35:2–13 The offer of wine to the Recabites
34:12a "And the word of the Lord came to Jeremiah, 'Thus says the Lord . . .'"	C. Prophetic Revelation Formula/ Messenger Formula	35:12a–13a "And the word of the Lord came to Jeremiah, 'Thus says the Lord . . .'"
(wayĕhî dĕbar- Yahweh el-Yirmĕyāhu mē'et Yahweh lē'mōr, kô-'āmar Yahweh)		(wayĕhî dĕbar- Yahweh 'el-Yirmĕyāhu mē'et Yahweh kô-'āmar Yahweh)
34:12b–16 Accusation: You have not obeyed me.	D. Divine Retelling of Incident with Accusation	35:13b–16 "But these people have not obeyed me."
34:17–20 To "all the people of the land" sword, pestilence and famine.	E. General Announcement	35:17 To "all the inhabitants of Jerusalem . . . I am bringing evil"
34:21–22 Re Zedekiah	F. Particularized Announcement	35:18–19[24] Re Recabites

A few comments can pinpoint some fascinating correspondences more clearly. In both narratives the prophetic revelation formula first introduces the incident and then in resumptive manner introduces the divine response (34:8, 12a; 35:1, 12a). The divine retelling of the precipitating incident in both narratives (34:12b-16; 35:12b–17) includes similar components, although not in the same sequence. These are:

[24] Nicholson (p. 34) compared a series of Jeremiah's sermons (chaps. 7, 11, 12, 24, 34, 35) with Deuteronomistic material to show that they owed their composition to the Deuteronomists. In the sermons Nicholson discerned a four-step sequence:
  1) introduction (e. g., 34:8–12; 35:1–12);
  2) Yahweh's command, call to obedience (e.g., 34:13–14; 35:13);
  3) description of Israel's apostasy and disobedience (34:15–16; 35:14–16);
  4) judgment announced (34:17–22; 35:17 [18–19]).
For a view that some of the prose speeches such as chaps. 34–35 are not Deuteronomistic but have a Jeremianic flavor see Helga Weippert, *Die Prosareden des Jeremiabuches* (Berlin: de Gruyter, 1973) 86–106, 121–191. The parallel structure for chaps. 34–35 is more elaborate than Nicholson indicates. Greater account needs to be taken also of the fact that the two chapters are juxtaposed.

1) Brief review of what transpired (34:15–16; 35:14–16)
2) Review of the divine action, namely, covenant making in the first incident (34:12) and the sending of prophets in the second narrative (35:15).
3) An accusation woven into each of the retellings: "You have not obeyed me" (34:17); and, "But these people have not obeyed me" (35:16, 17).
4) An accusation leveled in conjunction with the divine action: "Your fathers, however, did not listen to me or pay attention to me" (34:14); "but you have not paid attention or listened to me" (35:15).

The announcements, or verdicts of judgment (34:17–20; 35:17), which spin off the accusations have in common a takeoff on a key word in the preceding accusation. In the first account the announcement/verdict turns around a word play on "freedom" *(dĕrôr)*. God will let the sword swing free, for example. Freedom was the concrete issue in Zedekiah's story (34:8–16). In the second account, the announcement/verdict includes the charge, "they did not listen *(šmᶜ)*" (35:17). In the preceding formal accusation (35:12–16) the word *šmᶜ* occurs five times. Both accusation and announcement lean on the term *šmᶜ*. Beyond an announcement addressed to the general public, there is a specific announcement in each of the two accounts. Each ends by singling out for special mention the subject of the story: Zedekiah in the first account (34:21–22) and the Recabites in the second account (35:18–19); their destinies, however, are in marked contrast.

The stylistic patterning virtually betrays self-conscious shaping in that the basic components appear in each. Even details appear in common, e.g., the Zedekiah covenant was made in the house of the Lord (34:16), and it was also in the house of the Lord that the Recabites were tested for their obedience (35:4). Each of the stories might easily have been told quite differently, but they were not. In the present form they complement each other through parallel patterning and symmetric structural form. Thus chaps. 34 and 35 when analyzed for their narrative sequence are striking in that the components parallel one another. But the parallelism is not limited to content.

We turn to the question of the theme for these two chapters. If the two stories have stylistic parallelism, equally striking is the parallelism of theme. Here indeed the parallelism can be defined as "saying the same thing twice." The lead idea is integrity in covenant keeping. Zedekiah makes a covenant before the Lord in compliance with the command of Yahweh (34:15); when the political emergency passes, this fickle king breaks faith. The Recabites, however, keep their commitment to a stipulation anciently given to them by their forefather Jonadab and refuse to drink wine, even when Jeremiah the prophet invites them in the house of the Lord to drink wine (35:3–5); they maintain their commitment when it might be argued that they have good reason to make an exception. For King Zedekiah the issue is one of obedience to a covenent-making and a covenant-giving God: his action involves human freedom and human rights, to speak modernly. For the Recabites, the issue is also one of faithfulness, but in their case, faithfulness to a human forefather about a dietary matter. The accounts are essentially built around this contrast; however both end with similar words of indictment: "You have not listened" (34:17; 35:16). Thus, thematic considerations, and the stylistic device of parallel patterning, converge to indicate a deliberate joining of the story of Zedekiah's covenant-breaking (34:8–11) with the story of the Recabites (35:1–22).

The juxtaposition and the parallelism of these two stories suggest that chaps. 34–35 should be considered a unit for investigation at least at some stage in the interpretative process. Each narrative, though treated separately initially, must be exegeted in relation to its complement. As Kugel notes, with reference primarily but not exclusively to *parallelismus membrorum*, the two parts of a parallelism together make a statement. B is more than a repetition of A. The essence of parallelism, Kugel explains is that, "B, by being connected to A—carrying it further, echoing it, defining it, restating it, contrasting with it, *it does not matter which*—has an emphatic, 'seconding' character, and it is this more than any aesthetic of symmetry or paralleling, which is at the heart of biblical parallelism."[25] In this understanding of parallelism one needs to ask, What is the statement that the two parts (chaps. 34, 35) make together?

Certain theological features take on added signification when the two pairs are seen together. First, Yahweh's actions are a backdrop to both messages of judgment, even though these messages are occasioned by different events more than a decade apart. These actions include covenant making at the time of the exodus (34:13) but also Yahweh's ongoing work of sending prophets, even up to the present moment (35:15). Together the two accounts about God's actions embrace the whole of Israel's history.

Second, the indictment against King Zedekiah must be seen as going beyond Yahweh's displeasure with a single act of covenant breaking. Rather, Zedekiah's lack of integrity is symptomatic of a non-listening and non-obedient stance of the royal house and of the people generally toward God. The incident, while important in itself, is an illustration of a deep and long-standing problem, as is clear from the analysis put forward in connection with the Recabite story. To see it from another angle, these two chapters together give some specificity as to what is involved in Yahweh's frequent appeal to "listen," or "obey." "Listening" entails an

[25] Kugel, 51 (italics his).

attitude of commitment *and also* an adherence to concrete directives. Listening is worked out in specific acts. Still, at the base of both stories is a concern for loyalty and fidelity to Yahweh, and so in one story the concluding announcement to Zedekiah is about the sad fate of a disloyal people (34:21–22), while the Recabite story ends with a rewarding promise to a loyal clan (35:18–19).

The present stylistic literary arrangements call attention to the loyalty and integrity of an isolated remnant group, the Recabites. Indeed, the fidelity of the Recabites in dietary matters contrasts very sharply with the infidelity of the king in matters of national policies and justice. It is not too much to say, then, that the stage is set for dispensing with the disobedient people as a whole and for Yahweh to take up his purposes with a remnant. The remnant option, in Yahweh's pursuit of redemption history, surfaces abruptly.

The interpretation of two passages, when seen as a whole, in two parallel halves, brings about a different cast, a different flavor than when each is interpreted singly. The relationship between the two halves, only sketched here, is a fruitful area for further investigation. Enough has been suggested, however, to indicate that the two chapters are structured in paralleled fashion, a fact which has consequences for interpretation.

Narrative Parallelism in 36–38

Chaps. 36–38 relate Jeremiah's encounter with two kings: Jehoiakim and Zedekiah. In the first narrative Jeremiah's newly dictated scroll, already read before two audiences, is brought to Jehoiakim, who slices it in pieces and throws these into the fire (chap. 36). The second narrative recounts Jeremiah's personal encounter with King Zedekiah in a series of interviews. In the present literary arrangement, these two stories precede the account of the Babylonians' capture of Jerusalem (chap. 39). The two stories have similar features; but more than that, they exhibit an interesting pattern of sequencing.

36:1–32	SEQUENCE	37:1–38:28
36:1–4 king Jehoiakim, Jeremiah, and the scroll	A. Introduction	37:1–2 king Zedekiah, officials, and prophet
	B. Narrative in 3 movements	
36:5–10 first reading	First movement	37:3–10 first interview by a delegation (v 4, Jeremiah's whereabouts)
36:11–19 second	Second movement	37:11–21 second

reading in the scribe's chamber		interview with Zedekiah personally (vv 11–16 Jeremiah's arrest)
36:20–26 third reading before the king	Third movement	38:1–23 third interview with Zedekiah personally (vv 1–13 Jeremiah thrown into cistern, then released)
36:27–31 Jehoiakim's future	C. Message to the king	[38:14–23 Zedekiah's future]
36:32 destiny of the scroll	D. Concluding Note	38:24–28 destiny of the prophet

Certain niceties in the parallelism between the two parts (chap. 36 = A, chaps. 37–38 = B) are not immediately noticeable from the outline. In A the story turns around a king, Jehoiakim, with his officials, and a scroll. In B the story revolves around a king, Zedekiah, with his officials, and a prophet.[26]

In A one follows the vagaries of a book, which is read in the temple (36:5–10), read again in the scribe's chamber in the palace (36:11–19), and read the third time in the king's winter apartment (36:20–26), where it is systematically destroyed. In B one follows the vagaries, not of a book, but of a man. Just as the scroll is handed off from place to place, so Jeremiah is passed from one station to the next. He is at first free to move about (37:4), then arrested at the Ben'amin Gate (37:11), imprisoned first in Jonathan's house (37:14), then in the courtyard of the guard (37:21), and then (if one follows the account as it stands) in the cistern (38:6).[27]

In each section an attempt is made to destroy the word of God: in A the scroll, God's written word, is cut to pieces and burned; in B the prophet, who bears God's spoken word, is thrown into a cistern to die. In each section the potentially bad situation is salvaged: the scroll reappears, so to speak, thanks to Baruch; the prophet is rescued from death and reappears, thanks to Ebed-Melech.[28] In a summary, A tells of an unsuccessful attempt to destroy the message; B tells of an unsuccessful attempt to do away with the messenger.

[26] The label "prophet" for Jeremiah occurs nine times in chaps. 37–38 as compared to only one time in chaps. 34–35.

[27] John Bright (pp. 233–234) lists reasons for holding that 37:11–21 and 38:1–28a are essentially reports of the same series of events. Even so, he is cautious and "inclined not to insist upon it [the view]."

[28] It is these two, Baruch and Ebed-Melech, who at a later time will be the recipients of a favorable oracle—45:5, 39:16–18).

The three movements of each narrative are clearly marked. In A, as we have noted, the action unfolds at three different locations. In B there are three clearly marked verbal exchanges between Jeremiah and the king or his ambassadors. The first episode of A is linked to the first episode of B by an interesting antithetic contrast: the statement "Now Jeremiah was free to come and go among the people, for he had not yet been put in prison" (37:4, first interview with Zedekiah) seems to be a deliberate counterpart to the statement in A, "Then Jeremiah told Baruch, 'I am restricted; I cannot go to the Lord's temple'" (36:5). Attention to places characterizes both A and B.

Common to A and B is a threatening word by the prophet to the king. Jehoiakim is told that because he burned the scroll, he will have no descendants to sit on the throne, and Yahweh will bring disaster on Jerusalem (36:30–31). Zedekiah is told that if he refuses to surrender to the Babylonians, trouble will come to his family, his wives and children will be brought out to the Babylonians, and the city will be burned (38:22–23). Both parts contain a conclusion: the destiny of the scroll in A and the destiny of the prophet in B. Each conclusion conjoins the destiny (of scroll, of prophet) with the name of the respective king (36:32; 38:24–28). That the patterned sequence is so similar for A and B is hardly accidental, for one could easily relate either story without following a particular order.

Beyond the structural patterns, there is a key word of paramount importance: *sārāp*, "burn." The verb *sārāp* occurs five times in A and five times in B for a total of ten occurrences.[29] In A, the story in the narrative past is about the scroll that has been burned. In B, the announcement in the narrative future is that a city will be burned. In A Jehoiakim was urged not to burn the scroll (36:25), but he burned it nevertheless (36:27). The narrative sequel keeps the reader conscious of the burning [*sārāp*] (36:28, 29, 32). In B, Jeremiah's first response to the royal inquiry includes the news that the Babylonians will capture the city of Jerusalem and will "burn it down" (*sārāp*, 37:8, 10). The final interview repeats the message about the future burning of Jerusalem (38:17, 18, 23). One might suggest that the "Jehoiakim/burn" is a contrast to the "Nebuchadnezzar/burn" on the axis of "internal-external" threats to the witness of Yahweh in the world.[30]

Other resemblances may be noted. Each narrative names several officials: Elnathan, Delaiah, and Gemariah in Jehoiakim's court (36:12); Shephatiah, Gedaliah, Juhucal, and Pashhur in Zedekiah's court (38:1).

---

[29] The frequency of *sarap* in these two accounts is striking in comparison to only two occurrences (21:10; 32:19) in the first 33 chapters, despite the frequent discussion in those chapters about an enemy invasion.

[30] I owe this suggestion to John Gutierrez.

The word *sārîm*, "princes," occurs 13 times in A + B. As in the reading of the scroll the same message is given three times, so in the three interviews Jeremiah's message is thrice repeated. The material in A is dated to 605–604, a date which brings to mind immediately the large-scale battle at Carchemish where the Egyptians clashed with the Babylonians. Similarly in B, the two world powers were at war (37:11). The parallel pattern also calls attention to several differences: King Jehoiakim is decisive, King Zedekiah is indecisive; in A the officials are on the side of Jeremiah but in B they are not (more on this later).

That the two accounts are intentionally stylistically structured and compositionally arranged so as to correspond/complement to one another appears likely. Such an arrangement invites comparisons of the two narratives, as we have seen. More important, it invites close attention to the theology imbedded in the conjunction of the narratives. Proceeding on Kugel's understanding of parallelism, where A and B are to be viewed as a single whole, with B offering something more than A, we examine A and B for theological nuances.[31]

One of these has to do with God's word—written in A, spoken through the prophet in B.[32] The medium of the word of God is more compelling in B than in A. The reading of the scroll, has an effect on the hearers, to be sure; but in B one senses the powerful presence of a man who has come to represent God's word in his own person; he is the message incarnate, and as such a living, inescapable force. The attempt to do away with the word of God is therefore far more reprehensible in B than in A. The scroll can be disposed of, cut and burned; still, it can be rewritten. But a message embodied in a prophet cannot be eradicated without killing the prophet. B goes beyond A and completes A, for by threatening the life of Jeremiah, royal officialdom, which has unceremoniously set aside the basic message, now wishes to rid itself of the last vestige, the living vehicle of that message. But B together with A and one sees the seriousness of these successive rejections: the rejection of God's word is total.

To this rejection of the word of God there is a corollary. In both accounts the word is preserved: the scroll is dictated in a second edition;

---

[31] As Kugel (p. 8) notes, B goes beyond A in force or specificity. D. J. A. Clines, in a felicitious phrase in a public lecture, pointed to the "parallelism of greater precision."

[32] Kessler ("Form-Critical Suggestions on Jer 36"; "Jeremiah Chapters 26–45 Reconsidered") has noted that chaps. 26–36 deal with the story of the word of God. Cf. Nicholson (p. 109): "We have seen that the primary concern of the complex xxvi–xxxvi taken as a whole is a history of Yahweh's Word proclaimed by Jeremiah and the rejection of that word by Judah." But to stop with chap. 36 is to fail to see that in chaps. 37–38 the rejection moves to a second stage, the attempt to eliminate the human messenger of that word.

Jeremiah's life is spared. Robert Carroll suggests the point of the story in Jeremiah 38 to be that "Jeremiah escaped death, yet remained faithful to his uncompromising vision of Jerusalem's destruction if the king did not obey the divine word."[33] By taking the parallel structure into account, however, a theological point (as well as a biographical one) is made about the preservation of the Word of God, and that by strange means.

There is a second theological nuance. Parts A and B interpret each other at the point of contrast, especially with respect to the stance of the officials. The officials in Jehoiakim's court appear in a most favorable light; those in Zedekiah's court, by contrast, in a most unfavorable one. The officials mentioned in A not only make arrangements for King Jehoiakim to read the scroll, but they commend it to him. Elnathan goes so far as to make an effort to halt Jehoiakim's defiant destruction of the scroll. The officials work in Jeremiah's behalf. By contrast, the officials of Zedekiah's court, upon having Jeremiah brought to them by Irijah, are angry with Jeremiah, beat him and imprison him. Shephatiah, Gedaliah, Jehucal, and Pashhur are among the officials who say, "This man should be put to death." It is the officials who throw Jeremiah into the cistern. That we are to be alert to the importance of the officials in B is clear from the introductory statement, "Neither he [King Zedekiah] nor his attendants (ʿĕbādîm) nor the people of the land paid any attention to the words the Lord had spoken through Jeremiah the prophet" (37:2). Whereas in Jehoiakim's day the officials could not restrain the ungodly actions of the king, a decade later under Zedekiah they have become a direction-setting group apparently as powerful as the king: it is they who take the initiative in doing away with Jeremiah. The resistance to Yahweh's word has now permeated the entire cluster of leadership. In short, Judah is now more culpable because both the vacillating king and the responsible leaders are hostile to God's message and messenger. B has gone beyond A.

Announcements of judgment likewise become intensified. In chapter 36 we still hear of a "perhaps" (36:3; cf. v 7). But such contingent language is absent in chapters 37–38. Here, hope for a favorable prospect is all but gone. The escalation of rebellion, noted in the movement from A to B, justifies punitive action and is sufficient warrant for the destruction of the city which is reported (chap. 39). B not only functions as a persuasive addition to A, but brings closure to A.

If A and B taken together show the increased gravity of evil, they also make a statement about God. Already Jehoiakim deserved Yahweh's punishment; indeed God's judgment was announced (36:30–31). Yet it was only after another decade, when the total power structure had shown itself disobedient and defiant, that God moved to bring ultimate disaster.

---

[33] Robert P. Carroll, *From Chaos to Covenant* (New York: Crossroad, 1981) 156.

A and B, when taken together, declare God's patience and forebearance. God was not swift to retaliate. He made various approaches to a wayward people. In the conjunction of A and B there shines forth, as from behind dark clouds, something of God's mercy, especially his patience.

Theologically B is a "seconding sequence" to A for it carries forward the history of the Word of God, shifting from written word to a word-incarnate-in-a-prophet. Polk has in mind 8:4f, 10:17ff and passages such as chaps. 14–15 when he writes a summary which is equally applicable to our chapters: "[Jeremiah] comes personally to embody the divine-human event such that his life becomes a vehicle for the event's interpretation. Jeremiah's life becomes his message."[34] Kugel has shown that parallelism has to do with a second sequence such that B offers something more than A either by supporting it, elaborating it, or clinching A.

With such an understanding of parallelism we begin to understand the rationale of the overall arrangement of chaps. 34–38, a set of incidents which are told in non-chronological order, but which literarily and theologically score a forceful point by their very arrangement. Chapters 34–38 present a warrant for the awful catastrophe of Jerusalem's destruction which is told in chapter 39. Documentation for the assertion that Judah has disobeyed Yahweh is the account of Zedekiah who, though he attempts compliance to the Torah's stipulation about slaves, ends by reversing himself and disregarding the Lord's command (chap. 34). The "more" which the parallel account of the Recabites provides—an account carefully patterned in parallel to chapter 34—is the contrast of an obedient minority group. Here A and B together give definition to what specifically is meant by obedient/listening.

The second set of parallel narratives addresses the stance of the king and his court toward the word of God, with special attention to the medium of that word. Not only is the message disregarded by Jehoiakim and by Zedekiah together with his highly placed leaders, but the vehicles for that message, a written document in the one incident (chap. 36) and the person of the prophet in the other (chaps. 37–38), are attacked. Rejection of God's effort is total. The serial arrangement set up by the two sets of parallels leads to the impression that chaps. 36–38 are a seconding sequence to chaps. 34–35, so that in a larger sense B is again saying more than A. Thus in chapters 34–38, the stylistic parallelism features literary structure, semantic correspondence and thematic balance. By means of parallel patterning the initial message A is not merely restated in B but is reinforced in B. B added to A supplies power, force, persuasiveness and closure. In these chapters, parallelism is a stylistic technique of reinforcement for emphasis and persuasion.

Theologically, the two sets of parallel accounts (chaps. 34–35; 36–38)

[34] Polk, 125.

detail the obstinancy of a people and thus justify the judgment which God brings on Jerusalem. The argument of God's warrant for his announcement of disaster upon Jerusalem is already given in the earlier poetic sections of Jeremiah, but one should not miss the careful compositional arrangement of these chapters which precede the reports of Jerusalem's fall. The art form of parallelism is clearly in the service of a theology.[35]

[35]The writer pays tribute to Professor Brownlee, an esteemed instructor and friendly mentor. For this essay the writer expresses appreciation to his teaching colleagues, Professors Allen Guenther and John E. Toews, and to Professor John Gutierrez of Tyndale House, Cambridge, England, for their helpful suggestions.

NEW GLEANINGS FROM AN OLD VINEYARD: ISAIAH 27 RECONSIDERED

MARVIN A. SWEENEY
University of Miami
Coral Gables, Florida

Scholars have long recognized a direct relationship between Isa 27:2–5(6), the vineyard song of the so-called Isaiah Apocalypse (Isaiah 24–27), and Isa 5:1–7, generally regarded as the original Isaianic vineyard song. Both passages use the imagery of a vineyard as an allegorical representation of the people of Israel. At the end of the 8th century B.C.E., Isaiah of Jerusalem used the vineyard allegory as a means of announcing judgment against Israel and Judah.[1] He portrayed God as a vinedresser, patiently tending His vineyard in hopes of producing a good harvest of grapes. But when the vineyard produced sour grapes, i.e., when Israel produced violence and anguish instead of justice and righteousness, God decided to stop tending this unproductive vineyard, break down its walls, and allow briars, thorns, and wild animals to take it over. This, of course, referred to the impending Assyrian invasion. The author of the vineyard song in Isa 27:2–5(6), on the other hand, used the vineyard allegory as a means of announcing God's protection of Israel.[2] Here, God states that He will tend the vineyard, water it, and protect it from briars and thorns so that Israel can take root and blossom. Most scholars date this passage to the post-exilic period and understand it as an announcement of the eschatological restoration of Israel.[3] Thus, the new song of the vineyard is seen as a "late theological reflection upon prophecy and

---

[1] Scholars generally agree that Isaiah is the author of the vineyard allegory in Isa 5:1–7 (e.g., R. E. Clements, *Isaiah 1–39* [NCB; Grand Rapids: Eerdmans, 1980] 57–8; H. Wildberger, *Jesaja 1–12* [BKAT X/1; Neukirchen-Vluyn: Neukirchener, 1972] 166–7). Exceptions include J. Vermeylen, *Du prophète Isaïe à l'apocalyptique* (2 vols.; EBib; Paris: Gabalda, 1977–8), 1. 159–68, and O. Kaiser, *Isaiah 1–12* (OTL; 2nd ed.; Philadelphia: Westminster, 1983) 93–4, who see the oracle as a Deuteronomistic composition from the exilic period.

[2] H. Wildberger, *Jesaja 13–27* (BKAT X/2; Neukirchen-Vluyn: Neukirchener, 1978) 1008–9.

[3] E.g., Clements, 218–9; G. Fohrer, *Das Buch Jesaja* (3 vols.; ZB; 2d ed.; Zurich: Zwingli, 1966–67) 2. 1, 34–6; O. Kaiser, *Isaiah 13–39* (OTL; Philadelphia: Westminster, 1974) 224–26. Cf. Wildberger, *Jesaja 13–27*, 1008–12, who claims that the eschatological perspective is not original to the song.

its message which basically develops, and ultimately reverses, the verdict of Isa 5:6."[4] It is a reinterpretation of earlier prophecy in relation to the historical and theological circumstances of later times.[5] The old vineyard song was rendered obsolete by the events of the post-exilic era. Therefore, its message was transformed from one of judgment to salvation. In this respect, the new vineyard song seems well-suited to the context of Isaiah 24–27 since these chapters contain much reinterpretation of earlier prophetic texts.[6]

Yet, the new vineyard song poses many problems for its interpreters. There is a great deal of textual variation between the Masoretic Text and the other versions, especially the Septuagint, which hampers efforts to arrive at a precise understanding of the message of this pericope.[7] Furthermore, scholars have had much difficulty in relating the new vineyard song to its context in Isaiah 24–27.[8] The vineyard song seems to be thematically distinct from the preceding material. The imagery of God's protective care of the vineyard contrasts markedly with that of God's eschatological judgment of the world which, according to many scholars, reaches its climax in Isa 26:20–21 or 26:20–27:1.[9] Likewise, the new vineyard song lacks the mythological motifs and language that permeate the preceding chapters. Scholars have noted that the introductory *bayyôm hahû'* formula in v 2 distinguishes the song formally and associates it with the other constituent units of chapter 27 which include

---

[4] Clements, 219.

[5] R. P. Carroll, *When Prophecy Failed: Cognitive Dissonance in the Prophetic Traditions of the Old Testament* (New York: Crossroad, 1979) 148.

[6] For references to other prophetic passages which are reinterpreted in Isaiah 24–27, cf. Wildberger, *Jesaja 13–27*, 910.

[7] The passage presents numerous problems for the text critic (cf. Wildberger, *Jesaja 13–27*, 1007–8). The LXX's portrayal of the vineyard as a besieged city appears to be an interpretation of the song in light of the imagery of the desolate city of vv 10–11 and the besieged Jerusalem of Isa 1:4–9. In this case, it is unlikely that LXX represents a different text tradition from that of the MT. On the interpretative character of LXX Isaiah, see J. Koenig, *L'herméneutique analogique du Judaïsme antique d'après les témoins textuels d'Isaïe* (SVT 33; Leiden: Brill, 1982) 1–198.

[8] E.g., B. Duhm (*Das Buch Jesaia* [5th ed.; Göttingen: Vandenhoeck & Ruprecht, 1968] 189) claims that the song is a marginal gloss since it has nothing to do with its context.

[9] A number of scholars include Isa 27:12–13 with the climactic section, arguing that vv 2–11 are later. See, e.g., B. Duhm, 172; K. Marti, *Das Buch Jesaja* (KHAT X; Tübingen: J. C. B. Mohr, 1900) 201; O. Procksch, *Jesaia I* (KAT IX/1; Leipzig: A. Deichertsche, 1930) 331–36; and also W. Rudolph, *Jesaja 24–27* (BWANT IV/10; Stuttgart: W. Kohlhammer, 1933) 50–52. Fohrer (vol. 2., pp. 34–42) sees Isa 27:1–6, 12–13 as the concluding prophetic liturgy of the Isaiah Apocalypse. Isa 27:7–11 is held to be a later theological reflection (cf. "Der Aufbau der Apokalypse des Jesajabuches (Jesaja 24–27)," *Studien zur alttestamentlichen Prophetie (1949–1965)* [BZAW 99; Berlin: Töpelmann, 1967] 170–181, esp. 173–4).

similar formulas (i.e., Isa 27:1, 6, 12, 13).[10] Not only are these units perceived as having little relationship to chapters 24–26, they seem to have little or no apparent connection with the new vineyard song or with each other. Isaiah 27:1 uses the mythological motif of God's defeat of the sea dragon, Leviathan, as a means of describing His victory over the cosmic forces of chaos. Isaiah 27:7–9 discusses the exile of Israel as a punishment for its idolatry. Isaiah 27:10–11 describes an unnamed, fortified city which is now abandoned and desolate due to God's punishing it for its people's lack of understanding. Verses 12–13 describe the restoration of the exiled people of Israel to Jerusalem where they will finally worship God on His holy mountain. The absence of thematic and literary unity among these units has prompted many scholars to view them as a series of loosely related eschatological "impressions," written by various hands, which were added as supplements to chapters 24–26.[11]

This perceived fragmentary and supplemental character of Isaiah 27 has raised further difficulties, especially in regard to the unnamed city of vv 10–11. By interpreting the depiction of the guilt of Jacob in vv 7–9 as a reference to the Samaritans, a number of scholars have identified the city as Samaria.[12] Noting the reference to Jacob/Israel in v 6, they consequently understand God's battling the briars and thorns in the new vineyard song as a reference to the conflict between the post-exilic Jerusalem theocracy and the Samaritans. Verses 12–13 then express the hope for a reunification of Israel and Judah in worship at Jerusalem. But this view raises several problems. The post-exilic Jerusalem theocracy completely rejected the Samaritans, allowing them no possibility to join the Jerusalem community.[13] Furthermore, there is no indication that vv 2–6, 7–9, 10–11, or 12–13 were meant to refer exclusively to the Samaritans or even to the exiled northern kingdom of Israel. The original vineyard song in Isa 5:1–7 condemned both Israel and Judah (cf. Isa 5:7). The references to Israel and Jacob in vv 6, 9, and 12 are ambiguous,

---

[10] Wildberger, *Jesaja 13–27*, 903, 1008. Cf. O. Ploeger, *Theocracy and Eschatology* (Oxford: Blackwell, 1968), 71.

[11] Wildberger, *Jesaja 13–27*, 903–5. Cf. Clements, 199; Kaiser, *Isaiah 13–39*, 224; W. E. March, *A Study of Two Prophetic Compositions in Isaiah 24:1–27:1* (Th.D. Dissertation; Union Theological Seminary in New York, 1966) 187–98; M.-L. Henry, *Glaubenkrise und Glaubensbewaehrung in den Dichtungen der Jesajaapokalypse* (BWANT V/6; Stuttgart: W. Kohlhammer, 1967) 192–9.

[12] Clements, 220–1; Duhm, 191–2; E. Jacob, "Du premiere au deuxième chant de la vigne du prophète Esaïe, Réflexions sur Esaïe 27, 2–5," *Wort-Gebot-Glaube* (ed. H. J. Stoebe *et al.*; Zurich: Zwingli, 1970) 325–30; Vermeylen, *Du prophète Isaïe à l'apocalyptique*, 1. 378, 380; Wildberger, *Jesaja 13–27*, 1016–8. Ploeger (pp. 72–75) argues that Isaiah 27 originally focused on the reunification of Israel and Judah. The concern with Samaria, indicated by a gloss in v 10ax, is later.

[13] Cf. Kaiser (*Isaiah 13–39*, 225) who notes that various texts in Isaiah do not allow for Samaria's survival in the final age.

especially since these names are used throughout Deutro-Isaiah to refer
to all Israel, including Judah, and not exclusively to the northern kingdom.[14] One might expect a more explicit reference to Samaria in vv 10–
11 if the author had the Samaritans or the northern kingdom in mind.
Others see here a reference to Jerusalem which lay in ruins in the early
post-exilic period.[15] The people's lack of understanding mentioned in v
11 would correspond to the reason cited in Isa 1:3 for the punishment of
Jerusalem. But such a view of a desolate Jerusalem and a recalcitrant
people does not seem to fit well with the themes of protection and
restoration in vv 2–6 and 12–13. Some see vv 10–11 as a reference to the
vanquished world capital mentioned throughout chaps. 24–26 (cf. esp.
Isa 25:2),[16] but this is puzzling in the context of chap. 27 which focuses on
Israel. Others simply despair of identifying the city altogether.[17]

Clearly, the perceived lack of unity in chap. 27 has complicated the
interpretation of the new vineyard song and the other sub-units of the
chapter. Nevertheless, there are indications of thematic unity throughout
the chapter. It begins and ends with references to cosmic/international
events, i.e., God's defeat of the cosmic chaos monster in v 1 and the
ingathering of Israel from exile throughout the world to Jerusalem in vv
12–13. We have already noted the introductory eschatological formulas,
bayyôm hahû° (vv 1, 2), *habbā°îm* (v 6), and *wěhāyâ bayyôm hahû°* (vv 12,
13), which give the entire chapter a future orientation. Agricultural
imagery permeates most of the chapter. The vineyard song, of course,
employs such imagery throughout vv 2–5. Verse 6 includes references to
Jacob's "taking root," Israel's "blossoming" and "blooming," as well as
their "filling the world with fruit." The word *běsa°ssě°â* in v 8 presents
problems.[18] Most scholars understand it either as a contraction of *biš°â
sě°ă*, translating "measure by measure," or as a pilpel infinitive of a
hypothetical root *sw°*, translating "by her expulsion," but recognize that
neither solution is completely satisfactory. S. Daiches associates the word
with the Akkadian *sassu* and Talmudic Aramaic *s°s°* which refers to "the
top of an ear of corn."[19] While his interpretation of v 8 is problematic and
the precise meaning of the word remains unclear, its association with an
agricultural context is evident. Verse 9 contains *pěrî*, "fruit," and vv 10
and 11 contain *sě°ipêhā*, "its branches," and *gěsîrāh*, "its cuttings,"
respectively. Verse 12 contains the statement, *yaḥbōṭ yhwh miššibbōlet*

---

[14] Isa 40:27; 41:8, 14; 42:24; 43:1, 22, 28; 44:1, 21, 23; 45:4; 48:12; 49:5.
[15] Rudolph, 53–6; Fohrer, 2. 41.
[16] J. Lindblom, *Die Jesaja-Apokalypse: Jes. 24–27* (LUÄ NF I.34.3; Lund: Gleerup,
1938) 58.
[17] G. B. Gray, *A Critical and Exegetical Commentary on the Book of Isaiah I–XXVII*
(ICC; Edinburgh: T & T Clark, 1912) 459.
[18] Cf. Wildberger, *Jesaja 13–27*, 1014.
[19] "An Explanation of Isaiah 27.8," *JQR* 6/3 (Jan. 1916) 399–404.

hannāhār, "YHWH will beat out from the branch of the river." *Šibbōlet* is the singular form of *šibbōlîm*, "ears of corns," and *yaḥbōṭ* refers to winnowing corn. Finally, v 12 contains the verb, *tĕluqqĕṭû*, "you shall be gleaned," which refers to the gleaning of a grape harvest.

There are other indications of unity in Isaiah 27 in that references to Isaiah 17 and Isaiah 1 appear throughout the chapter. Vermeylen has already pointed to a number of references which associate Isa 27:9–11 with Isa 17:1–11 by using the same motifs and vocabulary.[20] Both texts treat the punishment of the northern kingdom of Israel, referred to as "Jacob" in Isa 17:4 and 27:9. He notes that *hammizbĕḥôt, wĕhāʾăšērîm wĕhāḥammānîm* in Isa 17:8 corresponds to *mizbēaḥ, ʾăšērîm wĕḥammānîm* in Isa 27:9b. The reference to *ʿārê . . . māʿuzzô kaʿăzûbat . . . ʿāzĕbû* in Isa 17:9 refers to *ʿîr bĕṣûrâ . . . wĕneʿĕzāb* in Isa 27:10. Both share the theme of harvest (*qāṣîr*) in Isa 17:5, 11 and 27:11. Finally, both texts (Isa 17:7; 27:11) presuppose that the people have betrayed their "Maker" (*ʿōśēhû*). He uses this evidence to argue that the "fortified city" (*ʿîr bĕṣûrâ*) of Isa 27:10 is none other than Samaria (cf. Isa 17:3, *mibṣār mēʾeprayīm*) and that the purpose of Isa 27:9–11 is to predict the punishment of this city "to expiate the guilt of Jacob" (Isa 27:9a). However, he has overlooked a number of other references to Isaiah 17 in chap. 27 which extend well beyond Isa 27:9–11. God's invitation to seize His protection (*ʾô yaḥăzēq bĕmāʿûzzî*) and make peace with Him stands in contrast to Isa 17:9–10, which describes a people who trust in their strong cities (*ʿārê māʿuzzô*) and have forgotten God, their rock of protection (*wĕṣûr māʿuzzēk*). The statement in Isa 27:6, that Israel will blossom and bloom (*ûpārah*) as a result of God's care, contrasts with the futile attempts of the people who try to make seed bloom (*ûbabbōqer zarʿĕk taprîḥî*) without divine support (Isa 17:11). The imagery of God's winnowing from the branch/ear of the river (*yaḥbōṭ yhwh miššibbōlet hannāhār*) and the gleaning of Israel so that they might return to Jerusalem (*wĕʾattem tĕluqqĕtû*) in Isa 27:12–13 contrasts with the punishment oriented gleaning of ears in the Valley of Rephaim (Isa 17:5). However, it compares favorably with the chaff of the nations which is blown away by the wind when God acts to protect His people in Isa 17:13 (cf. Isa 27:8). Likewise, the nations which threaten Israel roar like the roaring of the sea in Isa 17:12. God's rebuke of these nations calls to mind His defeat of the sea dragon Leviathan in Isa 27:1. Clearly, the association between chaps. 27 and 17 is intended not only to announce the condemnation of the people referred to in Isa 27:9–11, but to offer reconciliation once their punishment is over. Apparently, the full implications of the harvest imagery of Isaiah 17 come to fruition in chap. 27. Isaiah 17:5 notes that the initial harvest will mow down most of the people like standing grain.

[20] *Du prophète Isaïe à l'apocalyptique*, 1. 377–8.

But Isa 17:6–7 makes it clear that the gleanings which remain after the harvest is over will form the basis of a renewed relationship between the people and God. At that time, the people will look to their Maker for protection and ignore the Asherim and Hammanim[21] on which they previously depended. Isa 17:12–14 indicates that afterwards the nations which threatened Israel will be blown away like chaff. Isaiah 27 thus picks up this message from the final form of chap. 17 and applies it by associating its own themes of punishment and reconciliation.

Scholars have noted some connection between Isaiah 27 and Isaiah 1.[22] The reference to a people without undestanding in Isa 27:11 calls to mind the accusation against the people in Isa 1:3. However, most prefer to associate this statement with Ben Sira's appraisal of the Samaritans in Sir 50:26, which uses similar language to describe the people who live in Shechem.[23] But there are other thematic and semantic connections between these chapters. The fortified city which stands alone in Isa 27:10 ʿîr bĕṣûrâ bādād) resembles the besieged city of Jerusalem which is left alone in Isa 1:8. The comparison is particularly apt when one considers that the isolated Jerusalem is described "like a sukkah in a vineyard" (kĕsukkâ bĕkārem) and "like a besieged city" (kĕʿîr nĕṣûrâ). This language stands in contrast to the "delightful vineyard" (kerem ḥemed)[24] of Isa 27:2 which God watches over (Isa 27:3; ʾănî yhwh nōṣĕrāh, layĕlâ wāyyôm ʾeṣṣŏrennâ). Isa 27:7 questions the severity of the smiting which the people endured (hakkĕmakkat makkēhû hikkāhû) and this corresponds to the smiting mentioned in Isa 1:5 (ʿal meh tukkû). Isa 27:9 refers to both the guilt (ʿawōn) and the sin (ḥaṭṭāʾtô) of Jacob and these are prominently mentioned as reasons for the punishment of the people in Isa 1:4. Furthermore, there is a short oracle in Isa 1:29–31 which condemns the people of Jerusalem for their idolatrous terebinths and gardens. This is quite a contrast between the delightful vineyard (kerem ḥemed), protected by God, which produces so much fruit (Isa 27:6) and the parched gardens in which the people of Jerusalem delight (Isa 1:29; ʾăšer ḥămadtem). The leaves and branches of the terebinths and gardens are dry and will quickly burn with no water to quench the fire. In contrast, God waters His vineyard continuously (Isa 27:3) and burns any briars and thorns which might threaten it (Isa 27:4). Clearly, Isaiah 1 stands behind the descriptions of both the delightful vineyard of Isa 27:2–6 and Jacob's guilt and the solitary city of Isa 27:7–11. The description of

---

[21] Probably incense altars. Cf. Kaiser, *Isaiah 13–39*, 228.

[22] Cf. Kaiser, *Isaiah 13–39*, 230.

[23] E.g., Clements, 242.

[24] Most Hebrew manuscripts read *kerem ḥemer*, "a vineyard of wine" (cf. BHS; 1QIsaᵃ). Leningradensis' reading of *ḥemed* is to be preferred since it contributes to the positive imagery of the passage and agrees with both LXX, which employs generally negative imagery, and Targum Jonathan (cf. Amos 5:11).

the besieged Jerusalem and the idolatrous gardens in chap. 1 contrasts with the delightful garden of chap. 27. But these same images, with their explanation for punishment in Isaiah 1, resemble the isolated city and the explanation for Jacob's expiation of guilt in Isa 27:7–11.

These observations on the relationship between chap. 27 and chaps. 1 and 17 have several implications.

First, the references to chaps. 1 and 17 indicate that the various sub-units of chap. 27 can not be viewed as lacking a relation to one another. They are clearly intended to stand together.

Second, reference to chaps. 1 and 17 helps to clarify the conceptual relationship of the various sub-units of Isaiah 27. Isaiah 1 begins a scene of punishment that is the result of the people's wickedness in vv 2–17. Yet, vv 18–28 make it clear that the purpose of the punishment is to cleanse the people so that their relationship with God can be restored. Once the punishment is over and the cleansing has taken place, vv 29–31 indicate that the people will be ashamed of their former ways.[25] Isaiah 17 presents a similar situation. It begins by proclaiming judgment against Damascus and Ephraim, i.e., the northern kingdom of Israel. Most scholars see this as an oracle against the Syro-Ephraimitic alliance which threatened Jerusalem in 735-2 B.C.E.[26] Like chap. 1, the present form of this passage is not entirely concerned with judgment against these countries. Verses 6–8 make it clear that once the punishment is over, those few who survive will turn back to God. Furthermore, vv 12–14 indicate that God will eventually rebuke the nations which carry out this punishment, portrayed as cosmic forces of chaos, thus protecting those who return to Him. This demonstrates two things: 1) the purpose of punishment is to cleanse the people of their wickedness so that their relationship with God might be restored; and 2) this process of punishment leading to restoration is understood as having international or cosmic significance. These themes from chaps. 1 and 17 aid in understanding the seemingly unrelated images of Isaiah 27. The isolated city of vv 10–11 represents a scene of punishment whereas the delightful vineyard of vv 2–6 represents one of restoration. Verses 7–9 provide the link between them. They speak of punishment as expiation of guilt or sin which leads to Jacob's rejection of idolatrous practices. This paves the way for the restoration of their relationship with God. Verses 1 and 12–13 place this process of punishment leading to restoration in a cosmic, international

---

[25] For a detailed discussion of the structure, genre, and intent of the final form of Isaiah 1, see my *Isaiah 1–4 and the Post-exilic Understanding of the Isaianic Tradition* (Ph.D. Dissertation; Claremont Graduate School, 1983) 240–315.

[26] The extent of the original oracle is disputed. Various proposals have been put forward including vv 1–3, 1–6, 1–11, and 1–14. Others identify several Isaianic oracles in the chapter and some redactional additions. For a full discussion, see Wildberger, *Jesaja 13–27*, 633–77.

framework. The resulting ingathering of exiles from Assur and Egypt, made possible by the restored relationship with God, is portrayed as God's triumph over the forces of cosmic chaos.

Third, the many references to Isaiah 1 which appear in Isaiah 27 make it difficult to maintain that the solitary city of vv 10–11 is Samaria. Instead, it must be Jerusalem. Nevertheless, the vineyard itself must be understood as Israel and Judah as Isa 5:1–7 maintains. Chapter 17 deals with Israel, not Jerusalem, and Isa 1:8 makes it clear that Jerusalem stands in the midst of the vineyard. Once the people have been exiled and the city punished, the solitary city of Jerusalem will be repopulated as the exiles return.

These considerations, pointing to the unity of Isaiah 27, will aid in establishing the formal structure of the chapter. This will clarify the precise interrelationship of the sub-units which comprise Isaiah 27. By this means, the specific purpose or intent of the chapter can be determined.

The first sub-unit of chap. 27 is v 1. It is distinguished formally by its introductory *bayyôm hahû'* formula, indicating its genre as an eschatological announcement, and thematically by its focus on the sea monster Leviathan. A new sub-unit begins in v 2 which contains another introductory *bayyôm hahû'* formula. Verse 1 falls into two parts. Verse 1a contains the governing verb of the statement *(yipqōd)* and describes YHWH's attack on Leviathan. Verse 1b, with its *waw*-consecutive *wĕhārag*, describes the results of YHWH's attack, the slaying of the monster. The structure is as follows:

ESCHATOLOGICAL ANNOUNCEMENT: 27:1
YHWH'S DEFEAT OF LEVIATHAN

    I. YHWH's Attack on Leviathan   1a
   II. Result: Slaying of Leviathan   1b

The second sub-unit of Isaiah 27 is vv 2–6. It is distinguished formally by its introductory *bayyôm bahû'* formula, which indicates its generic character as an eschatological announcement, and thematically by its focus on the vineyard. Some have argued that v 6 should not be a part of this unit since it contains its own introductory formula, *habbám'îm*,[27] but this verse is necessary to explain the allegory in vv 2–5 which would otherwise be incomprehensible. Furthermore, vv 2–6 are cast in future-oriented, projecting language, whereas vv 7ff, which begin with a generically distinct rhetorical question, are oriented toward the present. Verses 2–6 deal with God's protection of Israel, allegorically portrayed as the vineyard. Verses 7ff take up the punishment of Israel.

---

[27] Wildberger, *Jesaja 13–27*, 1008, 1014–5.

Verses 2–6 fall into three sections, v2, vv 3–5, and v 6, each of which is formally identified by the perspective of its verbs. Verse 2 contains a masculine plural imperative verb, ʿannû. The speaker is apparently the prophet but the addressee is not identified. This verse serves as the introduction to the allegory which follows. Verses 3–5 contain the vineyard allegory proper and are formally distinguished by their first person plural singular form of address. The speaker here is God. Again, the addressee is not identified. The third person feminine pronouns refer back to the vineyard mentioned in v 2.[28] Verse 6 is cast in third person masculine form and explains the meaning of the vineyard allegory in vv 3–5. The speaker is not identified, but presumably, he is the prophet. The addressee is not specified.

The vineyard allegory in vv 3–5 contains two basic sections. Verse 3 contains direct statements concerning God's protection of the vineyard. Verse 3a specifies God's actions of guarding (v 3aα) and watering (v 3aβ). Verse 3b summarizes the purpose of God's guarding the vineyard with its subordinate clause in v 3bα, i.e., God guards the vineyard lest someone comes upon it. Verses 4–5 outline God's responses in the event that someone does come upon the vineyard.[29] Verse 4a states God's lack of hostility toward potential visitors. Verses 4b-5 describe the actual responses. If someone comes with hostile intent, expressed metaphorically in v 4bα as someone placing thorns and briars against God, then God will react with hostility, advancing against the vineyard and burning it (v 4bβ.[30] Verse 5, introduced by ʾô which expresses an alternative case, describes God's reaction to a peaceful visitor. If he grasps God's protection and attempts to make peace with Him (v 5a), then he will achieve this end (v 5b).[31] The third person feminine pronouns in v 4b indicate that God is waiting for the reaction from the vineyard itself. If the vineyard produces briars and thorns, God will destroy it. If it accepts God's protection, it will receive that protection. This indicates that the purpose of the allegory is to offer reconciliation to the vineyard, i.e., to Israel. It is up to the vineyard to respond.

[28] While kerem is normally masculine, the feminine pronoun in the statement ʿannû lāh, "sing of it," indicates that it is understood as a feminine noun here. Cf. Lev 25:3 where the feminine pronoun of tēbûʾātāh, "its produce," indicates that kerem is understood as feminine.

[29] The absence of a nomial subject for yipqōd indicates an unspecified subject, i.e., "should one come upon it." Cf. Wildberger, Jesaja 13–27, 1007.

[30] The feminine pronoun indicates that the vineyard will be burned. On the significance of the burning of the vineyard for the interpretation of the allegory, see below.

[31] The order of the words is significant here. Verse 5aβ places the verb yaʿăśeh first, indicating the condition that he must initiate action to obtain the desired result, peace. Verse 5b places šālôm first, emphasizing the result of his action, peace, which he will obtain only if he shows the proper initiative.

Verse 6 explains the meaning of the allegory. The vineyard is obviously Israel and this verse anticipates Israel's acceptance of God's offer of reconciliation. Jacob/Israel will take root, blossoming and blooming in v6a. The result will be a world filled with fruit in v 6b.

The structure of vv 2–6 is as follows:

ESCHATOLOGICAL ANNOUNCEMENT:
GOD'S OFFER OF   27:2–6
RECONCILIATION TO ISRAEL;
NEW VINEYARD ALLEGORY

I. Introduction	2
II. Vineyard Allegory Proper	3–5
A. God's statements of protection	3
1. specification of actions	3a
a. guarding	3aα
b. watering	3aβ
2. purpose of God's protection	3b
a. case: someone comes	3bα
b. consequence: God's protection	3bβ
B. God's offer of reconciliation	4–5
1. God's lack of anger	4a
2. alternative reactions	4b–5
a. hostile	4b
1) hostile response of people	4bα
2) hostile reaction of God	4bβ
a) advance against	4bβ1
b) kindle	4bβ2
b. peaceful	5
1) peaceful response of people	5a
a) seize protection	5aα
b) make peace	5aβ
2) peaceful reaction of God	5b
III. Explanation of Allegory	6
A. Jacob/Israel will be reestablished	6a
1. Jacob will take root	6aα
2. Israel will bloom and blossom	6aβ
B. Result: World filled with fruit	6b

The third sub-unit of Isaiah 27 is vv 7–13. The unit is distinguished formally by the introduction of a rhetorical question in v 7 which has no syntactic connection nor an apparent thematic relationship to the preceding material. Verses 8–9 begin a response to the concerns expressed in the rhetorical question of v 7. Syntactical connections at v 10 (*kî*) and vv 12 and 13 (*wĕhāyâ bayyôm hahû᾽*), however, indicate that the response does not end with v 9 but includes vv 10–11 and 12–13 as well. Chapter 28 begins a new formal unit apart from chaps. 24–27.

Verse 7 constitutes the first sub-unit of vv 7–13. This two-part rhetorical question, "Like the smiting of his smiters is he smitten? [v 7a] Like the slaying of his slain (is he) slain?" [v 7b], apparently compares the situation of Israel with that of her enemies. Obviously, the question presupposes that Israel has suffered at the hands of an enemy, but it also presupposes that her enemy has suffered far worse. In making this comparison, the question suggests that Israel's lot is not as bad as one might think. It could be far worse. It therefore challenges the assumption that Israel has been completely destroyed.

The response in vv 8–13 includes three sections distinguished by their contents. Verses 8–9 focus on the punishment of Israel as expiation for its guilt. Verses 10–11 focus on the image of the abandoned city whose people have no understanding. Verses 12–13 focus on the future restoration of Israel to Jerusalem.

Verse 8, despite the difficulties in understanding v 8a, addresses the current situation of the people. They are in exile, stated explicitly in v 8a[32] and metaphorically in v 8b through the imagery of removal by wind. Verse 9 uses projecting, future-oriented language to explain the purpose or outcome of this exile, i.e., the expiation of Jacob's guilt. This is basically stated in v 9aα. Verse 9aβ + b states the proof or result of the removal of Jacob's sin. A statement indicating proof appears in v 9aβ and introduces the two specifications of the proof which appear in v 9bα (when he crushes the altars) and v 9aβ (when Asherim and Hammanim do not stand).

Verses 10–11 describe the deserted city. The verbless clauses in vv 10a and 11bα indicate that, like v 8, these verses refer to a current state of affairs. Verses 10–11a contain the actual description of the city. This desolation of the city is basically stated in v 10a which claims that it is solitary (v 10aα) and abandoned (v 10aβ). Verses 10b–11a elaborate on this statement employing the images of a calf grazing in its midst (v 10b) and women gathering its dried cuttings for tinder (v 11a). Verse 11b explains the reason for this desolation. The people lack understanding (v 11bα). Consequently, God shows neither mercy nor favor (v 11bβγ).

Verses 12–13 describe the eschatological restoration of Jerusalem in two parts, each of which begins with the formula, *wĕhēyâ bayyôm hahûʿ*. Verse 12 focuses on the recovery of the exiles by using harvest imagery. God will beat out the exiled people from the Euphrates to the Nile (v

---

[32] The appearance of the second person statement, *bĕšallĕḥāh tĕrîbennâ*, "by expulsion, you contend against her," in a third person context indicates that it is an interpretative gloss, addressed to God, which is intended to explain *bĕsaʾssĕʾâ* in terms of exile. Cf. Clements, 221.

12a) which will result in the gathering (gleaning) of all the people of Israel (v 12b). Verse 13 focuses on the return of the exiles to Jerusalem. The return is described in a three-part sequence determined by the *waw*-consecutive verbal structure of the verse. First, the great *shôfar* will blow (v 13aα1). Second, the exiles will come from Assur and Egypt (v 13aα2 + β). Third, they will all worship God in Jerusalem (v 13b).

As noted above, the references to Isaiah 1 in vv 10–11 indicate that the desolate city is Jerusalem. This helps to clarify the relation of vv 12–13 to vv 10–11. Verses 12–13, with their future orientation, function in relation to vv 10–11 in a manner similar to that of v 9 to v 8. They explain the outcome of a current situation, i.e., they explain the future of the desolate city (Jerusalem) described in vv 10–11. Not only do vv 10–13 then form a structural parallel to vv 8–9, they represent a thematic development as well. Once the guilt of Jacob is expiated (vv 8–9), then the desolate Jerusalem will be filled with its redeemed inhabitants (vv 10–13).

Thus, vv 8–13 respond to the concerns posed by the rhetorical question of v 7. They refute the defeatist attitude which the question presupposes by explaining that the current situation of Israel, the exile of the people and the desolation of Jerusalem, will change for the better in the future. The exile is about to end and Jerusalem will be restored so that Israel is not so badly smitten after all. The purpose of this section is to encourage Israel, to convince the people that all is not lost in their present situation of defeat. Generically, vv 7–13 are therefore an exhortation to the people of Israel to maintain hope for their future restoration in Jerusalem.

The generic characterization of vv 7–13 as an exhortation to Israel aids in clarifying its relationship to the vineyard allegory of vv 2–6. As noted above, the purpose of the allegory was to offer reconciliation to the people of Israel. Should the vineyard/people react to God's offer with hostility, i.e., by producing briars and thorns, then God will respond with hostility by burning the vineyard (v 4b). Should the people/vineyard react peacefully by accepting God's protection, God will respond peacefully (v 5). The choice belongs to the vineyard, i.e., the people of Israel. As v 6 indicates, the allegory presupposes that the people will make the proper choice. By offering encouragement to the people, vv 7–13 reinforce the expectation of v 6. They give the people a reason to make the proper choice, i.e., to accept God's protection in expectation that their present desperate state will end when they are restored to Jerusalem. Thus, vv 7–13 apply the message of the allegory to the current situation of the people. Consequently, vv 2–6 and 7–13 constitute a single unit which exhorts the people to accept God's protection in anticipation of their restoration to Jerusalem. Verses 2–6 make the offer of reconciliation. Verses 7–13 encourage the people to accept the offer. The structure of vv 2–13 is as follows:

EXHORTATION TO ISRAEL TO ACCEPT GOD'S   .   27:2–13
OFFER OF RECONCILIATION

I. New Vineyard Allegory: Eschatological Announcement of God's Offer of Reconciliation	2–6
A. Introduction	2
B Vineyard allegory proper	3–5
1. God's statements of protection	3
2. God's offer of reconciliation	4-5
C. Explanation of allegory: Vineyard is Israel	6
II. Exhortation Proper: Application of Allegory to Israel	7-13
A. Rhetorical question challenging defeatist attitude of people	7
1. concerning smiting	7a
2. concerning slaying	7b
B. Response: Refutation of defeatist attitude	8–13
1. concerning exile of people	8–9
a. current situation: exile	8
1) expressed explicitly	8a
2) expressed metaphorically	8b
b. outcome of exile: expiation	9
1) basically stated	9aα
2) proof/result of expiation	9aβ + b
a) introductory statement	9aβ
b) specifications	9b
i. crush altars	9bα
ii. remove Asherim/Hammanim	9bβ
2. concerning desolation of city (Jerusalem)	10–13
a. current situation: desolation	10–11
1) description of desolate city	10–11a
a) basically stated	10a
i. solitary	10aα
ii. abandoned	10aβ
b) elaboration	10b-11a
i. grazing calf	10b
ii. women gather tinder	11a
2) explanation for desolation	11b
a) people lack understanding	11bα
b) consequences	11bβ

i. Maker shows no mercy	$11b\beta^1$
ii. Creator shows no favor	$11b\beta^2$
b. eschatological announcement: restoration of people to city	12–13
1) concerning recovery of exiles	12
a) God winnows foreign lands	12a
b) result: exiles are gathered	12b
2) concerning return of exiles	13
a) *shôfar* blast	$13a\alpha^1$
b) exiles come	$13a\alpha^2 + \beta$
c) worship God in Jerusalem	13b

Finally, the relation of Isa 27:2–13 to Isa 27:1 and Isaiah 24–26 needs to be addressed. Naturally, full discussion of this issue is not possible here, but a few tentative observations are in order.[33]

Isa 27:1 announces God's victory over the sea monster, Leviathan, the mythological symbol of the forces of cosmic chaos.[34] In the context of Isaiah 24–27 this refers to God's overturning the earth and His overthrow of the city of chaos.[35] Identification of this city is disputed, but it seems to be a mythological representation of the earthly power of the nations.[36] The defeat of this city is portrayed with imagery drawn from covenant curse traditions indicating violation of the Noachic covenant.[37] Once the defeat is accomplished, the nations turn to God at Mt. Zion. At this point, cosmic order is restored and this is symbolized through the defeat of Leviathan. A number of scholars see this as the climax of the Isaiah Apocalypse and question the role of Isa 27:2–13 which anticlimactically looks toward a restoration of Israel to Jerusalem.[38]

Yet, the defeat of the sea monster Leviathan and the restoration of Israel are linked together in other texts from Isaiah. We have already noted that Isa 17:12–14 ties the rebuke of the nations, portrayed in chaos sea imagery, to the restoration of Israel.[39] Isa 11:10–16 makes the connection explicit. The passage portrays God's gathering the exiles of Israel

---

[33] For a brief discussion of the superstructure of Isaiah 24–27, see *Sweeney*, 146–51.

[34] Cf. C. Gordon, "Leviathan: Symbol of Evil," *Biblical Motifs: Origins and Transformations* (ed. A. Altmann; Cambridge: Harvard University, 1966) 1–9.

[35] Cf. P. Redditt, *Isaiah 24–27: A Form Critical Analysis* (Ph.D. Dissertation; Vanderbilt University, 1972) 224.

[36] Clements, 202–3.

[37] Kaiser, *Isaiah 13–39*, 183–4.

[38] March, 170–5, 187–98; R. B. Y. Scott, "The Book of Isaiah: Chapters 1–39," *IB* 5.305.

[39] Note that Isa 24:13 cites Isa 17:6 to describe the destruction of the city of chaos. This indicates that the judgment against Israel, described in Isaiah 17, is now applied to the nations (cf. Isa 17:12–14), represented by the city of chaos. Cf. Kaiser, *Isaiah 13–39*, 181; Clements, 203.

and Judah from the nations and their restoration as a second Exodus. Verse 15 describes God's ban of the tongue of the sea of Egypt and His waving His hand over the River (i.e., the Euphrates). He then smites it into seven channels so that the people can cross dry-shod. The result is the return of the exiles. In Ugaritic and Hebrew mythology, Leviathan is portrayed as a seven-headed sea monster whom Baal/YHWH defeats to establish cosmic order.[40] According to Ps 74:13–14, God breaks the sea in pieces and crushes the heads of Leviathan to create cosmic order. This imagery apparently stands behind the statement in Isa 11:15 concerning the smiting of the Sea of Egypt/Euphrates River into seven channels. But in Isa 11:15–16, the order which results is the restoration of Israel. Similarly, Isa 27:2–13 portrays the restoration of Israel as the result of God's defeat of Leviathan.

There are other similarities between Isaiah 27 and Isa 11:10–16. The references to the River (Euphrates) and the Brook of Egypt (Nile) in Isa 27:12 correspond to similar references in Isa 11:15. The mention of Assur and Egypt in Isa 27:13 corresponds to the mention of Egypt and Assur in Isa 11:11 (cf. vv. 15–16). The "outcasts" (wĕhanniddaḥîm) of Isa 27:13 correspond to the "outcasts of Israel" (nidḥê yiśrā'ēl) in 11:12 and Jacob's "taking root" in Isa 27:6 calls to mind the "root of Jesse" in 11:10. But the most important point of comparison involves the role which the gathering of the exiles plays in relation to the nations. The gathering of the exiles is associated with God's "ensign to the nations," a sign of God's power to which the nations should look (cf. Isa 11:10). Thus, in Isa 11:11–16, the gathering of the exiles becomes the sign by which the nations will recognize the power of God.[41] That recognition will be complete when God, having defeated the forces of chaos (Tongue of the Sea of Egypt/ River Euphrates), brings the remnant of His people home. This aids in clarifying the relationship of Isaiah 27 to chaps. 24–26. The restoration of Israel is the climactic event in God's defeat of the forces of chaos on earth. Until Israel is restored, full cosmic order is not complete. The precise literary relationship between Isa 11:10–16 and Isaiah 27 is uncertain,[42]

---

[40] Cf. UT 67:I:1–3; 'nt: III:38–39.

[41] Cf. Isa 11:10; Kaiser, Isaiah 1–12, 262–5.

[42] While there are thematic and lexical similarities between these texts, there are also differences. Isa 11:10 employs royal Davidic imagery which does not appear in Isaiah 27. Isa 11:11–16 employs Exodus imagery whereas Isaiah 27 employs that of creation in describing the defeat of chaos. It therefore seems unlikely that these texts were written by the same author or redactor as Vermeylen maintains (Du prophète Isaïe à l'apocalyptique, 1. 279–80). It is also uncertain whether Isaiah 27 is literarily dependent on Isa 11:11–16 or vice versa. Wildberger (Jesaja 28–39 [BKAT X/3; Neukirchen-Vluyn: Neukirchener, 1982] 1572–73, 1575) assigns both passages to his final redaction category, but hesitates to assign both to the same redactor.

but they appear to share a similar concept that the restoration of Israel is the climactic act in God's restoration of order in the world.

Clearly, the new vineyard song of Isa 27:2–6 and the other sub-units of chap. 27 can not be viewed as a series of unrelated supplements to the Isaiah Apocalypse. There is a conceptual unity to these materials which offers hope for the future restoration of the post-exilic Jewish community.[43] This conceptual unity is based in a theological reflection on previous Isaianic tradition, not only on the vineyard song of Isa 5:1–7, but on chaps. 1 and 17 (and perhaps Isa 11:10–16) as well. In employing these older traditions, the writer of Isaiah 27 did not restrict their meaning to their original historical contexts in the 8th century B.C.E., but applied them to the circumstances of the post-exilic period. In this respect, the reinterpretation of older Isaianic tradition and its application to later historical circumstances testifies to the principle stated in Isa 40:8, "The grass withers, the flower fades, but the word of our God shall stand forever."[44]

---

[43] There is no indication that the sub-units which comprise Isaiah 27 were written by the same hand. There is no unified literary style or semantic consistency in the chapter and the imagery shifts from unit to unit. Instead, the chapter must be viewed as a redactional unity.

[44] I would like to thank my colleagues, Stephen Sapp and John T. Fitzgerald, Jr., for their assistance in the preparation of this paper.

"THE END OF THE DESOLATIONS OF JERUSALEM": FROM JEREMIAH'S 70 YEARS TO DANIEL'S 70 WEEKS OF YEARS

LESTER L. GRABBE
University of Hull
Hull, England

In two passages Jeremiah is credited with the prophecy that Jerusalem would be desolate and Judah taken captive for 70 years (Jer 25:11–12; 29:10). Exactly what was meant by this prediction is not completely clear; most likely it was only a general statement based on a stereotypical figure.[1] Like so many symbolic statements in the prophets, however, it became both a problem of fulfillment and an occasion of apocalyptic speculation. The most famous interpretation is that of the "seventy weeks prophecy" of Dan 9:24–27. The aim of my article is to examine the roots of Daniel's prophecy, both in Jeremiah and elsewhere in Israelite tradition. Because of the abundance of literature on the subject, I will only briefly summarize what can already be found in the standard commentaries and treatments and devote more attention to what may be genuinely new.

Old Testament Passages

Already in early post-exilic times Jeremiah's 70 years had become a hermeneutical problem. A straightforward reading of Jeremiah's prophecy says that the exile would last 70 years; one would assume that the period would thus have ended with the decree of Cyrus, or at least with the actual return of exiles a year or two later (Ezra 1). Zech 1:12 seems to say, however, that almost two decades after Cyrus' degree this period of time had still not come to an end. At this point the Israelites would still have been cognizant of the actual amount of time in exile, though in another century or so that information was evidently already to have become lost.[2] This seems to be the case by the time that 2 Chron 36:22–

---

[1] P. Grelot, "Soixante-dix semaines d'années," *Bib* 50 (1969) 169–86, esp. 173–78.
[2] L. L. Grabbe, "Chronography in Hellenistic Jewish Historiography," *SBL 1979 Seminar Papers* (SBLASP 17; Chico: Scholars, 1979) 2.43–68, esp. 55–58.

23 was written because it ties the exile to the sabbatical year, stating that the land was now able to rest for 70 years to make up for the many unobserved sabbatical years in the past. In the understanding of the Chronicler the Jews were exiled for the entire 70 years (contrary to the actual historical chronology as it is now understood), thus making the time end with the first year of Cyrus as king of Babylon.

The concept of the sabbatical year is described in Lev 25:2–7 and was known at least as early as the time of Jeremiah (Jer 34:8–11). Units of seven also feature in the very next chapter, Lev 26, though "seven times" (vv 18, 21, 24, 28) is most likely the measure of intensity. Nevertheless, the threatened punishments are also explicitly related to the failure to keep the seventh year rest (vv 34–35). While no direct statement is made, it seems likely that the 70 years of Jeremiah were thought of as ten sabbatical cycles.

It is probably one of the most established consenses of critical scholarship that Daniel 7–12 was composed by a writer of the Maccabean period, almost certainly in the year 165 or 164 BCE. The writer has two major thoughts on Jeremiah's 70 years: (1) the prophecy was not fulfilled by the decree of Cyrus, or at least it was only partially fulfilled by the Persian king's edict; (2) Jeremiah's prediction contains a cryptic reference to the Maccabean author's own time. The ten sabbatical years (10 × 7) of Jeremiah become ten *jubilee* cycles (10 × 49) by implication (cf. Lev. 25:8–12). Jeremiah's prophecy now no longer refers simply to the length of the exile but takes on a theological and cosmic dimension: it centers around the temple and its sanctity, rather than the land and the people (though the question of sin is central in both prophecies), and it refers to an apocalyptic endtime, not just the return of the exiles.

Clear historical references have long been seen in Dan 9:24–27: v 25 refers to the decree of Cyrus and the rebuilding of Jerusalem; the "anointed one, a prince" is often taken to be Jeshua or Zerubbabel. In v 26 the "anointed one" is usually thought to be Onias III who was slain at the instigation of Menelaus (cf. 2 Macc 4:33–34), while the "prince who is to come" is taken to be Antiochus IV. Antiochus' activities are further described in v 27: his agreement with the so-called "Hellenists," the stopping of the regular sacrifices, and the establishment of an "abomination of desolation." However, the prophecy is not just *ex eventu* since it is clear that Antiochus' death has not yet taken place and is predicted, a prediction which was of course incorrect (cf. especially Dan 11:40–12:3).

Unresolved Questions

What I have surveyed so far is not new; indeed, most of the comments are fairly accessible in the standard handbooks. However, there are still some loose ends which to my mind have never been tied up or, it seems, even clearly recognized as problematic. These fall into two major areas:

1. Despite the clear references to historical events, the passage still fits uneasily into the category of *ex eventu* prophecy. That is, even though the author of Daniel did make some genuine predictions (the death of Antiochus, the elimination of the abomination of desolation, and the resumption of the regular sacrifices), the bulk of the prophecy refers to events which had already taken place. Thus, apart from the "half of the week" (i.e., 3½ years) and the vague "decreed end" of v 27, most of vv 24–26 are usually interpreted as *post eventum*. Yet whereas the historical references of the long *ex eventu* prophecy of chapter 11 can generally be sorted out without too much trouble, much of 9:24–27 does not clearly and easily fit the known historical context. This is highlighted by practically all the major commentaries which resort to a great deal of emendation in order to make the statements correspond with history.[3]

2. Even though certain elements of linguistic usage are highly characteristic of the author, other aspects are foreign to him. One cannot draw far-reaching conclusions from such *hapax legomena* as "determine" (*ḥtk*, 9:24), "moat" (*hārûṣ*, 9:25), or "distress" (*ṣôq*, 9:25). On the other hand, the word "anointed" (*māšîaḥ*), used twice in this passage but nowhere else in the book, is especially significant (note also the verb *mšḥ* in v 24). In addition, the word "covenant" (*běrît*) elsewhere in Daniel always refers to the holy covenant between God and the righteous Israelites (9:4; 11:22, 28, 30, 32), whereas here it seems to refer to the alliance between Antiochus and the Jewish "Hellenizers". Further in v 25 the expression "the many" (*rabbîm* with the article) for the "Hellenist sinners" is a usage unique in Daniel. For the author of Daniel the noun with the article seems to have a semi-technical meaning of "the multitude," with reference to the mass of the Jews who are not blatant sinners (11:33, 39; 12:3). Only here is this specific word used of those whom the Danielic author would have regarded as the apostate Israelites.

It does not seem possible to explain these examples of a difference in usage as mere coincidence or due to a desire for variety in expression. There are other occasions when one would expect the author to have used "anointed" if it were part of his normal idiolect (e.g., 11:22). As for the word *běrît* the author does not use it of secular alliances, either with other powers (11:17, 23) or with the Jewish "Hellenizers" (11:30, 32, 39). On the contrary, Antiochus and the Hellenizers are described as those

[3] See R. H. Charles, *A Critical and Exegetical Commentary on the Book of Daniel* (Oxford: Clarendon, 1929); J. A. Montgomery, *A Critical and Exegetical Commentary on the Book of Daniel* (ICC; Edinburgh: T & T Clark, 1927); L. F. Hartman and A. A. Di Lella, *The Book of Daniel* (AB; Garden City: Doubleday, 1978).

who violate the covenant (11:28, 30, 32). Thus, it seems unlikely that the Maccabean author would have used *bĕrît* to describe what he saw as an abominable agreement between Antiochus and Jewish sinners; whatever the range of meaning of *bĕrît* in other Hebrew sources, it seems to be an exclusively religious term in the normal usage of the author of Daniel 7–12. Similarly, the author had the opportunity to use *hārabbîm* of the Hellenizers elsewhere if it had had no technical meaning for him (11:30, 32).

Thus, we are faced with a difficulty apparently not recognized up to this time, viz., a passage which refers in part to the known historical period of the author's time and with his characteristic linguistic usage, yet one which in part ill fits this interpretation and which has linguistic usage completely uncharacteristic of the author. How can one explain this? It seems to me that there is a reasonable solution: *the author of Daniel 7–12 has taken over and adapted an earlier oracle known to him.*

This proposal resolves the difficulties noted above but immediately raises a major question of its own: Is there any evidence of independent oracles in circulation at this time which might serve as examples or analogues? The answer is, Yes. First of all, we know that a number of oracles based on the figure 70 existed before or about the time of the Maccabean revolt. Even before the time of Jeremiah an inscription of Esarhaddon used the symbolic figure of 70 for a time of punishment.[4] The prime example in Jewish literature is the Animal Apocalypse (*1 Enoch* 85–90) which divides history from Adam to Judas Maccabeus into 70 stages of no fixed length. This prophecy seems to date from about 165–163 BCE[5] and is thus roughly contemporary with Daniel 7–12. There are other Jewish texts which have a similar structure to Dan 9:24–27[6] but these are probably also directly dependent on the passage in Daniel.

Secondly, the figure of ten is prominent in several oracles, which is important if the interpretation of Daniel's 70 weeks as ten jubilees is accepted. The Apocalypse of Weeks (*1 Enoch* 93:1–10; 91:11–17) divides history into ten weeks. A recent study argues that the apocalypse is no later than 167 BCE and thus a few years older than Daniel 7–12 and the Animal Apocalypse.[7]

Interestingly, a climax comes at the end of the seventh week, making the number seven as well as ten important for this writing. The *Fourth*

---

[4] Grelot, 173–175. For the text and a translation of the relevant passage see B. Albrektson, *History and the Gods* (Coniectanea Biblica, OT Series, 1; Lund: Gleerup, 1967) 91.

[5] J. C. VanderKam, *Enoch and the Growth of an Apocalyptic Tradition* (CBQMS 16; Washington: Catholic Biblical Association, 1984) 161–63.

[6] F. F. Bruce, *The Teacher of Righteousness in the Qumran Texts* (London: Tyndale, 1957) 16–17.

[7] VanderKam, 142–49.

Sibylline Oracle contains a section which divides history into ten generations (lines 49–101). While Sibylline Oracle 4 dates from around 80 CE,
this section seems to be based on an old oracle from the early
Hellenistic period.[8] Thus, it is much older than Daniel 7–12 and probably originally non-Jewish in origin.

Thirdly, Josephus tells us of several oracles in circulation in his own
time. Especially important is the one in *War* 6. 311–13:

> Thus the Jews, after the demolition of Antonia, reduced the
> temple to a square, although they had it recorded in their oracles
> that the city and the sanctuary would be taken when the temple
> should become four-square. But what more than all else incited
> them to the war was an ambiguous oracle, likewise found in their
> sacred scriptures, to the effect that at that time one from their
> country would become ruler of the world.

The exact source of these oracles has been much debated. There are
several scholars who argue that Dan 9:24–27 is being used, however, at
least for the oracle about the temple being made into a square and for the
phrase "at that time."[9] There is something compelling about the idea of a
connection between Dan 9:25 and the statement about the temple
becoming "four-square." On the other hand, the passage in its present
form would appear to be rather far removed from Josephus' interpretation, which argues against the canonical text being the basis of the
"ambiguous oracle." However, if an original oracle which mentioned
rĕhôb ("plaza," "street") in a more prominent way was the basis of Daniel 9
but also continued to circulate independently, it could also be the origin
of Josephus' "ambiguous oracle."

This is only speculation but it illustrates my point that a variety of
oracles—not necessarily biblical in origin—were extant in the last centuries of the Second Temple. The few preserved plus the occasional
references to others makes us aware of the wealth of oracular material
which was available to the Jews of the time. The Seventy Weeks Prophecy, far from being unique, is only one of many which made the rounds in
Jewish circles. A number of these were not even Jewish in origin but
were taken over and used by Jewish apocalyptists for their own needs.
This being so, it would hardly be surprising if the Danielic author
adapted pre-existent material for his own purposes.

---

[8] J. J. Collins, "The Place of the Fourth Sibyl in the Development of the Jewish
Sibyllina," *JJS* 25 (1974) 365–80 esp. 370–76; D. Flusser, "The Four Empires in
the Fourth Sibyl and in the Book of Daniel," *IOS* 2 (1972) 148–75, esp. 148–53.

[9] F. F. Bruce, "Josephus and Daniel," *ASTI* 4 (1965) 148–62, esp. 155; U. Fischer,
Eschatologie und Jenseitserwartung im hellenistischen Diasporajudentum
(BZNW 44; Berlin/New York: de Gruyter, 1978) 158–66; cf. Grabbe, 57–58.

Summary and Conclusions

The Seventy Weeks Prophecy of Dan 9:24–27 is explicitly an inter-pretation of the Seventy Years Prophecy of Jeremiah and is a good example of the hermeneutical process already attested in the canonical text itself. However, this is not the first attempt to explain Jeremiah's 70 years, as Zech 1:12 and 2 Chron 36:22–23 show. Further, this may not be the first attempt to explain the 70 years as 70 weeks of years, for I have proposed that Dan 9:24–27 represents an old oracle which has only been adapted by the author of Daniel. There are several reasons for advancing such a hypothesis:

1. Like Daniel 11 the Seventy Weeks Prophecy is clearly connected with known historical events at certain points, but contrary to chapter 11 a surprising amount of the prophecy cannot be easily related to Macca-bean history. The incongruous nature of much of the passage is tacitly acknowledged by the many emendations proposed to make the *ex eventu* part of the prophecy match the historical data.

2. While some of the linguistic usage is characteristic of Daniel 8–12, certain expressions seem to be used contrary to the author's attested usage, especially "covenant," "the many," and "anointed."

3. A variety of oracles before or roughly contemporary with Daniel demonstrate that 9:24–27 was by no means unique. Some of these oracles use the figure 70 or ten, showing that oracles with such symbolic num-bers were commonplace. An oracle in Josephus bears an uncanny re-semblance to Daniel without being clearly based on the canonical text; this could be explained by the continued independent existence of an oracle which was also taken over and modified by the author of Daniel.

Attempts to delineate the hypothesized oracle further would only be speculation. Suffice it to say that this hypothesis explains certain features of Daniel's prophecy and does not seem to create new problems of its own. If so, the author of Daniel was not interpreting Jeremiah directly but simply took a pre-existing interpretation and deftly made it a part of his own message. Such a hypothesis would imply that the process of interpreting Jeremiah's 70 years was a continual one and that the Danielic writer was not the first to interpret the 70 years as *weeks* of years.

In my files on Daniel are old notes from some of Professor Brownlee's seminars, a reminder of his interest in that book. I last saw him at his retirement party in Claremont in 1982, at which time he was looking forward to a long and profitable retirement. Sadly, that was not to be. It is an honor to pay this small tribute to his memory.

THE OLD TESTAMENT AND ITS INHERITORS*

". . . at once perfect and perpetually incomplete."

KENT HAROLD RICHARDS
Iliff School of Theology
Denver, Colorado

We take for granted our language. What was spoken and written at home becomes our speaking and writing. We inherit the accents, syntax, grammatical frailties, idioms and some suggest even the tonal qualities. How many times has a daughter or son answered the phone, turned to you and with some indignation said, "they think I'm you!"

We do not inherit our language systematically, but rather in a hit and miss fashion. We are not instructed first to distinguish the imperative from the indicative—and many will not in their adult years be familiar with these terms—yet most three year olds know all too well the imperative mood!

There are some occasions when we can *not* take our language for granted. These situations are startling and profound. They cause us to reflect upon the marvelous inheritance we call language. For example, seeing an autistic child isolated—however explained—from the inheritance of language. Walking into a cardiac unit of a hospital where someone we know lies there incapable of expressing through their inheritance the words and expressions once so facile. These are dramatic experiences which call us to reflection on many dimensions of life. We may think that these reflections are beyond language. They bring us face to face with who we are and one might say with our finiteness. Yet even the recognition of one's finiteness is formed by language. Language shapes experience just as much as experience shapes language.

Less dramatic but equally revealing is the experience of learning a new language or visiting a country whose language we do not know. We are reminded in those contexts of both the convenience of language and what *The New English Bible* calls the "babble of the language of all the world" (Gen 11:9). Until we meet the boundaries we are seldom jostled

---

*Installation address as Professor of Old Testament delivered on 12 October 1983 at Iliff School of Theology

into considering this inheritance we call language. We rarely of our own volition take the initiative. Linguists, who are trained in these matters and have a curiosity for these issues, recognize that research on a well-known language can yield surprises. I have always been under the assumption that "near" is a preposition in phrases like "near the wall." I had never accounted for the fact that in standard English one can say "nearer the wall" or "nearest the wall." We all know that prepositions don't have comparative or superlative forms, therefore, "near" must be functioning as an adjective, or more precisely, as one linguist suggests, a transitive adjective.[1] These examples where we lack knowledge and seem insensitive to the familiar could be multiplied.

If one can understand language as an inheritance it may provide an analogue in seeing the Old Testament (hereafter OT) as an inheritance. Just as with language, there are enormous variables in what each of us has inherited of the OT. Some may not be sure whether the book of Psalms is a part of the OT or not since the practice of printing the Psalms with the New Testament has a long history. Others may have inherited the Jonah story as a narrative about a whale and a man, when in fact no whale is mentioned. Others will have as their OT inheritance the awareness that the Greek text of the Jeremiah book is one eighth shorter than the Hebrew text. Most of us will have inherited the OT in a haphazard fashion just as we did our language. Until we are thrust into the necessity—for whatever reasons—of confronting the OT we all too frequently accept it as a matter of fact. The acceptance can range between those who see it as an ancient pagan classic or, if in one religious community or another it might be understood as canon, scripture or sacred book.

Inheritance is a peculiar and fascinating phenomenon. On this occasion it seemed appropriate that I might examine what the OT suggests about inheritance and from that point of departure determine the implications for those of us who understand ourselves as inheritors of this library of books.

My critical, reflective work in the OT dates back almost exactly twenty-five years ago this Fall at the University of Southern California in one of my only two undergraduate religion courses. I had met this library of books before that time. In fact, I still have the Bible I was given in third grade at Sunnyside Presbyterian Church. It is not marked up like many of those I use today. Its binding is still intact. I do have one text marked in that King James Version but that is because I had to read it in fifth grade in public worship. I remember having Bible stories read to me (the one that I remember most vividly was the Joseph story and what we now call the "technicolor robe"). I heard the great Howard Thurman and

---

[1] Arnold M. Zwicky and Geoffrey K. Pullum, "Cliticization vs. Inflection: English NT," *Language* 59 (1983) 502.

Henry Hitt Crane read it. My grandfather, a Church of the Brethren pastor and teacher of homiletics, comes to mind as one of the voices who read it. But twenty-five years ago amidst all the furor of being a sophomore in college the OT took on a new shape. I could say the initial inheritance as a child was sufficient yet incomplete. I did not have to throw out the old, OT which I had more haphazardly encountered. I do not think I was as cognizant then as I am now that my "haphazard stage" was in continuity with this new critical reading as a sophomore. Nevertheless I think there were clear indications then as now that my inheritance of the OT was changing but not in a way that was focusing on the disjunction of understanding. My work in seminary and graduate school, as well as my teaching over the last fifteen years could be placed in much this same framework.

This is the context in which I would like to place these observations on the OT and its inheritors. First, I will discuss the inheritance traditions found in the Hebrew canonical literature. Second, the focus will turn to several implications for the contemporary inheritors.

*   *   *   *   *

There is no single Hebrew term which contains the inheritance traditions within the OT. Rather there are over a half dozen words which contribute to the meanings of inheritance. These words are sometimes found by themselves which can demonstrate the distinctive qualities of each term. Other times they appear in parallel. These parallel structures indicate a degree of synonymous meaning, that is indicative of the interconnection of the terms.

Surprisingly little critical scholarship has been devoted to the individual terms or their interrelationships. One rarely finds the term inheritance in a subject index of an introductory OT textbook. Bible dictionaries do not treat it as a major entry. The new theological wordbooks are forced to have articles on the separate terms since most of the words occur more than sixty times. These wordbooks infrequently cross reference the terms despite the numerous passages where more than one of the words appears.

There are two reasons these words surrounding inheritance have not been studied together. On the one hand, the immediate inclination is to view inheritance solely within the legal sphere. That is, to examine testamentary activities, transference of possessions and comparative juridical practices in the ancient Near Eastern world. This is an immense, rich and complicated enterprise in which few are trained sufficiently to deal with the wide range of languages. It also takes a certain degree of nerve to jump into this arena. One colleague observed, who wants to study inheritance? The most you could get out of it might be a novel paragraph for your will!

The other reason the terms have not been taken together is that several of them overlap and play into other concepts of long standing interest. One of these is the idea of promise. A concept important not only to Hebrew scripture (promise to the partriarchs, house of David, etc.) but also, within the Christian tradition, a theological concept used to link the testaments.

Before turning to the Hebrew terms one additional comment may be helpful. I have opted for the English word inheritance knowing that there are other terms that might have been used. Many would suggest that "heritage" is a better term since I am dealing with "something transmitted by or acquired from a predecessor." One of the key Hebrew terms, *naḥălāh*, is occasionally translated with the word heritage. Others might suggest "legacy," although this term is not used in many translations. Its older and more primary meanings surround the office of legate. Much of the discussion and some of the English biblical translations focus on yet another term, "patrimony." Historically and culturally, most of the property inheritance in the OT is derived from "fathers." Yet the fundamental issues and implications as I see them are not gender oriented. Inheritance is intended as a generic term which enables me to speak of the *act* of dispensing and acquiring, as well as the *content* of what is dispensed and acquired. It encourages an examination of the total perspective.

There are six Hebrew words which I have placed initially into this complex. First, *hlq*, usually translated "portion" or "share." It can be used in a very straightforward, unreflected manner to refer to part of the whole piece (Gen 14:24). However, in Ps 50:16–18 the wicked are characterized as those whose portion or inheritance is with adulterers as opposed to the righteous who may reside near God and take on their lips the covenant. Here two kinds of inheritance—good and bad—are set in opposition. A second term, *gôrāl*, is usually translated "lot," as in the casting of lots. Joshua at Shiloh casts lots to apportion land. He says, "I will cast lots for you (Israel) here before the LORD our God" (Josh 18:6). However, in the next verse one finds "lot" identified with the first term I mentioned, "the Levites have no inheritance or portion *(hlq)* among you, for the priesthood of the LORD in their inheritance *(naḥălāh)*. "Lot" and inheritance are synonymous.

This introduces the third term, *naḥălāh*, which has been the focus of most of the previous inheritance discussions in the secondary literature. Two quite different passages let us see the interconnection of the three terms.

> Their lot shall be portioned *[hlq]* according to the inheritance *[naḥălāh]* between the larger and smaller.
>
> Num 26:56

> The LORD is my portion and my cup,
>   You increase my lot

> The lines fall for me in pleasant places,
> Yea, my inheritance is beautiful.
>
> Ps 16:5–6

Without a detailed exegesis one can readily ascertain the interconnection, if not synonymous quality of these terms. They designate what is dispensed and acquired.

The fourth term, *segūlah*, occurs only eight times in the OT. The biblical interpreter is always delighted to find a term that occurs so sparingly since massive theories can be evolved best from minuscule data! One writer said of this Hebrew term, "it is filled with theological and spiritual treasures"! Whatever the case, the term does emerge in some intriguing passages which would need to be located in the complex of ideas under discussion.

Listen to the usage in this famous Exodus text.

> You have seen what I did to the Egyptians and how I bore you on eagles' wings and brought you to myself. Now therefore, if you will obey my voice and keep my covenant you shall be my own possession *[segūlah]* among all peoples.
>
> Exod 19:4–5

Inheritance terms occur frequently within the promises to the patriarchs. The fifth word, *'aḥūzah*, surfaces in this promise context.

> I will give to you, and to your descendents after you, the land of your sojournings, all the land of Canaan for an everlasting inheritance *['aḥūzah]*, and I will be their God.
>
> Gen 17:8

The word appears in two other quite different, but interesting texts. Psalm 2, usually designated a royal psalm, has the king reporting what the LORD has said to him.

> . . . you are my son, today I have begotten you. Ask of me, and I will make the nations your inheritance *[naḥǎlāh]*, and the ends of the earth your possession *['aḥūzah]*.
>
> Ps 2:7–8

These terms are found together in a number of places, further substantiating their interconnection. This is also the case in the second passage which deals with women inheriting property rights. The text deals with a question raised by the daughters of Zelophehad on the occasion of their father having died in the desert, but with no sons. Moses reportedly brings this case to the LORD to which part of the response is the following.

> The daughters of Zelophehad are right; you shall give them possession *['ăḥūzah]* of an inheritance *[naḥǎlāh]* among

their father's brethren and cause the inheritance [naḥǎlāh]
of their father to pass to them.

Num 27:7

A final Hebrew term, yrš, depending upon grammatical form and
context, is translated "to take possession" or "inherit." In the nominal
form it can mean an "heir." In Genesis 15, Abram complains that he has
no offspring except a slave who is born in his house. God responds, "This
man shall not be your heir; your own son shall be your heir (15:4). Or
later in this passage God says

> "I am the LORD who brought you from Ur of the Chaldeans, to
> give you this land to possess [yrš]."

Gen 15:7

This overview of the six Hebrew words gives some impression of the
complex of terms identified with the inheritance traditions. The focus has
been on the connection of the terms, not their individuality or
uniqueness. To the English reader there is displayed a range of meanings
which include possession, boundaries, portions, lots, limits and numerous nuances which deal with dispensing and acquiring.

One might expand the range of these terms by calling attention to
the content of what is inherited. Several of the examples illustrated the
inheritance of land. These examples could be expanded if one listed the
numerous promise texts. Other passages cited point to the people as the
inheritance of the LORD. The largest number of occurrences fall into
this category. Two of the examples cited designate the LORD as that
which is inherited. In fact the Joshua passage which was quoted distinguishes the land inheritance of the tribes from the Levites' inheritance
of the LORD. The inheritance even comes to signal what one might call
"destiny." One of Job's "dear" friends, Zophar, speaks of the destiny of
the wicked

> The possessions of his house will be carried away,
>   dragged off in the day of God's wrath.
> This is the wicked one's portion [hlq],
>   The inheritance [naḥǎlāh] decreed for him.

Job 20:29

Or Job says in his final defense,

> What would be my portion [hlq]
>   from God above,
> And my inheritance [naḥǎlāh] from
>   the Almighty on high?

Job 31:2

Still other passages speak of inheritance in an eschatological context. That
which was inherited spans an enormous spectrum in the OT. It can

designated a specific plot of ground and a particular possession. Or it can encompass the issues of individual and communal destiny.

Inheritance traditions in the OT were influenced by the juridical understandings. One can observe martial contexts of inheritance as well. However, the most striking factor comes in what one scholar called the "richly theologized" usage. I would prefer to call it a secondary, reflected richness. By this I mean, after working through over 500 occurrences of these Hebrew words one walks away, not with a sense of having fallen into the pit of technical inheritance cases and laws, but rather of being thrust into the necessity of grappling with those competing, complementing, multifaceted dimensions of dispensing and acquiring even life itself.

*   *   *   *   *

The implications of this all too brief overview of inheritance in the OT are manifold. Had I found a limited perspective the task would have been simple. A novel paragraph here or there in a will would have been fun! If inheritance had been understood with one or at most two Hebrew terms the conclusions might have been neat and precise. Some will complain that this is typical of the so-called biblical scholar who always finds "things" more ambiguous and complicated than anyone else! It is possible to point toward several implications. While these may not be elementary, they can be transparent and understandable.

First, there is a tension which pervades the texture of inheritance in the OT which is not fully expressed in the overview of terms. The point is that there is a *reciprocity between the inheritor and the inherited*. This reciprocity or mutuality resides deep in the social fabric of the people of The Book.

Inheritance is not something you take or leave. Jewish law assumes that children become the inheritors. Children are heirs *eo ipso*. They may not renounce their inheritance, since one cannot waive what one already possesses. Through the laws of transference an inheritance may be conveyed but never waived. One might say inheritance is automatic and immediate.

This is not terribly comforting to a time and culture which so emphasizes individual freedom. We want to make up our own minds about what we inherit and from whom we inherit it. The focus upon individuality seems pervasive except for our desire to have Dior ties, a Sassoon hairdryer, Izod shirts and a pair of Jordache jeans!

One historian in examining early 19th century American usage of the Bible points to what he calls the "individualization of conscience." He gives several alluring examples. One is the Reverend Elhanan Winchester, a famous Baptist preacher who when fighting the Calvinists on their unwillingness to accept Universalism (the idea that all persons are eventually saved) proposed a method of resolving theological issues.

His method was to lock the door of his study and come to grips with the Bible for himself.

> I shut myself up chiefly in my chamber, read the Scriptures and prayed to God to lead me into all truth, and not suffer me to embrace any error; and I think with an upright mind, I laid open to believe whatsoever the LORD had revealed. It would be too long to tell all the Teaching I had on this head; let it suffice, in short, to say, that I become so well persuaded of the truth of Universal Restoration, that I determined never to deny it.[2]

I suppose one could argue that the Reverend Winchester really understood OT inheritance best of all since he was so close to his Bible. The problem with this free-flowing individualism, which I think is still riding a crest in twentieth century America, is that I doubt that there is much reciprocity between the inheritors and that which is inherited. The focus of individualism is upon the inheritor deciding in isolation what to inherit and not allowing in any genuine way that which is inherited to shape the inheritor.

Another dimension of this reciprocal relationship which produces ambiguity and some tension, has been seen in the overview of Hebrew terms. These words seem to refer to an ever widening number of inheritances.

Therefore when one asks, what is the inheritance of the OT? There is no single answer. One cannot say it is the land or the people or the LORD or even human destiny. Each of these interconnect. It is not that there are no distinctions in inheritance. The overview of terms pointed to some of these and one could accumulate numerous examples.

There is embedded within the OT from a very early time the comprehensiveness of the LORD's inheritance. This comes to light in one of the earliest Hebrew psalms. God sits in the divine council and asks those around him how long they will judge unjustly. God goes on to pass judgment on them. The psalm ends with God no longer speaking but being called,

> Arise O God, judge the earth
> for to thee belong *[nḥl]* all the nations!
>
> Ps 82:8

Here all the "nations" are God's inheritance. It is on this basis that God is called to pass judgment. Inheritance moved to this level certainly affirms the fundamental reciprocity between inheritor and the inherited.

One further observation on this point may be significant for our

---

[2] Nathan O. Hatch, "*Sola Scriptura* and *Novus Ordo Seclorum*," in *The Bible in America: Essays in Cultural History* (eds. Nathan O. Hatch and Mark A. Noll; New York: Oxford University, 1982) 62.

contemporary context. If one sets aside the problem of the "individu-alization of conscience," there still exists a dilemma. Who are the inher-itors of the OT? Several groups will step forward. Certainly Judaism will stand as an inheritor—not under the name OT—but of the Hebrew scripture. Islam will find a place. The Christian Church sometimes haltingly has laid claim to this literature. It is the new group of literary critics which present an interesting case for their inheritance. One of these critics, Harold Bloom, bemoans the current course of literature saying,

> Everyone who now reads and writes in the West . . . is still a son
> or daughter of Homer. As a teacher of literature who prefers the
> morality of the Hebrew Bible to Homer, indeed who prefers the
> Bible aesthetically to Homer, I am no happier about this dark
> truth than you are.[3]

Some have thought that Bloom and others around him constantly reflect on origins, or I would say on inheritance. Some think the key to Bloom may be found in his quote from Kierkegaard, "He who is willing to work gives birth to his own father."[4] Here the reciprocity between inheritance and the inherited takes on yet another twist.

This leads directly to my second and final point. Our inheritance of the OT is *at once perfect and perpetually incomplete.* Deep into my work on the inheritance terms and after submitting the title of this lecture I began to wonder why so many different Hebrew words were emerging to express some dimension or another of the OT understanding of inheritance. I would work through a group of texts, begin to see, for example, how the inheritance of land worked. The inheritance was expressed usually in a context of promise. One received the inheritance not on the basis of inheritance in a strict sense but because of what God had done. God had been faithful therefore the inheritance could be grasped.

I understood inheritance and that set of texts seemed clear enough. It worked perfectly. Here is where the problem emerged. I had to go to some other set of texts and words in order to finish my work. Then I ran into other issues and overlapping problems. The inheritance wasn't the land, it was destiny or even God. Given the context in which I found each of these it seemed perfect. It worked, but why the variation? How could I explain this?

My first answer came in a less refined although similar point to the one I have already mentioned regarding the reciprocity between the

---

[3] Harold Bloom, *A Map of Misreading* (New York: Oxford University, 1975) 33.
[4] Susan A. Handelman, *The Slayers of Moses: The Emergence of Rabbinic Interpre-tation in Modern Literary Theory* (New York: SUNY, 1982) 182.

inheritor and the inherited. The inheritance is in part new and in part
old. The occasions on which Israel inherited something provided a new
and dangerous time in which the old became present. Each new inheritance then in its turn became part of the old. Variation was inevitable so
long as the inheritor and the inherited contributed mutually. One might
suppose that if you could find the penultimate inheritance they would all
be waiting there to be swooped into the same grand finale. There were
those in Israel (and there have been many since) who tried but failed
because they forgot they were a fallible link in the inheritance. After this
attempt I came upon the comment of Louis Finkelstein regarding the
nature of Torah. He said that

> . . . the text is at once perfect and perpetually incomplete; that
> like the universe itself it was created to be a process rather than a
> system—a method of inquiry into the right, rather than a codified
> collection of answers . . .[5]

This provided an analogue for my understanding inheritance in the
OT. Furthermore, it helped me understand my own inheritance of the
OT. Inheritance is a "method of inquiry" not a collection of codes.
Inheritance is—so to speak—continually completing itself. The structure
for this continuing project is found in the reciprocal relationship between
the inheritor and the inherited.

Finkelstein went on to say more about the Torah. It is there ". . . to
discover possible situations with which it might deal and to analyze their
moral implications in the light of its teachings . . ." He contended that
this "is to share the labor of the Divinity . . ."

This certainly is an awesome plane on which one may place our responsibility, but it is equally certain that this is a part of our unending
inheritance.

[5] Louis Finkelstein, "Introduction," in Solomon Schechter, *Aspects of Rabbinic
Theology: Major Concepts of the Talmud* (New York: Schocken, 1961; originally
New York: Macmillan, 1909) xix–xx.

PART TWO

THE FUNCTION OF SCRIPTURE IN INTERTESTAMENTAL LITERATURE

THE BIBLICAL TEXTS IN THE QUMRAN COMMENTARIES: SCRIBAL ERRORS OR EXEGETICAL VARIANTS?

GEORGE J. BROOKE
University of Manchester
Manchester, England

I. *Introduction*

The purpose of this essay is to raise once again the question of variants in the biblical quotations in the Qumran commentaries. That question concerns whether those variants should be considered as accidental scribal errors or as deliberate alterations of a received textual tradition; it may be that some variants are errors, some exegetical alterations. In addition some variants may not be fairly categorized in either camp, but represent orthographic and stylistic differences amongst Jewish writers of different times and places.

Because of the limits imposed upon me, it is necessary in this study to restrict my enquiry somewhat. Firstly, since William H. Brownlee himself has done so much work on this topic in relation to 1QpHab,[1] that manuscript is not considered here. In general he has concluded that much more attention should be paid to the exegetical traditions in and behind the non-stylistic variants in the text of Habakkuk as it is represented in 1QpHab. Secondly, it is not even possible within the limits of this article to list and discuss all the variants in the commentaries apart from 1QpHab;[2] as a result I have concentrated deliberately, but somewhat arbitrarily, on what may be deemed major variants. Thirdly, in order to argue more persuasively that the Qumran commentator was intentionally altering the biblical text within certain rules to accommo-

---

[1] Especially in "Biblical Interpretation among the Sectaries of the Dead Sea Scrolls," *BA* 14 (1951) 54–76, *The Text of Habakkuk in the Ancient Commentary from Qumran* (JBL Monograph Series 11; Philadelphia: SBL, 1959), and *The Midrash Pesher of Habakkuk* (SBL Monograph Series 24; Missoula: Scholars, 1979).

[2] Not all variants are cited even in M. P. Horgan's extensive work: *Pesharim: Qumran Interpretations of Biblical Books* (CBQMS 8; Washington: Catholic Biblical Association of America, 1979); hereafter cited as *Pesharim*. All references to the Qumran commentaries in this essay are according to Horgan's numbering of the fragments, columns and lines.

date his interpretation, I propose to consider for the most part textual variants which are not known in the traditions of the MT or versions.

Since in my opinion such a concentration immediately puts the balance of the argument in favor of recognizing exegetical devices at work in the biblical citations in the commentaries, it is necessary to state unequivocally that not all variants are the result of deliberate exegetical decisions by the commentator: not every variant is an exegetical reading. In relation to variants not previously known two illustrations help prevent any misconception. In 4QpNah 3–4 ii 3–4 Nah 3:3 is quoted. In the MT it includes the phrase *wlhb ḥrb wbrq ḥnyt*, but in 4QpNah the phrase reads solely *lhwb wbrq ḥnyt*, even though at the appropriate place in the interpretation of this verse there is an explicit mention of the sword (*ḥrb*) of the nations (4QpNah 3–4 ii 5). It seems that even the careful Qumran exegete could omit a word by mistake. R. Weiss reckoned[3] that this is because of homoioteleuton, both *lhb* and *ḥrb* ending in *b*, and this is indeed most likely. If that example shows that the Qumran scribe could omit a word, 4QpNah 3–4 iv 7 suggests that he might also represent his own variant tradition with no exegetical bias. In the MT and versions Nah 3:11bβ reads *mᶜwz mᵓwyb;* in 4QpNah it is *mᶜwz bᶜyr mᵓwyb*. This immediately precedes an interpretation which includes the phrase *ᵓwybyhm bᶜyr* (4QpNah 3–4 iv 8). Since *mᶜwz* can denote a city of refuge, it is not strictly necessary for the interpreter to include in the text of Nah 3:11 explicit mention of a city. Elsewhere in 4QpNah, especially in 3–4 i 1–3, there is mention of Jerusalem in the interpretation with no use of any general term such as *ᶜyr* or any other more explicit term naming the place in the preceding biblical text. The one use of *ᶜyr* in Nah 3:1 is interpreted cryptically of "the city of Ephraim, the seekers after smooth things" (4QpNah 3–4 ii 1–2). It seems as if in 4QpNah 3–4 iv 7 the commentator has anticipated his interpretation and inadvertently slipped an extra word into his text of Nahum.

Together with the probability that there are some scribal errors in the biblical texts in the commentaries it must be noted that in many instances the biblical texts in the commentaries support a variant known already. This has led many scholars to suppose that all or nearly all the variants in the biblical texts in the commentaries are witnesses of different recensions or traditions[4] which the commentator plays upon to his

---

[3] "A Comparison between the Massoretic and the Qumran Texts of Nahum III, 1–11," *RevQ* 4 (1963–64) 435; followed by J. Strugnell, "Notes en marge du volume V des «Discoveries in the Judean Desert of Jordan»," *RevQ* 7 (1969–71) 209.

[4] E.g., F. F. Bruce, *Biblical Exegesis in the Qumran Texts* (Grand Rapids: Eerdmans, 1959) 12; most recently, D. Dimant, "Qumran Sectarian Literature," *Jewish Writings of the Second Temple Period* (ed. M. E. Stone; CRINT 2/2; Philadelphia: Fortress/Assen: Van Gorcum, 1984) 505. G. Vermes' view seems to oscillate: *for* exegetical variants is his "The Qumran Interpretation of Scripture in

advantage; few scholars go as far as to suggest that the Qumran commentator actually introduced variants himself.

Within the tradition of the Hebrew text the occurrence of variants of no immediate use to the Qumran commentator is best exemplified by the tendency in the commentaries, as in the targumim, to follow the *qěrê* rather than the *kětîb*, as for example in Isa 10:32 (MT: *byt*; 4QpIsa*a* 2–6 ii 25: *bt* as in 1QIsa*a*), 29:11 (MT: *hspr*; 4QpIsa*c* 15–16:3: *spr*; 1QIsa*a* has *spr* with *h* added above the line), Nah 3:3 (MT: *ykšlw*; 4QpNah 3–4 ii 4: *wkšlw*), and possibly in Mic 1:8 (MT: *šyll*; 1QpMic 11:2: *šll*); indeed, this tendency enables Horgan[5] to restore confidently the *qěrê* of Hos 6:10 in 4QpHos*b* with support from 4QTestim 27 and 1QpHab 9:1 *(kětîb: šᶜryryh; qěrê: šᶜrwryh)*.

Variants which represent the *Vorlage* of the LXX are also frequent in the biblical quotations in the commentaries. Most often these are minor syntactical, grammatical and other stylistic variants. The name of the Lord is often caught up in stylistic variants in the LXX; there are several non-sectarian variations on this also in the Qumran commentaries. In a few instances in the discussion which follows the LXX is used as corroborative evidence for a major exegetical variant, but for the most part my concern is with variants not attested elsewhere in contemporary texts.

In addition to some major and minor variants known already, the biblical texts in the commentaries abound with orthographic variants, some of which variously recur in the medieval witnesses to the MT. The significance of these variants has as yet to be assessed fully;[6] some of them may be of exegetical value.

What follows is an attempt to show that in more cases than are usually recognized the variants in the biblical texts in the Qumran commentaries have been deliberately caused by the desire of the Qumran commentator to make his text conform with his exegetical understanding. Recognition of these early exegetical traditions within the biblical text has some significant ramifications for those Qumran scholars interested in making restorations in the commentaries, for text critics who seldom take adequate account of exegetical traditions in their descriptions of the processes behind the stabilization of the Hebrew text at the end of the Second Temple period, and for historians who sometimes seem to use the commentaries with little appreciation of the subtlety of their content.

its Historical Setting," *Post-Biblical Jewish Studies* (SJLA 8; Leiden: E. J. Brill, 1975) 44, 46; *against* such variants is his "Interpretation, History of: At Qumran and in the Targums," *IDBSup* (1976) 441a.

[5] *Pesharim*, 156.

[6] On the significance of these for establishing the MT see M. Breuer, *The Aleppo Codex and the Accepted Text of the Bible* (Jerusalem: Mosad Harav Kook, 1976).

II. *Major Exegetical Variants in the Qumran Commentaries*

1. The first group of textual differences to be considered appears as kinds of syntactical and grammatical variants; rather than simply being explicable as scribal errors or the repetition of a different recension, these variants can be explained as deliberate alterations of the Hebrew consonantal text. There are four kinds of variant in this category.

(a) Firstly there are variants containing a change in person. In the quotation of Ps 37:10 in 4QpPs*a* 1–10 ii 7 the verb which in the MT (*htbwnnt*) and versions is second person is first person in 4QpPs*a*. Though H. Stegemann supposes this alteration to be the restylization of the text to make it a divine speech,[7] there is nothing to refute the possibility that the commentator is referring to himself. In the interpretation of the text there is an indirect biographical comment: "Its interpretation concerns all the wicked at the end of forty years. They will be destroyed and no wicked man will be found on the earth." Most commentators[8] align this forty year period somehow with that of CD 20:14–15 and 1QM 2:6–14. If the Psalms commentary is meant to be read as if written by the Teacher of Righteousness, then here is supportive evidence for P. R. Davies' thesis that in CD 20:13b–22a the death of the Teacher ushers in the age of wrath (40 years) but does not diminish the continuing effect of the Teacher's words in the community[9]. In this way not only is the Psalm text prophetic[10] concerning the apostates, but also the Teacher is himself prophetic about the duration of the period of apostasy. Whether or not he will actually see the defeat of the wicked is beside the point. Extra justification for this exegetical alteration at v 10 comes from the use of the first person in all four hemistichs of Ps 37:35–36 (4QpPs*a* 1–10 iv 13–14 and versions;[11] MT has a third person verb in one hemistich); the interpretation of these Psalm verses concerns the demise of the Man of the Lie, the Teacher's opposite number.

Another change of person occurs in 4QpIsa*c* 8–10:3 where Isa 14:8 reads "against them" as opposed to "against us" of the MT, versions and 1QIsa*a*. Though the interpretation of the Isaiah text is badly damaged, the impression given is that the taunt against Babylon is a taunt against

---

[7] "Der Pešer Psalm 37 aus Höhle 4 von Qumran (4QpPs 37)," *RevQ* 4 (1963–64) 248 n. 45.

[8] For a list of authors and their various interpretations see D. Pardee, "A Restudy of the Commentary on Psalm 37 from Qumran Cave 4," *RevQ* 8 (1972–75) 174–75.

[9] *The Damascus Covenant* (JSOTSup 25; Sheffield: JSOT, 1982) 189.

[10] As Stegemann suggests ("Der Pešer Psalm 37," 241 n. 20); on the psalms as prophecy see D. N. Freedman, "Pottery, Poetry, and Prophecy: An Essay on Biblical Poetry," *JBL* 96 (1977) 21–22.

[11] Followed by *NEB*, *RSV*. Pardee ("A Restudy," 192) argues that the evidence of Ps 37:35–36 is sufficient to account for the variant in v 10; Pardee treats all the variants in 4QpPs*a* on the level of lower criticism.

the community's oppressors and the cypresses and cedars of Lebanon that rejoice at their own lack of oppression in Isaiah, rejoice in the commentary at the end of the oppression of the people and the land (Isa 14:6–7). The purpose of this exegetical alteration is to assert that not just the council (identified as Lebanon in 1QpHab 12:3–4) but the whole community is to be free from external persecution.

In 4QpNah 3–4 ii 10–11 the verbs of Nah 3:5 are represented in the second person rather than the first person of the MT and versions. This alteration means that rather than God himself being responsible for the abominations of the apostates and those they lead astray, the apostates themselves are. Punishment duly follows with God as subject in the quotation and interpretation of Nah 3:6–7a in 4QpNah 3–4 iii 1–5.

(b) Some variants concern a deliberate change in number. In 4QpNah 3–4 i 6 Nah 2:13b reads *wymlʾ ṭrp] ḥwrh wmʿwntw ṭrph;* in the MT *mʿwn* is plural as the suffix shows: *wmʿntyw*. Horgan thinks that 4QpNah gives the same feminine plural as the MT with a defectively written suffix.[12] Defectively written suffixes occur five or more times in 1QpHab[13] and in 4QpNah 3–4 ii 1,[14] but *mʿwntw* is likely to be a singular in 4QpNah 3–4 i 6 because otherwise the noun itself is also written defectively as Horgan acknowledges; yet the overwhelming tendency in the commentaries is for feminine plurals to be written *plene*. A singular noun brings Nah 2:13b into line with 2:12; the purpose of the alteration is to underline that there is just one Lion of Wrath, whoever he is, and that he has just one den which seems to be Jerusalem (cf. 3–4 i 2, 11).

In 4QpNah 3–4 iii 2, 5 the verbs associated with *kwl* are plural. Whilst they are collective singulars and grammatically correct in the MT, the author of the commentary seems to have broken the grammatical rules in order to make it explicit in the biblical text that the subject of *ndd* in the interpretation is plural: "the simple ones of Ephraim." Since the interpretation contains *ydwdw*, it seems likely that the author of the commentary has anticipated his interpretation and altered his biblical quotation to fit it.

In 4QpIsaᶜ 11 ii 4 the plural *ʾnw bny* (over against *ʾny bn* of MT and 1QIsaᵃ) is consistent with the plurals in the context in Isa 19:11–12. This stylistic improvement, which also represents the *Vorlage* of the LXX, may have had exegetical consequences but nothing is preserved of the passage's interpretation.

(c) Some variants concern a difference in gender. In 4QpNah 3–4 i 4 (Nah 3:13aα) *gwr* appears as a masculine plural (rather than MT's feminine) and the word for lion in the second hemistich is not the feminine

---

[12] *Pesharim*, 176.
[13] 3:6, 7, 8:5 (twice), 8:7; cf. 3:9, 4:10, 13.
[14] *ṣyrw* which is the interpretation of the plural *wmlʾkyw*.

lb³h of the MT but *lby³* which can be either masculine or feminine. Since the commentary speaks of "his great ones" *(gdwlyw)* and "the men of his counsel" *(³nšy ʿṣtw)*, it is fitting for their textual counterparts to be masculine too.

Later in the same column in the text of Nah 2:14 the commentary reads *kpyrykh* over against *kpyryk* in the MT. In the interpretation that follows it is clear that the interpreter has wanted to read the suffixes as masculine, since he talks of "his lions" *(kpryw;* 4QpNah 3–4 i 10). If the commentator's original consonantal text was written defectively, then it seems as if he has deliberately chosen to read the suffixes as masculine, not feminine as is the case in the MT. Perhaps this is not so much a gender change as differing traditions resolving a textual ambiguity in different ways.

(d) Early in the discussion of 1QpHab it was pointed out by J. van der Ploeg and others[15] that the sequence of verbs in the scriptural citations and especially in the interpretations is significant. Two changes of tense in biblical texts in the minor commentaries can be mentioned here. In 4QpIsa*b* 1:1–2 there is a badly mutilated quotation of Isa 5:5bβ–6a which in the MT as rendered in the RSV reads: "I will break down its wall, and *it shall be trampled down.* I will make it a waste; it shall not be pruned or hoed and briers and thorns shall grow up." 4QpIsa*b* reads *wyhy lmrms* where MT has *whyh lmrms* and so implies a reading of Isaiah 5 in which the vineyard is already destroyed but the final judgment is yet to come; *wʿlh šmyr* (Isa 5:6aβ) is preserved in line 3 of the Qumran fragment, implying a future desolation. As with the tendency in the other commentaries the effect of this alteration is to portray the community as standing between an initial destruction and a future judgment. These events may be the past defilement of Jerusalem by its inhabitants whose future demise will be the community's vindication; or these events may be the ravaging of the community itself, possibly by apostate members ("wild grapes:" Isa 5:4), and the situation will get worse before the pleasant planting, the house of Judah, can bear fruit. Too little remains to enable positive identification, but the verb change in 4QpIsa*b* 1:1 may show how the prophecy of Isaiah is slotted into an eschatological perspective that reckons that the latter days are already under way.[16]

A similar textual variant occurs in 4QpHos*b* 11–13:5 in the subsidiary quotation of Hos 8:6b. In the MT *ky sbbym yhyh ʿgl šmrwn* is most likely

---

[15] "L'usage du parfait et de l'imparfait comme moyen de datation dans le Commentaire d'Habacuc," *Les Manuscrits de la Mer Morte* (Paris: Presses Universitaires de France, 1957) 25–35; this discusses other earlier literature, as does J. Carmignac, "Notes sur les Peshârîm," *RevQ* 3 (1961–62) 533–38.

[16] Cf. the eschatological use of Isaiah 5 in Mark 12:1–9, Matt 21:33–41, Luke 20:9–16.

to be translated so that Samaria's calf is to be destroyed in the future. In 4QpHos[b] the text of Hos 8:6b reads *hyh* instead of the MT's *yhyh;* by implication Samaria's calf has already been destroyed, perhaps an allusion to the destruction of the Samaritan temple by John Hyrcanus (Josephus, *Ant.* 13.9.1 § 254–58), perhaps an allusion to something less specific.

2. A second group of exegetical variants concerns omissions from the biblical text being interpreted. This is more widely recognized as reflecting the arbitrary interpretative interests of the Qumran commentator, so my purpose in this section is to support my contention for the text of 2 Sam 7:11–14 in 4QFlor that when writing a commentary on a continuous passage of scripture, the Qumran commentator only made omissions if he could justify them through the deliberate use of an exegetical device.[17] The process was less arbitrary than might be supposed; what has sometimes been seen as an accidental omission because of scribal error may rather have been the deliberate use of a technique which the modern text critic identifies as a reason for the error.

In 4QpHos[a] 1:7–8 Hos 2:8bα is apparently not cited. The content of the excluded Hosea phrase is "and I will build a wall against her." In CD 4:19 the wall-builders *(bwny hhys)* are the apostates who follow after Ṣāw, a pseudonym for their leader probably taken from Hos 5:11. In CD 4:12 Mic 7:11 ("A day for the building of your walls") is partially cited; again the end-time is the time after the wall has been built.[18] Building on the work of Stegemann and others, P. R. Davies has suggested that a well developed exegetical tradition lies behind the various phrases in CD concerning the builders of the wall; that tradition involves Ezek 13:8–10, Mic 2:11, 7:11, and Hos 5:11. In conjunction these passages describe the enemies of the community.[19] Here then is the reason for the exegetical removal of Hos 2:8bα from 4QpHos[a]: it describes Yahweh as a wall builder! Both Hos 2:8bα and β begin with *w* so, to put it anachronistically, there may have been the deliberate use of homoioarchton to justify the omission.

In 4QpHos[a] 1:15–16 there is another omission. There is not enough room at the start of line 15 to restore more than Hos 2:9b, as Allegro, Strugnell and Horgan all agree.[20] Strugnell suggests that the omission has occurred because of homoioteleuton: *tmṣ'* is the final word of Hos 2:8 and also of 2:9a. Perhaps if Hos 2:8bα was so unfitting for what the

[17] *Exegesis at Qumran: 4QFlorilegium in its Jewish Context* (JSOTSup 29; Sheffield: JSOT, 1985) 111–12, 138.

[18] Hos 2:8 uses *gdr* for "wall" as does Mic 7:11 and Ezek 13:5.

[19] *The Damascus Covenant*, 103–104, 166–68; also B. E. Thiering, *Redating the Teacher of Righteousness* (ANZSTR 1; Sydney: Theological Explorations, 1979) 14.

[20] DJD V, 31; "Notes," 200; *Pesharim*, 143, respectively.

commentator wanted to say, 2:9a might be similarly inappropriate and deliberately excised through what text critics traditionally recognize as a scribal error. In the interpretation of Hos 2:11–12 (4QpHos^a 2:12–14) the lovers are identified with the nations on whom "they" had leaned for support. That suited the commentator's purpose well but he could not at the same time suggest that if the lovers were to see the bride's nakedness (2:12), they were also incapable of being found (2:9a).

In 4QpIsa^b the citation of texts jumps from Isa 5:14 to 5:24b with only a line of interpretation between them. Unless 4QpIsa^b is really a thematic rather than a continuous commentary[21] or unless Isa 5:24b–25 is a subordinate quotation in this section of the commentary, then it could be that 5:15–24a have been deliberately omitted through homo-ioteleuton: in 4QpIsa^b Isa 5:14 ends with ‘lyz b’ and in the MT 5:24a ends with y‘lh ky (ky’ in the more usual Qumran orthography), phrases which in Hebrew script look very much alike. The omission could be to prevent repetition (e.g., concerning drunkenness: Isa 5:11, 22), but more importantly it enables the crowd in Jerusalem (Isa 5:14) to be identified as those who rejected the law (Isa 5:24b) with a minimum of interpretation; in any case Isa 5:15–23 is more general in tone than either what precedes or follows it.

In what is extant of 4QpIsa^c there appear to be at least three omissions. In Frgs. 4, 6–7 i 6–9 there is no room for Isa 9:11b–12, in Frgs. 6–7 column ii begins with Isa 10:12 and since column i ends with 9:20, it seems as if Isa 10:1–11 has been deliberately omitted, and in Frgs. 8–10:3–5 it seems as if the commentator has jumped from Isa 14:8 to 14:26 with only a brief interpretation in between, probably containing an identification of something in Isa 14:8. The length and frequency of omissions in 4QpIsa^c is clearly intentional and may mean that it should not be classified simply as continuous pesher;[22] indeed in 1:4 Jeremiah may be quoted, in 8–10:8–9 there seems to be a subsidiary quotation from Zechariah, in 21:7–8 there seems to be an allusion to Zech 11:11, and in 23 ii 14 on Isa 30:15–18 there may be a quotation from Hos 6:9. In general for the omissions from 4QpIsa^c there is not enough surviving text to determine what device was used to justify them, though it could be that none was needed if the genre of the commentary was subtly different anyway.

3. The third group of variants concerns various kinds of par-

---

[21] As noted summarily together with other pecularities by Horgan, *Pesharim*, 86–87; cf. W. R. Lane's emendation of 4QpIsa^b 1:1 to a scribal error in order to make 4QpIsa^b conform to the usual structure of the continuous pesharim ("Pešer style as a reconstruction tool in 4Q Peser Isaiah *b*," *RevQ* 2 [1959–60] 281–83).

[22] Horgan (*Pesharim*, 95) implies this too.

onomasia.[23] Because of the very slippery nature of word-plays it is difficult to catalog these variants precisely; indeed, the alterations of person, number, gender, and tense listed in the first group above may as well have been categorized under this heading.

(a) There are at least three examples of metathesis[24] in the commentaries other than 1QpHab. In 4QpNah 3–4 iii 2 the last word of Nah 3:6 (MT: kr^2y) is k^2wrh and the interpretation supports the reading with wk^2rwm (line 4). Rather than seeing here a scribal error or an understanding of kr^2y as either "like light" or as from ^2rh, "to pluck," most scholars propose reading the scroll as from k^2r, a by-form of k^cr, which in mishnaic Hebrew means "to be dark, ugly, repulsive."[25] Since this verb has the overtones of indecency,[26] it fits the context of Nah 3:5 well and makes for better parallelism in Nah 3:6 itself. The MT's kr^2y can be vindicated on the basis of r^2yk in Nah 3:7a and its representation in the versions. It seems as if the Qumran interpreter has made a deliberate alteration in his received text.

In 4QpNah 3–4 i 9–10 the interpretation of Nah 2:14 begins by requoting a word *(rwbkh)* from the text; it is followed by *hm*, the pronoun frequently used to introduce statements of identification. Unfortunately the actual text of Nah 2:14 is only partially extant. Horgan restores *rwbk]h* in place of MT's *rkbh*.[27] Since the scroll is supported indirectly by the LXX *(plēthos sou: ?rbk)*, it is difficult to determine at what stage in the tradition the metathesis occurred; indeed, the alteration may have taken place only in the consonantal tradition of the MT, perhaps through assimilation to *mrkbh* in Nah 3:2.

For Isa 9:18 MT reads n^ctm $^2rṣ$ whereas 4QpIsa^c 4, 6–7 i 17 reads [nt]^cm (as also at 1QIsa^a 9:9). Nothing of any interpretation remains to inform our understanding of the interpreter's thoughts. Given the difficulty that lexicographers have had with the form in Isa 9:18 (MT), the proposal of Horgan to take it in Qumran tradition as a nithpael from ^cmm is to be welcomed, since "to be black" fits the context well.[28] Since there

---

[23] For the increasing recognition of all manner of word-plays in Jewish exegetical traditions see, e.g., J. Frankel, "Paranomasia in Aggadic Narratives," *Scripta Hierosolymitana* 27 (1978) 27–51.

[24] Cf. 1QDeut^b 13 ii 4 (Deut 31:1) where *wykl* of Qumran supports the LXX over against *wylk* of the MT.

[25] Horgan, *Pesharim*, 185–86; R. Weiss ("A Comparison," 437 n. 13) also notes the metathesis but does not say whether he thinks it was deliberate or accidental. Cf. *Tg.* Nah 3:6: mk^cr.

[26] M. Jastrow, *A Dictionary of the Targumim, the Talmud Babli and Yerushalmi, and the Midrashic Literature* (republished: Brooklyn: P. Shalom, 1967) Vol 1, p. 656.

[27] *Pesharim*, 179.

[28] *Pesharim*, 109; with some discussion of the lexicography, esp. W. L. Moran, "The Putative Root ^cTM in Is. 9:18," $\bar{C}BQ$ 12 (1950) 153–54.

is no versional support for the proposal, it would seem to be a local variant introduced through metathesis deployed exegetically to overcome a text difficult to understand.

(b) Closely related to metathesis is anagram, the movement of letters to form different words. In 4QpIsa^b 2:6 Isa 5:14bβ reads *wš°nh ʿlyz b°*; in the MT it reads *wš°wnh wʿlz bh*, as also in 1QIsa^a, though there *wʿl[z]* is slightly damaged. Though the anagram is not precise, the play on words in the interpretation seems clear enough: *wš°nh* may have been written defectively so that it might more easily be interpreted as *°nšy*, *ʿlyz* may have been written without the conjunction so that it might both be punned as *hlṣwn* (involving the further technique of *°al tiqrē°*) and also be connected with the preceding word from which it could borrow the *hē°*. In other words, not only is the interpretation a play on some words in the scriptural text, but the text itself may have been adjusted in minor ways in order the more easily to accommodate the play on words.

This particular understanding of the interrelatedness of text and interpretation is supported by 1QpHab 7:3–5 where *yrwṣ* ("may run") of Hab 2:2b may be punned in the interpretation with *rzy* ("mysteries of");[29] here might be an example of *ṣādê* and *zayin* changing places. Furthermore in 4QpPs^a i 27 the Teacher is called *mlyṣ dʿt*, *mlyṣ* probably being a pun on *mṣlyh* of Ps 37:7; some such contrasting interpretation may be in the back of the mind of the interpreter of Isa 5:13–14 in 4QpIsa^b since in Isa 5:13 the exiled people are described as wanting knowledge (*dʿt*) which presumably the scoffers in Jerusalem could not provide. The contrast in the interpretation is thus twofold. On the one hand the men of scoffing are those who imitate the "man of scorn" (*°yš hlṣwn*) of CD 1:14; over against this man of scorn stands the Teacher of Righteousness who interprets knowledge (4QpPs^a i 27; 1QH 2:13). The "dripper of lies" (*mtyp hkzb*: 1QpHab 10:9) who spouts "waters of deceit" (*mymy kzb*: CD 1:14–15) stands over against the "one who rains down" (*mwrh*: "teacher") righteousness. On the other hand the verbal play also shows how the tumultuous exultation (*š°wn*: Isa 5:14) is really to be seen as scoffing (*lṣwn*: 4QpIsa^b 2:6). With so rich an exegetical tradition reflected in these few phrases it would be hazardous in the extreme for the text critic to adjust Isa 5:14 in light of 4QpIsa^b. Fortunately the existence of 1QIsa^a which represents the MT letter for letter makes this unlikely, but given the bland way variants in the commentaries are usually listed, it may be proper for text critics to realize the extent of the likely exegetical adjustment of the scriptural text before that text is used as a straightforward witness to the history of the text.

[29] W. H. Brownlee, *The Midrash Pesher of Habakkuk*, 111; cf. L. H. Silberman, "Unriddling the Riddle: A Study in the Structure and Language of the Habakkuk Pesher (1QpHab)," *RevQ* 3 (1961–62) 344–45.

(c) In the previous example the play on words could have involved in part an implied use of *ʾal tiqrēʾ*: for the *zayin* of *ʿlyz* should be read the *ṣādê* of *lṣwn*. But in that instance such a proposal does not involve the alteration of the text itself. However there are examples where the use of *ʾal tiqrēʾ* has caused emendation of the text. The most well-known example is in 4QpPsᵃ 1–10 iii 5a. Vermes writes: "The author introduces an important change into the text of verse 20b, rendering it 'those who *love* the Lord' instead of 'those who *hate* the Lord.' The artificiality of this alteration is evident from the broken context."[30] Because of the LXX support for the MT it can be seen that this alteration almost certainly represents the deliberate change of *ʾyby* to *ʾwhby*: for *yôd* read *hēʾ*.[31] A phonological shift may have facilitated the change but does not of itself suggest that the change was unintentional.[32]

Another example of this method in 4QpPsᵃ may be found at 1–10 i 25–ii 1: in the text of Ps 37:7 MT reads *ʾl tthr* whereas the commentary has *ʾl thr*. The Massoretes understood the verb as the hithpael imperfect from *ḥrh*, "to be angry." While it is possible to derive the scroll reading from the qal of the same verb,[33] the interpretation does not mention anger, but rather the deceit of the man of the lie whose followers will perish by the sword, famine and plague. It is possible that such an interpretation is suggested to the commentator by his taking *thr* from *ḥwr*: in Isa 29:22 Jacob will no longer "grow pale" (*yḥwrw*) because justice will be delivered against the scoffer (*lṣ*: Isa 29:20; cf. *lmlyṣ*: 4QpPsᵃ 1–10 i 27) who led many astray (*tʿy rwḥ*: Isa 29:24; cf. *htʿh*: 4QpPsᵃ 1–10 i 26). Or again, the commentator could be making an allusion to Ezek 14:21–15:5 which mentions sword, famine and pestilence,[34] and also used the verb *ḥrr* (15:4, 5) to describe the burning of the useless wood of the vine. By implication the commentator's audience is warned against being consumed with those who follow the one who makes his way prosperous (*mṣlyḥ*: Ps 37:7) because it prospers them nothing (*hyṣlḥ lmlʾkh*: Ezek 15:4: "Is it useful for anything?" RSV). Although the textual allusions are far from certain, some such association may be at work as the Qumran commentator adjusts his biblical text to give it his particular interpretation.

---

[30] *The Dead Sea Scrolls in English* (Harmondsworth: Penguin, 1968³) 243.

[31] Stegemann ("Der Pešer Psalm 37," 251 n. 78) recognizes a word-play here.

[32] As Pardee proposes ("A Restudy," 192); he quotes with approval the description of the shift by J. D. Amoussine ("Observatiunculae Qumraneae," *RevQ* 7 [1969–71] 533–35) who proposes *ʾwby* as a likely middle term that could have been ambiguous for the Qumran commentator; cf. *ʾwb* of 4QPs 89:6 (v 23).

[33] So Stegemann ("Der Pešer Psalm 37," 247 n. 38); Pardee ("A Restudy," 190) classifies this as a minor grammatical variant and proposes either niphal or qal with a semantic shift akin to that of *ʾnp* in both qal and hithpael.

[34] As do many other passages in Jeremiah and Ezekiel in particular.

Similarly Ps 37:14 in the MT contains the hiphil infinitive *lhpyl*, "to cause to fall"; in 4QpPs*a* 1–10 ii 16 this is simply *lpyl*. Although there are several instances of the apparent elision of the *h* of the hiphil infinitive,[35] it is possible that such elision gave here the deliberate alteration to the root *pll*, "to judge, punish." In the interpretation the wicked of Ephraim and Manasseh are handed over to the ruthless of the Gentiles for *judgment*, a neat reversal of the impending time of trial for the priest and the men of his council. Further support for such an exegetical possibility lies in the extended meaning of *pll/pwl*, "to search";[36] the commentary (4QpPs*a* 1–10 ii 18) talks of those who "seek" *(bqš)* to lay hands on the priest and his partisans. The irony of the interpretation is that those who seek will indeed find justice!

In 4QpNah 3–4 i 6 Nah 2:13b contains the likely reading *ḥwrh*; the MT reads *ḥryw*, "its dens." Though it might be possible to see here a scribal error on the part of the commentator as Horgan suggests,[37] in the light of the interpretation with its phrase *kpyr hḥrwn*, "lion of wrath," it seems more probable that the commentator has altered Nah 2:13 so as to read part of *ḥrh*, "to be angry."

Or again, in 4QpNah 3–4 iii 6 Nah 3:7 could just as well read *śwrdh*, "escaped, abandoned" (pual) as *šwddh*[38] like the MT's *šddh*, "wasted." Such a use of *ʾal tiqrēʾ*[39] is suggested and supported by *dwršy*, "seekers of," the first word of the interpretation derived from *śrd* through an anagram. This also fits the immediately preceding context of 4QpNah which describes those who will *abandon* their deceivers. Another interchange of *dālet* and *rêš* occurs in 4QpNah 3–4 iv 2: Nah 3:10 in the commentary has *ywrw* where MT has *ydw*. Both verbs can mean "to cast lots," but the alteration in 4QpNah would seem to reflect the preference in QL for *yrh*, as in the title of the Teacher;[40] even the lot will fall against Manasseh, not just the Teacher's interpretation of scripture.

---

[35] 1QpHab 3:1; 4:13; 6:8; 8:12; 10:10, 11, 11:8; 1QpMic 10:5; 4QpNah 3–4 iii 7. *lpyl* here is classified by Pardee ("A Restudy," 191) as a minor grammatical variant due to syncopation; M. H. Goshen-Gottstein ("Linguistic Structure and Tradition in the Qumran Documents," *Scripta Hierosolymitana* 4 [1958] 110) suggests that the elision is the result of the impact of Aramaic.

[36] Jastrow, *A Dictionary*, Vol 2, p. 1141; though far-fetched, it may be worth mentioning that in Neh 3:25 a certain Palal is one of the builders of the wall of Jerusalem: see the discussion of the omission of Hos 2:8bα above.

[37] *Pesharim*, 176.

[38] For *šwddh:* Strugnell, "Notes," 209; Horgan, *Pesharim*, 187.

[39] H. Yalon ("Review" of *The Dead Sea Scrolls of St. Mark's Monastery, Kirjath Sepher* 27 [1951] 175) was the first to notice a use of *ʾal tiqrēʾ* in 1QpHab 11:3 where there is a deliberate *dālet-rêš* substitution in Hab 2:15.

[40] According to Horgan (*Pesharim*, 190) *ydd* does not occur in QL. R. Weiss ("A Comparison," 439 n. 28) cites the idiomatic interchange of *ydh* and *yrh* in Job 38:6/Lam 3:53 and in 1 Chr 10:3/Jer 50:4; he also lists many instances of *dālet-rêš*

Another use of *ʾal tiqrēʾ* may lie behind the variant in Hos 2:14 in
4QpHos*a* 2:18, a passage of Hosea which contains paronomasia in its own
right. There *ʾtnm* is read in the commentary over against MT's *ʾtnh* (a
hapax legomenon), giving the overall sense: "of which she said '*I will be
given them*, they are mine, which my lovers have given me'." Perhaps
here is the Qumran commentator's deliberate alteration of a text which
was no longer comprehensible.

(d) In several instances a consonantal text gives rise to a verbal play
because of the ambiguity of the Hebrew word; these are puns proper.
Most obviously is this the case in 4QpIsa*d* 1:3–6. Isa 54:12a contains
šmštyk (4QpIsa*d* 1:4: *šmšwtyk*) which the commentator takes as both
"pinnacles," the twelve men of the council of the community, and as
"sun," since they are the ones who give light.[41] This pun in the use of Isa
54:12a is support for supposing that in the earlier partly preserved
section of the commentary there was a deliberate play on the two
meanings of *bpwk* (Isa 54:11b). It seems that the context demands that it
is to be understood as some kind of jewel and yet its use with *ʿyn* in the
interpretation preserved in 4QpIsa*d* 1:1 suggests it was also understood
as "mascara, black paint for the eye."[42]

In 4QpNah 3–4 iii 10–11 *ḥyl* of Nah 3:8 is interpreted as "power"
rather than "rampart."[43] This reading is proposed in BHS, perhaps to
reflect the LXX's *archē*, but the parallelism of *ḥwmth* (4QpNah: *ḥwm-
wtyh*), "her walls," makes it unlikely that the sense of "rampart" was
completely lost. In translation (LXX) and interpretation (4QpNah) the
ambiguities of the Hebrew consonantal text are either resolved one way
or the other or played upon.

In 4QpHos*b* 11–13 the difficulty of *šbbym* of the MT has been
resolved, so it seems, by taking this word in Hos 8:6b to be from *šwbb*,
"apostate." It is represented in 4QpHos*b* as *šw[bby]m*, and is to be taken
from the root *šwb* rather than from the barely attested *šbb*, "flames" or
"fragments."[44] Support for this understanding at Qumran comes from Jer
3:14 and 22 where *šwbbym* refers to the faithless one of Israel (i.e.
Samaria) which is also the referent in Hos 8:6: "the calf of Samaria." In
the LXX this word has been interpreted paraphrastically, *planōn ēn* (cf.
Syr. *ltʿnwtʾ*).

---

interchange in the scrolls which he reckons helped facilitate this deliberate
emendation.

[41] So J. Carmignac, *Les Textes du Qumrân traduits et annotées* (Paris: Letouzey et
Ané, 1963) Vol 2, 47.

[42] So Horgan, *Pesharim*, 126–27.

[43] So *NEB*; L. H. Brockington (*The Hebrew Text of the Old Testament: Readings
adopted by the translators of the NEB*, London: Oxford University, 1973, 259)
cites only this scroll as support for the *NEB* translation of Nah 3:8.

[44] Job 18:5; Hos 8:6; Aramaic: Dan 3:22; 7:9; cf. Arabic *sb*.

(e) Sometimes it seems as if textual variants occur in the commentaries because some additional text is in the mind of the commentator
and functions as a parent for the variant. These allusions are obviously
difficult to ascertain. In 4QpHos*a* 2:9 there is a syntactical variant in Hos
2:11. The MT reads *ṣmry wpšty lkswt*, "my wool and my flax which were
to cover"; in 4QpHos*a* Hos 2:11 reads *ṣmry wpyšty mlkswt*, "my wool and
my flax from covering." Overall there is no real difference in meaning but
it could be that in considering the position of Israel as the adultress of
Hosea 2, the commentator has in mind by way of contrast the picture of the
good wife of Proverbs 31. In Prov 31:13 the good wife seeks "wool and
flax" *(ṣmr wpštym)*. Here may be the cause of the appearance of the *mêm*
in Hos 2:11 in 4QpHos*a*—contrasting assimilation to Prov 31:13. Over
against the adultress is set the picture of the good wife.

III. *Conclusions*

Although the suggestions in this study are not all of the same degree
of probability and although many puzzles remain to be solved, at the
least the phenomenon of exegetical interpretation taking place within the
biblical text itself is sufficiently widespread and recognizable that some
significant conclusions may be drawn.

1. Scholars concerned with the restoration of the biblical texts in the
Qumran commentaries should always be mindful of the close association
of scriptural citation and interpretation, to the point that the interpretation may be anticipated or depend upon a variant in the biblical text. It is
good to see that Horgan proposes[45] to restore *ḥyyt* in Ps 68:31 (MT *ḥyt*)
in 1QpPs 9:2 because the interpretation begins *pšrw ḥyyt q[nh*, but it
may nevertheless be better to leave unaltered the text to be restored for
surprisingly the text of Nah 1:4b in 4QpNah 1–2 ii 5 contains *lbnn* over
against the MT's *lbnwn*, even though the interpretation in line 7 reads
lbnwn.

Conversely before restorations are made in the interpretation of the
scriptural passage, the biblical text itself should first be searched for
variants or any other clues which may yield some justification for the line
of interpretation that follows the biblical text. For example, Horgan's
restoration of *šbṭ* in 4QpIsa*a* 2–6 ii 19 on the basis of CD 7:20, 1QSb 5:20
and 1QM 5:1[46] seems questionable given that *šbṭ* in the text of Isa 10:24
which is being interpreted refers to the rod of Assyria used against the
people of Zion. More likely is the "prince of the congregation" to have
been identified with the Lord's staff *(mṭhw;* 4QpIsa*a* 2–6 ii 14), especially
as *yswr* follows shortly afterwards in both biblical text and interpretation.
All in all intricacy with which biblical quotation and interpretation are

---

[45] *Pesharim*, 70.
[46] *Pesharim*, 79.

bound together must cause anyone proposing a restoration in the commentaries to hesitate and exercise great care in any proposal.

2. Likewise scholars interested in the history of the biblical text should be very cautious in their use of the variants in the biblical quotations in the commentaries in any reconstruction of the overall history of traditions. Many variants may be local and unique to the particular commentary; only indirectly can they be used for the understanding of textual recensions. Recently S. Talmon has written: "What is especially required . . . is a careful collation of the MT and the Vss with the text preserved in Qumran biblical mss and fragments, in the Pesher literature, and in quotations from the bible which abound in the covenanters' non-biblical writings." Such a collation, he suggests, will be conducive "to a better understanding of scribal techniques, and of human failings and weaknesses which affected the text of the Bible in the long history of its transmission."[47] Talmon has long wished to allow for exegetical alterations in the Qumran biblical texts and elsewhere in the transmission of the text; as a result he has often argued for the blurring of the distinctions between higher and lower criticism.[48] This study supports from another angle his numerous and much more significant insights.

Furthermore, as part of the dissolution of the boundaries between criticisms, text critics must allow that to discern an example of homoioteleuton or letter-change or some other particular phenomenon which the handbooks usually label as scribal errors[49] may be to miss the deliberate editing of a text in one tradition or another. A classic example of this is to be found in Isa 40:7–8.[50] 1QIsaᵃ supports the shorter text of the LXX translator who had been accused of scribal error (homoioteleuton). It is now possible to posit that it is just as likely that at some time the MT recension was intentionally glossed through the conscious use of an exegetical device. Support for that also comes from 1QIsaᵃ in which a corrector has added the extra words to make 1QIsaᵃ conform to the MT tradition.

[47] "The Ancient Hebrew Alphabet and Biblical Text Criticism," *Mélanges bibliques et orientaux en l'honneur de M. Mathias Delcor* (AOAT 215; eds. A. Caquot, S. Légasse, M. Tardieu; Neukirchen-Vluyn: Neukirchener, 1985) 401.
[48] See, e.g., his "Aspects of the Textual Transmission of the Bible in the Light of Qumran Manuscripts," *Textus* 4 (1964) 125–32; "The Textual Study of the Bible—A New Outlook," *Qumran and the History of the Biblical Text* (eds. F. M. Cross, S. Talmon; Cambridge, Mass.: Harvard University, 1975) 321–400.
[49] E.g., E. Würthwein, *The Text of the Old Testament* (London: SCM, 1980) 105–110; R. W. Klein, *Textual Criticism of the Old Testament* (Philadelphia: Fortress, 1974) 76–80; J. Weingreen, *Introduction to the Critical Study of the Text of the Hebrew Bible* (Oxford: Clarendon, 1982) 46–64.
[50] Noted, e.g., by Würthwein, *The Text of the Old Testament*, 142.

It could be that in light of the use of the biblical text in the commentaries at Qumran it is now time for a complete reconsideration of all the additions and omissions, as well as the alterations, in the various recensions so that exegetical traditions as well as scribal errors can be properly described.

3. Scholars interested in reconstructing the history of the Qumran community, or the parts of it to which the commentaries belong, have an almost impossible task on their hands when it comes to the proper use of the commentaries in any such reconstruction. There are still many exegetical puzzles to be solved, many perhaps beyond solution, before the referents of all the interpretations in the commentaries can be adequately identified. The work of Allegro, Strugnell and Horgan, together with numerous other suggestions by scholars, has enabled over the last thirty years an adequate description of the commentaries, but the more complex analytical work of unravelling the intentions and precise meanings of the exegetical combinations of scriptural text and interpretation, and the way the two interrelate, has only partly begun; William Brownlee's work, especially that on 1QpHab, was and remains pioneering in this field.

THE QUMRAN TEACHER—ANOTHER CANDIDATE?

JOHN C. TREVER
School of Theology at Claremont
Claremont, California

The Friday evening before Dr. William Brownlee was to go into the hospital for surgery in July, 1983, he and I were traveling together to a meeting. During the forty-five-minute drive, I had hoped to discuss with him three words on which I was engaged in some research that had interested me for some time. The words were *neḇûʾāh*, *Diadochi*, and *Kittim*. Unfortunately, we arrived at the meeting place shortly before we had finished discussing the first one, and that not very adequately. Then the tragedy of his untimely death closed the door to my gaining the benefit of his perceptive insights that I cherished so much. Little did I realize then how those three disparate words would, almost a year later, catapult me into an exciting new adventure with the Qumrân documents.

After many months of interruption from a self-imposed commitment to editing some of Dr. Brownlee's materials,[1] I began working on this memorial article, feeling that the three words I had hoped to discuss with him that evening might be woven into a suitable article. In this way I

---

[1] Dr. Brownlee's death barely two weeks later came as such a shock that I set aside my own research to tackle another task I felt impelled to undertake in his memory. Several months before, we had discussed at a luncheon with a Ph.D. student from Saudi Arabia a plan to issue five small booklets in which we would gather together our lectures and sermons on our common concerns about the continuing crisis in the Middle East from a perspective of our biblical research in that area. After our seven eventful months there as fellows of the ASOR in 1947–48, each of us made six additional trips at various times. By that Friday my booklet had just come from the press (*The Bible and the Palestinian-Israeli Conflict* [Middle East Fellowship of Southern California, 1983]), while Dr. Brownlee's had to be postponed because of the needs of several of his Ph.D. students whom he had been guiding at the time of his retirement the year before. For the sake of my beloved colleague in the Scrolls, I plunged into the task of editing his materials, condensing them into three memorial booklets which appeared during the next eight months: *The Rights of the Palestinians* (Public Affairs Series 22; New York: Americans for Middle East Understanding, 1983); *The Lion that Ravages Palestine* (PAS 23; 1984), and *Israel and the Ten Commandments* (PAS 24; 1984).

could express my deep appreciation for his friendship, his dedicated academic spirit, and his significant contributions to biblical scholarship.

It was after several weeks of intense study of the three words that so intrigued me, and while relaxing (June 9, 1984) with a book on Old Testament history, that suddenly, without any apparent connection with what I was reading, the words came into focus as a question flashed into my mind: Could the author-compiler of Daniel have had a direct relation to the origin of the Qumrân Scrolls?

Practically every scholar who has studied the Qumrân documents in depth and published at any length on the subject has drawn attention to the book of Daniel as somehow related to words, expressions, or passages in the Scrolls. Not one could I find, however, who went on to suggest that there might be a direct connection between the two. Dr. Brownlee, for instance, had approached this idea in 1964 when he said in his first book: ". . . Daniel is believed to have been written by a member of the Hasideans (or Hasidim) . . ."; and again, "The Qumran literature stands so close to the Hasidic tradition . . ."[2] Recently B. Z. Wacholder has written, "The Book of Daniel . . . may perhaps be counted among the works that are related to the scrolls."[3]

Furthermore, the three words began to focus in on that very period of history—those twenty years when ". . . a root of planting . . . from Israel and Aaron . . . they were like blind men groping for the way" (CD 1:9–10)—about 164–145 B.C.; and it soon became apparent that there was a possibility that the author-compiler of the book of Daniel might also have been a part of that "root of planting," to become the "Teacher of Righteousness," or "Right Teacher"[4] who founded the Qumrân Community.

---

[2] *The Meaning of the Qumrân Scrolls for the Bible* (London/New York: Oxford University, 1964) 106. F. F. Bruce comes very close, but stops just short of it, in his "The Book of Daniel and the Qumran Community," in *Neotestamentica et Semitica—Studies in Honor of Matthew Black* (eds. E. E. Ellis and M. Wilcox; Edinburgh: T. & T. Clark, 1969). G. Behrmann, as early as 1894, took the position that Daniel, on the basis of Josephus' descriptions of the Essenes, originated in that reform movement of Hasidim: "Unsere Behauptung, dass das Danielbuch aus der essäischen Richtung der Asidäer hervorgieng . . ." (*Das Buch Daniel* in D. W. Nowack, *HKAT* III, 3 Band 2, xxv–xxvi). But James Montgomery, in 1927, swept it aside with ". . . but too long a lapse exists between the bk. and our first sources for Essenism to pass judgment" (*The Book of Daniel* [ICC; Edinburgh: T. & T. Clark, 1927] 87).

[3] *The Dawn of Qumran* (Cincinnati: Hebrew Union College Press, 1983) 33.

[4] On the basis of the statement in 1QpHab 7:4–5, I prefer to follow Theodor Gaster's translation here. See his *The Dead Sea Scriptures* (Anchor Books; Garden City: Doubleday, 1956) 5 and n. 2. Brownlee often preferred "Teacher of Right"; see his major work, *The Midrash Pesher of Habukkuk* (SBLMS 24; Missoula: Scholars Press, 1979) 53 and often. For the origin of the title see Frank Cross, *The Ancient Library of Qumran* (Garden City: Doubleday, 1961) 148, n. 82. Cf. G. W.

Late in the period of the Diadochi, after the battle of Panias in 198 B.C., the Jews began to feel increasing pressure of Greek Hellenization upon them, an experience they had felt only minimally under the Ptolemies who had ruled Palestine for over a century. Naturally they turned to the writings of their Prophets, searching for guidance, viewing them more in the sense of n^ebû'āh ("prediction from revelation") than in the original sense of nābî' ("proclaim or preach")—"foretelling," rather than "forthtelling."[5]

It was in the spring of 168 B.C. that an incident occurred which introduced the "Kittim" briefly into that Greek period. The Seleucid king, Antiochus IV, Epiphanes, was attempting a second time to conquer Egypt under King Ptolemy II, Philometor (Dan 11:29). Alarmed by that development, the Roman Senate sent their Consul, Gaius Popillius Laenas, to Egypt by means of "ships of Kittim" (via Cyprus?—Dan 11:30) to stop Antiochus. Thus the three words came into focus in the historical period which saw the appearance of Daniel and a few decades later the origin of the Qumrâm Community, according to the archeological and manuscript evidence.

The Book of Daniel and the Seleucid Greeks

For over a century scholars have been aware of the fact that behind the cryptic language of Dan 11:21–39 is a clear outline of the tyrannical rule of Antiochus IV, Epiphanes, from 175 to about 165 B.C., with only a few uncertainties.[6] In these verses we are clearly dealing with *prophetia* (or *vaticinia*) *ex eventu*. From 11:40–45, on the other hand, no known historic events can be detected. These verses represent pure prediction of events that their author, on the basis of his vision, sincerely expected must occur, given the tragic direction of Antiochus' heinous crimes

---

Buchanan, "The Office of Teacher of Righteousness," *RevQ* 9 (1977) 241–243, who adds 2 Chr 15:3 as a source. For another suggestion see J. C. Trever, "The Book of Daniel and the Origin of the Qumran Community," *BA* 48 (1985) 89–101.

By the time the first draft of this article was completed, the significance of its scope had become such that it seemed wise to divide the accumulated material into two articles, in the first of which (see ibid.) the main thesis has now been directed toward a wider readership. Here I am providing some elaboration of the evidence and more supporting documentation.

[5] See ibid., sidebar on pp. 97–98.

[6] Should there be any lingering doubts about the all-important reference to the "fourth kingdom" as meaning the Greek period of Alexander and the Diadochi in the five dreams and visions in Daniel, one need but study H. H. Rowley's exhaustive work, *Darius the Mede and the Four World Empires in the Book of Daniel* (Cardiff, Wales: University of Wales Press Board, 1959) 70–137. There the issue is so thoroughly handled from every angle that it should leave no question that the final editing of Daniel occurred about 167–165 B.C.

against the Jews. Furthermore, they are followed immediately by an eschatological prediction in 12:1–3 of the angel Michael's appearance.[7] Dan 11:45 provided, therefore, the *terminus ad quem* of the author's generation, which he clearly expected to occur within a few years. This sequence of events, despite all the sincere attempts to interpret them otherwise, cannot cover any other period than that of the life of Antiochus IV, or that of the *Diadochi*. Obviously no transition to another person or age was intended by the author. To insert such a shift to the "Anti-Christ" anywhere in these verses, as some still do at verse 36,[8] it seems to me, is dishonest biblical hermeneutics. Much of that vision in Daniel is clearly focused on the Greek period (from 11:15 on). A long delay would have been unthinkable for our author.[9]

When he learned, about 164 or 163 B.C., that Antiochus had died a miserable death far away in Persia,[10] his faith in what he had believed to be Divine revelation must have suffered a shattering blow. His angelic informant swore "by him who lives forever" that it would be within "a time, two times, and half a time" (12:7), quite probably intended to mean three and a half years, or about 1095 days, covering from some point in Antiochus' militant abuse of the Jews to his death. In verse 11, probably added by him about seven months later, the 1290 days he specified as being counted from the date of the desecration of the Temple in December, 168 B.C. In verse 12 he extended it a month and a half to 1335 days, as he was struggling to hold on to his faith in his vision. When the 1335 days passed without the beginning of the heavenly drama, he apparently set his book aside as disillusionment overwhelmed him.[11]

[7] John J. Collins, *Daniel* (Grand Rapids: Eerdmans, 1984) 103, puts it succinctly: "The expression 'at that time' indicates continuity with the events of ch. 11." F. F. Bruce (see *supra*, n. 2) suggested in 1969 that "the Qumran Rule of War (1QM), parts of which may not ineptly be regarded as a sort of Midrash on . . ." Dan 11:40–12:3, represents the earliest known attempt to interpret these verses as referring to some other person and time (p. 233), a process that was developed by the early Christians and has been continued to the present. Cf. G. Vermès, *The Dead Sea Scrolls in English* (New York: Penguin Books, 1975) 122–123, where he says: "The primitive work [of 1QM 1 and 15–19] draws its inspiration from Daniel xi, 40–xii, 3 and describes the final battle against the Kittim."
[8] See Edward Young, *A Commentary on Daniel* (Grand Rapids: Eerdmans, 1949) 241 and 246; and now the cautious approach of William La Sor, *The Truth about Armageddon* (New York: Harper & Row, 1982) 113 and 123–124.
[9] Christians should have been aware of this fact since the 3rd century from the writings of Porphyry which Jerome preserved in his *Commentary on Daniel* in the 4th century. See *PL* 25:491–584, and P. M. Casey, "Porphyry and the Origin of the Book of Daniel," *JTS*, n.s. 27 (1976) 25–33.
[10] Sources for the date of Antiochus' death waver between 164 and 163 B.C.: 1 Macc 6:8–16 (163 B.C.); 2 Macc 11:23 (164 B.C.); Josephus *Ant.* 12.357–361 (163 B.C.).
[11] Admittedly these additions do not equate precisely with the recorded dates for Antiochus' death; but this approach seems reasonable even if the verses were added before (or after) his death, since we do not know precisely when the

Any sensitive reading of Daniel should make one realize that the authors must have suffered a great disappointment, if not a serious psychological upset, when the reality of history dawned upon them.

There seems to be no discussion among the many scholarly analyses of Daniel that even attempts to penetrate what might have happened to our author-compiler beyond the implications of Dan 11:12.[12] When one seeks to identify and empathize with him in his dilemma, some important aspects of his feelings and his spiritual odyssey, it seems to me, emerge to relate him to the scrolls from the Qumrân caves.

As already suggested in my *BA* article (see *supra*, note 4), when the Qumrân Damascus Document referred to a transitional period of twenty years (CD 1:10) prior to the founding of the Qumrân Community, it offered a natural implication that it was the pietistic Jews (pacifist Hasidim) who suffered a spiritual malaise caused by the period of oppression under Antiochus. Here, it seems to me, both the author-compiler of Daniel and Founder of the Qumrân Community seem to be drawn together in one scenario. Both were apparently a part of that movement of Hasidim, who may have migrated to Judea from Babylon early in the second century B.C. to help their Judean brethren resist the rising Hellenistic pressures begun by Antiochus III.[13] The crisis that produced the Maccabean revolt in 167 B.C. apparently also saw the division

---

completed book was first circulated. Other unexpected events could have prompted these additions, after which the psychological reaction suggested below may have begun. Cf. Collins, *Daniel*, 104: "These revisions must have taken place after the rededication of the Temple by Judas Maccabee." Note Dan 8:11–14, where 1150 days (v. 14) are mentioned specifically to cover the period from the desecration of the Temple (Dec., 168) to its rededication (Dec., 165 B.C.), actually a little over three years.

[12] Dan 12:13, it has been suggested (see *BA* 48 [1985] 97–98 under "Use of the word *maśkîlîm*"), was added by one of the men of Qumrân as a tribute long after the death of their teacher, when the book of Daniel was being revived.

[13] There have been many suggestions about how the Qumrân Teacher fits into the events of known history. See Cross, 127–160, and G. Vermès, *The Dead Sea Scrolls: Qumran in Perspective* (Cleveland, OH: Collins-World, 1978) chap. 6, with its fine bibliography. The widely accepted approach of J. Murphy-O'Connor, "The Essenes and their History," *RB* 81 (1974) 215–244, identifies the Teacher as the "senior member of the Zadokite family" during the rule of Jonathan, 159–152 B.C., when there was no high priest. When Jonathan was made high priest in 152 B.C., "the ejected Zadokite took refuge with the Essenes," whom he traces to the "ultra-conservative branch of Babylonian Jewry." ("Damascus" in the Scrolls, he says, "is a symbolic name for Babylon," which he bases on Amos 5:26–27 as preserved in CD 7:14–15.) These Essenes had been attracted to Judea by the events there in the early 2nd century B.C., and they joined the Hasidim during the beginning of the Maccabean revolt in 167 B.C. If the Teacher did not become the leader of the Essenes until after 152 B.C., he could hardly meet the requirements for the thesis presented here; but a Zadokite priest could have been the author-compiler of Daniel and a pacifist Hasidic Jew whose efforts led to the Essene movement sometime after 163 B.C., but before 152 B.C.

between the militant Jewish pietists and at least some pacifist members, including the author-compiler of Daniel and others who escaped into the wilderness of Judea away from the conflict. It seems reasonable to assume that it was the author-compiler of Daniel who became the leader of that pacifist group after a new and "glorious vision" (1QPrayers 2:6), prompted by his study of the Prophets, especially Habakkuk and Isaiah, laid a new foundation for his eschatological expectations.

The Sixth Danielic Vision

Since our author believed himself to be a prophet,[14] it was natural for him to turn to the early Prophets for guidance. Was it the book of Habakkuk that triggered a new sense of direction in the mind of our disillusioned author? If one reads the first chapter of Habakkuk in the light of the Antiochid persecutions, an experience parallel to that of our author seems apparent. The dismay of Habakkuk over the tragic death of the dedicated King Josiah in 609 B.C. at the hand of the Egyptian Pharaoh Necho prompted that prophet to raise what to him was an overwhelming problem—theodicy—perhaps for the first time in recorded history. Even the first few verses of Habakkuk, in fact, were perfectly suited to address the dilemma of our author. He could identify easily with Habakkuk's dilemma. The fragmentary first two columns of the Habakkuk *pesher* offer the possibility that it was indeed Habakkuk who turned around the troubled faith of our author.

If Dr. Brownlee's reconstruction and translation of the first two columns of the Habakkuk *pesher* are correct (other scholars who have published translations of that scroll seem to agree, with only minor differences), one cannot help feeling that a kinship exists there between Habakkuk, Daniel, and the Founder of the Qumrân Community—all three kindred prophets who suffered under similar tests of faith. The three seem to flow together in the beginning of the Habakkuk *pesher:*

1:16   (1:5) *[Look, O traitors, and see;/*
17   *wonder and be astonished!*
         For He is working a work in your days

---

[14] Daniel is referred to as a "prophet" in Matt 24:15 and Josephus *Ant.* 10.5:249, 266–269. Now our earliest reference to the "prophet Daniel" is from Qumrân, 4QFlor (esch. Midrash), where it says: ". . . as it is written in the book of Daniel the prophet," followed by quotations from Dan 12:10 and 11:32—see John Allegro, *DJD* 5 (Oxford: Clarendon, 1968) 54 (4QFlor 2:3).

Apparently it was the men of Qumrân who started the tradition of "Daniel the Prophet," some time after the death of their Teacher, when Dan 11:30 was being interpreted as a true prediction rather than a *prophetia ex eventu*, thus applying it to the Romans about the time of Pompey or later. Only one Ms. of Daniel from Qumrân dates from the early period (Ia—*ca.* 140–100 B.C.; see Cross, 43—was it a first edition?), for all the other seven date from Period II (*ca.* 4 B.C.—A.D. 68) over a century later.

2:1   *ye will not believe, though]/ it be foretold.*
         The prophetic meaning of the passage concerns
2   *those who were traitors along with the Man of/ Lies,*
         for they [did] not [believe the words of] the Teach-
3   *er of Right (which came) from the mouth of/ God. It*
         also concerns those who were trait[ors to the] New
4   *[Covenant,] f[or] they were not / faithful to the*
         covenant of God, [but profaned] His [h]oly na[me] ./
5   *And thus the prophetic meaning of the passage [con-*
6   *cerns] also [the trai]tors of the last / days. They*
         are vio[lators of the coven]ant who will not believe/
7   *when they hear all that is com[ing upon] the last*
8   *generation from the mouth of / the priest in [whose*
         heart] God has put [understandi]ng to give the pro-
9   *phetic meaning of all / the words of His servants*
10   *the prophets, [through] whom God foretold/ all*
         that is coming upon His people and[His] c[ongre-
         gation]. [15]

These two columns of the Habakkuk *pesher* provide a good introduction to the nature of the community that produced the Scrolls. Inspired by a "Right Teacher," who also was a "priest," [16] he was endowed by God, they (and he) believed, with "understanding" of Scripture that provided special eschatological insights for the "last generation" of God's people who were faithful to the "New Covenant." When one adds the impact of what 7:1–5 says about Habakkuk [17] in relation to the Right Teacher— ". . . its interpretation [of Hab 2:2] concerns the Righteous Teacher to whom God has made known / all the mysteries of the words of His servants the prophets" (4–5, Brownlee's translation)—it is very apparent that this testimony of the Teacher's followers, who wrote down his re-

[15] *Midrash Pesher*, 53. Cf. M. Burrows, *The Dead Sea Scrolls* (New York: Viking, 1955) 365; T. Gaster, 318; and Vermès, *DSSE*, 233.

[16] Most scholars have assumed the Teacher was a priest from line 8 of this passage and 4QpPs[a] 3:15: "The priest, the Teacher of . . .", but also from the line of Zadok—CD 5:4: ". . . until the coming of Zadok." Note also 2 Chr 15:3, where Azariah said to Asa, "For a long time Israel was . . . without a teaching priest (*ûlĕlōʾ kōhēn môreh*)."

[17] Brownlee (*Midrash Pesher*, 107) makes the interesting suggestion that the bottom line of col. 6 had on it *ḥăbaqqûq yitpallēl lĕdaʿat hannihyôt bĕʾaḥărît hayyāmîm*, ". . . / Habakkuk prayed that he might know the things which would happen in the last days." In his notes (p. 109) Brownlee draws a parallel with Dan 2:28–29 and 45 about the "God in heaven Who reveals mysteries." In his "Introduction," p. 30, he compares the degrees of revelation to Daniel, Habakkuk and the Teacher, the latter of whom he calls "a charistmatic exegete" of whom it is even said he "spoke from the mouth of God" (1QpHab 2:2–3). He concludes by saying that "the Righteous Teacher in his role as interpreter functioned like the Prophet Daniel. . . ." He might have gone a step further.

membered words about a century after his death, raises the Teacher to a level equal to, or perhaps even above, the ancient Prophets. Such testimonies make the author-compiler of Daniel a likely candidate from the second century B.C. for being that person. Most scholars have come to believe that 1QpHab represents the remembered interpretations of the Teacher himself, passed down for several generations by the devout men of Qumrân.[18] It was such a level of devotion to the words of their ancestors that produced canonical Scripture during those centuries.[19]

Habakkuk's words (2:1–3) could have prompted our author to await a new vision,[20] since end-time had not arrived as he expected. Dr. Brownlee translated the Teacher's interpretation of Hab 2:3a (1QpHab 7:7–8): "Its prophetic meaning is that the last time will be long in coming but will excel all / that the prophets predicted, for the mysteries of God are to be surpassingly wonderful."[21] This statement suggests a very important experience.

The Teacher's interpretation of Hab 2:3b that follows in lines 11–14 is very suggestive of what may have happened to the author-compiler of Daniel to restore his faith and to lead him to a sixth vision. Brownlee translated these lines:

10 . . . Its prophetic meaning concerns the men of
11 truth, / the doers of the Law, whose arms will not
12 be relaxed from the service of / truth, when to
13 them the last time seems to be delayed; for / all
    God's times will come in their measured sequence,
14 just as He decreed / for them in the mysteries of
    His providence.[22]

In this passage we note one of many references in the Scrolls to what became a major focus of the order of community life that resulted from the Teacher's new vision; namely, persistent keeping of Torah which would assure him and his followers a part in the delayed but certain end-

---

[18] Only a single copy of the Habakkuk *pesher* has been discovered in the eleven caves. It is the best preserved of all the *pesharim* (about fifteen), of which each represents a single copy. Do they constitute a kind of Mishna of the Qumrân Community? Also, it seems possible that the reason the scrolls of Isaiah "A," the Rule of the Community and the Habakkuk *pesher* were the only ones found together in a jar against the back of the first Qumrân cave was just because of their special importance to the men of Qumrân.

[19] Apparently interest in the book of Daniel was revived at Qumrân during the early first century A.D., since all but one copy of the eight scrolls discovered are from that period. 1QDanᵃ is one of the latest of the Qumrân documents. It seems likely that it was the influence of the men of Qumrân that had much to do with Daniel's becoming a part of the canonized Kethubim.

[20] *BA* 48 (1985) 93.

[21] See *Midrash Pesher*, 114, and his "Exposition," 115–117.

[22] Ibid., 118.

time.[23] Thus Habakkuk's words may well have inspired the pattern of life that was adopted at Qumrân.[24]

If Habakkuk formed the bridge for our author's spiritual transition, apparently it was the book of Isaiah (especially 40:1–11) that supplied the spark for a "sixth vision of Daniel," especially the words of verse 3: "A voice cries, 'In the wilderness prepare the way of the Lord, make straight in the desert a highway for our God'" (RSV; cf. 1QS 8:10–14).[25] That vision is the one referred to in a liturgical prayer (1Q34bis, Prayers) which may have been used on the most holy day of the Qumrân calendar year, Yom Kippur. Whether it was used on that day or not depends upon the proper location of the small fragment on which the last words of one prayer and the first words of another begin with: "A prayer for the day of atonement, 'Remember, O Lord. . . .'"[26] In 2:5–6 appear the words:

> But in the time of Thy goodwill Thou didst choose for Thyself a people. Thou didst remember Thy Covenant and [granted] that they should be set apart for Thyself from among all the peoples as a holy thing. And Thou didst renew for them Thy Covenant (founded) on a glorious vision and the words of Thy Holy [Spirit], on the works of Thy hands and the writing of Thy Right Hand, that they might know the foundations of glory and the steps toward eternity . . . [Thou didst raise up] for them a faithful shepherd . . .[27]

Paradoxically, this very fragmentary scroll was discovered fused to the top of four other leather fragments of two Daniel scrolls.[28] Apparently the three scrolls had been torn in pieces by the Roman conquerors of Qumrân in A.D. 68, and crushed together underfoot. The matted mass of nine layers of leather was recovered from Qumrân Cave I in August or September of 1948 by some members of the St. Mark's Syrian Orthodox monastery in Jerusalem.

---

[23] See now the "Temple Scroll" which some are calling the "Sectarian Torah," which is discussed below.

[24] Many years later, probably in period II (*ca.* 4 B.C.–A.D. 68), even after the Habakkuk Pesher had been prepared (*ca.* 40 B.C), some Qumranian may have penned in Hebrew the enigmatic "Habakkuk" passage, now known only from the LXX of Daniel, "Bel and the Dragon" (14:33–39). See *Supra*, note 19.

[25] *BA* 48 (1985) 93–94.

[26] Cf. Jean Carmignac's suggestion ("Le recueil de Prieres liturgiques de la Grotte 1," *RevQ* 14 [1963] 271–76) that the fragment should be placed to the right of the first of the two columns, which may have therefore been the beginning of the prayer that continues on col. 2. See my comment in "Completion of the Publication of some Fragments from Qumran Cave I," *RevQ* 19 (1965) 325. Also see J. T. Milik, *DJD* 1 (Oxford: Clarendon, 1955) 153–155.

[27] Vermès, *DSSE*, 206.

[28] See *RevQ* 19, 323–344.

The "glorious vision" must have had an important part to play in the life of the Qumrân Community to appear in such an important liturgical prayer recited annually. Also in some passages in the *Hodayoth* Scroll (1QH) that are considered to be the compositions of the Teacher, some lines seem to reflect the experience of a great spiritual awakening, or a "glorious vision":

> . . . for Thou hast unstopped my ears
>   to marvellous mysteries.
>
>   (1:21, Vermès, *DSSE*, 151)
>
> . . . for Thou hast illumined my face . . .
>
>   (4:1, Vermès, 160)
>
> Thou hast revealed Thyself to me in Thy power
>   as perfect Light . . .
>
>   (4:23, Vermès, 162)
>
> Through me Thou hast illumined
> the face of the Congregation . . .
>
>   (4:27, Vermès, 163)
>
> . . . and hast shown Thyself mighty within me . . .
>
>   (4:28, ibid.)

In one case the Teacher seems to refer to both his vision and the depression that preceded it:

> . . . Upon my [. . .] lips
>   Thou hast laid a reply.
> Thou hast upheld my soul,
>   strengthening my loins and restoring my power . . .
>
>   (2:7–8, Vermès, 153)

In the poetic lines that occupy the last two columns of the "Rule of the Community" (1QS 10–11), which has been defined as a "Hymn of the Initiants,"[29] or the "Master's Hymn,"[30] are found two passages which may reflect the Teacher's "Vision":

> For my light has sprung
>   from the source of His knowledge;
> my eyes have beheld His marvellous deeds,
>   and the light of my heart, the mystery to come.
>
> . . . .
> . . . and from His marvellous mysteries
>   is the light in my heart.
> My eyes have gazed
>
>   (1QS 11:3–6, Vermès, 92)

[29] Gaster, 125.
[30] Vermès, 72.

Apparently the "sixth vision" was one that redirected our author's thinking, turning him away from writing more apocalypses to writing what might be called eschatological exegesis, with a focus on a "New Covenant" relationship with God,[31] all of which led to the founding of the community with his followers, who were inspired by his new vision and teaching.

The new focus of his ministry is reflected in the *Hodayoth* Scroll (1QH):

> I thank Thee, O Lord,
>   for Thou hast illumined my face by Thy Covenant.
> (4:5, Vermès, 160)
> . . . the Law engraved on my heart by Thee . . .
> (4:10, Vermès, 161)

It is very prominent in the Rule Book of the Community, where Isa 40:3 is quoted and followed by the words: "This (path) is the study of the Law which He commanded by the hand of Moses . . ." (1QS 8:14–15, Vermès, 86).

The words *Tôrāh* and *běrît* appear repeatedly in 1QS and 1QH and other documents that make it clear that end-time is delayed to allow for the development of a Torah-focused community in preparation for the age to come, as the Rule of the Community clearly shows: ". . . the men of the Community shall be set apart as a House of Holiness for Aaron. . ." (1QS, 9:5–6, Vermès, 87). In fact, the Rule of War (1QM) is more Torah-inspired than apocalyptic, even though it might be called the book of Revelation of the Qumrân Community.[32]

The order of the community constituted a group of devout, disciplined, Torah-focused men in a context of eschatological expectation. In fact, they seem to have lived in daily expectation of the end of the age, spanning a period of almost two hundred years. So great was the influence of the "sixth vision" of the Teacher that this amazing community continued its rigid discipline and Torah-focused life for over a hundred years after his death. It might be said that much of the unique Qumrân literature, especially the *pesharim* documents, constituted a new genre of sectarian Jewish literature. It was the expression of a community that believed itself to be a living reality of the new age that would be ushered in at the close of the cosmic struggle of "light" with "darkness," in which they felt they were already involved.[33]

---

[31] It seems probable that Jer 31:31–34 played a part in shaping the Teacher's eschatological approach to Torah that is so prominent in the Qumrân documents. Perhaps this passage was also involved in the "sixth Danielic vision."

[32] J. J. Collins, *The Apocalyptic Imagination* (New York: Crossroads, 1984) chap. 5.

[33] Collins (ibid., 140) aptly puts it: "The war of Light and Darkness is already raging

Summary of the Evidence

As indicated at the beginning, the purpose of this article is to document and expand the implications set forth in the *BA* article, which outlined the main thesis for a wider reading audience (see note 4). There, twelve supporting points were outlined briefly. Here some additions have been made to the approach to the thesis, but now the twelve supporting points need further documentation and some further observations added as the research has continued.

1. *The Hasidim*. Shortly after the discovery of the Qumrân Scrolls scholars began to point to the Hasidim as the likely source of their origin and to relate the name "Essene" to that pietistic group of Jews.[34] The author-compiler of Daniel had already been traced to that same sectarian, pietistic movement.[35] Many Hasidic Jews, whether originating in Babylon (see note 13) or indigenous to the Holy Land were apparently pacifists,[36] who based their hope on divine judgment, or retribution against evil in creation.

Given the circumstances surrounding the nature of the Antiochid

---

in the hearts of humanity. . . . The eschatological assertions of Qumran presuppose a coherence in the structure of the universe—past, present, and future. . . . Insights into the pattern of present experience can then be used to illuminate the future, and eschatological doctrines can disclose meaning in the present."

[34] For the relation of "Essene" to Hasidim through the East Aramaic word *ḥasen*, see Cross, 51, n. 1. Recently, however, Stephen Gorenson ("Essene; Etymology from   ," *RevQ* 44 [1984] 483–498) has made a strong case for relating the name to *ʿwsym* ("doers") on the basis of the frequent occurrences of the expression *ʿwsy htwrh*, "doers of the Torah," a prime focus of the community (1QS 6:6, etc.). Both etymologies are indeed descriptive of the Qumrân Community. Perhaps the name "Essene" from *ʿwsy* arose from the "sixth vision of Daniel" after the author's new sense of direction focused his eschatology on preparation for end-time through closer attention to the study and keeping of Torah (cf. 1QS 8:14).

[35] For a summary of the evidence see L. F. Hartman and A. A. Di Lella, *The Book of Daniel* (AB 23; Garden City: Doubleday, 1978) 43–45.

[36] See Montgomery (ICC; n. 2 *supra*) 87, where he wrote: "Our bk. represents the principled pacifistic wing of the party"; and see Hartman and Di Lella, 42–43: "The Book of Daniel as a whole may rightly be viewed as a pacifistic manifesto of the Hasidim" (p. 43). Many scholars have pointed to the expression, "they shall receive a little help" (Dan 11:34), as a cryptic indication of our author's disdain for violence. See G. von Rad, *Theologie des Altes Testaments* (Munich: Kaiser, 1960) 2.328 for a fine statement. Collins (*Daniel*, 101) rejects the identification of Daniel with the Hasidim on the grounds that they are called "mighty warriors of Israel" in 1 Macc 2:42, preferring to identify them with the *maśkîlîm* as a separate sect. The position that seems more reasonable to me is that the Hasidim divided into two parties during the tragic Antiochid persecutions. Cf. 4QFlor 1:16–17 (after quoting Ezek 44:10), which may reflect the division of the Hasidim when it says, "They are the Sons of Zadok who [seek their own] counsel and follow [their own inclination] apart from the Council of the Community" (Vermès, 244).

persecutions of the Jews, very few pacifists could have survived; and probably many joined the leadership of Judas Maccabeus in the revolt, leaving a very small number of potential candidates for the author-compiler of Daniel and the Qumrân Teacher and his followers.[37] The spiritual and other qualities exhibited by the author-compiler of Daniel and the Right Teacher in the face of those circumstances must have been so unusual that it seems logical to suggest that they could have been the same person.

2. The *pesher* method. It was Dr. Brownlee who first called attention to the frequent use of *pesher*[38] in the manuscript he was working on in February–March, 1948, and thereby identified the nature of the Habakkuk "Commentary," as he called it at first. More recently he used what he felt was the more accurate expression, "midrash pesher," as in the title of his monumental research project.[39]

Although the Hebrew form of this word is not found in the visions of Dan 7–12,[40] where it might be expected, it could be said that the author-compiler of Daniel introduced this new method for interpreting Scripture to the Qumrân Community as the Right Teacher.[41] Basically the same method of interpreting Scripture is found in both Daniel and about fifteen *pesharim* scrolls from the eleven Qumrân caves. The Teacher's eschatological method of interpreting Scripture was apparently used at Qumrân throughout its almost 200-year history.[42]

3. The *maśkîlîm*. The late Victor Tcherikover, a noted historian at

---

[37] The excavations at Khirbet Qumrân, period Ia (*ca.* 140–100 B.C) revealed a small community of no more than fifty participants.

[38] A loan word from Aramaic, *pĕshâr* occurs thirty-two times in Dan 2:4b–7:28. It appears in pre-exilic Hebrew as the verb, *pātar* (9 times), and noun, *pittārôn* five times), only in Genesis 40–41, in the stories about Joseph's interpretation of dreams.

[39] See *supra*, n. 4. See also his *The Meaning*, 65, n. 6.

[40] The Hebrew form appears in the O.T. only in Qoh 8:1. In the Hebrew portions of Daniel various forms of the verbs *bîn* and *śākal*, or the nouns *bînâh* and *śekel*, are used in relation to the interpretation of the visions, but the structures of the composition may account for the different words used. Or perhaps it was the result of translation Hebrew, done many years later when the book of Daniel became popular again.

[41] According to Brownlee, ". . . the Righteous Teacher in his role as interpreter functioned like the Prophet Daniel . . ." (*Midrash Pesher*, 30). See also his *The Meaning*, 48 (and n.6) and 65–69. See now B. Z. Wacholder (n. 3 *supra*), who suggests (p. 195) that both CD and 1QpHab were composed about 176 and 170 B.C. respectively, even before the book of Daniel. Such a suggestion seems to be anachronistic and lacking sufficient evidence.

[42] Cf. Andre Lacoque, *The Book of Daniel* (Atlanta: John Knox, 1979) 233, where he says, "This eschatological aspect of the text (of Daniel) did not escape the attention of the sectarians at Qumran. 1QM is a midrash on our text." (See especially 1QM 1:4–7). Also see F. F. Bruce's statement quoted in n. 7 *supra*.

the Hebrew University in Jerusalem (d. 1958), wrote that "the Ḥasidim were the chief scribes and authoritative interpreters of the regulations and commandments of the Torah."[43] Though he did not mention the *maśkîlîm* as a class of the leaders of the Ḥasidim, he seemed to be pointing directly toward them and Daniel *and* the Teacher who laid out the strict rules for the men of Qumrân. In fact, in Dr. Brownlee's discussion of the Hebrew word *maśkîl*,[44] he, too, comes very close to relating Daniel directly to the Qumrân Community:

> The Qumrân literature stands so close to the Hasidic tradition, it is entirely probable that the Hasidic use of *maśkîl* as a title for "teacher" was transmitted into its own community life directly, quite apart from the influence of Daniel. This means that the Qumrân usage of the term must be taken seriously as pointing to a special class of person, if not more specifically to a particular official of this title.[45]

Then he goes on to conclude that a better translation of *maśkîl* would be "Cantor." It seems to me that, when Brownlee wrote the words ". . . quite apart from the influence of Daniel . . .," he veered away from what should have seemed obvious; i.e., that it indeed was the author-compiler of Daniel, a leader among the Ḥasidim, who was himself the *maśkîl* who later founded the Qumrân Community.[46]

4. References to "Kittim." As already discussed, the single occurrence in Daniel of the name "Kittim" (11:30) applied to a minor event involving a Roman consular official during the rule of Antichus Epiphanes[47] in the Greek period of the "Diadochi." All thirty-three occur-

---

[43] *Hellenistic Civilization and the Jews* (Philadelphia: the Jewish Publication Society, 1961) 197.

[44] *The Meaning*, 104–107. On p. 106 he says, "The word *maśkîl* is a causative participle in Hebrew; and therefore its . . . meaning should be 'make wise.'"

[45] Ibid., 106. Cf. also F. F. Bruce, 229.

[46] Collins (see n. 7 *supra*) 28, after quoting Dan 11:33–35 says, "There is no serious doubt among scholars that the author of Daniel 7–12 understood himself as one of the *maśkîlîm*, or wise teachers." On p. 57, however, he adds: ". . . but this group (*maśkîlîm*) cannot be identified with the chief scribes and authoritative interpreters of the Torah." Thus he separates the *maśkîlîm* completely from the Ḥasidim. See n. 31 *supra*, 89–90. It seems just as reasonable to suppose that the Ḥasidim divided into those two groups over the issue of how to solve the persecution they all suffered, a matter that produced both Daniel and the Qumrân Community. It is perfectly clear that both pacifism and scribalism with authority of interpretation of Scripture are basic to Daniel and the Qumrân 200-year tradition.

[47] See Emil Schürer, *The History of the Jewish People* (new edition by Vermès and Millar; Edinburgh: T. & T. Clark, 1973) 1.151–152 and n. 35, for the historical record of the event.

rences of *Kittîʾîm*[48] discovered so far in the Qumrân Scrolls,[49] on the other hand, refer to the later period of Roman suzerainty over the eastern Mediterranean countries shortly before or after 63 B.C.

It is also clear that the men of Qumrân assumed that it would be in imperial Roman times when end-time would take place (see especially 1QM, cols. 1 and 15). It might even be said that the Qumrân Community lived in daily expectation of the coming end of the Age, especially during the Roman imperial period. Thus the eschatological implications of 1QpHab, 4QpNah, 4QpIsa and 1QM fall between 63 B.C. and probably before A.D. 68. Since at least two Daniel scrolls (1QDana,b) from the Qumrân caves are among the last scrolls copied at Qumrân, it is possible that they were being circulated again just because they believed that the message of Daniel was soon to be fulfilled with the beginning of the first Jewish revolt,[50] the next great crisis in the history of the Jews.

Most scholars are agreed that the author-compiler of Daniel 11, using his new hermeneutical approach to Scripture, was interpreting Num 24:24 as being fulfilled in the "ships of Kittim" which had brought the Roman consul to Egypt. Given the cryptic nature of the book of Daniel, it is easy to understand how that somewhat incidental event in 168 B.C. was overlooked by the men of Qumrân many years later. Thus "Kittim" in Dan 11:30 came to be interpreted as referring to the later imperial period of Rome.[51] Perhaps it was the author-compiler of Daniel himself who, before his death in the latter part of the second century B.C., had forgotten that incident in 168 B.C. that influenced his writing Dan 11:30.

---

[48] The longer form is usually used in the Scrolls, fifteen times in the *pesharim* documents (twice in 4QpNah—once only partially; and four times in 4QpIsaa— twice partially, but quite probable), and eighteen (four partial, but certain) in the 1QM.

[49] All but one of the 1QM occurrences are in cols. 1 and 15-19, called "the primitive work" by several scholars: see Vermès, 122–123, who follows J. Van der Ploeg, *La Rouleaude la querre* (Leiden: Brill, 1959) 11–22. For detailed treatment see Y. Yadin, *The Scroll of the War of the Sons of Light against the Sons of Darkness* (tr. B.C. and Rabin; Oxford: Oxford University, 1962) esp. 10–14, 21–26.

[50] See J. C. Trever, "1QDana, the Latest of the Qumran Manuscripts," *RevQ* 26 (1970) 277–286.

[51] Cf. F. F. Bruce's statement quoted in n. 7 *supra*. Brownlee, in 1964 (*The Meaning*, 66, n. 8) said, "The best article on this subject is still Roger Goosens, "Les Kittim du Commentaire d'Habacuc," *La Nouvelle Clio* (1952) 137–170. Now J. J. Collins (see n. 31 *supra*) 74–78, illustrates this process further from the Sibylline Oracles (4:49–101), which mention a schema of four kingdoms (Assyrian, Median, Persian, and Macedonian) in an early Jewish form to which a fifth (Rome) was added in the late fifth century work of another author. Also he refers to the *Dynastic Prophecy* from Babylonian sources, which give a four-kingdom schema. All of this suggests that the authors of Daniel's visions may have been influenced by the "world of political prophecy" (p. 77) in the Near East during the period of the Diadochi.

But it is certain that when he seized upon his new hermeneutical method to help his suffering people in 168–165 B.C., he never dreamed that his book would become the key for applying "Kittim" to the Roman persecutions that came more than two centuries later.

  5. More linguistic affinities. Scholars have shown many additional words and phrases that suggest a continuity between Daniel and the Qumrân Scrolls—the word *raz,* for instance (cf. Daniel 2 and 4:9 [H6] and often in 1QH 1 and other columns). Alexander Di Lella adds a poignant illustration from the "Apostrophe to Zion" (11QPsª 22:6, 8, 13–14),[52] of which several key words and phrases "show a remarkable relationship to Dan 9:24. . . ."[53]

  In fact, one might go further in this case to suggest that the "Apostrophe to Zion" was a composition by the author-compiler of Daniel—or at least inspired by him—during the early period of the Qumrân Community's life in the barren wilderness by the Dead Sea, where they were isolated from their beloved Jerusalem which they had abandoned in protest against the violations of Torah by the Hasmonian rulers. Just a few lines from the first strophe clearly suggest the pathos and longing of the men of Qumrân for the Holy City:

> I remember thee for blessing, O Zion;
> with all my might have I loved thee.
> May thy memory be blessed forever!
> Great is thy hope, O Zion;
> that peace and thy longed-for salvation will come.
>
>   .   .   .   .
>
> Those who yearn for the day of thy salvation
> that they may rejoice in the greatness of thy glory.
>
>   .   .   .   .
>
> The merits *(ḥsdy)* of thy prophets wilt thou remember and in the
>   deeds of thy pious ones *(ḥsydyk)* wilt thou glory.[54]

A careful comparison of Dan 11:40–12:3 with 1QM col. 1 and in several points of cols. 15–19, as G. Vermès has pointed out (see *supra,* end of note 7), reveals many words and phrases which imply a very close relationship.[55] Further studies of the Qumrân documents with Daniel's

52 See J. A. Sanders, *DJD* 4 (Oxford: Clarendon, 1965) 43, 86–89 and pl. XIV; or *The Dead Sea Psalms Scroll* (Ithaca, NY: Cornell University Press, 1967) 76–77.
53 Hartman and Di Lella, p. 45. Cf. Collins, *Apocalyptic Imagination,* 120–21.
54 J. A. Sanders' translation. See *DJD* 4, 87.
55 See B. Z. Wacholder (*supra,* n. 3), 80–81, where he gives numerous other verbal relationships. He says, "The War Rule is clearly dependent upon the Book of Daniel" (p. 80).

special words, phrases and ideas in mind doubtless will add considerably to this dimension of the evidence for their direct relation.[56]

6. Historical sequence. As has been pointed out in my *BA* article and early in this article, the relation of Daniel and the origin of the Qumrân Community to known history of the period from ca. 168-140 B.C. provides significant evidence that the two may be directly related. Now, according to the recent publications of the late Dr. Yigael Yadin,[57] the "Temple Scroll" provides another important link in that chain of historical sequence. The Temple Scroll may have been the *magnum opus* of the author-compiler of Daniel and inspired by the "sixth" Danielic vision.

Since already the origin of that scroll as proposed by Dr. Yadin has been challenged by some scholars,[58] it is too early to consider his conclusion as supporting evidence to our overall point of view, even though it is tempting to do so. A careful literary study of Daniel in comparison with the "Essene torah," however, might be valuable for both Yadin's as well as my thesis.

7. Apocalyptic chronology. In Daniel, dating of events as they unfold (Dan 1:1, 21; 2:1; etc.) is similar to the usage of the pre-Exilic prophets, like Jeremiah (1:1–3) and Ezekiel (1:1–2); but Daniel's apocalyptic chro-

---

[56] See M. Delcor, *Le Livre de Daniel* (Paris: Gabalda, 1971) 17–19.

[57] *The Temple Scroll* (Jerusalem: Israel Exploration Socity, Hebrew edition, 1977; English edition, 1983) 3 vols. Cf. his posthumous article, "The Temple Scroll," *BAR* 10:5 (Oct., 1984) 32–49.

[58] Ibid., 12 and 14. In this same issue Jacob Milgrom reviews the English edition of Yadin's three-volume work. Milgrom says concerning the composition date of 150–125 B.C.: "Some scholars prefer a later date and others an earlier one, so perhaps Yadin did not stray from the truth! Nevertheless, in this writer's opinion, an earlier date must be given very serious consideration" (p. 12b). He calls the scroll "the constitution of the Qumran sect" and gives a few somewhat weak reasons why it should be dated in the time of Antiochus III, or about 200 B.C.
    Now B. Z. Wacholder (see n. 3 *supra*) has elaborated this position in a detailed book. He bases his historical outline on the 390 years (from Ezek 4:5) after Nebuchadnezzar's destruction of Jerusalem in 586 B.C. (CD 1:5) as an accurate historical reference to 196 B.C., when the Teacher, Zadok, first appeared (CD 5:4, ". . . until the coming of Zadok"), announcing the discovery of the *sēper Torah* (the "Temple Scroll"—Wacholder calls it "the Qumranic Torah"), which had been hidden and was considered superior to the Mosaic Torah (p. 31). He had composed it a few years before (p. 203)! Zadok appeared as "the anointed one" and believed that the eschaton had begun. The twenty years was a period for gaining Israel's acceptance until he could "enter triumphantly into the holy city" (pp. 185–186). Onias III was the "Wicked Priest" (!) who was accepted at first but went astray by his pursuit of wealth (p. 194). The absence of any consideration of archeology or paleography in Wacholder's closely reasoned outline will appear as an obstacle to acceptance by many scholars, including this one; but it is apparent that another "battle of the Scrolls" has begun.

nology, as exhibited in such statements as "seventy weeks of years" (Dan 9:24), is quite another matter. Di Lella[59] shows how the author drew upon Scripture to derive his long-range prediction by combining Lev 26:18 ("sevenfold") and 33–35 ("sabbaths"), and 2 Chr 36:21 to expand Jeremiah's "seventy years" of Exile (25:11–12 and 29:10) to get 490 years. Scholars have for many years recognized this literary method as an ingenious and legitimate device for our author.[60] But at Qumrân this apocalyptic chronology was used in a much larger way that seems to have stimulated the growth of apocalyptic literature.[61] It seems reasonable to suppose that this long-range prediction procedure was a by-product of our author's "sixth vision" and contributed directly to the Qumrân Community as a hermeneutical method for interpreting Scripture.

8. Dreams and visions in Daniel. In Daniel at least one dream (chap. 2) and four visions (chaps. 7–12) are related by the authors, the last two of which (9:21–27 and 10–12) seem to have been the work of the final author and compiler of Daniel. Only one vision is noted in the Scrolls, but it is interpreted here as the "sixth vision" of Daniel, for it suggests that visions constituted a point of direct contact. The "sixth vision" is presented here as one that changed the direction of our author's approach to eschatology—toward a Torah-based hope.

9. Angelology in both sources. In Daniel it is angels who interpret the dreams, while in the Scrolls apparently the Teacher interpreted his vision from revelation. The angels Michael and Gabriel appear in both. If G. Bampfylde is correct in his analysis of the angelology of Daniel and the Qumrân documents,[62] this ideological evidence may add further weight to the claim that the author-compiler of Daniel was directly involved in the Qumrân Community and its thought patterns.

10. Imminence of end-time. Fragmentary as it is, 4QFlor, called an "eschatological midrash," summarizes the focus on end-time that dominated the Qumrân Community throughout its history.[63] In a very per-

---

[59] Hartman and Di Lella, 249–250.

[60] It should be noted that if Daniel were indeed a prophet writing in the 6th century B.C., it would be difficult to conceive a reason for his changing Jeremiah's "seventy years" to "seventy weeks of years" as we find in Dan 9:24–27. It would have been quite inconsistent with prophetic practice *at that time*. But for a prophet writing pseudonymously in the second century B.C., to use Jer 25:11–12 and 29:10 in this way was quite consistent with the veneration of the Hebrew Prophets and the hermeneutics of our author. Thus the "seventy weeks of years," or 490 years, was clearly a literary device.

[61] Cf CD 1:3–10; 1 QM 1 and 15; and 1QpHab 2–4, etc.

[62] "The Prince of the Host in the Book of Daniel and the Dead Sea Scrolls," *JSJ* 14 (1983) 129–134.

[63] See *JBL* 77 (1958) 350–354; and *DJD* 5, 53–57, pls. xix–xx.

ceptive chapter, J. J. Collins[64] has recently made a careful distinction between "eschatology" and "apocalyptic" when he concludes: "It is not inappropriate, then, to refer to Qumran as an apocalyptic community or as an example of apocalypticism, although it cannot be taken as a typical setting for the production of apocalypses."[65] Although the community may not have produced apocalypses as such, their voluminous literature was greatly infused with an eschatological outlook. The Founder-Teacher had a strong sense of imminent end-time during the period of the Diadochi and deeply infused that expectation into his followers. For the author-compiler of Daniel it is also clear that he believed he was living in end-time which would be during his lifetime. Thus the two are in harmony again. The only difference to be noted is that the men of Qumrân shifted that expectation to the Roman period, at least after 63 B.C., when most of the pertinent documents were written. The key seems to have been the reference to "Kittim" in Dan 11:30, shifting it to imperial Rome a century after the Teacher.

11. Devotion to Scripture. It is perfectly evident that both our author's and the Qumrân Teacher's lives were devoted to the study of the Hebrew Scriptures. The Community Rule emphasizes as a basic community requirement, very probably laid down by the Teacher, the constant study of Scripture:

> And in whatever place the ten are, there shall not cease to be a man who expounds the Torah day and night / continually (expounding) orally each to his fellow. And let the Many keep awake in Community a third of all the nights of the year in order to read aloud from the Book and to expound laws / and to bless in Community (1QS 6:6–8).[66]

Again this similarity points toward a direct relation.

12. "Daniel" as a pseudonym.[67] Since "Daniel" was clearly a

---

[64] *Apocalyptic Imagination*, chap. 5.

[65] Ibid., 140–141. But see now Philip R. Davies, "Eschatology at Qumran," *JBL* 104 (1985) 39–55.

[66] Dr. Brownlee's early, literal translation in *The Dead Sea Manual of Discipline: Translations and Notes* (Supplementary Studies, nos. 10–12; New Haven: A.S.O.R., 1951) 22, 24. See also Millar Burrows' translation in *The DSS*, 378, or that of G. Vermès, *DSSE*, 81.

[67] In my *BA* article, 48 (1985) 91–92, the last piece of evidence was a suggestion about an archeological possibility not yet explored. Perhaps another item might be added under that rubric; namely, 4QPrNab, published by J. T. Milik in 1956 ("'Prière de Nabonide' et autre ecrits d'un cycle du Daniel," *RB* 43 [1956] 407–15). Although its paleography is too late (*ca.* 50 B.C.) to relate it directly to the Founder of the Qumrân Community, perhaps it was a copy of a document which

pseudonym for the authors of the book, and the Qumrân Community
maintained anonymity for both its Founder-Teacher and its members for
some 200 years, one must assume that there was a reason for this
practice. Perhaps it points toward a possible direct relation, given the
eleven other pieces of evidence which have been cited. Or could Isaiah, a
favorite at Qumrân, have had an influence from ʿavdî in its "Servant
Songs" (42:1; 49:3, 5, 6; 52:13), or even malʾākî from Mal 3:1, to continue
this practice at Qumrân?[68]

Hopefully, further study of the thesis presented here may bring forth
additional evidence, and perhaps this and the *BA* article may inspire
those who are working on the hundreds of unpublished fragments to
watch for other points that might suggest a direct link between the
author-compiler of Daniel and the Right Teacher.

Regardless of who the Right Teacher was, it is certainly true that
Daniel, the Teacher and the Qumrân Community represent a 200-year
dedicated experiment in eschatology, the hopes for which failed 1900
years ago. I feel sure, therefore, that Dr. Brownlee would have wanted to
join all biblical scholars in proclaiming: Qumrân and biblical eschatology
urgently need a new message of hope—perhaps a seventh Danielic
vision.[69] In the face of the military and political realities of this late

---

the Teacher had brought to the community a century earlier and thus preserved
by his admiring followers. It may, therefore, have archeological significance for the
thesis (cf. Cross, 166–68).

[68] In a posthumously published paper, "The Wicked Priest, The Man of Lies, and
The Righteous Teacher—The Problem of Identity," *JQR* 18 (1982) 1–37, Dr.
Brownlee wrote that as long ago as 1952 he concluded that Judah the Essene (cf.
Josephus, *War* 1.77–80; also *Ant.* 13.311–313) was the Righteous Teacher, a point
of view which was first published by J. Carmignac in *RevQ* 38 (1980) 235–246.
Josephus' reference is to an event during the reign of Aristobulus (105–104 B.C.)
and the only named Essene from our historical records. Such a date would make
the Teacher about eighty years of age. Brownlee suggests that he died between 95
and 88 B.C., which would make him almost a hundred, an unlikely age for that
period of history, even given the austere and disciplined life of the men of
Qumrân. The only point of probability available is the fact that Josephus mentions
Judas the Essene as a respected "prophet," and he implies he was an "old man." If
Carmignac and Brownlee are right, it does not affect the point of view presented
here since no given name for the Teacher is necessary. But the historical timing
might be stretched too far to be reasonable. Brownlee supports his conclusion
from the reference to "Judah" in 1QpHab 12:4–5 and 4QpMic fragments which
interpret Mic 1:5 as referring to the Teacher. Also in the introductions to several
hymns in 1QH that are considered by some scholars to be compositions by the
Teacher, he sees cryptic references to the name "Judah." But see now Wacholder
(*supra*, n. 3), whose thesis forces the Teacher back to about 240 B.C. for his birth!

[69] Such a vision could be based on God's words to Moses, kîʾehyeh ʿimmāk (Exod
3:12; cf. Deut 31:6, 8, 23; also 33:27), or Isaiah's ʿimmānûʾel (7:14 and 8:8, 10); i.e.,
the "withness" of God.

twentieth century, when a human-created eschaton seems almost imminent through, God forbid, a human-sparked nuclear holocaust, it is self-evident that our Creator is counting on all people of faith to help prevent such a reality. We need now earnestly to seek new beginnings, rather than to hope for a hypothetical "rapture," as so many Christians do.[70]

---

[70] Gen 8:20–22, if handled properly, could provide a new beginning and help overcome the lethargy created by the old eschatology for many Christians, some Jews, and even Muslims. See J. C. Trever, *The Dead Sea Scrolls: A Personal Account* (Grand Rapids: Eerdmans, 1978) 178–181.

INTERPRETATION AND INFALLIBILITY:
LESSONS FROM THE DEAD SEA SCROLLS*

WILLIAM SANFORD LA SOR

Professor Emeritus
Fuller Theological Seminary
Pasadena, California

— I —

During the latter half of the period of the Second Jewish Common-wealth there was considerable interest in eschatological subjects. It was during that time that most of the Jewish apocalyptic materials were produced. The nameless "son of David," who had been a guiding star of hope in the canonical prophets, received a more definitive title, which later became a name, "the Messiah."[1] The "son of Man" figure which first appeared (or so I believe) in the book of Daniel was elaborated upon in the Similitudes of Enoch (chaps. 37–71). The tribe of Levi, and more specfically the Aaronic priesthood, moved into a position that vied with the tribe of Judah, so that a messianic priest seems to have taken the place of the messianic king, or at least to have taken precedence over the Davidic Messiah.[3] Chronological systems were established in order to calculate the time which God had determined for the end of all things.[4] Complex angelologies and demonologies were developed.[5] The doctrine of resurrection, together with the concept of rewards and punishments, was elaborated.[6] Perhaps most important, there was a growing sec-tarianism, or perhaps it would be better called particularism—the idea of a people of God that enjoyed a privileged position.[7]

*The influence of William H. Brownlee's work, notably in *The Meaning of the Qumrân Scrolls for the Bible*, will be apparent at several points in this study. I wish to record my appreciation of his scholarship and his friendship.

[1] *1 Enoch* 48:10; 52:4; *Pss. Sol.* 17:36. R. H. Charles translates the term "His Anointed" and "anointed of the Lord" in *APOT*.

[2] *1 Enoch* 46:2–3.

[3] Cf. *T. Levi* 18:2–14. In *T. Jud.* 21:3 we read, "For to me [Judah] the Lord gave the kingdom, and to him [Levi] the priesthood, and He set the kingdom beneath the priesthood" (*APOT* 2:322). Cf. *T. Sim.* 7:1–2.

[4] Cf. *Jub.* 50:1–5; Ezra 7:27–44; *1 Enoch* 92–105.

[5] Cf. *1 Enoch* 6–16; 1QM 12:1–9; 13:9–13; 17:6–8.

[6] *1 Enoch* 51:1 (and often in *1 Enoch*); *T. Benj.* 10:6–8; *Abot* 2:1–2, 19–20.

[7] *1 Enoch* 58:1–6; 60:6; 61:12–13, cf. the Qumran literature.

A survey of the literature that was produced in this period will show that there were diverse systems of eschatology—if "system" can be applied to these materials. It would probably be incorrect to assume that the various presentations represented various sectarian groups, but certain tendentious statements are found that suggest strong differences of opinion.[8] On one point we can be reasonably certain that there was a developing rift, namely on the heavenly Son of Man in contrast to the human Davidic Messiah views, for the Judaism that gained ascendancy after the destruction of the Second Temple opted for the Messiah-concept and discarded the idea of a superhuman deliverer, a kind of *deus ex machina* to come down from heaven and complete the redemption of Israel.

It has been pointed out[9] that interest in eschatology increases in time of stress. The Jews returned from Babylonian exile with hopes of becoming once again an independent nation. Subsequent to the reforms under Ezra there was a belief on the part of some of the returnees that they had paid for the sins of the fathers, that they were now a purified people, obedient to the law of the Lord, and that the blessings promised by the prophets were soon to be poured out. But things did not work out that way. Foreign rulers waxed worse and worse. Jewish leaders who rose up to deliver the people proved disappointing. And as the picture darkened, the hope of final deliverance—whether led by a Davidic Messiah or by a Son of Man from heaven, whether by God Himself or by His angels—burned more brightly.

There is a parallel between the closing period of the Second Temple and the present day. I am not suggesting that this is the only time in history that there has been such a parallel; I simply wish to deal with the present. With World War I, there was a rise in interest in the end times. This tapered off until the rise of Hitlerism, when it again became strong. And at the present time, with the threat of nuclear war or other nuclear tragedy, there is an eschatological fervor (or fever) in many parts of the world. Some have attempted to calculate when this end will come (*similiter Jubilees*). Others discuss whether there will be a messianic kingdom on earth. (*sim. Testaments*) or not (*sim. 4 Ezra*). Still others are greatly concerned with the eschatological war or apocalyptic deliverance[10] (*sim.* War of the Sons of Light vs. the Sons of Darkness [1QM]).

[8] For an example of analyzing such tendentious materials, cf. Y. Yadin, "The Dead Sea Scrolls and the Epistle to the Hebrews," *Scripta Hierosolymitana* 4 (1958) 36–55.

[9] Cf. *APOT* 2.ix–x; J. Moltmann, *Theology of Hope* (trans. J. W. Leitsch; New York: Harper & Row, 1975) 15–19, 124–128; W. S. LaSor, *The Truth about Armageddon* (San Francisco: Harper & Row, 1982) 1–9.

[10] Cf. W. S. LaSor, D. A. Hubbard, and F. W. Bush, *Old Testament Survey* (Grand Rapids: Eerdmans, 1982) 661–662; G. E. Ladd, "Apocalyptic Literature," *ISBE* 1 (1979) 151–156.

There is a growing sectarian attitude that says, in effect, We are the people of God; we will escape the holocaust. Frequently it develops into an intolerance of other views and interpretations.

In this study I propose to take an ancient sectarian group that displayed a number of these attitudes. History proved that its interpretation of the scriptures was at points incorrect. Hence it may prove valuable to us to see just where and how this group went wrong. The group I refer to, of course, was the Qumran Community.

— II —

The Qumranians believed that they lived in the end of days. They were "the Congregation of Israel in the last days" (1QSa 1:1), "the last generation" (CD 1:10). God was about to wield His sword "in the end time of judgment" (1QH 6:29). It was to be a "day of Vengeance" (1QS 10:19), a "day of Slaughter" (1QH 15:17), a "day of Judgment" (1QpHab 13:2–3), when God would be glorified "in the judgment of the wicked" (1QH 2:24).

This conviction had been reached by mathematical calculations based on certain scriptures. It is not important that we are unable to understand precisely the method used by the Qumranians. They believed that "three hundred and ninety years He had given them into the hand of Nebuchadnezzar, king of Babylon," the Lord caused this "root" to grow forth (CD 1:6–7; cf. Ezek 4:5). Twenty years later God raised for them a "teacher of righteousness" (CD 1:11).

They were convinced that they were the people of God. God had raised up men of understanding and wisdom (CD 6:2–3). They volunteered to be separated from the congregation of the men of unrightousness to become a community in the Torah (1QS 5:1–2). They were the Congregation of Israel, whereas the others were the Congregation of Belial. They described Jerusalem as the city of priests "who will heap up wealth and unjust gain from the plunder of the people" (1QpHab 9:4–5), where "the wicked priest did works of abomination and defiled the Temple of God" (12:7–9). The "dominion of Belial" (1QS 1:18) was composed of "sons of perversion" (1QS 1:31), "men of the pit" (1QS 9:22). There are many other passages, spread throughout Qumran literature, indicating that the Qumran community was not only separatist and schismatic, but cultic in their belief that they alone were chosen of God and they alone possessed the truth.

This separationism was extreme, bordering on the fanatical. The members of the community were not only "to love all the sons of light," but even "to hate all the sons of darkness" (1QS 1:11). Something like a double predestination is expressed in the Thanksgiving Scroll: as for the righteous, "Thou hast created the righteous one and from the womb

Thou hast established him for the appointed time of [His] will"; whereas "the wicked men Thou hast created for [the end-times of] Thine [ang]er, and from the womb Thou hast set them apart for the day of slaughter" (1QH 15:14–19).[11] The covenanters of Qumran had received a special knowledge from God, by which they were instructed to walk in God's way; they were forbidden to argue or dispute with "the men of the pit," but rather "to conceal the counsel of the law in the midst of the men of error" (1QS 9:16–17).

A principal figure was the Teacher of Righteousness.[12] There is actually very little said directly about him in the Qumran literature, unless we infer that all of the first-person passages in the Hymns are autobiographical.[13] There are certain points that can be made unequivocally. The Teacher was *not* the founder of the sect, but was raised up "twenty years" after its founding (cf. CD 1:4–11). And the Teacher was not the Messiah, for it is clear that the Teacher had died (or had been "taken up") and the community was still looking for the coming of the Messiah of Aaron and Israel (CD 19:1).[14] However, when we have excluded the extreme claims that have been made concerning this teacher, we still must recognize that he left his imprint on the Qumranians in a way that no other person had done.

In particular, the Teacher of Righteousness was the interpreter of the Scriptures, the one "whom God caused to know all the mysteries of the words of His servants the prophets (1QpHab 7:4–5). It might reasonably be assumed that he was responsible for the *pešārîm*, the "interpretations" of a number of portions of Scripture.[15] If the Hymns contain autobiographical material (an acceptable inference, if carefully controlled), then the following pasages may be attributed to the Teacher: "These things I know from Thy understanding, for Thou hast opened my ears to wondrous mysteries" (1QH 1:22); "Thou hast appointed me an ensign to

---

[11] In 1QS 3:13 ff. the doctrine seems to be less deterministic. God has placed two spirits in man, leaving the possible inference that man makes the decision. Yet even in this passage the choice is God's, cf. 4:23 ff.

[12] Usually *môrè haṣṣedeq*, which can be translated either as an objective genitive ("the one teaching righteousness") or as a subjective genitive ("the teacher who is righteous").

[13] A. Dupont-Sommer was particularly prone to use this method. For a critcism and a study of the Teacher of Righteousness in the Qumran texts, see W. S. LaSor, *The Dead Sea Scrolls and the New Testament* (Grand Rapids: Eerdmans, 1972) 106–130.

[14] The Teacher was a priest (4QpPs37 2:15–16). If the view that the Qumranians expected a priestly messiah is established, the Teacher might be identified with that figure, but CD 19:1 seems to distinguish between the "Unique Teacher" and the coming messiah.

[15] Cf. M. P. Horgan, *Pesharim: Qumran Interpretations of Biblical Books* (Washington: Catholic Biblical Association, 1979) 308 pp.

the righteous elect, an interpreter of knowledge in wondrous mysteries" (2:13).[16]

The Qumranians believed that the Messiah was coming to deliver them from the Kittim and to restore the kingship on earth. "The dominion of the Kittim shall come to an end" (1QM 1:6).[17] That this Messiah was Davidic and not Aaronic is clearly stated. In a fragment known as the Patriarchal Blessings we read, "For 'the staff' is the covenant of kingship, [and the thousan]ds of Israel they are 'the feet,' until the coming of the Messiah of Righteousness, the sprout of David, for to him and to his seed has been given the covenant of kingship unto the generations of eternity" (4QPatrBless 2–5). In another fragment known as the Florilegium there is the following statement, "This is the sprout of David, the one standing with the Seeker of the Law who [shall arise] in Zi[on in the la]tter days, 'And I will raise up the tabernacle of David which is falling'—that is the tabernacle of David which is fall[ing and whi]ch shall stand to save Israel" (4QFlor 1:11–13). In the Order of the Congregation there is an enigmatic passage—further complicated by the fact that it is broken in several places—which may possibly be restored to read, "When [God] shall beget the Messiah with them" (1QSa 2:12). If this restoration and translation is correct, it seems to be a reference to Psalm 2, which was believed by the Jews to be a messianic Psalm. However, great caution must be used in dealing with this text.

Since the idea of a Davidic Messiah is an integral part of the Judaism that was developing in the period under consideration, it is possible to connect other Qumranian statements with the messianic idea. There was to be an earthly kingdom, "an end-time of dominion for all the men of His lot" (1QM 1:5), when the people of God could claim the ancient promises: "Fill Thy land with glory and Thine inheritance with blessing" (1QM 12:11). The Temple and its ritual would be restored (1QM 2:1–6). But before this kingdom is established there will be a time of God's wrath, a time when "Belial shall be let loose upon Israel" (CD 4:13). It was not developed systematically, and attempted reconstructions have not been in full agreement, but we may possibly see the death of the

---

[16] J. Carmignac is of the opinion that "without doubt" the Teacher of Righteousness composed 1QS, 1QSa, 1QSb, 1QH, and 1QM; cf. *Les Textes de Qumrân* (Paris: Letouzey et Ané, 1963) 52. Many would disagree.

[17] For the identification of Kittim as Romans, despite the association with Assyria, cf. Y. Yadin, *The Scroll of the War of the Sons of Light against the Sons of Darkness* (trans. B. and C. Rabin; London: Oxford University Press, 1962) 22–25. J. Carmignac (*La Règle de la Guerre* [Paris: Letouzey et Ané, 1958] 4), argues that the Kittim, who figure eighteen times in the War Scroll are neither Greeks, nor Seleucids, nor Romans, but simply "Gentiles." It should be noted that the "Kittim in Egypt" (1QM 1:4) and "Kittim of Assyria" (1:2; cf. 11:11) are mentioned, possibly suggesting some connection with the Ptolemies and Seleucids.

Teacher of Righteousness as the beginning of the period of wrath, and the duration of that period "about forty years" (CD 20:14–16). This "time of wickedness" ends with the coming of "the Messiah of Aaron and Israel (12:23–13:1).[18]

The period of wrath on Israel (meaning those who had not gone out with the covenanters of Qumran) was a time when it was possible for "penitents of Israel" (CD 4:3) to join this elect group, but when this epoch is completed, there is no further chance of uniting with "the house of Judah" (CD 4:10–11). Following this period of wrath on Israel, it would seem, there is the war against the sons of darkness, when the dominion of the Kittim shall come to an end (1QM 1:5–8). According to Yadin's reconstruction, the war takes place in three phases: the first in "the wilderness of Jerusalem" (1:1–3); the second against the Kittim in Egypt (1:4a); and finally against "the kings of the north" (1:4b).[19] This warfare occupies forty years, but during the sabbatical years there is respite, so there are five periods of warfare of six years each and a final period of five years, each separated from the other by a sabbatical year. The end of the scroll is lacking, so we can only assume that the victorious people of God returned at last to a purged Jerusalem,[20] as portrayed in the victory hymn to "the Mighty One of War" (1QM 12:9–15). Then because of God's covenant they will live "a thousand generations" (CD 7:6), and Yahweh will reign for ever and ever" (4QFlor 1:3, quoting Exod 15:18).

The Messiah is not mentioned once in the extant texts of the War Scroll.[21] At the head of the Sons of Light were the Chief Priest and his Second (1QM 2:1), together with priests and Levites. The duties of the Chief Priest and his coterie were religious rather than military, to lead in prayer and praise and to blow the trumpets (which might be included in the military operations, since the trumpets sound certain commands). The military operations were led by the angel Michael, accompanied by other angels (17:5–9). The forces of the Sons of Darkness were led by

[18] For the purpose of the present study, the question of whether there was one Messiah ("the Messiah of Aaron and Israel") or two ("the Messiahs of Aaron and Israel," cf. 1QS 9:11) is of no major concern. The expression "the Messiah of Aaron" does not occur in the Qumran texts. Elsewhere I have given my reasons for rejecting the doctrine of two Messiahs in Qumran literature, cf. W. S. LaSor, "The Messiahs of Aaron and Israel," VT 6 (1956) 425–429; "The Messianic Idea in Qumran," in Studies and Essays in Honor of Abraham A. Neuman (M. Ben-Horin, B. D. Weinryb, and S. Zeitlin, eds.; Leiden: Brill, 1962) 354–356. The priority of the priests in Qumran I do not question.

[19] Cf. Yadin, War of the Sons of Light, 19.

[20] Ibid., 225.

[21] The word $m^e\check{s}\hat{\imath}h\check{e}k\bar{a}$, "thine anointed ones," occurs in 1QM 11:7, but the context indicates that it applies to previous seers who foretold the times of the wars and not to the "messiahs" of the Sons of Light.

Belial. A reference to Gog (1QM 11:16) suggests that the idea of this great battle was drawn from Ezekiel 37–38.

Several other points of the eschatological beliefs of the Qumranians could be mentioned, but these provide sufficient background for our present study. Our starting-point, mentioned above, was that this Community, so devoutly committed to the study of the Scriptures, had come to the conclusion on the basis of that study that they were the last generation: the end was at hand. There would be a terrible battle, lasting forty years, but at the end the forces of Belial would be completely destroyed, sin would be no more, and the people of God would dwell in peace. The kings of the Gentiles would bring tribute to Jerusalem, there would be abundance of cattle, silver, gold, and precious stones, and Zion would rejoice exceedingly (1QM 12:11–13).

These things did not happen. They were not the last generation. The Kittim were not defeated; instead the Romans crushed the Qumran community on their way to besiege Jerusalem. Some Qumranians may have escaped to Masada, perhaps taking some scrolls with them,[22] only to die there. The "wicked priests" of Jerusalem continued to exist after the destruction of the Second Temple, and laid the foundations of post-Temple Judaism. Some of those "sons of Belial," indeed, became members of the early Church while the Temple was still standing. The Qumranian interpretation of Scripture was *wrong*. Why? What can we learn from them that may be of value in the present time of end-time predictions?

— III —

At least five factors contributed to the Qumranian interpretations that proved to be erroneous.

1. There was a single interpreter. This is an argument from silence, I admit, and therefore must be handled cautiously. From the extant Qumran materials we know only of the Teacher of Righteousness, who came along about twenty years after the rise of the sect and who died, leaving them looking for a future teacher (CD 19:35–20:1; 20:14). Since he is consistently presented as the one "whom God caused to know all the mysteries of the words of His servants the prophets" (1QpHab 7:4–5; cf. 1QpHab 2:1–3, 6–9; CD 20:13; 4QpPs37 3:33–34 [on 37:23–24]) and no other teacher is referred to, the conclusion appears to be reasonable. Other scholars have added to this explicit material details that they find implicit in other texts. Some believe that the Thanksgiving Hymns (1QH) were composed by the Teacher of Righteousness or by one of his disci-

---

[22] Cf. Y. Yadin, *Masada* (trans. M. Pearlman; London: Sphere, 1971) 168–189.

ples, that the first-person passages are autobiographical.[23] It is generally agreed that the *Pesharim* are unique works, i.e. only one copy of each has been found, and that they are probably the work of the recognized interpreter, the Teacher of Righteousness.[24]

In this connection we should note the terms *rāz*, "mystery," and *pišrô*, "its interpretation." In the book of Daniel God made known a "mystery" to Nebuchadnezzar (2:27–28) and its interpretation He made known to Daniel (2:30, 36). But in the Qumran literature, God made known both the mystery and the interpretation to the Teacher of Righteousness. This is apparent in a passage from the Habakkuk Commentary: "And God told Habakkuk to write the things which were to come on the last generation, but the completion of the era He did not make known to him. And where it says, 'That he who reads may run,' its interpretation (is) the Teacher of Righteousness whom God caused to know all the mysteries of His servants the prophets" (1QpHab 7:1–5).

If the Hymns contain autobiographical elements we may add other references. "These things I know from Thine understanding, for Thou hast opened mine ears to marvelous mysteries" (1QH 1:21). "Thou didst appoint me an ensign to the righteous elect, and an interpreter of knowledge with (*b*-) wonderful mysteries" (1QH 2:13).

There is, obviously, no cross-check on such a situation. Jesus imposed this judgment on Himself: "If I bear witness to myself, my testimony is not true" (John 5:31). He appealed to the testimony of John the Baptist and to the witness that was borne by the works he did, as well as to the words of the Father and the Scriptures (5:32–39). I recognize that the acceptance of the words of Jesus is a matter of personal faith on the part of members of the Christian community. However, I do not find the Teacher of Righteousness appealing to the members of his community to apply any test to his claims.

2. There is no historical perspective in Qumran eschatology. Everything in Scripture refers simply to the last days. F. M. Cross expressed it well: "All biblical prophecy is normally taken to have eschatological meaning. The 'prophets,' Moses as well as Amos, the Psalmist as well as Jeremiah, speak regularly in open or veiled language of the 'last days.' "[25]

---

[23] This is developed at length in A. Dupont-Sommer, *Le Livre des Hymnes découvert près de la mer Morte (1QH). Traduction intégrale avec introduction et notes* (Paris: Maisonneuve, 1957; 120 pp.), and *The Essene Writings from Qumran* (trans. G. Vermès; Oxford: Basil Blackwell, 1961) 200ff. *et passim*. For my criticisms, see *The Dead Sea Scrolls and the New Testament*, 111–114.

[24] Cf. J. T. Milik, *Ten Years of Discovery in the Wilderness of Judaea*, tr. J. Strugnell (London: SCM, 1959) 40–41; F. M. Cross Jr., *The Ancient Library of Qumran and Modern Biblical Studies* (Garden City, NY: Doubleday, 1958) 84f. This is challenged by Horgan, *Pesharim*, 3.

[25] Cross, *The Ancient Library of Qumran*, 82.

In an account of the Israelite period of wilderness wanderings, there is a Song of the Well: "Spring up, O well!—Sing to it!—The well which the princes dug, which the nobles of the people delved, with the scepter and with their staves" (Num 21:17–18). There can be doubt that, according to the tradition of the Israelites, this had to do with a historical situation at Beer, where God gave the people water (21:16). But in the Qumran quotation of this passage, the "well" is interpreted as the law, and those who dug it were "the penitents of Israel who went out from the land of Judah and sojourned in the land of Damascus" (CD 6:5), in other words, the Qumran covenanters (6:2–3). The "staff" of the biblical passage is interpreted to mean "the searcher of the law," a play on the meanings in the semantic range of the root *hqq*, from "to dig, hollow out, a tool for performing this work" to "engrave, write, the laws or statues that are written, the person writing these statues." All has to do with the last days.

Similarly, the reference to the exile under Nebuchadnezzar (CD 1:5–6) finds its only relevance to the Qumranians. The "remnant of Israel" that remained (1:4–5) is identified as "Aaron and Israel"—terms used of the Community—from which God cased a root to sprout, and for his people God raised up the Teacher of Righteousness. The "epoch of wrath" (1:5) was terminated when God "remembered the covenant of the forefathers" (1:4). In the Bible "The covenant with their forefathers" (Lev 26:43) is mentioned in a passage which foretells the penalties of disobedience, and applies to all of Israel, but the Qumran covenanters appear to have applied it only to themselves. The figure 390 probably was taken from Ezekiel, and had to do with "the punishment of the house of Israel" (Ezek 4:5); the Qumranians used it for the point of origin of their sect (CD 1:7).

3.   In order to support their views the Qumranians broke the scriptural texts in fragments, with little or no regard for the larger context. The Commentary on Habakkuk is illuminating, since it is an extended treatment of a single prophetic book.

The background of the prophecy, as I understand it, is the violence and oppression under king Jehoiakim. Jeremiah had spoken out against this (Jer 22:13–17, cf. v 18). Habakkuk's problem was from a different angle: How could Yahweh, the righteous God of Israel, allow this to happen? (Hab 1:2–4). The Lord replied, "I am rousing the Chaldeans, that bitter and hasty nation . . ." (1:6). This raised a second and graver problem for Habakkuk: How can God, whose eyes are too pure to behold evil, allow the wicked to swallow up the righteous? (1:12–13). God's reply was, Be patient: the righteous shall live by his faithfulness (2:4).

But to the Qumran commentator the prophecy is a disjointed collection of proof texts. "The wicked surround the righteous" (Hab 1:4) in a broken text is interpreted to mean "[the wicked is the Wicked Priest and the righteous] is the Teacher of Righteousness" (1QpHab 1:10–11). "I am doing a work in your days" (Hab 1:5) is explained: "This means those who acted treacherously together with the man of the lie, for they did not heed the words of the Teacher of Righteousness from the mouth of God . . ." (1QpHab 1:14—2:3). The "Chaldeans" are the Kittim (1QpHab 2:10–12). Habakkuk's statement, "Thou who art of purer eyes than to behold evil . . ." is interpreted as follows: "God will not destroy His people by the nations, but by His elect ones[26] He will make judgment on the nations" (1QpHab 5:3–4). The "faithless men" (the Chaldeans), who were objectionable to Habakkuk, is taken to mean "the house of Absalom and the men of his council who kept silent in the chastisement of the Teacher of Righteousness, and did not aid him against the man of the lie . . ." (1QpHab 5:9–11). It would be possible, of course, to take the historical meaning of the passage and draw from it lessons for another time, making clear that the interpreter is so doing. But the Qumranian interpreter does not do this.

In the Damascus Document, a passage from Isaiah is quoted: "There shall come upon you and your people and the house of your fathers days which have (not) come since Ephraim went out from Judah" (Isa 7:17). The additional words in Isaiah, "the king of Assyria," are not included in the quotation. The Damascus Document uses the word pišrô, "its interpretation," only once (CD 4:14); however, the work is replete with interpretations, similar in exegesis to those in the Pesharim. This passage from Isaiah is explained as follows: "When the two houses of Israel were separated, Ephraim prevailed over Judah." This exegesis depends on the similarity of the words sûr, "turn aside, depart," and śar, "be prince, rule." That the one was written with sāmek and the other with śîn was of no consequence; neither was the explicit reference to Assyria in Isaiah's text.

4.   The Qumran author(s) made the passages fit the desired interpretation however the Scripture had to be manipulated. We have seen some of this in the previous illustrations.

The well-known Star-and-Scepter passage from Numbers (24:15–17) is quoted in the War Scroll. The scriptural passage is composed in distichs, star and scepter being parallel terms, and Judah and Israel likewise. In Rabbinic literature,[27] as in Christian, the passage is considered to be a Messianic prophecy, although the interpretations are varied. In the passage in Numbers, the immediate application is to the defeat of Moab and the sons of Seth. In the War Scroll this is applied to "the

---

[26] The text reads BHYRW, which can be pointed as either a singular, —ô, or a plural, – āw. I understand it to be parallel with "his people."

[27] Cf. C. G. Montefiore and H. Loewe, A Rabbinic Anthology (New York: Schocken, 1974) 262.

[order] of the battles of Thy hands . . . to make the troops of Belial fall"
(1QM 11:6–9), a clear reference to the Qumran war against the Sons of
Darkness. The passage is also quoted in the Damascus Document, where
the star is identified as "the searcher of the Law" and the scepter as "the
prince of all the congregation" (CD 7:18–20). Both here and in the War
Scroll the reading *wqrqr*, "and he shall tear down," agrees with MT of
Num 24:17. In the Testimonia, however, we find *wqdqd*, "and the crown
(of the head)" (4QTest 12–13), which agrees with the reading in the
Samaritan Pentateuch and in Jer 48:45, and fits the parallelism better.

A similar prophecy is found in Genesis (49:10), "The scepter shall not
depart from Judah, nor a lawgiver (ruler's staff, *mᵉhôqēq*) from between
his feet, until Shiloh (?) come; and unto him shall be the gathering
(obedience?) of the peoples." In the Blessing of Jacob this is rendered as
follows: "A ruler shall ‹not› depart from Judah. When the rule is Israel's
[the coven]ant shall return to David, for the *staff* is the covenant of the
kingship, and the [trib]es of Israel, they are the *feet*, until the Messiah of
righteousness comes, the branch of David. For to him and his seed has
been given the covenant of kingship of his people unto everlasting
generations, the [interpreter] of the law with the men of the Community" (4QPatrBless 2–7). The scriptural passage can easily be adapted
(or distorted) in this case, for *šebet* can mean "tribe" or "scepter," *mᵉhôqēq*
can mean "prescriber of laws" or "commander's staff," and *šîlôh*, which
has been much debated, could mean "that which belongs to him" or it
could be taken as a cryptic word for "Messiah."[28]

A portion of the Damascus Document makes use of four portions of
Scripture, giving us a fairly good idea of how the sacred words could be
handled to bring the desired meaning. The passage (CD 7:10–21) contains quotations from Isaiah (7:17, considered above), Amos (5:26f.; 9:11),
and Exodus (24:17). The first passage from Amos contains the references
to "*sikkût* your king, and *kiffûn* your star-god." Reference to commentaries will show that this text has several problems: the reading *sukkat*,
"tabernacle," is supported by LXX, Vulgate, and Syriac; it has been
suggested that both words have been vocalized on the pattern of *šiqqûs*,
"abomination,"[29] and that we should read *kêwān*, "Kaiwan." In the
Qumran passage, "the books of the Torah are the tabernacle *(sukkat)* of
the king" (CD 7:15–16). This is supported by a quotation from Amos 9:11,
"I will raise up the tabernacle of David which is falling." Then "Kiyyun
your images" of the previous quotation is taken to mean "the books of the
prophets" (CD 7:17). Finally, the passage from Exodus (24:17) is inter-

---

[28] *Sanh.* 98*b* (late); F. Delitzsch, *New Commentary on Genesis* (trans. S. Taylor;
Edinburgh: T. & T. Clark, 1889) 2.377.
[29] Cf. W. R. Harper, *Amos and Hosea* (ICC; New York: Scribner's 1915) 139.

preted, "the star is the searcher of the Law" (7:18), the "scepter is the prince of all the congregation, and when he arises he shall crush all the sons of Seth" (7:20–21).

Allegory is used in order to obtain a desired meaning. In Habakkuk, there is mention of "the violence done to Lebanon" (Hab 2:17). The allusion is not clear; possibly Habakkuk was thinking of the ravaging of the forests by the Chaldeans for military purposes.[30] But to the Qumranians "Lebanon is the council of the community, and "the beasts are the simple ones of Judah, the doers of the law" (1QpHab 12:4–5).

I do not suggest that the Qumranians had a library of textual materials and a science of textual criticism. It is quite likely, however, in view of the textual variants that are extant, that there were various textual traditions (probably oral), and that the Qumran interpreters simply latched on to the readings that best suited their purposes—a custom not entirely unknown at the present time.

5.   The Qumranians were a sect. They believed that they and they alone were the elect, the people of God. This is evident in their literature and has already become apparent in passages quoted above. They were "the men of the community who have offered themselves to turn from all evil and to lay hold of all that he commanded according to his will, to be separated from the congregation of the men of error, to become a community in law and in wealth, answering when asked by the sons of Zadok, the priests who keep the covenant, and when asked by the majority of the men of the community, who lay hold of the covenant" (1QS 5:1–7).

There is nothing in this statement that by itself is wrong. It is the application that leads to error, for they considered the priests of Jerusalem to be wicked (1QpHab 12:7–9), and those outside the Qumran community to be the men of Belial's lot (1QS 2:4–5). In this study I have not entered into the efforts to identity the historical situation, for the many scholars who have done so have not yet achieved a consensus. This much, at least, can be said: there was a schismatic mood, observable not only in the Qumran literature but also in the Pseudepigrapha and in the New Testament. Whether the Qumranians were the only complete separatists we cannot properly say—but they were definitely cut off from the rest of Israel by their own choice.

The fact that some of the extracanonical writings of the time of the Second Temple have been found among the Dead Sea Scrolls has led to speculation about the relationship between the Qumranians and other Jewish sectarians. Their emphasis on the primacy of Levi over Judah seems to connect them with whoever was responsible for the *Testaments*

---

[30] C. F. Keil, *The Twelve Minor Prophets. Biblical Commentary on the Old Testament* (C. F. Keil and F. Delitzsch, eds.; trans. J. Martin; repr. Grand Rapids: Eerdmans, 1949) 2.88–90.

of the Twelve Patriarchs—although the date of composition of the latter is in much dispute. But the high level of social and moral implications of the Law, as presented in the *Testaments*, is not found in the Qumran writings. Their calendar appears to be that of the *Book of Jubilees*. But no breach with the Jerusalem priesthood or cultus is found in Jubilees. Moreover, the last battle which leads to the age to come is not found in Jubilees. We can only assume that the Qumranians were aware of various movements among the Jews of that period, but set themselves apart from other Jews. They were "a house of community for Israel" (1QS 9:6). They were the people Israel whom God had chosen from all the peoples of the lands: a people of holy ones of the Covenant" (1QM 10:9–10).

— IV —

Certain lessons may be drawn from this study that should be useful for our own day.

1. It is dangerous to listen only to a single voice. This is just as true of those who derive their eschatology solely from A. Schweitzer or C. H. Dodd as it is of those who read only the Scofield Bible. In place of an individual we might substitute a school. In the past century or so there have been a number of schools of scholarship, such as the Barthian or the Bultmannian, in each of which there is a distinctive viewpoint. And in place of a school we might substitute Protestant, or Catholic, or Christian vis à vis Jewish interpretation. The more one is tied to a certain position on any subject, particularly in eschatology, the greater the possibility of error due to lack of corrective viewpoints.

2. The study of biblical eschatology, as in the case for other biblical doctrines, requires historical perspective. Those who believe in a God who acts should be as careful in the study of how God has acted in the past as they are in the theories or dogmas of how He is going to act in the end time. This, too, is bidirectional. I find as much to criticize in the writings of those who rule out all biblical eschatology, as I do in the works of those who ignore history. The biblical viewpoint presents a God whose redemptive activity leads from an age of sin and death to an age of righteousness and life. The Scriptures, whether we study the Miqra as a Jew or the Old and New Testaments as a Christian, present a goal toward which God is leading His people.[31] At any point in our study we need to keep in mind the greater truth, we need to keep all doctrines in this historical perspective.

[31] Cf. K. Barth: "If Christianity be not altogether and unreservedly eschatology, there remains in it no relationship whatever to Christ" (*Der Römerbrief,* 2d ed. [1922] 298, quoted in Moltmann, *Theology of Hope,* 39. Moltmann does not accept Barth's thesis, and I find it necessary to understand what Barth means by "eschatology," but in principle he is right. Eschatology is the central nervous system of biblical theology.

3. The use of proof texts taken out of context, the effort to employ certain terms uniformly as keys to unlock a mystery, the bending of scripture to support an interpretation—such methods can only lead to error at best, and, if carried to a logical conclusion, to schism. Within my scholarly lifetime I have seen proof-texting not only by the apocalypticists of a fundamentalistic position, but also by ethical monotheists, by proponents of the myth-and-ritual school, and more recently by the scavenger hunters of wisdom everywhere in the Bible. By a skillful manipulation of texts and terms it is possible to prove that there will be an earthly kingdom of God (a millennium) or that there will be no earthly kingdom; that there will be a messianic king on the throne of David in Zion, or that the kingdom will exist only in the spiritual realm, or that the kingdom is within us. The Qumranians developed only one system from their study of Scripture; an analysis of the eschatology of the books of the Pseudepigrapha will show that several other systems were likewise founded on the same Scripture.

4. Similar to the previous point, but from a different approach, is the effort to make the Scriptures fit a theory. In the one case, the method of interpreting the Scriptures leads to a system; in the other, the system leads to the method (or lack of method) of interpretation. Both are found in the Qumran writings. Both are found today. Quite possibly, the faulty method first leads to the faulty interpretation, and then, once the results are accepted, the system that has been derived dominates the interpretation.

Historically, Christian Chiliasm (the view that a millennial kingdom will be established on earth) appears to have been the earliest system derived from the Scriptures. This was rejected, about the fifth century of our era, one reason given that it was "too Jewish." To defend this antimillennial position, on the one hand, all sorts of methods of exegesis and interpretation have been employed. To reestablish a millennial position, on the other hand, all sorts of methods of exegesis and interpretation have been employed. Modern scholars who insist that a hermeneutic (system of interpretation) should first be established are certainly right. The question that remains to be answered is simply this: Will the hermeneutic that is set up be distorted by a prior system that is being defended?

5. The most serious possibility of error is from sectarianism. This has occurred in many forms, and indeed still does. By sectarianism I mean either the belief that one's viewpoints are completely self-sufficient, or that other viewpoints are of little or no value, or a combination of the two.

This attitude can be found in many areas. Take German theology, for one example. Read through almost any German book and glance at the footnotes. There will rarely be a reference to any work that is not in German. Or look at Protestant works in almost any area of biblical studies and note the absence of references to Catholic writers, or to the Church Fathers, or to Jewish and rabbinic studies. The Jewish rejection of apocalyptic elements, possibly a tendentious result of how the early Christians used these materials, is another illustration. This attitude is not as marked today as it was when I first started my studies more than fifty years ago.

In biblical eschatology the most notable sectarianism is the almost total lack of knowledge on the part of Christian scholars of Jewish and rabbinic teachings, and only a slightly less ignorance of the Old Testament. This has been noted by Jewish writers, particularly with reference to the redemption of the material world. G. Scholem states: "Judaism has always maintained a concept of redemption as an event which takes place publicly, on the stage of history and within the community."[32] But Christian eschatology, which came strongly under the influence of the Neoplatonism of Augustine and the triumphalism of his *City of God,* relegated Chiliasm to an attic of ideas that had failed, and looked upon apocalyptic as "an utter lack of faith and hope in the present, arising from 'a persecution complex.'"[33] The works of P. D. Hanson are a welcome and healthy corrective to this view.[34]

— V —

We have traced the methods of the Qumranians that led to the belief that they were the last generation, that the end of the age was upon them. As Jews they believed that the Scriptures were from God and infallible in matters of faith and life. As sectarians they cut themselves off from others who also believed in the Scriptures as God's word.

We live in a day when there are many who believe that this is the end of the age, that Armageddon—whether it be a military invasion of Israel or a nuclear holocaust—is about to explode. The sectarian attitude affects both sides, for while the apocalypticists often cut themselves off from all who disagree with them, the rest of us usually pay no attention to the Scriptures that evoke such apocayptic ideas. We would do well to remember that a firm faith in God's ultimate victory is our best basis for hope in an uncertain age. As a rule of faith and life the Scriptures are never wrong; interpreters and their systems are frequently wrong. We need to distinguish between the two.

---

[32] G. Scholem, *The Messianic Idea in Judaism* (New York: Schocken, 1971) 1. Cf. Also J. Klausner, *The Messianic Idea in Israel: From Its Beginning to the Completion of the Mishnah* (trans. W. F. Stinespring; London: Allen and Unwin, 1956) 10. Klausner exempts the early Christian Chiliasts (rightfully) from his criticism.
[33] S. B. Frost, *Old Testament Apocalyptic* (London: Epworth Press, 1952) 5.
[34] P. D. Hanson, "Apocalypse, Genre," *IDBS* 27–28, "Apocalypticism," *ibid.* 28–34.

THE PSEUDEPIGRAPHA AS BIBLICAL EXEGESIS

JAMES H. CHARLESWORTH
Princeton Theological Seminary
Princeton, New Jersey

Biblical exegesis during the period of Early Judaism, circa 250 B.C.E. to 200 C.E., was once thought to be primarily reflected in the Targumim and Midrashim;[1] but then we learned that each of these is too late to help us understand the Jewish interpretation of the "Old Testament" prior to the destruction of the Temple in 70. With the discovery of the Dead Sea Scrolls we turned our attention to an attempt to understand the Pesharim and a reexamination of the possible early nature of Aramaic translations and interpretations of the scriptures, thanks to the recovery of Targumim in the Qumran caves. A study of Qumranic biblical text types awakened us to the reality that the adjective "Septuagintal" must no longer be used only to refer to Greek variants, but may refer to

---

[1] Even Emil Schürer, the erudite late nineteenth-century and early twentieth-century expert on Early Judaism succumbed to this tendency. In his justly famous *A History of the Jewish People in the Time of Jesus Christ* he tended to treat early Jewish exegesis in isolation from the study of the apocrypha and pseudepigrapha and, for example, contended that the Targumim in their present form were only "about one hundred years after the time of Christ" (div. 1, vol. 1, p. 118). Schürer unduely restricted his treatment of Jewish exegesis to haggadah and halakhah, which were too narrowly defined (cf. div. 2, vol. 1, section 25). It is now slowly becoming clear that to study the pseudepigrapha is to examine Jewish exegetical work on Tanach. Only to a minor extent did Schürer observe this insight (cf. div. 2, vol. 3), and he failed to integrate into his study of early Jewish exegesis the Jewish pseudepigrapha he labeled "sacred legends" (namely *Jubilees* and the *Martyrdom of Isaiah*). These pseudepigrapha are *not* adequately categorized as "modes of enriching the sacred story" (div. 2, vol. 3, p. 134); they are *interpretations* of Torah by reciting and expanding the stories, and thereby making them more meaningful and paradigmatic for daily life.

Some pseudepigrapha probably did rival and replace canonical works in some communities, for example in the groups that produced the *Books of Enoch* (cf. also 11Q Temple and 1QpHab); but the pseudepigrapha should not be portrayed as rivals of canon. They are supporters of it. Random comments by Schürer indicate that he may well have agreed with this insight; but he did not adequately integrate his voluminous and brilliant (at times) reflections. Of course, the precursor is seldom the perfector.

very early Hebrew traditions that are not reflected in the Biblia
Hebraica.

We are now in a totally new era in the study of biblical exegesis in
Early Judaism. Interpretation begins not with the writings separate from
the Old Testament; it does not even begin with the pointing of a text. It
begins with the choosing of consonants in Semitic manuscripts. The
subsequent expansions or deletations in the Hebrew text of the Bible
itself is unexpected and impressive, and is not limited to the Qumranic
fragments of Jeremiah and Samuel.[2]

In the present study I shall try briefly to illustrate that another
chapter in early Jewish biblical exegesis is reflected in the production of
the so-called pseudepigrapha. In the second volume of *The Old Testament Pseudepigrapha* I have arranged a group of documents under the
title "Expansions of the 'Old Testament' and Legends." Here are collected writings reminiscent of another type of biblical exegesis found at
Qumran, reflected for example in the Genesis Apocryphon. The documents are the following:

Letter of Aristeas
Jubilees
Martyrdom and Ascension of Isaiah
Joseph and Aseneth
Life of Adam and Eve
Pseudo-Philo
The Lives of the Prophets
Ladder of Jacob
4 Baruch
Jannes and Jambres
History of the Rechabites
Eldad and Modad
History of Joseph

The *Letter of Aristeas* celebrates the translation of the Hebrew scriptures
into Greek, but the other writings placed under "Expansions of the 'Old
Testament' and Legends" illustrate how Early Judaism was a religion of
the Book and how the Old Testament narratives were clarified, enriched,
expanded and sometimes retold from appreciably a different viewpoint.

There is certainly no space here to illustrate how each of these
documents takes the Hebrew Bible seriously and reinterprets portions of
it. Fortunately the reader can consult the introductions to and transla-

---

[2] See the brilliant discussions by F. M. Cross, not only in his classic work *The
Ancient Library of Qumran and Modern Biblical Studies* (Garden City, NY:
Doubleday, 1961 [revised edition] and recently reprinted) but also in his recent
articles in *Bible Review*. In "New Directions in Dead Sea Scroll Research: Original
Biblical Text Reconstructed From Newly Found Fragments," *Bible Review* 1
(1985) 26–35 Cross demonstrates dramatically that "4QSam[a] preserves lost bits of
the text of Samuel" (p. 26).

tions of each of the documents in the new edition of the Old Testament Pseudepigrapha. For the present it must suffice merely to pull out two examples.

First, *Pseudo-Philo* (extant in Latin and also in a late Hebrew version) is something like a haggadic midrash on Genesis through 2 Samuel. A significant expansion is the moving lament attributed to the daughter of Jephthah (cf. Judg 11:30–40).

According to the biblical narrative we hear neither about the name of Jephthah's daughter nor about her words of lamentation to God. Jephthah had promised to sacrifice to the Lord the first who should come out of his house to greet him after his victorious battle. Jephthah had promised to offer this male, "him" *(weha͎ͨalîthihû)*, to the Lord; it had never entered his mind that he would be greeted by his only child, a daughter, who came forth dancing and singing about his victories over the Ammonites.

In *Pseudo-Philo* we find the name of the daughter, Seila, and her lamentation. Note the opening lines of Seila's threnody:

> Hear, you mountains, my lamentation;
> and pay attention, you hills, to the tears of my eyes;
> and be witnesses, you rocks, of the weeping of my soul.
>
> (40:5)[3]

As intimated above, this passage is an example of biblical exegesis by expansion. It is paradigmatically different from the longer versions of Samuel that were once part of one form of the ancient Hebrew text. It is an expanded legend; they are precious remnants of what was later deleted.

Second, *Jubilees* (preserved in full only in Ethiopic) is a type of midrash on Gen 1:1 through Exod 12:50. It rewrites these portions of the Tanach from a different perspective. In this rewritten Bible angels play a much more dominant role, the lunar calendar is discredited, and the Sabbath is elevated and described as written on heavenly tablets (obviously the author desires to correct the habit of some Jews who do not, in his opinion, properly observe the Sabbath). The author treats the biblical text with astonishing liberties: names and places are now supplied seemingly at will, and unattractive actions are explained; for example, Abraham commands Rebecca to love and cherish Jacob more than Esau because he had seen Esau's deeds and perceived that Jacob was the rightful heir.

In the present paper I shall try to show that most of the Jewish pseudepigrapha, which were written from circa 250 B.C.E. to 135 C.E., are related because they are exegetically rooted in the Old Testament.

---

[3] Translated by D. J. Harrington in *The Old Testament Pseudepigrapha*, edited by J. H. Charlesworth (Garden City, NY: Doubleday, 1985) 2.354.

They should not be categorized as the result of some modern desire to collect them together in a pseudo category; they are important for the study of Early Judaism and are a product of the early Jewish desire to stand under the Bible. They are an essential part of early Jewish exegesis.

It gives me considerable pleasure to dedicate these reflections to the memory of Bill Brownlee. We both studied under W. F. Stinespring. He preceded me as a professor at Duke University; and we both taught courses on the Dead Sea Scrolls. He was a fine colleague and contributor to my collection of essays on the relationship between the Dead Sea Scrolls and the Gospel of John. And perhaps most importantly he was a dear friend with whom I often slipped away from the noisy business of the academy to relax and enjoy a quiet meal and to discuss the meaning of our research and the challenge of our faith.

The Problem of Abundant Writings

The major problems are how to procede and what to include as Jewish writings clearly antedating the demise of Bar Kokhba. The second problem, when solved with some confidence and caution, leaves us with far too many writings to discuss in a paper such as the present one. To choose only one or two documents to examine would fail to make the major point, namely that the pseudepigrapha are almost always shaped in some way by the force of the Old Testament. To discuss each of the documents would result in a desultory and perfunctory treatment of the subject.

In order to avoid these potentially misleading methodologies I have reviewed the documents and assessed how each seems to depend on the Old Testament. Four categories have emerged:

1) *Inspiration.* The Old Testament serves primarily to inspire the author, who then evidences considerable imagination, perhaps sometimes under influences from other writings.

2) *Framework.* The Old Testament provides the framework for the author's own work. The original Old Testament setting is employed for appreciably other purposes.

3) *Launching.* A passage or story in the Old Testament is used to launch another, considerably different reflection. The original Old Testament setting is abandoned.

4) *Inconsequential.* The author borrows from the Old Testament only the barest facts, names especially, and composes an appreciably new story.

Inspiration

The best example of this exegetical method is found in the category labeled "Prayers, Psalms, and Odes." The "More Psalms of David" are

structured according to the poetry of the Davidic Psalter, and are frequently indistinguishable from them. The Psalms are the inspiration for
these additions to it. Psalm 151A also evidences the characteristic of the
second category; it uses 1 Samuel 16 and 17 as the framework for four
verses. Note the following translation of the Hebrew (11QPsᵃ 151):

> I was the smallest among my brothers,
> and the youngest among the sons of my father;
> and he made me shepherd of his flocks,
> and the ruler over his kids.
>
> (151A:1)
>
> . . .
>
> He sent his prophet to anoint me,
>   Samuel to make me great;
>
> (151A:5)
>
> . . .
>
> But he (God) sent and took me from behind the flock,
> and he anointed me with holy oil,
> and he made me leader for his people,
> and ruler over the sons of his covenant.
>
> (151A:7)

These lines are based upon 1 Sam 16:1–11, 17:14, and 2 Sam 7:8; and
perhaps also on Pss 78:70–71 and 89:20. It is understandable why the
Hebrew of this psalm contains the title "A Hallelujah of David the Son of
Jesse."[4]

The next psalm, 151B (11QPsᵃ 151), is also based on the Davidic
Psalter, and on another episode in the life of David, one which is
recorded in 1 Sam 17:8–25. A translation from the Hebrew is as follows:

> Then I s[a]w a Philistine
>   who was uttering taunts from the ra[nks of the
>   enemy . . .].

The Syriac recension is not so fragmentarily preserved:

> I went out to attack the Philistine,
> and he cursed me by his idols.
> But after I unsheathed his sword, I cut off his head;
> and I removed the shame from the sons of Israel.

Other verses in the additional psalms, or Psalms 151 through 155, are
also inspired by the Davidic Psalter and by episodes in the life of David.

The Prayer of Manasseh, one of the most beautiful penitential psalms
ever written, was composed in the century before the destruction of the

---

[4]The translations are by Charlesworth and are printed in *The Old Testament
Pseudepigrapha*, 2.612–13.

Temple by a devout Jew who wished to supply the prayer of Manasseh
described in 2 Chronicles 33. Note this comparison:

2 Chronicles 33	Prayer of Manasseh
[Manasseh] . . . provoking	I provoked
his [Yahweh's] anger	your fury (or anger)
[Manasseh] . . . placed	I set up
. . . the idol . . . in the	idols
Temple	I am ensnared
Manasseh with hooks	I am bent by a multitude
. . . in	of iron chains
chains . . .	I am bending
humbling himself	the knees of my
deeply	heart before you
before	God of our fathers.
the God of his ancestors	

Here we confront a prayer composed pseudonymously to provide the
prayer mentioned in 2 Chr 33:11–13. The Prayer of Manasseh, therefore,
is an exegesis of an Old Testament passage using the model of both
inspiration, because it is structured according to the style of the Psalter
and other Hebraic poems, and framework, because it intends to use the
story in 2 Chronicles to compose a new psalm or prayer.

Framework

The best examples of the type of exegesis called "Framework" are
found in the *Fourth Book of Ezra, 2 Baruch,* and in the *Testaments*
collected in the Pseudepigrapha. In each of these documents an Old
Testament passage provides the basis, or framework, for an entirely
different story. The apocalypse in *4 Ezra* begins as follows:

> In the thirtieth year after the destruction of our city, I, Salathiel,
> who am also called Ezra, was in Babylon. I was troubled as I lay
> on my bed, and my thoughts welled up in my heart, because I
> saw the desolation of Zion and the wealth of those who lived in
> Babylon.
>
> (*4 Ezra* 3:1–2)[5]

The author has used the framework of the story of the destruction of
Jerusalem, Zion, by the Babylonians in the sixth century B.C.E. to tell
the story of the devastation wrought by the Romans in the first century
C.E. The author of this passage knew well the traditions related to and
based exegetically in 2 Kings 25, according to which Nebuchadnezzar,
king of Babylon, attacked and conquered Jerusalem.

[5] Translation by B. M. Metzger in *The Old Testament Pseudepigrapha* (Garden
City, NY: Doubleday, 1983) 1.528.

The same source, combined with Jeremiah traditions, produced the apocalypse called *2 Baruch*. Note in particular 6:1–2.

> Now it happened on the following day that, behold, an army of the Chaldeans [=Babylonians] surrounded the city. And in the evening I, Baruch [=Jeremiah's scribe], left the people, went outside, and set myself by an oak. And I was grieving over Zion and sighed because of the captivity which had come upon the people.[6]

Scholars often explain the use of "Babylon" for "Rome" because of the need to hide from the Romans the Jewish polemic against them. This attractive suggestion does not exhaust the possibilities or reasons for such pseudepigraphical writing. In my opinion, an equally important one is the powerful paradigmatic force of the biblical text and the traditions related to it. By using an exegesis of 2 Kings and Jeremiah as the framework for articulating the search for meaning in a new day it was possible to stress that as once growth sprang up from the ruins of 587 so it will be possible—indeed certain in light of the vision revealed to Baruch—for the new to begin again, thanks to the fact that God was indeed in control of the destruction of his Temple and is about to bring in the promised eschaton.

The source for the testamentary literature is the account of Jacob's last word, or testament, to his sons; and in particular the record of that scene described in Genesis 49.

> Then Jacob called his sons, and said, "Gather yourselves together, that I may tell you what shall befall you in days to come.
>
> Assemble and hear, O sons of Jacob,
>   and hearken to Israel your father."
>
> (Gen 49:1–2; RSV)

A Jewish document, probably composed around 100 B.C.E. and redacted by a Christian sometime in the second century C.E.,[7] reflects this

---

[6]Translated by A. F. J. Klijn in *The Old Testament Pseudepigrapha*, 1.622.

[7]There is considerable controversy over the Jewish or Christian origin of the *Testaments of the Twelve Patriarchs*. It is clear that at least two testaments, one attributed to Levi and the other to Naphtali, are Jewish and pre-Christian, since fragments of each were found in medieval manuscripts in the Cairo Geniza and also in Cave IV at Qumran. It is also clear that these testaments are not identical to the Greek testaments in the critical text of the *Testaments of the Twelve Patriarchs*. The crucial question is now whether a document of twelve testaments was composed by a Jew or a Christian. Acknowledging that the distinctions between "Jewish" and "Christian" are now blurred, and that the Jewish fragments mentioned above are not identical with the critical text of the *Testaments of the Twelve Patriarchs* M. de Jonge and I have tended to differ on assessing the origin of the document. He continues (since 1953) to favor the possibility that a Christian

memorable story in Genesis 49. A Jew composed testaments for each of
the twelve sons of Jacob by using the account of how Jacob called his
twelve sons around his death bed and exhorted and blessed them.
Genesis 49 was the framework for composing testaments for each of
Jacob's twelve sons. What Jacob had done on his death bed for his sons,
each of them did for their sons, but the content shifted markedly in the
direction of thought so prevalent in Early Judaism; large apocalyptic
sections filled out the brief statement by Jacob ("that I may tell you what
shall befall you in days to come," Gen 49:1).

Both the old framework and the new content is pellucidly represented in the *Testament of Levi;* note the following excerpts:

> A copy of the words of Levi: the things that he decreed to his sons
> concerning all they were to do, and the things that would happen
> to them until the day of judgment. He was in good health when
> he summoned them to him, but it had been revealed to him that
> he was about to die. When they all were gathered together he
> said to them: (1:1–2) . . . "At this moment the angel opened for
> me the gates of heaven and I saw the Holy Most High sitting on
> the throne. And he said to me, 'Levi, to you I have given the
> blessing of the priesthood until I shall come and dwell in the
> midst of Israel'" (5:1–2).[8]

The *Testaments of the Twelve Patriarchs* thus evolves out of the Old
Testament narrative, especially Genesis 47 through 50, and in that sense
belongs within the broad study of exegesis within Early Judaism.

The *Testament of Job*, which was written in the century before the
destruction of Jerusalem, also evolves out of an exegesis of Joshua's
testament. As R. P. Spittler perceives, the Old Testament provided for
the composition of the *Testament of Job* the following framework features:

---

conceived the idea of twelve testaments in the second century. He is certainly
correct to stress that with the Greek document we are faced not with interpolations by with redactions, with extensive deletions as well as additions, of the
Jewish sources; I, however, am more convinced that the Jewish strata is far more
extensive that he thinks and that it is found behind each of the twelve testaments.
My conviction that a Jew composed a document which contained twelve testament is now confirmed, in part at least, by the discovery of a *Testament of Judah*
among the fragments of the Dead Sea Scrolls. This discovery was presented to
specialists in Cambridge and Uppsala and will be published in the near future.

The most recent publications on this debate are the following: M. de Jonge,
"The Testaments of the Twelve Patriarchs," in *The Apocryphal Old Testament,*
edited by H. F. D. Sparks (Oxford: Oxford University Press, 1984) 505–12. H. C.
Kee, "Testaments of the Twelve Patriarchs," in *The Old Testament
Pseudepigrapha,* 1.775–80. J. H. Charlesworth, *The Old Testament
Pseudepigrapha and the New Testament: Prolegomena for the Study of Christian
Origins* (SNTSMS 54; Cambridge: University Press, 1985).

[8] Translation by H. C. Kee in *The Old Testament Pseudepigrapha,* 1.788–90.

the blessing from father to sons (Gen 47:29–50:14):
an ill father (Gen 48:1),
who is near death (Gen 47:29),
and on his death bed (Gen 47:31),
calls his sons (Gen 49:1),
disposes of his possessions (Gen 48:22),
and issues a forecast of future events (Gen 49:1).
The father dies (Gen 49:33),
and a lamentation completes the framework of the story (Gen
  50:2–14).[9]

This framework provides the basis for the genre, loosely defined, that
unites the Jewish testaments, namely the *Testaments of the Twelve
Patriarchs*, the *Testament of Job*, and to a lesser extent the *Testament of
Abraham* and the *Testament of Moses* (cf. also *1 Enoch* 91:1–19, Tob
14:3–11, Acts 20:17–38, 1 Timothy 4:1–16, and John 17:1–26). Here is the
opening to the *Testament of Job* (which is extant in Greek):

> Now on the day when, having fallen ill, he (Job) began to settle his
> affairs, he called his seven sons and his three daughters (cf. Job
> 1:2), ... And when he had called his children he said, "Gather
> round, my children. Gather round me so that I may show you the
> things which the Lord did with me and all the things which have
> happened to me" (1:2–4).[10]

As can be surmised from the last clause, "that I may show you the things
which the Lord did with me and all the things which have happened to
me," this testament is basically a recital of Job's life. It, therefore,
contrasts with the *Testament of Levi*, and constantly returns, after expan-
sive narratives, to the biblical framework and book of Job. In essence, the
Testament of Job is an imaginative exegesis and legendary expansion of
the biblical book. For example, Job's wife has a speech of only two lines in
the Hebrew text, which is expanded in the Septuagint to a full paragraph;
in the *Testament of Job* she is named—Sitis—and shares a rather lengthy
dialogue with Job. As I stated long ago, the *Testament of Job* is a type of
midrash in the form of a testament on the canonical book.[11] It is an
example of the early phases of what will later be called midrashim.

The *Testament of Abraham* (extant only in Greek) continues in the
direction taken by the author of the *Testament of Levi* and away from that
followed by the author of the *Testament of Job*. It does not expand on the
life of Abraham; it describes how Abraham refuses to die. Michael is sent

---

[9] See Spittler's discussion in *The Old Testament Pseudepigrapha*, 1.831–32.
[10] Translation by R. P. Spittler in *The Old Testament Pseudepigrapha*, 1.839.
[11] Charlesworth, "Testament of Job," in *The Pseudepigrapha and Modern Research
with a Supplement* (SBL Septuagint and Cognate Studies Series 7S; Chico: Scholars, 1981) 135.

by God to help Abraham prepare for death and to write a testament; eventually Michael is to collect his soul. Abraham, however, refuses to die and forces Michael to take him on a celestial journey (somewhat reminiscent of the journeys of Enoch). In contrast to the *Testament of Job*, as E. P. Sanders states, virtually nothing from the Old Testament is found in the *Testament of Abraham*, other than the obvious and relatively insignificant references which can be traced back to Genesis.[12] Surprisingly, in light of the vast iconographical and documentary evidence, there is no clear reference to Abraham's attempt to sacrifice Isaac. With the authors of many apocalypses and apocalyptic writings the author of the *Testament of Abraham* is interested in the cosmic dimensions of Jewish theology.[13]

The *Testament of Moses* (extant in only one Latin palimpsest) received its present form in the first half of the first century C.E. It is similar to the *Testament of Abraham* and the *Testament of Levi*, in that it does refer to the future acts of God, but it is more similar to the *Testament of Job*, in that it also concentrates not upon the predictions of the future but on a recitation of the past history of God's people. In a farewell discourse to Joshua Moses describes the history of Israel and the Jews from the time of the conquest of Palestine through the rebuilding of the Temple after the sixth-century exile to the subsequent apostasy (perhaps due to the hellenizing priests or the "kings" of the late Hasmoneans). The work, as extant in its fragmentary form, continues with an eschatological hymn which celebrates the destruction of the evil one by Israel's guardian angel, and the final exaltation of Israel.

The close relationship between the *Testament of Moses* and Deuteronomy, especially chaps. 31 through 34, leads J. Priest to suggest that it is "a virtual rewriting of them. This is true not only with respect to general outline but also regarding specific allusions and theological perspective. Deuteronomy 31–34 is clearly the author's model, though he has recast his own work in light of the history of the people from the conquest to his own day and through the prism of his own apocalyptic outlook."[14] What Priest calls "model" I have been referring to as "framework"; yet the *Testament of Moses* shares much with the apocalyptic dimensions of the *Testament of Levi* and another model of exegesis, namely "Expansions of the 'Old Testament' and Legends." Each of these are different methods used by the early Jews to comprehend and make contemporary the biblical message.

[12] Sanders, "Testament of Abraham," in *The Old Testament Pseudepigrapha*, 1.879.
[13] See Charlesworth, "The Cosmic Theology of Early Judaism," in *The Old Testament Pseudepigrapha and the New Testament*, 65–67.
[14] J. Priest, "Testament of Moses," in *The Old Testament Pseudepigrapha*, 1.923.

Launching

The best examples of using a passage in the Old Testament for launching forth into a new setting are the *Books of Enoch*. The books gathered together now into what is called *1 Enoch* and *2 Enoch* are based upon two verses in Genesis 5:

> Thus all the days of Enoch were three hundred and sixty-five years. Enoch walked with God; and he was not, for God took him (Gen 5:23–24; RSV. [See also Sir 44:16]).

From these brief comments the early Jews developed exegetically the ideas that Enoch must be somehow associated with the solar calendar of 365 days, that he was perfectly righteous, and that he did not die, but is with God.[15] Since Enoch then tends to transcend time and place—his place is either unknown or hidden (cf. *1 Enoch* 12:1–2)—he is the perfect candidate for ascending through the heavens and viewing the world below, its history, and the future ages.

According to *1 Enoch* (extant in its full form only in Ethiopic, although early Aramaic Qumran fragments have been found) he receives from the angels a vision; he states "I heard from them everything and I understood. I look not for this generation but for the distant one that is coming" (1:2).[16] Enoch falls asleep and has a dream and visions, according to *1 Enoch* 13:8. According to *2 Enoch* (extant only in Slavonic) he is awakened from his sleep and guided by "two huge men" (*2 Enoch* 1:4). Subsequently in both works Enoch journeys through the heavens.

Another passage in the Old Testament has significantly influenced the thought of the authors of *1 Enoch* and *2 Enoch*. It is the story of the fall of the watchers found in Gen 6:1–4. In *1 Enoch* 1–36 this story is considerably reworked and expanded. In *2 Enoch* 18 [J] the fallen angels are seen being punished in the fifth heaven and others are in the second heaven, "imprisoned in great darkness."[17]

Another passage in Genesis—which is exceedingly important for understanding early Jewish exegesis, because of a Qumran scroll, Philo, Josephus, and Hebrews—has considerably shaped the ending of *2 Enoch*, which unfortunately was excised by R. H. Charles. *2 Enoch* 71–72

---

[15] A careful study of the origin of apocalyptic thought and the role of Enoch in its development is J. C. VanderKam's *Enoch and the Growth of an Apocalyptic Tradition* (CBQ Monograph Series 16; Washington, DC: Catholic Biblical Association, 1984).

[16] E. Isaac, "1 (Ethiopic Apocalypse of) Enoch," in *The Old Testament Pseudepigrapha*, 1.13.

[17] See F. I. Andersen, 2 (Slavonic Apocalypse of) Enoch," in *The Old Testament Pseudepigrapha*, 1.130–32.

describe the miraculous birth of Melchizedek; these chapters, like 11Q Melchizedek, are similar to the early midrashim and to the "Expansions of the 'Old Testament' and Legends." They are an exegesis, with fantastic expansions, of Gen 14:17–24, according to which a mysterious individual, Melchizedek King of Salem, priest of God Most High, offers bread and wine to Abraham and blesses him. Abraham subsequently gives him a tenth of his spoils from battle.

Inconsequential

Some pseudepigrapha have only an inconsequential relation to the Old Testament. The *Sibylline Oracles* are not essentially shaped and created by biblical exegesis, even though the third book is influenced by Psalms 2 and 48, Isaiah 11, and the traditions about the pilgrimage of the gentiles to Jerusalem in the eschaton (cf. Isa 2:1–4, Mic 4:1–4, Zech 14:16–21). Likewise books four, five and eleven are only to a certain extent influenced by the Old Testament.

Similarly the *Treatise of Shem* and the *Apocalypse of Adam* received from the Old Testament little more than the name pseudepigraphically linked with the document. In fact the astrological interest of the former and the present gnostic nature of the latter expose the vast differences between these two pseudepigrapha and the Old Testament, even if it is a library of widely differing documents.

The best example of a block of documents that belong under this category are those organized under "Wisdom and Philosophical Literature." This insight should come as no surprise to one who has studied Greek philosophy, observing the paradigmatic difference between this literature and the biblical books, and who has read the Wisdom literature of the Old Testament, noting how the key biblical idea of *Heilgeschichte* is noticeably absent in such writings. At times it is apparent that Israelite wisdom and the biblical books have influenced the writings gathered under this new category; but in most passages it is simply impossible to be certain that the thought is clearly and peculiarly Jewish. That feature is a central characteristic of universal wisdom and morality; it transcends the boundaries of race and creed. It is, therefore, by definition clear that the Old Testament may have only an inconsequential influence on the following documents: 3 Maccabees, 4 Maccabees, *Pseudo-Phocylides,* and *Syriac Menander.*

The Pseudepigrapha Which Are Expansions of the Old Testament

As stated at the beginning of this essay, and noted intermittently throughout it, there is a group of pseudepigrapha which has a special relation to the Old Testament. The documents in this group are almost always characterized by expansions and re-writings of the biblical narrative. Most of these documents, in various ways and degrees, start with a passage or story in the Old Testament and rewrite it, often under the imaginative influence of oral traditions linked somehow to the biblical narrative. It is simply not possible here to delve into this deep and vast area of early Jewish exegesis; it will be prudent, however, to list the documents with the sections of the Tanach that are re-written.

Here are the documents which are "Expansions of the 'Old Testament'" along with the portion of scripture that is rewritten:

Jubilees	Gen 1:1–Exod 12:50
Martyrdom of Isaiah	1 and 2 Kings (esp. 2 Kgs 21:16)
Joseph and Aseneth	Genesis 37–50
Life of Adam and Eve	Genesis 1–6
Pseudo-Philo	Genesis to 2 Samuel
Lives of the Prophets	Kings, Chronicles, the Prophets
Ladder of Jacob	Genesis 28
4 Baruch	Jeremiah, 2 Kings, 2 Chronicles, Ezra, Nehemiah
Jannes and Jambres	Exodus 7–8
History of the Rechabites	Jeremiah 35
Eldad and Modad	Num 11:26–29

These writings are related in their free exegetical use of the Old Testament. As one might have expected from reading the documents of Early Judaism, which emphasize above all God as the creator, the major source for these writers was Genesis. The preoccupation with Jeremiah is not yet perceived and assessed.

These writings use a somewhat similar methodology. The Old Testament is often treated in a cavalier fashion; the text, or portions of it, without constraint is frequently condensed, omitted, expurgated, explained, supplemented, and radically recast.[18]

Conclusion

The life of the early religious Jews was defined by and circumscribed by the Book, the Torah.[19] The pseudepigrapha generally do not reflect an attempt to replace the Tanach; they demonstrate how significant was the canon, rapidly taking final and definitive form during the period of Early

[18] See the comments on *Jubilees* by Wintermute in *The Old Testament Pseudepigrapha*, 2.35–41.

[19] In *Das Wesen des Judentums* (Köln: J. Melzer, 1960 [sixth edition]) Leo Baeck astutely asserted that all religiosity and tradition has its firm emphasis in the lively existence of the Holy Book. "In der Bibel hat das Judentum sein sicheres, unverrückbares Fundament" (p. 16).

Judaism.[20] While the Tanach tended to define life and reflection, it was not treated in anyway like it is today by the biblical fundamentalists. It could be expurgated, even re-written. The popular (and ancient) contention that prophecy ceased with Ezra fails to grasp the fluid exegetical techniques employed in most segments of Early Judaism. To rework the Torah, as in the documents collected in the Pseudepigrapha and in the Qumran corpus (especially 1QpHab 7 and 11Q Temple), is to assume a pneumatical exegesis.[21] The Pseudepigrapha, like all early Jewish religious writings, generally tended to be in some way exegetical.[22]

[20] M. McNamara correctly observes that recent scholars agree that "in the books composed during the post-exilic age, both proto-canonical and deutero-canonical, there is a fair degree of dependence one earlier books of the canon." He continues by emphasizing a fact often overlooked in some fairly recent American books: "While often there seems to be a question of dependence on actual written texts, at times there may be more a question of dependence on the tradition itself without it being clear whether the later writers had access to this in its written or oral form." McNamara, *Intertestamental Literature* (Old Testament Message 23; Wilmington, DE: Michael Glazier, 1983) both quotations are from p. 33.

[21] See the pertinent and insightful comments in the following books: D. Patte, *Early Jewish Hermeneutic in Palestine* (SBL Dissertation Series 22; Missoula, MT; Scholars, 1975); W. H. Brownlee, *The Midrash Pesher of Habakkuk* (SBL Monograph Series 24; Missoula, MT: Scholars, 1979), G. J. Brooke, *Exegesis at Qumran: 4QFlorilegium in its Jewish Context* (JSOTSup 29; Sheffield: JSOT, 1985).

[22] Philo and Josephus, despite some claims to the contrary, are both exegetically shaped by the Old Testament. H. W. Attridge has persuasively argued that Josephus interpretively presents scriptural narratives. His "theology is very much an apologetic one, which reworks Jewish tradition in categories derived from and comprehensible to a Greco-Roman public." See Attridge, *The Interpretation of Biblical History in the* Antiquitates Judaicae *of Flavius Josephus* (HDR 7; Missoula, MT: Scholars, 1976) 17. Likewise, as R. D. Hecht has attempted to show, Philo is "exclusively engaged in deducing the reasonableness of the Law." See Hecht, "The Exegetical Contexts of Philo's Interpretation of Circumcision," in *Nourished with Peace: Studies in Hellenistic Judaism in Memory of Samuel Sandmel* (eds. F. E. Greenspahn, E. Hilgert, and B. L. Mack; Homage Series 9; Chico, CA Scholars, 1984) 51–79; the quotation is from p. 79.

PART THREE

THE FUNCTION OF SCRIPTURE IN THE NEW TESTAMENT

JESUS AND THE MESSIANIC WAR

WILLIAM KLASSEN
University of Toronto
Toronto, Ontario

Among Bill Brownlee's last publications were his papers concerning
Palestinian rights and peace in the Middle East.* I welcome these
studies not simply because they contribute to the dialogue necessary for
a genuine and lasting peace in the Middle East, but also because we have
in these studies a fine example of biblical scholarship rendered acutely
relevant to the needs of our explosive and dangerous modern society. In
my estimation Professor Brownlee's work has fulfilled the requirements of
the task of relevant scholarship as given in the Prologue to Sirach: "It is
the duty of those who study the scriptures not only to become expert
themselves, but also to pursue their scholarship for the practical benefit
of the outside world through both the written and spoken word" (NEB).

As biblical scholars we have taken the first part of this task quite
seriously: We have become experts. We have an abundance of journals
and scholarly tools which demonstrate to all who are interested that we
can meet the standards of scholarship. All of it exists, of course, not to
convince anyone that we are experts, but for what we believe our main
task to be: to illuminate the dark corners of the text. But we must also
strive to make our scholarship relevant, to make it speak to our society.
We must not abdicate this responsibility and allow the non-experts to
(mis)interpret and distort the legacy of the Bible to suit popular and
nationalistic agendas. It is with this concern in mind that this paper,
written in honor and memory of William H. Brownlee, seeks to make a
contribution.

* *The Rights of the Palestinians* (Public Affairs Series 22, Moral Appeals Concerning
Palestine 1; New York: Americans for Middle East Understanding, 1983); *The Lion
that Ravages Palestine* (Public Affairs Series 23, Moral Appeals Concerning Pal-
estine 2; New York: Americans for Middle East Understanding, 1983); *Israel and
the Ten Commandments: An Appeal to the Conscience Based upon the Modern
History of Palestine* (Public Affairs Series 24; New York: Americans for Middle
East Understanding, 1984). The volumes are edited and introduced by John C.
Trever.

1. *Yahweh as God of War*

One of the aspects of our legacy is Yahweh as Warrior, which includes the Holy War or, what for our purposes will be called, the Messianic War. At least three scholars have in recent times addressed themselves to the topic of war and violence with respect to the Hebrew Scriptures[1] and in doing so have made important contributions to an international discussion of some importance. This is not the place to assess their work in detail, nor am I the person to do so. Anyone familiar with the literature in this field will know how complicated the issues are and will join me in gratitude for the competence with which the issue is treated by our colleagues.

My interest is rather more specifically with Jesus. What part of this legacy appealed to him? My question presupposes that Jesus like the rest of us had to filter the legacy which came down to him; he had choices to make. He was a Jew, which means that he had a tradition which formed him but which also allowed him considerable freedom. Certainly first-century Judaism was no monolith and to affirm that Jesus was a Jew means that he likely held some Messianic expectations, though it does not help us to draw a portrait of the Messiah he looked for. I also assume that Jesus had more access to the intellectual cross-currents of Hellenistic Judaism and of Stoic-Cynic thought (at least via the former) than is usually recognized.

The texts known to us from the Hebrew Bible were obviously in his memory. The idea that Yahweh was a warrior and that he had intervened on behalf of his people was undoubtedly a given for him. No doubt he knew of the confidence expressed by Judas Maccabeus that victory in battle depends not upon the size of the army but on strength from heaven (I Macc 3:19). Judas had expressed the conviction that God himself would crush their enemies before them, and that therefore they need have no fear (3:22). His faith in Divine intervention was rewarded and Judas was triumphant in that battle. Perhaps he also knew the story of Judith and how the beauty of a woman who relied upon God caused Holofernes to lose his head—literally. Such stories of Yahweh's involvement in war, it can be assumed, were as well known to Jesus as the stories of God's intervention on behalf of the allies were known to us as Canadian children during the wars of our century. I remember as a child my relief when it became clear that God was on our side!

---

[1] Peter Craigie, *The Problem of War in the Old Testament* (Grand Rapids: Eerdmans, 1978); Waldemar Janzen, "God as Warrior and Lord: A conversation with G. E. Wright," *BSOR* 220 (1975) 73–75; idem, "War in the Old Testament," *MQR* 46 (1972) 155–166; Edward J. Crowley, "The Old Testament," in *Non-violence—Central to Christian Spirituality* (J. T. Culliton, ed.; Toronto Studies in Theology 8; Toronto: Edwin Mellen, 1982) 11–33.

It cannot be said that the attitude of Jesus towards the Messianic war has absorbed the attention of scholars. Hans Windisch was the first to give it major attention in 1909 and since then only Otto Betz has given the topic detailed study after the discovery of the scrolls at Qumran.[2] The fact that four different scrolls, termed war scrolls were found there made such an investigation inevitable.

Before looking at the way in which the theme appears in the first century it should be observed that the Jewish cultural and religious tradition contained no glorification of war.[3] It could indeed be argued that the only war which Judaism considered legitimate was the war to end all war—the Messianic war—waged to bring about God's will upon earth through his chosen instrument, the Messiah.

No spokesman for Judaism put it as eloquently as Josephus: At the beginning of the war against Rome in 66 C.E. the appeal is placed on the lips of Agrippa: Agrippa deals with the two possible motives for the war: (1) Revenge for injustice; (2) finding servitude intolerable.

On the first he warns that the most effective way to deal with injustices is not war:

> "The powers that be should be conciliated by flattery, not irritated; when you indulge in exaggerated reproaches for minor errors, you only injure yourselves by your denunciation of those whom you incriminate; instead of maltreating you, as before, in secret and with a sense of shame, they will now debase you openly. There is nothing to check blows like enduring them and the gentleness of the wronged victims diverts the wrongdoers from their action" (*War* 2.352, last sentence my translation).

Here Josephus prescribes an approach almost identical to what Seneca recommends as the Stoic way:

> ". . if the conflict comes, he is the better man who first withdraws. The vanquished is the one who wins. If someone strikes you, step back; for by striking back you will give him both the opportunity and the excuse to repeat his blow; when you later wish to extricate yourself it will be impossible" (*de ira* 2.34.5).

He agrees also with Philo who used a similar line of reasoning when discussing how war is to be averted. Either war will not pass through the godly people at all (compare Leviticus 26) or when justice is one's

---

[2] Hans Windisch, *Der messianische Krieg und das Urchristentum* (Tübingen: J. C. B. Mohr, 1909); Otto Betz, "Jesu Heiliger Krieg," *Novt* 1 (1956) 116–137.

[3] There is, however, some truth in the statement that Judaism, Christianity (and Islam) "shamefully added an ingredient missing totally in antiquity, namely the concept of the religious war" (Wilhelm Nestle, *Der Friedensgedanke in der antiken Welt* [Leipzig: Dieterich, 1938] 76).

irresistible ally war will dissolve and fall to pieces when the enemy perceives the nature of the opponents. "For virtue is majestic and august and can unaided and silently allay the onset of evils however great" (de praemiis et poenis 93).

In a later speech Josephus himself appeals to the Zealots inside the city and he draws on deeper theological motives as well as repeating some of the arguments he had earlier placed on Agrippa's lips.

With respect to vengeance he asks:

> Ah, miserable wretches, unmindful of your own true allies, would you make war on the Romans with arms and might of hand? What other foe have we conquered thus, and when did God who created, fail to avenge, the Jews, if they were wronged? (War 5.376–377).

He then portrays in detail the way in which God has avenged his people, protected them and above all proven true to this holy place, the Temple, by intervening on their behalf. Beginning with Abraham, Josephus tells the history of his people as a saga of nonviolent resistance. The exodus was achieved without Israelites raising their swords. The victory over the Syrians and Philistines was brought about by God:

> God's leadership it was that brought our fathers this triumph, because, without resort to hand or weapon, they committed the issue to his decision (War 5.386).

He concludes his summary of the history of his people:

> In short, there is no instance of our forefathers having triumphed by arms or failed of success without them when they committed their cause to God; if they sat still they conquered, as it pleased their judge, if they fought they were invariably defeated (War 5.390).

Later on he states that:

> Invariably have arms been refused to our nation, and warfare has been the sure signal for defeat. For it is, I suppose, the duty of the occupants of holy ground to leave every thing to the arbitrament of God and to scorn the aid of human hands, can they but conciliate the Arbiter above (War 5.400).

At the end of the speech he urges them to fling away their weapons and to kill Josephus's own mother and wife instead of the Romans:

> Slay them, take my blood as the price of your own salvation! I too am prepared to die, if my death will lead to your learning wisdom" (War 5.419).

When all allowances are made for dependencies on Stoicism and the self-interest of Josephus living in Rome as he wrote, it still strikes us as evident that Josephus rejects war as something willed by God to keep his people alive.

The history of God's people could be told from the standpoint of the Messianic war. It could also be told from the perspective of God himself being the Warrior who overrules all that humans do. That is how Josephus prefers to tell it in his old age. What his own views were on the Messiah cannot be seen from his writings.

About the time Jesus was living, perhaps around the year 28, the *Assumption of Moses* was written by a group which shared Josephus's perspective. Moses is portrayed here as the mediator who intercedes for the people and although the question of vengeance is raised, Moses appears as the Mediator who "every hour, day and night, had his knees fixed to the earth, praying." Taxo, the representative of the Pharisaic community (?), a man from the tribe of Levi takes his seven sons with him into the cave, "let us die rather than transgress the command of the Lord of Lords, the God of our fathers. For if we do this and die, our blood will be avenged before the Lord." Such vengeance he sees in 5:1 as arising from the "kings who share their guilt." The eternal God alone will appear to punish the Gentiles and will destroy all their idols (10:7).

It is interesting that Josephus refers to the days of Pompey, for we have from that time the *Psalms of Solomon* which give a clear picture of the way in which the people of the community that lies behind the Documents—probably Pharisees—transformed the idea of the Messianic war in Pompey's day.

Chapter 17 succinctly describes the group's Messianic hope: Basic is their affirmation of the kingship of God himself. Their hope is placed in

> God, our deliverer; for the might of our God is for ever with mercy, And the kingdom of our God is forever over the nations in judgment (17:3).

The writer describes the destruction and shame wrought by Pompey. The alien ones even trampled the Holy Place with their sandals (2:2) and even the children of the Covenant defected:

> They that loved the synagogues of the pious fled from them, as sparrows that fly from their nest. They wandered in deserts that their lives might be saved from harm (17:18ff).

There is, however, no hint that they are attracted to armed revolt as Josephus thinks they should have been. They have a different way.

2. The Messiah as God's Warrior of the Word.

The community of the *Psalms of Solomon* prays for the raising up of their king, the Son of David that he may rule over Israel, shatter unrighteous rulers, purge Israel of nations that trample her down to destruction. He will,

> Destroy the pride of the sinner as a potter's vessel. With a rod of
> iron he shall break in pieces all their substance, He shall destroy
> the godless nations with the word of his mouth (17:24–28).

This king will gather together a holy people and he shall not allow
unrighteousness to lodge anymore among them. All shall be called sons
of God, and "neither sojourner nor alien shall sojourn with them anymore" (17:31). The heathen nations will serve under his yoke and the
nations shall come from the ends of the earth to see his glory, bringing as
gifts her sons who had fainted (17:34). He shall be a righteous king,
taught of God, over them and all shall be holy and their king will be the
anointed of the Lord (17:36). He shall not put his trust in horse and rider
and bow, nor multiply for himself gold and silver for war (17:37). Nor shall
he gather confidence from a multitude for the day of battle. The Lord
himself is his king, the hope of him who is mighty through his hope in
God (17:38). Nor is his rule confined to Israel, for all nations will be in
awe of him for he will smite the earth with the word of his mouth forever,
blessing the people of God with wisdom and gladness, keeping himself
pure from sin so that he can rule a great people. He will rebuke rulers,
and remove sinners by the might of his word. Since he so totally relies
upon the Lord himself none will be able to prevail against him (17:44).
The Psalm ends with a prayer that the Lord may soon deliver "us from
the uncleanness of unholy enemies" (17:51).

What is remarkable in this Psalm is the clearly expressed hope that
the Messiah will gain his objectives, ruling over the people in righteousness and mercy and over the nations of the world without a Messianic
war. For he does not put his trust in horse and rider and bow. Basing
one's trust on armaments as a strategy was rejected by the Deu-
teronomist (Deut 17:16 ff), by at least two Psalm writers (Pss 20:9; 44:7),
and by the prophet Isaiah (Isa 2:7; 36:9).

The *Psalms of Solomon* base their hope on that root of Jesse announced by Isaiah (chap. 11) which will spring forth and rule in such a way
as to bring in a period of uninterrupted peace not only for the people of
Israel but also for the nations of the world who will rally around the signal
of the scion from the root of Jesse (*Pss. Sol.* 17:39f.).

This chapter of Isaiah, entitled by a modern commentator, "The
Messiah and the Kingdom of peace,"[4] predicts that in the future an ideal
king will come from the Davidic line. Such predictions of a king who will
bring peace and justice are not unknown among other writers of the
ancient Near East and thus this account can hardly be considered
unique. While questions may be raised about Isaianic authorship, it is
also possible that the poem was composed by Isaiah, as was chapter nine,

---

[4] Hans Wildberger, *Jesaja 1–12* (BKAT X/1; Neukirchen-Vluyn: Neukirchener,
1972) 436ff.

as a result of his disillusionment with the Davidic dynasty, in particular, with Hezekiah. Thus he expects this new king to come from Jesse, not David himself.

A similar portrait of the Messiah can be found in other texts. Yahweh is portrayed as someone who serves as the advocate for the poor and the oppressed. The king-messiah will need to represent Yahweh and therefore will do the same.

The ruthless will be struck down with the rod of his mouth, and with a word he will slay the wicked. Noteworthy is the weapon used by this Messianic king. Hosea's task was to "slay" the people, and God used him to "lash them to shreds" (Hos 6:5). For the words of Yahweh are the words of the prophet (Jer 1:9; 15:19; 30:2) and with those words he builds and destroys. These words can be described as deadly weapons (Amos 7:17ff; Isa 9:8) and Jeremiah is told:

> I will make my words a fire in your mouth; and it shall burn up
> this people like brushwood (Jer 5:14).

The same prophet describes the words that have gone forth from the Lord as "a scorching wind, a furious whirlwind" (Jer 23:18) and warns against the false prophets who promise hope. "See what a scorching wind has gone out from the Lord, a sweeping whirlwind. It whirls round the heads of the wicked; the Lord's anger is not to be turned aside, till he has finished and achieved his heart's desire" (Jer 30:23–24). "If the prophet has a word, let him speak my word in truth. What has chaff to do with grain?, says the Lord. Do not my words scorch like fire? says the Lord. Are they not like a hammer that splinters rock?" (Jer 23:28–30).

Second Isaiah also considers himself elected from birth, called and named from his mother's womb:

> He made my tongue his sharp sword, and concealed me under
> cover of his hand (Isa 49:2).

On the other hand the imagery of the word is also applied to the growth imagery, of imparting life as in Isa 55:10–12:

> As the rain and snow come down from heaven and do not return
> until they have watered the earth, making it blossom and bear
> fruit, giving seed for sowing and bread to eat, so shall the word
> which comes from my mouth prevail. It shall not return to me
> fruitless without accomplishing my purpose or succeeding in the
> task I gave it. You shall indeed go out with joy and be led forth in
> peace.

In a similar vein, Isaiah 31 promises that Assyria will be defeated:

> Assyria shall fall by the sword, but by no sword of man; a sword
> that no man wields shall devour him. And this will happen when

> Israel comes back to him whom they have so deeply offended.
> Then the Lord of Hosts will come down to do battle and like a
> bird hovering over its young, will be a shield over Jerusalem; he
> will shield her and deliver her, standing over her and delivering
> her (Isa 31:4–9 quoted in 1QM 11:11–14).

In a number of these texts, then, the symbol of power—"the sceptre
of his mouth,"—which characterizes this king forms the key to what the
Messiah does and what is expected of this king. Hans Wildberger has
designated this a "spiritualizing" which is similar to the usage found in
other Near Eastern texts, and considers it likely that it entered Israelite
royal ideology in Jerusalem before Isaiah's time.[5] The power of this word
and its usage is determined not by the king-Messiah himself but by God
who inspires it. Whether it gives life or destroys is decided by the way
the recipient responds.

Even the usage of this imagery as life-depriving must be seen
alongside of the dialectic relationship between life and death observed
keenly by the prophets. For Hosea the "killing" function of the word may
have meant not the literal death and therefore end of Israel but rather the
death or end of that style of life which she follows so avidly but which
really invalidates the covenant.[6] The day of discipline or punishment will
lead to God's enduring loyalty in contrast to hers which is like the
morning mist.

Along similar lines the *Epistle of Aristeas* answers the question:
What is the goal of speech? "To convince your opponent by showing him
his mistakes in a well-ordered array of arguments. For in this way you will
win your hearer, not by opposing him, but by bestowing praise on him
with a view to persuading him. And it is by the power of God that
persuasion is accomplished" (*Ep. Arist.* 266).

The importance of speech is also recognized by the writer of *Pseudo-
Phocylides* who urges:

> Practice speaking good words, which will greatly benefit all.
> Speech is to man a weapon sharper than iron. God alloted a
> weapon to every creature; . . . but reason to man as his protec-
> tion. . . Better is a wise man than a strong one (*Ps. Pho*. 123–30).[7]

---

[5] Wildberger, 454. The word "spiritualize" is not adequate to cover the reality.

[6] H. W. Wolff, *Dodekapropheten 1 Hosea* (BKAT XIV/1; Neukirchen-Vluyn: Neukirchener, 1961) 152, who observes that the imperfect of the verb *yaza* describes
the intended result. The expression, "their tongues are as sharp swords" (Ps 57:4)
is used to describe the terror which the tongue can inflict.

[7] P. W. van der Horst notes that the ideas expressed here are a common place
among both Greek and Hebrew writers; cf. *The Sentences of Pseudo-Phocylides*
(Leiden: Brill, 1978) 97, 136. 2 Esdras 15:22: "Thus says, the Lord God, . . . my
sword will not cease from those who shed innocent blood upon the earth" and
verse 25 refers likewise to a pollution as does 1:26.

When we look at this imagery of the word in the light of the Gospel portrait of Jesus we find first of all a striking contrast between John the Baptist's expectations and Jesus actions. John proclaimed judgment: "You viper's brood! . . . Already the axe is laid to the roots of the trees; and every tree that fails to produce fruit is cut down and thrown on the fire" (Luke 3:7–9; Matt 3:7–10). "He will baptize you with Holy Spirit and with fire. His shovel is ready in his hand, to winnow his threshing floor and gather the wheat into his granary; but he will burn the chaff in a fire that can never go out" (Luke 3:17; Matt 3:12).

The Gospel narratives indicate that what John the Baptist prophesied did not happen. Of the various models of the Messiah available to him, John had made his choice. Jesus does not seem to meet those expectations but invites John's emissaries to present him with the evidence (Luke 7:18–28). John's fate, like that of Jesus, was to die without seeing his expectations fulfilled.

In the Gospels Jesus is depicted as confronting the demonic in a struggle which began at the beginning of his life and did not end till his cry of victory (dereliction) from the cross. These accounts have both a dynamic and martyrological dimension.[8] By choosing the way of death Jesus defied every expectation of the Messiah known to him: By dying he disqualified himself as the Messiah by any definition known to his contemporaries.[9]

It should, however, be stressed again that Jesus had to choose from many concepts of the Messiah available to him. He chose those elements from his Jewish heritage which stressed that God alone is sovereign. Difficult as it was for him to understand and to walk that path, he chose it and adhered to it to the end. He proclaimed the kingdom of God, not the installation of a Messianic king. All of those actions and sayings which are used to argue that Jesus saw himself as a militant messiah appear before the Gethsemane struggle: especially the entry into Jerusalem and the cleansing of the temple, both of which demonstrate that he is prepared to allow the people to join in the acclaim of his mission.

His cleansing of the temple, whatever we make of it, must always be compared with the approach used by Menachem, the Zealot, some thirty-three years later (66 C.E.) in which the Chief Priest was murdered. There is in any case considerable evidence that the transaction of business in sacrificial objects had been newly introduced and that Jesus was not alone in his opposition of this practice.[10] The act itself serves as a

---

[8] R. Leivestad, *Christ the Conqueror: Ideas of Conflict and Victory in the New Testament* (London: SPCK, 1954).

[9] Windisch, 33: "The death of the war-like Messiah is the proof of his deception and the demise of his cause. Jesus, however, chose death, in order that his cause might triumph (Mark 10:35–45)."

[10] The best detailed study of this event is still Jean Lasserre, "Un Contresens

powerful illustration that Jesus did intervene for the disadvantaged at some risk and that he did not adopt a stoical approach to evils around him. That the incident is so often cited to justify the violence of terrorism and armed struggle points up the poverty of our understanding of the way in which Jesus dealt with evil. At the very most one might appeal to it as a method for cleaning out God's place of prayer. If I am going to release bulls in a public place, I know as a farm boy that a whip is essential to keep them from trampling on bystanders. The fact that Jesus hastily made a whip from the cords which bound the animals indicates not that he had lost his cool and was prepared to begin thrashing the merchants but rather his profound respect for all the people there and his desire to protect them from the trampling of the bulls. John notes with some surprise that having made the whip he cast them all out, both the sheep and the bulls (John 2:15). Presumably the former did not need the whip. Just because the artists have enjoyed portraying this scene as Jesus whipping the merchants does not mean that we should distort the text. Nor should we take a practice from a shepherd and justify preparation for a nuclear war!

Jesus' action may have had Messianic connotations for those standing around. Hardly was it seen as an action which transformed Jesus into a Zealot revolutionary. It is best to interpret it as a symbolic act in line with the prophetic acts of the Old Testament, many of which also got the prophets into considerable trouble.

3. The Messiah as Son of Joseph

The Messiah as Son of Joseph who conquers by means of a war to end all wars and thus ushers in an endless era of peace was the third model of Messiah available to Jesus. According to Joseph Klausner, "the one name which recurs most frequently (but much less in the pre-Hadrianic time) is 'Son of David'."[11] With respect to a military Messiah he concludes:

> "Throughout the earlier periods of the Messianic idea, Israel's best minds thought of the *Messiah as king and a warrior.* Like any ordinary king, the Messiah must lead his assembled people in the last battle and bring them to victory over foes. . . . The Messiah

---

Tenace," in *Cahiers de la Reconciliation* (Paris, October, 1967) 10. In short form his conclusions are stated in *War and the Gospel* (Scottdale: Herald Press, 1962) 45–49. Victor Eppstein ("The Historicity of the Gospel Account of the Cleansing of the Temple," ZNW 55 [1964] 42–58) points out that the establishment of the transaction of business in sacrificial objects inside the temple was introduced in the spring of 30 C. E. by Caiaphas. He considers the event as historical with Jesus taking action possibly the same week it was introduced.

[11] Joseph Klausner, *The Messianic Idea in Israel* (London: Allen and Unwin, 1956) 461.

must, therefore, be a military hero in the fullest sense of the term."[12]

The Messiah ben Joseph who was to lead in the war against Gog and Magog and who kills in battles is considered by most writers to have emerged as a result of the split between those who held to a peaceful Messiah and those who believed in a more war-like figure. That may have taken place before Hadrianic times but our sources do not allow us to arrive at firm conclusions on that point.[13]

This is the Messiah who is called the Messiah of War (*Messiach milchamah*) in contrast to the descendant of David and although we cannot date its origin it is hardly a product of fantasy. According to van der Woude: "More likely it may go back to an ancient concept of the Messiah, which the synagogue could or did not wish to repress." It is surely evidence that the Messianic ideas of the time of Jesus were much more complicated than we can demonstrate from the sources available to us. The fact that some see the war-like Messiah as particularly strong in Galilee may suggest that the term originated and was most popular there.[14] Jesus, it seems, followed those who did repress the notion of a warring Messiah.

It is ironic that the name of Joseph appears here, since the literature depicts him the mildest of all the twelve sons of Jacob. Through his innocent suffering he was able to enter into the enemy camp and not only survive himself but also attain such power that he was able to help his whole clan to survive. He even forged an alliance with the enemy by marrying Aseneth, daughter of an Egyptian priest. Some Jewish writers highly praised Joseph and made him a model of how innocent suffering can be used for the benefit of the whole people. They held up not only Joseph but also Aseneth as a model of goodness in her refusal to respond vindictively to those who had tried to do her harm. To be sure Joseph continued faithfully in his Jewish customs in Pharaoh's court, but the narrator states that when his brothers came he did not eat with the Egyptians because "the Egyptians hold it an abomination to eat with Hebrews" (Gen 43:32). In the story, *Joseph and Aseneth,* she instructs Simon, her brother-in-law, in the Hebrew doctrine that vengeance belongs to God alone and the good person must instead forgive and heal the wounded attacker (18–19).

---

[12] Klausner, 493.

[13] Klausner, 483–501.

[14] A. S. van der Woude, *TWNT,* 9. 518. On the "war-Messiah" see S. Mowinckel, *He that Cometh* (New York, Abingdon, 1955) 291; 314; See also Klausner, 483–501. The term appears in *Pesikta* 51a; *Pesikta Rabbati* 15.75z; *Canticles Rabbah* on 2:13 according to Mowinckel, 291.

This writing, which Jeremias predicted some thirty years ago "will be playing a considerable part in further investigation in the religious environment of the New Testament,"[15] begins with the story of Joseph's marriage to Aseneth and depicts her as a Gentile who warmly embraces Judaism but as a Jew rejects the notion that it is ever justified to return evil for evil. The just man does not harm his enemy and six times the statement is repeated that he never repays evil with evil (*Jos. As.* 23:9; 28:3, 5, 10, 14; 29:3). Aseneth by her own behaviour and her refusal to be avenged testifies to the depth of her conviction that God will fight on her behalf and that vengeance must be left in his hands.[16] She is supported in her position by Levi against the more aggressive stance of Simon.

A similar approach is taken in the Jewish ethical treatise, *Pseudo-Phocylides*. He admonishes:

> If you gird on a sword, let it not be to murder but to protect. But
> may you not need it at all, neither without the law nor justly. For
> if you kill an enemy, you stain your hand (32–34).

The author here indicates that killing is fundamentally wrong, although he recognizes that it may be justified in self-defence. Describing the position as "a rather exceptional point of view in antiquity" van der Horst describes these lines as having "undeniably a pacifist ring about them."[17]

Klausner is correct in his assertion about kingship being essential. There are, however, nonviolent models of kingship (e.g. Joseph) in the ancient world which deserve scrutiny. The *Epistle of Aristeas* is an unusual Jewish source in which Jewish sages are depicted as advising a pagan (Egyptian?) king. They suggest that the highest degree of security for a nation is not a well-trained army, but rather the strength of a king who embodies justice and above all generosity towards all friends and foes.

Dating from between 127–118 B.C.E., the *Epistle of Aristeas* has attracted scholarly interest primarily for its relation to the LXX. It is doubtful that the author's own interest lies there; more likely it is in the political and ethical values of the Jews.[18] We have here an interpretation to the Greeks of what it means to be a Jew, cast in the form of answers by Jewish wise men to questions by the Egyptian king. The main question is: What is an ideal king? In his questions the king naturally asks repeatedly about the matter of security, both internally and from external

---

[15] Joachim Jeremias, "The Last Supper," *ExpTim* 64 (1952/53) 91.

[16] "Ethical rigor combines with a hellenistic-stoically influenced wisdom theology with its ideal of the wise person who is pleasing to God and the Hebrew concept of being a child of God" (Dieter Sänger, *Antikes Judentum und die Mysterien* [Tübingen: Mohr, 1980] 203).

[17] van der Horst, 136.

[18] See Norbert Meisner, *Aristeasbrief* (Gütersloh: Gerd Mohn, 1973) 38.

foes. The Jewish sages answer that the greatest protection of his kingdom comes from securing just and prudent men as his advisers (*Ep. Arist.* 125).

Moses their legislator taught them that Jews "must be just and effect nothing by violence and refrain from tyrannizing over others in reliance upon their own strength" (*Ep. Arist.* 148); "our law forbids us to injure anyone either by word or deed" (168). "Our whole system aims at righteousness and righteous relationships between man and man" (169). If the king desires to keep his empire secure he can do so best by imitating the generosity of God (118), for God draws all men to himself by his generosity (207), and so the king too must be generous to offenders. As God is the benefactor of the whole world, so too the king must imitate him and be void of offence (210).

The king asks: How can I despise my enemies? "if you show kindness to all men and win their friendship, you need fear none" (225). Such generosity is to be shown not only to friends, "but I think that we ought to show the *same keen spirit of generosity* to those who are opposed to us (enemies), that by this means we may win them over to the right and to what is advantageous to ourselves. But we must pray to God that this may be accomplished, for he rules the minds of all men" (277). If this is done, "it is impossible for you to fail, for you have sown in all men the seeds of gratitude which produce a harvest of good will, and this is mightier than the strongest weapons and guarantees the greatest security" (231). If any man does fail, he must never again do those things which caused his failure, but he must form friendships and act justly. For it is the gift of God to be able to do good actions and not the contrary (231). "It is necessary to recognize that God rules the whole world in the spirit of kindness and without wrath at all and you, O King, must of necessity copy his example" (254).

One pre-Christian text which addresses this matter quite differently is the *Testament of Asher*. It too uses the model of God's behavior. It would seem to be from the Zealot group and the theme of the two ways is given a peculiar twist. Although he clearly delineates the sharp division between the two ways, he also affirms that actions sometimes wear two faces. Instead people themselves should wear a single face although

> "For persons who are good, who are single-minded—even though they are considered by the two-faced to be sinners—are righteous before God. For many who destroy the wicked perform two works—good and evil—but it is good as a whole, because evil is uprooted and destroyed. One person hates the man who, though merciful, is also unjust, or who is an adulterer, even though he fasts, and thus is two-faced. But his work is good as a whole, because he imitates the Lord, not accepting the seeming good as though it were the truly good (4:1–3).

In a work which has so consistently affirmed the love commandment and ruled out all hate it is indeed remarkable to find here this stress on hatred and killing. The theme of imitating God (*T. Ash.* 3:3) provides, along with the reference to zeal, the clue to the social context from which it comes. For all of this is explained by the writer with the conclusions:

> For they walk in zeal for the Lord and abstain from what God also hates and forbids by his commandments, thus delineating the evil from the good (*T. Ash.* 3:5).

What the Zealot like Phineas or Judas Maccabeus did when he killed a fellow Jew who was compromising his faith may on the face of it have looked evil. But done in the zeal of the Lord and following in God's own example of hating evil and destroying the evil-doer the deed could be done by good men, for the *whole* deed is good.[19]

Like *Pseudo-Aristeas* the author appeals to the motif of imitating God. It is clear, however, that Jesus who also appealed to the behavior of God stands in the tradition of the *Epistle of Aristeas* and followed that concept of love for the neighbor and even the enemy which is found throughout the rest of the *Testaments of the Twelve Patriarchs*.

Nevertheless it is also clear that Jesus saw his life as a struggle with evil. Although the war metaphor is not predominant he forged a peculiar weapon from his own tradition which was particularly designed for the conflict before him: The parable.

It has been recognzied for some time that the elaborate parables played a significant role in the teaching of Jesus and particularly that they were used by Jesus "in the first place as weapons of controversy."[20] What is the significance of this weapon? It is a weapon selected because its use never deprives the antagonist of either self-respect or the freedom to respond. It is selected because it always pays tribute to the opponent's ability to receive a word and to respond in a way which the curse cannot.

In the Synoptic Gospels the parable is introduced after the first evidence of opposition to Jesus is noted. Whatever the historical facts may have been, there is a distinct possibility that the writers saw Jesus as following in the footsteps of Socrates in using the spoken word as a "weapon" in his struggle against demonic powers. It is certainly clear that Jesus saw his life as wrestling with a "strong man" and it also seems clear that he never identified specific human beings as demonic. His life

---

[19] Jürgen Becker, *Die Testamente der Zwölf Patriarchen* (JSHRZ 3; Gütersloh: Gerd Mohn, 1974).

[20] J. Jeremias, *The Parables of Jesus* (London: SCM, 1954) 99. The book by Arland J. Hultgren, *Jesus and His Adversaries* (Minneapolis: Augsburg, 1979), does not touch upon this aspect at all, although he does conclude that the parables probably accurately display the way in which Jesus dealt with his enemies.

was rather spent in purging people of demons and instructing them in the new ways in which God's power might be made available to them.

In his analysis of the literary form of the Bible, Auerbach noted that one of the features that sets it off from other ancient literature is the abundance of direct discourse.[21] This is a feature which certainly is noticeable in the New Testament where Jesus directly addresses the demon(s), the sick, his disciples, his opponents, God himself and even Judas his betrayer. While the military imagery is not very abundant in the Gospels, it is evident that Jesus is engaged in an intense struggle. There are occasions in which the imagery is so striking that the thesis has often reasserted itself that Jesus had never totally cut his ties with the Messianic war motif. It would seem clear, however, that of all the paths of serving God available to him, or the one which comes closest to his approach, is the picture which Isaiah draws of the suffering servant.

If Matthew is right in his interpretation of the style of Jesus' work, then the way he meets opposition combines a gentle style or ("He will not strive") with a normal voice ("he will not shout"); nor will his voice be heard on the streets, but he will lead justice on to victory by this quiet peaceable manner. He is not defensive, although he is persistent in freeing those who are enslaved by sickness or demons (Matt 12:18–21).

4. The Suffering Servant who Bears the Sin of the People.

The prophets of Israel identified with their people by bearing the sins of the people. This meant that they suffered in solidarity with them as they took that suffering upon themselves and sought to deliver their people from punishment. Thus Moses intercedes on behalf of the people and offers his own life to save them. 2 Esdras concedes that about mankind as a whole God knows best,

> But I will speak about thy people for whom I am in pain. I lament about their inheritance; about Israel I agonize; about the seed of Jacob I am troubled (8:15ff.).

This strand of Israelite thought is so pervasive that it must be recognized as normative and the one which Jesus selected. It is, therefore, only natural that in Rachel Rosenzweig's recent book on *Solidarity with the Suffering One in Judaism*,[22] Jesus and Paul are both treated as representatives of Judaism.

Like other prophets Jesus was sent to Israel and he expressed solidarity with his people. That solidarity is expressed in the words:

---

[21] "I do not believe that there is a single passage in an antique historian where direct discourse is employed in this fashion in a brief direct dialogue" (Erich Auerbach, *Mimesis* [Princeton: Princeton University, 1953] 40).

[22] Rachel Rosenzweig, *Solidarität mit den Leidenden im Judentum* (Berlin: de Gruyter, 1978).

> The sight of the people moved him to pity: they were like sheep
> without a shepherd, harassed and helpless.

It has been observed that the verb here translated "moved to pity" is a
peculiar construction, not used in Greek literature, and is obviously an
attempt by the Matthew 9:36 translators to render the Hebrew (Num
27:17; 1 Kgs 22:17; 2 Chr 18:16; Ezek 34:5–7; Zech 10:2; Jdt 11:19). The
verb is confined to Jesus in his attitude towards the people and graph-
ically demonstrates the degree of solidarity he felt for those who suffered.
Like his contemporaries, Johanan ben Zakkai and R. Zadok, this compassion led Jesus to do everything in his power to avert the tragedy which
he, like they, foresaw. R. Zadok did it by fasting and warnings, Johanan
ben Zakkai by trying to persuade the Zealot terrorists to prevent them
from carrying out their plans (ʾAbot R. Nat. 23).

Jesus clearly did not proclaim himself the Messiah. It is hard to
imagine that he even thought of himself in such lofty terms. As a servant
of Yahweh he served the people of Yahweh and he did so by announcing
that God's rule had been established and was available to them. In doing
so he made such an impact that people began to raise the question of his
Messiahship and his credentials. In each case he engaged them in
discussion about the nature of his work and what it might bring about.

The one text which comes closest to a discussion of the Messianic war
is Matt 11:12. This dark text which has defied so many attempts to
illuminate it can be translated as follows:

> From the days of John the Baptist till now violence is done to the
> kingdom of Heaven and violent people plunder it.

The words stand in the context of Jesus' discussion of John the Baptist.
He has high praise for John, yet the lowest in the kingdom is greater than
he (Matt 11:11). John announced the coming of the kingdom, Jesus is
more. He is the eschatological warrior fighting for the kingdom, dispensing its power, and making it visible. With his activity the Messianic war
has begun even though the victory has not yet been won. The evidence
that the war has been declared is given in 11:5:

> The blind receive their sight, the lame walk, lepers are cleansed
> and the deaf hear, the dead are raised up, and the poor have the
> Gospel preached to them.

Belial, or the Prince of Demons who has ruled over these domains is
being routed and God is re-establishing his sovereignty over humans and
nature. The connection with this war and demonic possession is especially clearly drawn in Matt 12:28: "If, I by the Spirit of God, cast out
demons, then the kingdom of God has come upon you." He has entered
the domain of the strong man and proved himself the stronger.

Like the Qumran sectarians who saw their opponents as sickness and death, storm and wind, so too Jesus engages these powers in conflict. Jesus conquers over the Prince of Evil when he brings a roaring sea to silence by his command (Matt 8:26).

The men of violence referred to in Matt 11:12 may be of the same ilk as the men of violence referred to in the Qumran scrolls. They belong to the tribe of violent warriors mentioned in Isa 49:25–26 and in other OT texts who appear as the oppressors of the little people and seek to destroy them (Pss 37:32; 54:5; 86:14).

In Isa 29:5–8 the violent ones, the nations, camp about the city of David, Mount Zion, and storm its gates. God who has instigated the siege will also deliver them from it.

In Matthew too the kingdom is seen as a fortress. The violent ones seek to plunder it. They are the agents of the Prince of Devils and as at Qumran they can take the shape of human beings, so likewise Jesus may be speaking of all those who oppose the inception of the kingdom.[23] As Adolf Schlatter already noted the violent ones are the demonic hosts as well as earthly powers who serve them.[24] Herod is certainly one of them.

The battle with the demonic powers has come to a decisive point. Jesus is not only re-establishing God's sovereignity over life but also freeing others from serving the Prince of Evil and inviting them to join him in his holy war.[25]

The Prince of Evil is therefore depicted as being on the defensive rather than on the offensive. The same imagery is seen in the promise to Peter that the church will be built and that the "gates of hell" will not be able to storm it.

There is another difficult saying, which has been taken by S.G.F. Brandon[26] and others as clear indication of Jesus being a militant Messiah:

> I have not come to bring peace but a sword (Matt 10:34; Luke 12:51).

This is surely one of the most arresting statements preserved by the early Christians. If it is a declaration that Jesus is a Messiah who stands in the Zealot tradition and that his agenda is revolt against Rome, the editors of our two Gospels were very careless in what Brandon refers to as their pacification of Jesus. Either they realized that it had a different meaning or else they created a very difficult situation for the early church in its dealings with Rome.

---

[23] In the above I am following Betz, 126ff.
[24] A. Schlatter, *Der Evangelist Matthäus* (Stuttgart: Calwer, 1957) 368.
[25] Leivestad, 40ff.
[26] S. G. F. Brandon, *Jesus and the Zealots* (Manchester: University Press, 1967) where it appears on the frontispiece 202, 320 but no exegesis is given.

The clue to its meaning is in the explanation which follows both in Matthew and in Luke. Jesus is using the image of the sword to describe the havoc which the kingdom will bring to the family and the exclusive claims which he must have on the disciple's loyalty. Both Judaism and such Stoics as Musonius valued the family very highly. Peace and tranquillity in the family is the foundation on which the peace of the world rests according to Musonius.[27] For the Jews it is so important that there is a delightful story, called to my attention by Lloyd Gaston, that even God on one occasion told a lie in order to avert a family crisis between Sarah and Abraham. Family peace is more important than God's own commitment to truth![28] Paul himself argues that "we are called to peace" and therefore a marriage is to be dissolved if the tension between unbeliever and believer is so high that the former desires to separate (I Cor 7:15).

But the more distant background of this statement is to be found in the great war poem of Tyrtaeus, the first and perhaps still most eloquent call to battle originating in Sparta in which the soldier is urged to break all sentimental ties with family and leave for war realizing that he may never return and that therefore this decisive act which is necessary for the good soldier may be construed as an act of hatred on his part for the family.[29]

In the sayings of Epictetus the same call using the analogy of a battle is made to the true seeker after wisdom. He cannot be deterred by sentimental obligations to loved ones and certainly dare not think that the most important thing he has to do is "to bring a few ugly-snouted children into existence." There will be enough others to do that. The lover of wisdom has more important things to do![30]

Jesus, no doubt was more deeply influenced by the precedents set for the priority of the family by the Old Testament law. It prescribed that if members of the family lead one into apostasy that then "You shall have no pity on them . . . your own hand shall be the first to be raised against them" (Deut 13:6ff). This piece of legislation was taken seriously by both the Qumran sect and also by the Zealots who were particularly keen on dealing with those of their own people who were leading them astray. For Jesus a closer analogy may well have been the vow of the Levite: who said of his parents, I do not know them, who did not acknowledge his brothers, nor recognize his children (Deut 33:9). These words Philo used

---

[27] "Thus, whoever destroys human marriage destroys the home, the city and the whole human race" (14, Lutz, 93).

[28] *Perek Haschalom*, 59b: "Great is peace, for we find that the Torah modified a statement in order to maintain peace between Abraham and Sarah."

[29] Bruno Snell, *Tyrtaios und die Sprache des Epos* (Göttingen: Vandenhoeck & Ruprecht, 1969) 50f.

[30] III. 3.5–10; 22.77.

to describe the fugitive state of the Levites "who have, for the sake of being well-pleasing to God, forsaken parents and children and brothers and all their mortal kindred . . . so that they may without distraction minister to Him who is" (de fuga et inventione, 17.88–89).

This zeal of the Levites is expressed in Exod 32:25ff where Moses calls upon the Levites to be the executioners against those who have worshipped the calf, and after they had killed 3,000 Moses commends them with the words: "Today you have consecrated yourselves to the Lord completely, because you have turned each against his own son and his own brother and so have this day brought a blessing upon yourselves" (Exod 32:27–29).

In the *Embassy to Gaius* Philo even ventures that not only the Levites but the people as a whole value the sanctity of the shrine so much if the statue is not taken out, "I believe they would kill their whole families—wives and children and all—and finally sacrifice themselves on top of the bodies of their kinsfolk" (308).

One needs to look only at what the Zealots did with their families at Masada to see how far Jesus is from their point of view. For in those fateful last days of their stand when their religious zeal had driven them to the end of their quest for freedom Eleazar's speech, the genuine kernel in it, comes to terms with the guilt that they had in having begun the war. Now God has rendered his verdict on their act and since the sacrifice is to be made, let it be made by their own hands and not by the hands of the pagan Romans. It is not suicide Eleazar recommends, but the fathers killing their families. In this way the Zealots attempt one final act of zeal and of atonement for their act. Josephus calls Eleazar ben Yair a tyrant (*War* 2.447), but he was perhaps merely a religious zealot who lost his (holy) war. Yahweh did not come to his rescue and with that he was left with one step: to express his loyalty to Yahweh by sacrificing his family and his own life as well.

Jesus may have spoken about "hating" one's loved ones (Luke 14:16ff). But it is clear that the war to which he called and the sword which he brought into the midst of the family was of a different order.

If we take such texts in isolation it is possible to interpret Jesus as a traditional Messianic warrior. But instead he is using metaphors and images of his time to declare the rigour of his kingdom and the fact that the kingdom will not come without a struggle. As Paul expressed it later, the battle was not against flesh and blood but rather against the powers which determine the levels of our existence. It takes faith to believe that God is king, especially when Pilate and Herod and other kings make their presence so forceful. But it is precisely to this realm of faith that he invites.

The Sermon on the Mount can be described as a call to arms. It is a military manual much different from the War Scroll at Qumran for it calls for unlimited use of one weapon, *the weapon of love.* The ultimate weapon is contained in those words, "love your enemies," and by speaking them Jesus parted ways with all Zealots and all revolutionaries and placed himself squarely in the mainline Jewish tradition. It is simply incorrect for John Piper to say that a "perceptive Jew must have viewed Jesus' love command as an attack on the Torah, first because it contradicted his understanding of Lev 19:18 and, second, because it seemed in general to devaluate the distinction between Jew and Gentile—a distinction grounded in the Torah. Jesus' command to love the enemy as well as the friend contained the seed for the dissolution of the Jewish distinctive."[13]

Such statements can only be made when one has ignored the impressive materials in the Old Testament on loving one's enemies: Abraham's haggling with God for the lives of the sinners at Sodom and Gomorrah, Joseph's treatment of his brothers, Jonah's mission to Nineveh, Elisha's treatment of the Syrian soldiers, and the book of Proverbs. The evidence from such Jewish writings as *Joseph and Aseneth, Pseudo-Phocylides,* the *Testaments of the Twelve Patriarchs,* and the *Epistle of Aristeas* is too overwhelming to ignore. It is not good historical scholarship to attribute all such material to Stoic influences on Judaism or, worse yet, to later Christian interpolations! In clear agreement with this approach is the story told about Rabbi Meir who was being harassed by highway men. When he prayed that they might die, his wife Beruria said to him: "How do you make out that such a prayer should be permitted? Because it is written, let sins cease? Is it written 'sinners'?" Further look at the end of the verse: and let the wicked men be no more. Since the sins will cease, there will be no more wicked men! Rather pray for them that they should repent, and there will be no more wicked. He did pray for them and they repented" (*b. Ber.* 10a).[32]

Above all we lose sight of the way in which as early as Thucydides (4.19.1–4; 7.68.1–3) generosity was seen as the greatest weapon to overcome the enemy. This strain in Greek literature in which a military term is used to describe the effect of love is widespread and is also present in Judaism (Sir 29:12–13; *Ep. Arist.* 231). Jesus is saying in effect, if you want to conquer the enemy, meet him and love him. All of his instructions take the enemy seriously and he did not share the rosy optimism of the *Didache* (1:3), which promises if you love your enemies, they will disappear! Rather he suggests that the disciple partake of the strength of God's love and when he receives that love he will be able to do as God does, who overwhelms his enemies with generosity. It is precisely be-

---

[31] John Piper, *Love Your Enemies* (Cambridge: University Press, 1979) 91–92.
[32] Soncino edition, 1948.

cause that love is sovereign that in this "holy" war family love must take second place.

Conclusion

Jesus embraced the Messianic war idea but followed those of his Jewish colleagues who saw it as a struggle in which suffering love even to the point of dying for one's enemies could bring liberation. He may have been totally misguided and had he joined his Zealot friends, might have been able to unite the Jewish people as a whole and remove the rule of Rome from Palestine.[33] Or he might have died with Eleazar on Masada. He was neither a pacifist who spent his time denouncing war nor a social activist who trained his disciples in techniques of nonviolent resistance. Rather he lived in close communion with God and allowed God's will to remain sovereign and his love to flow freely through him. His way, as George Bernard Shaw said; has not so much been tried and found wanting but is still wanting to be tried. Given the options which our world presents to us today and given the history of our attempts to emasculate, by individualizing or spiritualizing, his approach one wonders whether his invitation to join the Messianic war may not be our only option left. At least it deserves consideration.[34]

---

[33] David M. Rhoads has analyzed the various parties and the positions they took with regard to the war. The situation was obviously quite complex and it is not impossible that Christians were strongly attracted to those who felt armed resistance was the only way (see his *Israel in Revolution* [Philadelphia: Fortress, 1976]).

[34] An earlier version of this paper was read as a Presidential address to the Canadian Society for Biblical Studies.

A NEW TESTAMENT HERMENEUTIC FABRIC: PSALM 118 IN THE ENTRANCE NARRATIVE

JAMES A. SANDERS

School of Theology at Claremont
Claremont, California

The records of Jesus' "royal" entry into Jerusalem in the four gospels have varying points of emphasis. But all four accounts agree on a major component for understanding the import of the entrance into Jerusalem: they all four cite portions of Psalm 118. Matthew and John cite also Zech 9:9. The confluence of these two Old Testament passages signals a particular context of ideas the importance of which for understanding the accounts should not be overlooked.

According to the synoptics, the entry into Jerusalem would have marked the first time Jesus in the years of his ministry had been to the historic city of David. The significance of the entry is thus heightened in the first three gospels because it is presented as an event of unique import. I am pleased to dedicate the following study to the memory of my esteemed colleague and friend, William H. Brownlee.

Zechariah

All four gospels force one's attention to the claim that Jesus was the king expected, the one who was to come; and the two OT passages here brought together emphasize the royal dimension of the claim. The Zechariah passage (9:9) points to the expectation of the messianic son of David riding into Jerusalem on an ass, claiming the heritage of kingship.

> Rejoice greatly, O daughter of Zion!
> Shout aloud, O daughter of Jerusalem!
> See, your king comes to you;
> a righteous one and saved is he,[1]

---

[1] The citations of Zech 9:9 in Matthew and John exhibit the typical fluidity of the period in quotation of Scripture. Neither bothers with the second or fourth colon (stichos) of the six in the verse. The second is in synonymous parallellism to the first and is easily dropped. But omission of the fourth, "a righteous one and saved is he," is interesting. The LXX translates it "righteous and saving," most witnesses reading the *autos* with the following (fifth colon). The resignification in the LXX

> humble and riding on an ass,
>   on a colt, the foal of an ass. (So the MT)

And Psalm 118 points to the mode of entry of kings in antiquity, providing rather specific particulars on what was said and recited by the king, priests, and people when the royal procession approached the eastern gates of the city, passed through them, and went into the temple precincts. All four gospels cite expressions from verse 26 of Psalm 118, and all but Luke the Hosanna of v 25; but a full understanding of the function of the psalm in the gospel tradition depends on the reader's knowledge of the whole psalm to grasp the full significance of the entry as a symbolic act.

A word of caution is in order. Modern readers of the NT should not attribute their possible ignorance of Scripture, that is the Scripture of the first-century church, to either the NT writers or to their congregants. There is every reason to believe that common to all programs of instruction upon conversion in the early churches was assiduous reading of Scripture, what we call the OT, as well as Jesus traditions. Scripture for them was not so much Jewish as it was sacred, especially the Septuagint in the hellenistic world, but also other less formal-equivalence, more spontaneous translations such as those evidenced in some NT literature, as well as in much Jewish literature of the period. Such readings were typically done aloud in groups for the benefit of the illiterate, who were perhaps a majority of early Christians.

The synoptics make the point that Jesus reached Jerusalem from the east. This is quite significant because of the tradition that the Messiah would approach Jerusalem from the area of the Jordan valley.[2] But they also make it clear that Jesus did not ride the ass until he reached the

---

from "saved" to "saving" indicates lack of knowledge on the part of the LXX translators of association of Zech 9:9 with the liturgical events expressed in Psalm 118. Matthew and John, who often reflect loose translations of a Hebrew text instead of the LXX both omit any vestige of the fourth colon. It may be they or their sources did not know of the LXX resignification of "saved" to "savior"; or it may be that they wanted to get on with the image of the humble one riding. Matthew reflects a belabored literal translation of a (proto-MT) Hebrew text of the last two cola while John reflects a typically trimmed down version. Neither seems to know the LXX.

See other points discussed in J. D. M. Derrett, "Law in the NT: the Palm Sunday Colt," *NovT* 13 (1971) 241–58; H. Patsch, "Der Einzug Jesu in Jerusalem. Ein historischer Versuch," *ZTK* 68 (1971) 1–26; and O. Michel, "Eine philologische Frage zur Einzugsgeschichte," *NTS* 6 (1959) 81–82.

[2] See the excellent study by Joseph Blenkinsopp, "The Oracle of Judah and the Messianic Entry," *JBL* 80 (1961) 55–64, especially on the importance of Gen 49:8–12 in understanding traditions of messianic expectation as well as for understanding how riding the ass would have been variously interpreted by the Romans on the one hand and by different Jewish groups on the other.

eastern bounds of the city at Bethphage and Bethany. Riding the ass into Jerusalem is presented, therefore, as a symbolic act.[3] In ancient Israel the heir of David to be anointed rode the royal ass to coronation. Thus was Absalom's riding on the mule or ass, when he was hanged by the great tresses of the hair of his head, symbolic of his claim to the kingship he wished to wrest from his father David (2 Sam 18:9). Thus was poor Mephibosheth's riding on an ass approaching the city a symbol of the claim he would have made for the old house of Saul if Absalom's insurrection had succeeded (2 Sam 19:26). Thus was it necessary for Solomon to ride on the royal mule or ass in the Kidron Valley to the sanctuary at Gihon in order effectively to counter Adonijah's claim to the throne and to secure his own accession (1 Kgs 1:33 ff.).

On the historical level Jesus apparently went out of his way to demonstrate his claim to fulfillment of these ancient royal traditions. On the gospel level, however, it is clear that the reader is not to miss the royal claim established by the account of the trip to Jerusalem. Every gesture reported had a significance which traditionists would have understood very well indeed.

The fact that all three synoptics include in the account the spreading of garments *(himatia)* on the way in front of Jesus as he rode, confirms the royal claim by its apparent allusion to the anointing of Jehu (2 Kgs 9:13) where it is said that after the young prophet from Elisha had privately anointed Jehu, the latter's lieutenants and close associates spread each his garment (**LXX:** *himation*) on the steps of the sanctuary, blew the trumpet and exclaimed, "Jehu is king."[4]

Psalm 118

In the time of Jesus Psalm 118 was recited at the time of the Festival of Tabernacles or Booths in the fall, at the time of Passover in the spring, that is, the fall and spring equinoctial festivals, and also at Hanukkah.[5] In

---

[3] See J. Dom Crossan, "Redaction and Citation in Mark 11:9–10 and 11:17," *BR* 17 (1972) 33–50. Crossan's discussion is the clearest I have seen to date on the necessity of seeing both the entry and the cleansing in the light of the prophetic symbolic acts recorded in the OT.

[4] On the royal/messianic dimension of the entry narrative see P. van Bergen, "L'Entrée messianique de Jésus à Jérusalem," *Questions liturgiques et paroissiales* 38 (1957) 9–24; A. George, "La Royauté de Jésus selon l'évangile de Luc," *Sciences ecclésiastiques* 14 (1962) 57–69; and R. Bartnicki, "Das Zitat von Zach ix, 9–10 und die Tiere in Bericht von Matthäus über dem Einzug Jesu in Jerusalem (Mt xxi, 1–11)," *NovT* 18 (1976) 161–66.

[5] See *m. Pesaḥ.* 5:5 and 10:6; and *b. Pesaḥ.* 117a, 118a and 119a, *b. Sukk.* 45a and *b. ʿArak* 10a. In the last mentioned reference Rabbi Jochanan (d. 279) noted the Hallel, Psalms 113–118, were recited on 18 days of the year in Palestine 8 days of Succot, 8 days of Hanukkah, the first day of Passover and the first of Weeks (sic)), and 21 days in the diaspora (9 Succot, 8 Hanukkah, 2 Passover and 2 Weeks).

pre-exilic times, however, Psalm 118 was a royal psalm which would have been recited on the occasion of the annual enthronement of the king at the time of the fall equinoctial celebration of the New Year.[6] In the first century it was during the fall celebration of Tabernacles that palm branches would have been available to everyone in Jerusalem for the building of the succot or booths, probably marketed from sources in Jericho or elsewhere east and south of Jerusalem. Unless the Jerusalem entry episode was somehow first related in gospel tradition to the Festival of Tabernacles in the fall, we must simply suppose either historically that Jesus and the disciples transported a considerable quantity with them in the spring as they came up from the eastern valley (which seems unlikely), or that the symbols involved purposefully point to the ancient royal dimension of the reference.[7] The validity of the latter view seems to be confirmed by the fact that the citation from Zechariah would bring to mind the Festival of Tabernacles, mentioned explicitly in Zechariah (14:16), during which the Lord, Yahweh, would appear on the Mount of Olives: "On that day Yahweh's feet shall stand on the Mount of Olives which lies before Jerusalem on the east" (Zech 14:4).

The admixture of the Zechariah and Psalm 118 passages, and their citation in the Entrance Narrative (in Matthew and John), would have been about as explosive as any such fusion could be. The fact that all three synoptics follow the entrance and temple-cleansing sequence with the raising of the question of authority (Mark 11:27–33; Matt 21:23–27; Luke 20:1–8) is significant, indeed. For, of all the acts attributed to Jesus, either in the ministry materials or in the Passion Accounts, the entry into Jerusalem, with the royalist claims implied, would have been taken as a challenge and even an offense to the establishment of his day, an establishment precisely represented by those who raised the question of authority—the priests, elders and scribes. It would have been all right to recite it as one among many psalms in celebration of a festival, but it would have been blasphemous to re-enact it with its original royal meanings to those not otherwise convinced of the claim. Such a re-enactment was surely not to be done until Messiah came to make his royal entry into city and temple when the authorities would by some grand re-enactment of the psalm receive and acknowledge their messianic king.[8]

[6] See the several remarks by Sigmund Mowinckel about Psalm 118 and its pre-exilic cultic function in *The Psalms in Israel's Worship* (New York: Abingdon, 1962), Vol. 1, 118–21, 170, 180–81, 245; and in Vol. 2, 30. See also Mitchell Dahood, *Psalms III* (AB; Garden City: Doubleday, 1970) 155; and Earle E. Ellis, *The Gospel of Luke* (NCB; London: Nelson, 1966) 191.

[7] See B. A. Mastin, "The Date of the Triumphal Entry," *NTS* 16 (1969) 76–82.

[8] See again the discussions to the point, above in notes 2, 4 and 6, and especially in Blenkinsopp and van Bergen.

The fact that the evangelists or their sources expected their readers and hearers to have in mind the whole of Psalm 118, and more importantly to know its significance,[9] is indicated by the fabric of thought that is woven when the Entrance Narrative is taken seriously on its own Scriptural or canonical terms. What the evangelists record might be thought of as the warp with the psalm and other Scriptural allusions as the woof which together make up the weftage of the gospel accounts.

Hans-Joachim Kraus' discussion of the relation in Psalm 118 between the individual and communal elements demands a clearer answer than has heretofore been offered.[10] Rabbinic efforts at seeing in Psalm 118 a liturgical dialogue offer clues for the following suggestion as to how the psalm functioned in pre-exilic temple ritual.[11]

As a hymn of royal entry Psalm 118 would have been recited in Iron Age Jerusalem as the king entered the city and the temple on the occasion of an annual rite of re-enthronement. He would already have endured the rite of humiliation and now approached the city with his account of how the Lord God had delivered him from evildoers, the humiliators. As he approached the city the people would have shouted,

---

[9] See Ed. Lohse, "Hosianna," *NovT* 6 (1963) 113–19.

[10] Hans-Joachim Kraus, *Psalmen 64–150* (BKAT; Neukirchen-Vluyn: Neukirchen, 1972) 800–809.

[11] There are three efforts, to my knowledge, in rabbinic literature to elaborate the liturgical aspects of Psalm 118, those in *b. Pesah* 119a, the Midrash to Psalm 118 and the Targum to Psalm 118. English translations of the talmud and midrash texts may be consulted in *The Babylonian Talmud, Seder Mo'ed*, by I. Epstein (London: Soncino, 1938) ad loc., and in William G. Braude, *The Midrash on Psalms* (New Haven: Yale University, 1959) 2.242–45. Those in the talmud and targum are historicizing, that is, they suggest who originally said or spoke the several parts of the psalm; the midrash seems to suggest who should recite which parts in future, perhaps at Messiah's arrival.

The midrash indicates that the first halves of vv 15, 16, 25, 26, 27 and 28 will be recited by "the men of Jerusalem inside the walls" while the second halves of those verses will be recited by "the men of Judah outside the walls." Then both groups would recite all of v 29. Curiously the midrash mentions that "David said" what is v 19a.

The talmud and targum scan the psalm in quite similar ways but with different people taking the different parts. They agree, however, at two places: both see Samuel as having said v 27b and David v 28a.

The talmud notes that David said vv 21a, 25b, and 28a; Jesse vv 22a and 26a; David's brothers (priests, presumably?) vv 23a and 25a; and "all of them" vv 27a and 28b.

The targum notes that "the builders" said vv 23a, 24a, 25a and 26a; the sons of Jesse (priests?) vv 23b and 24b; Jesse and his wife v 25b; the tribes of Judah v 27a; Samuel vv 27b and v 29; and David v 28.

These ancient perceptions of the dramatic/liturgical nature of Psalm 118 suggested the effort here elaborated. See again Mowinckel, *Psalms*, 180–81, and R. Press, "Der Gottesknecht im AT," *ZAW* 67 (1955) 90.

"Give thanks to the Lord, for his mercy (*ḥesed*, in royal theology meaning promise, perhaps, or providence) endures forever" (v 1). In antiphony the people, the priests and the "Yahweh-fearers" would then sing in turn the refrain of vv 2 to 4, "For his *ḥesed* endures forever." Then after an initial general recital of his humiliation experience (vv 5–7), a chorus, perhaps, or the king and the people together would have sung forth the "It is better" affirmations of vv 8 and 9.[12]

The king would have resumed his recital in vv 10–13 but this time in the more specific terms of the "event" of humiliation. Thereupon the people or a chorus would join him in the glad affirmation of v 14.[13] Such an affirmation of faith would incite the following song, as recorded in vv 15 and 16, sung by all present! One can almost hear the solo voice of, or for, the king in *obligato* rise above the song with "I shall not die . . ." of vv 17–18. After some dramatic move, turning to face the temple gates, the king would intone v 19, "Open to me . . ." Quite ponderously would a select group of priests from within the temple intone v 20 reminding one and all, quite liturgically, that they were guardians of the gate of the Lord's House and had sole authority for granting admission.

For response the king would make appeal directly to the saving act of God which marked the salient day of ceremony by engaging in the act of thanksgiving of v 21. Thereupon would the chorus and perhaps all the people sing out the account of wonder of divine election of the Davidic king, a wonder never ceasing to astound and amaze, generation to generation, even year to year—indeed that very marvel (*niphlat*, MT— *thaumastē*, LXX v 23) being celebrated in the joyous ritual. It is difficult to determine if the traditional (LXX and following) understanding of v 24 is the correct one, that is, affirming that God had indeed created that very special day of celebration and re-affirmation of election; or if Mitchell Dahood and the New English Bible are correct in seeing v 24 as affirming that the day was indeed special in that God had once more committed a mighty saving act in saving the king from death and re-affirming his election.[14] This portion of the hymn sung by chorus and people (vv 22–25) concludes with the stirring plea to God of the *Hoshi‘ah-na’*, later in Greek to be called the Hosannah (v 25).

At the conclusion of the plea, which may in actual ceremony have been much longer full of joy and wonder, the priests, who had earlier fulfilled their role as gate-keepers (v 20), now joyfully intone the great "Blessed be he who enters . . .", thereby officially recognizing and

---

[12] Psalm 118, vv 1, 8, 9, 15, 16 and 29 are examples of common liturgical phrases that were adaptable to more than one hymn or song. Cf. 11QPs^a 17:1–6.

[13] Ps 118:14 is found verbatim also at Exod 15:2a and Isa 12:2b, another example of common liturgical phrases used in different hymns.

[14] See Dahood, *Psalms*, 159.

receiving the one arriving as indeed the king. The climax of the ceremony has been reached. The king is once more king. It would appear, as
has been noted, that Yahweh's kingship is in part expressed in the earthly
Davidic king so that the very presence of the king is the divine gift of
light, and so the chorus and people affirm the point (v 27).[15] Verse 27b
indicates the commencement of offering sacrifices of thanksgiving and
may perhaps have been intoned by the priests.

The hymn concludes with the re-affirmation of faith by the king and
all the people (v 28) and finally the reverberation of the incipit of v 1 as
now the refrain of the whole hymn in *inclusio*.

People   1. Give thanks to the Lord, for he is good;
                his hesed endures forever!
            2. Let Israel say: his *hesed* endures forever.
            3. Let the house of Aaron say: his *hesed* endures forever.
            4. Let the Yahweh-fearers say: his *hesed* endures forever.

King   5. Out of distress I invoked Yah;
                Yah answered me with largesse.
            6. When Yahweh is with me I have no fear.
                What could a mere mortal do to me?
            7. When Yahweh is with me as my helper,
                then I look with confidence at my enemies.

People   8. It is better to take refuge in Yahweh
                than to trust in humans;
            9. It is better to take refuge in Yahweh
                than to trust in princes!

King   10. All nations surrounded me;
                in the name of Yahweh I cut them off.
          11. They surrounded me, they were all around me;
                in the name of Yahweh I cut them off.
          12. They surrounded me like bees,
                they blazed like thorns on fire;
                in the name of Yahweh I cut them off.
          13. I was hard pressed about to fall,
                but Yahweh helped me!

King and 14. Yahweh was my strength and my song;
people   he was with me as salvation.[16]

---

[15] Ps 118:27 calls to mind the priestly benediction and the light of the presence of
God, here expressed in the presence of the king as a gift of God.

[16] The verse can, as has become customary, be translated in the present tense to
emphasize God's ever-present strength and salvation. I have put it in the past

All	15. A shout of joy and salvation throughout the tents of the righteous: the right hand of Yahweh acts valiantly, 16. the right hand of Yahweh is exalted, the right hand of Yahweh acts valiantly.
King	17. I shall not die but shall live to recite the deeds of Yah! 18. Yah disciplined me sorely, but he did not hand me over to death. 19. Open for me the gates of righteousness; I shall enter through them, I shall give thanks to Yah!
Priests	20. This is the gate that belongs to Yahweh; only the righteous may enter through it.
King	21. I give thanks to you for you answered me; you were with me as salvation.
People	22. The stone the builders rejected has become the cornerstone. 23. This is Yahweh's own doing; it is a marvel in our eyes. 24. This is the day on which Yahweh has acted; let us rejoice and be glad in him. 25. Pray, O Yahweh, grant salvation; pray, O Yahweh, grant prosperity.
Priests	26. Blessed by the name of Yahweh be he who enters! We bless you from the House of Yahweh.
People	27. Yahweh is God and he has given us light!
Priests	Bind the festal sacrifice with ropes onto the horns of the altar.
King and People	28. You are my God and I do give you thanks, O, my God, I extol you.
All	29. Give thanks to Yahweh for he is good; his *ḥesed* endures forever!

The psalm so conceived would have been at the heart of the annual ceremony of the humiliation and exaltation of the king, itself a liturgy of re-affirmation of Yahweh as God and King. The heart of the psalm is

---

tense here to show that it may also be seen as the grand conclusion to the recital of vv 10–13, a summation of the presence of God in the event of humiliation.

expressed in the two verses cited in the gospel accounts: the Hosanna plea of v 25 which affirms the sovereignty of the acting, humbling and exalting God, who has in this New Year's experience of the king demonstrated his sovereignty by a new mighty act; and the welcome in v 26 to the king expressed by the priests from the temple steps.

The Entrance

The warp and the woof weave a pattern which bears a message of barely subdued excitement. The messiah has arrived and been acclaimed king. He has been recognized as king by acclamation not of those with power or authority but by a rather scragly crowd of disciples and followers. Typical biblical themes abound in the pattern.

The approach to Jerusalem was from the east, by tradition.[17] Bethphage and Bethany, modern Et-tor and Esariyeh are located on the eastern slopes of the Mount of Olives, a location which none of the synoptics takes for granted but all specify since the Mount of Olives had eschatological meaning, as we have seen. At this point the references in Zechariah 14 are important in complement to the locales mentioned. The references in this regard are probably more eschatological than geographic, though actual historicity is also highly possible. On the gospel level, however, all history culminates here. The commission to fetch the colt depends upon the glad expectation expressed in Zechariah 9 as well as upon acquaintance with Scriptural traditions about coronation. The episode of the colt is as much eschatological in dimension as historical.[18] The rhetorical mode of recounting the fetching of the colt heightens the mystery or divine dimension of the mission.

The references to the garments spread before the one riding the donkey provide a striking pattern of royal dimension. This is a king riding to coronation. "As he was drawing near, at the descent of the Mount of Olives, the whole multitude of the disciples began to rejoice and praise God with a loud voice for all the mighty works they had witnessed" (Luke 19:37). Subtly woven in is reference to the Kidron Valley in preparation for the recitation and enactment of Psalm 118. The phrase *peri pason dunameon*, for all the mighty works, would refer not only to the OT gospel story of God's mighty acts toward his elect people Israel, but more directly to his election and traditional acts toward David, and his heirs, as recited in Psalm 118. Pursuant to basic NT hermeneutics all those traditional divine acts are now contemporized in Christ's humiliation-exaltation story to be recounted in the Passion Account. Luke and John

---

[17] Again see the seminal study by J. Blenkinsopp (above, n. 2).
[18] See again the study by H. Patsch (above, n. 1).

include the epexegetic *ho basileus*, the king, to clarify who it was that was coming or arriving.

The Hosanna

It would be well at this point to trace the texture of the woof suggested in the Hosanna (which Luke omits). First, it is a citation of Ps 118:25, which in the ancient royal use of the psalm was both the king's and the people's full recognition or confession of the kingship of Yahweh.

Specifically, it was a plea both for mercy and for justice before the king. In the psalm it was a plea to God for salvation and prosperity for the following year; it was also ancient Israel's affirmation of the kingship or sovereignty of God even in the ceremony of the enthronement of the earthly Davidic king. But the *Hoshi-ah-na'* also has another context. It was the cry of the litigant as he or she entered the court of the king to submit a brief and plead a case (2 Sam 14:4 and 2 Kgs 6:26). The opening formula as the litigant entered the presence of the king sitting in judgment of cases in the city gate (sic) was the phrase, *Hosha'-na'/Hoshi'ah-na'*. It was a cry both for justice and for mercy at the same time. But the important observation is that it was a formula used when entering the presence of the king as judge. In the psalm it was spoken by the people when the humiliated exalted king entered the temple gates of Yahweh, the Gates of Righteousness. Lohse is undoubtedly right that it had attained a messianic meaning as a *Zuruf* in pre-Christian Judaism.[19]

In the gospels, except Luke, it is spoken by the disciples or the people before the temple after Jesus' entry into the gate of the city. It is then repeated in the phrase "Hosanna in the highest" just after the recitation of Ps 118:26, the "Blessed be he. . . ," in both Mark 11:10 and Matt 21:9. Matthew then brings it in a third time just after the Entrance when the people in the temple react to Jesus' healing of the blind and the lame by shouting "Hosanna to the son of David." Luke omits the Hosanna but has the epexegetic *ho basileus* in citing v 26 of the psalm. Mark, who has the Hosanna (11:9), adds after the citation of Ps 118:26, "Blessed be the coming kingdom of our father, David" (11:10). John, who has the Hosanna, further notes the royal dimension by adding, "and the king of Israel" (12:13) after citation of the psalm.

In the synoptics this recognition and acknowledgment of the king as judge in the city gate, is immediately followed by Jesus' proceeding into the city and entering the temple, precisely that which is indicated in Ps 118:25–26. In the Davidic royal entry, the king's arrival was marked by the exclamation of the priests from the temple steps, "Blessed by the name of Yahweh be he who arrives (or, comes); we bless you from the

House of Yahweh." Thereafter follows in 118:27 the sacrifice of the festal victim(s) and the affirmation that Yahweh is El. This final event indicated in the psalm is reflected in Matt 21:12 and Mark 11:15 in the mention of "those who sold pigeons" for sacrifice. Even Luke has "drive out those who sold" also in the pericope on the cleansing of the Temple.

Stones and the Temple

The sequence of the disciples' recitation of Ps 118:26 and Jesus' first act of judgment as eschatological king within the temple, against those who had made it into a den of robbers, is interrupted in Luke by the intrusion of verbal exchange between Jesus and the establishment (which occurs in Matthew after the cleansing of the temple). Some Pharisees are reported to have chided Jesus to rebuke his blasphemous disciples. Jesus' reply was that if the disciples did not say the "Blessed be he . . ." (which the temple priests should have recited) then the very stones would recite it. Some students of this passage understand this pericope in Luke to be placed by the evangelist on the Mount of Olives overlooking the city and understand the stones to be those of the path or road from Bethany. Such a view puts geography above theology; here, as in much of the rest of the gospels, we have theological or eschatological geography.

It is quite clear from the fuller context of the Lucan warp and woof, from Psalm 118, that the stones refer not to the pebbles of a rocky path but to the building stones of the temple, the destruction of which Jesus prophesies at the end of the intruding pericope. Luke 19:45, immediately following, indicates that Jesus was already in the city (contrast Mark 11:11 and Matt 21:10) and now enters the temple for judgment. What Jesus is saying to the Pharisees, according to Luke, is that the part of the royal entrance liturgy, which according to Psalm 118 the priests from the temple steps were supposed to have recited (namely the "Blessed be he . . .") would have been recited by the stones of the temple if it had not at least been recited by the disciples (see a similar kind of theological affirmation in Luke 3:8). It is as though Jesus responded, "I'm sorry, friends, this event is happening, and the roles indicated have to be filled." Such high, objective theology is a Lucan characteristic.

A Theophany

The fabric woven of the warp of the new act of God (jeshu῾ah— sotēria) recorded in the gospels, and of the woof of the earlier acts of God heralded in the psalm, is canonical in texture and eschatological in design. Christ, according to the gospel claim, was the long-expected king unrecognized upon his arrival by the authorities of his day. From them he

won no credentials, and the gospel accounts faithfully reflect the understandable rejection by the authorities of the claims Jesus and the early
church laid to the authority of the Scriptural (OT) traditions. As the king
uncrowned, Jesus passed judgment on the church and state of his day,
very much as Yahweh had done through his prophets of old. And as with
those prophets, his judgments and blessings went unheeded by his
contemporaries, save for a few disciples and followers. On the one hand,
Jesus' symbolic act was no more compelling or convincing than the
earlier prophetic symbolic acts had been. On the other, however, this
later act, like its prophetic predecessors, was offensive to the responsible
authorities, those precisely charged with the burdens of the continuity of
tradition. The claim to kingship was messianic, but the effect was a
prophetic challenge.

Luke has two phrases emphasizing the claim to Davidic kingship as a
reign of peace. Just after the citations from Psalm 118 in the mouths of
the disciples, Luke adds the expression, "Peace in heaven and glory in
the highest" (19:38), very similiar to the phrase he attributes to the
heavenly chorus at the Bethlehem theophany (2:14), perhaps suggested
to him by the *en tois hupsistois* in Mark/Matthew. And in Jesus' lament
over the city Luke employs the time-honored pun on the name Jerusalem by reporting Jesus as saying of the city, "Would that you knew the
things that make for peace!" The word *eirēnē*, peace, occurs more often
in Luke than in any other New Testament book: it is apparently a Lucan
interest.

In another sense also Jesus' entry into Jerusalem is a theophany for
Luke. Luke as much as any other NT writer attributes to Jesus in the NT
what the OT says of Yahweh. The entry into Jerusalem is apparently more
eschatological in dimension in Luke than in the other synoptics, all of
which are eschatological enough. The stones of the temple might indeed
welcome Jesus, according to Luke, if no one else did. According to the
psalm the priests from the temple steps should have greeted Jesus after
the disciples shouted the Hosanna, but they did not; so the disciples also
went on and shouted the "Blessed be he. . . ." Why did the priests not
receive this "king" at his so-called triumphal entry? Because, as the
prophetic intrusion says (Luke 19:41–45), Jerusalem did not know the
time of its visitation, that is, the *kairos* of divine judgment. They could
not recognize, they could not see that in this little parade the king had
entered the gates of city and temple and thereby entered into judgment
with his people. They simply did not believe that the time of judgment
had arrived with the arrival of the messianic king riding on the ass's colt
from Bethany. They lacked the vision the disciples gave witness to. This
is not to say that on the historical level the disciples and followers knew
what they were doing in terms of the eschatological significance of the

enactment. On the contrary, there is a canonical dimension to God's resignifying what humans otherwise do.

What from the standpoint of the established institutions and recognized authorities of the day was a misguided, scandalous demonstration by a fringe group of society, in the divine economy, according to the gospels, was a theophany, the arrival of a king and the presence of God.

Luke says that when "he entered the temple and began to drive out those who sold," Jesus said to them, "It is written, 'My house shall be a house of prayer'; but you have made it a den of robbers" (Luke 19:45–46). Matthew's and Mark's picture of the arriving king's judgments in the temple is even more dramatic; according to Mark Jesus "overturned the tables of the money-changers and the seats of those who sold pigeons and he would not allow anyone to carry anything through the temple" (Mark 11:15–16). The citations or authoritative references for Jesus' acts of judgment against the established authorities were significantly enough to Isaiah (56:7) and Jeremiah (7:11). According to the book of Isaiah the temple should be a house of prayer for all peoples but like Jeremiah Jesus upon entering it found it a den of robbers. The offense to the authorities was unmistakable. Jesus thrust the rapier of prophetic judgment to the heart of the church, and the reaction of the "chief priests and the scribes and the principal folk of the people" (Luke 19:47) was later in the week to bring charges against him, much like those their predecessors had brought against Jeremiah; both were charged with sedition and blasphemy (Jeremiah 7 and 38).

A Canonical Re-reading

We cannot blame Jesus' contemporaries. On the contrary, we should identify with them. This enactment of the psalm as a prophetic symbolic act would have been no less blasphemous and scandalous to those responsible for Israel's traditions (and they would have known them well) than similar symbolic acts performed by the prophets in the late Iron Age. One thinks of Isaiah walking about in Jerusalem naked and barefoot for three years (Isa 20:3–4) to dramatize his message; or of Jeremiah's and Ezekiel's similarly dramatic acts in order to press the points of their messages (e.g., Jer 13:1–11; 16:1–9; 18:1–11; 19:1–13, etc.; Ezek 4:1–17; 5:1–4; 12:3–20, etc.). Such prophetic acts were also called "signs" (as in Ezek 12:11). They in all cases challenged the religious and political authorities of the day, and brought alienation, pain and suffering upon the prophets who enacted them.

In all such passages modern readers who have responsibility for the traditioning of Scripture, both preserving and presenting it, should by dynamic analogy identify with their appropriate counterparts in the

Scriptural narratives, so as to experience and hear the message conveyed. This is as much the case in reading the gospel accounts of this prophetic enactment as in reading the prophets. With the priests, scribes and elders in Mark 11:27, Matt 21:15 and 23, and Luke 20:1, we should be induced by our reading of this offensive act to ask by what authority Jesus did "these things." The precious psalm was not to be read and enacted in that way until Messiah came. Would there be a single judicatory of any Christian community today that would have been on those temple steps to recite the "Blessed be he . . ."? I dare say not. It is not until Christians learn to monotheize while reading the New Testament, that is, refuse to engage in good-guys-bad-guys hermeneutics, that they will be able to read it for what it canonically says.

One of the remarkable things about the gospel reports of the offense taken by the Pharisees and the other religious authorities at Jesus' teaching of Scripture and his various kinds of acts, symbolic and otherwise, was their continued willingness to dialogue with Jesus right on up to the point of being able to take no more. They knew very well the Scripture passages he preached from, taught from and re-presented by word and deed; they simply had a quite different hermeneutic by which they understood them. One wonders how many modern Christians would be as tolerant of Jesus' scandalous interpretations and re-presentations of Scripture as the Pharisees were. "And some of the Pharisees in the multitude said to him, 'Teacher, rebuke your disciples.'" They were still willing even after this offense to discuss it with him.

But Jesus' response was in effect to say that while debating Scripture, indeed a very Jewish vocation, was important, this time it was not just a matter of debate, God in fact was bringing it to fulfillment before their very eyes. The event was happening and that part of the liturgy (Ps 118:26) which was supposed to have been recited by the priests on the temple steps was at least being recited by the unauthorized followers of Jesus. And even then, should they have balked, the stones of the temple steps would have taken the role. Such is Luke's theocentric, objective theology.

Finally, after Jesus' even more offensive act of daring to disrupt the customary temple procedures which facilitated the purchasing of animals so that the common people, particularly those on pilgrimmage, could have the opportunity to offer their sacrifices, the priests and scribes had taken as much as they could tolerate and still be responsible to their office. They had finally themselves to take action. And so on with the Passion Account.

THE PROPHETIC USE OF THE SCRIPTURES
IN LUKE-ACTS

JACK T. SANDERS

University of Oregon

Eugene, Oregon

The person who would understand Luke-Acts must stay close to the concordance. This necessity was well demonstrated by Hans Conzelmann in his justly famous study of the theology of Luke-Acts,[1] when, in order to understand Luke's concept of proclaiming the gospel, he pursued Luke's use of words on the stems, *aggel-*, *kērys-*, *leg-*, etc., at some length.[2] The method is indispensable. If, for example, we are interested in learning how Luke portrayed the Jews, the concordance will lead us at once to the fact that a distinct change occurs in Luke's use of the term, "the Jews," after Acts 8; or, we need just a few minutes with the concordance to learn that what Luke says the Jews wanted to do with Jesus he also says they wanted to do with various Apostles and other early Christians—to "do away with" them *(anaireō)*.[3]

If we apply this method to Luke's use of the Bible—that is, to what would have been called in his day "the Scriptures *(hai graphai)*" or "the Law and the Prophets *(ho nomos kai hoi prophētai)*"—or perhaps "the Law, the Prophets, and the Psalms," as in Luke 24:44—then we immediately find that Luke thinks of all the Scripture as something to be fulfilled—that is, as prophetic.[4] Thus the risen Jesus explains to his strolling companions on the Emmaus Road that "it is necessary for

---

[1] H. Conzelmann, *The Theology of St Luke* (New York: Harper & Brothers, 1960).

[2] Ibid., 218–25.

[3] Cf. Luke 22:2 and, e.g., Acts 2:23; 5:33; 23:15, 21. These themes and related ones are pursued, not surprisingly, in my forthcoming study, *The Jews in Luke-Acts*.

[4] Cf. the discussion of this point in J. A. Fitzmyer, *The Gospel According to Luke (I–IX)* (AB 28; Garden City: Doubleday, 1981) 180. Fitzmyer has, quite naturally, followed the "concordance method" of Lucan study here. I realize that Luke's use of Scripture is not entirely defined by the designation, "prophecy (to be) fulfilled"; cf. esp. M. Rese, *Alttestamentliche Motive in der Christologie des Lukas* (SNT 1; Gütersloh: Mohn, 1969), and *idem*, "Die Funktion der alttestamentlichen Zitate und Anspielungen in den Reden der Apostelgeschichte," *Les Actes des Apôtres: Tradition, rédaction, théologie* (ed. J. Kremer; BETL 48; Gembloux: Duculot; Louvain: University Press, 1979) 61–79. That point, however, is not directly germane to the issue being pursued here.

everything written about me in the Law of Moses and the Prophets and the Psalms to be fulfilled" (Luke 24:44); and he then seeks to help them to understand "the Scriptures" (v 45). Since Luke quotes no text here— nor earlier in v 27, where the same point is made, nor in Acts 17:2–3 and 18:28, where there are similar statements—we are readily able to con- clude that Luke was of the firm conviction that Jesus' Messiahship and his death and resurrection were foretold in "the Scriptures," probably in "all the Scriptures" as a unit, whether any particular text is cited or not. That is to say that it would appear that Luke would have that conviction even if he were unable to quote a single verse of Scripture.

Naturally, Luke does know quite a few verses of Scripture, and he is often able to cite them as being fulfilled.[5] He has Jesus claim that Isa 61:1–2 + 58:6, quoted in Luke 4:18–19 in Jesus' Nazareth sermon, is fulfilled (v 21); and in Acts he also cites specific prophecies as being fulfilled, e.g., Joel 2:28–32 in Acts 2:16–21, which the Lucan Peter introduces by saying that "this [i.e., the outpouring of the Spirit] is what was spoken by the Prophet Joel"; or Isa 6:9–10 in Acts 28:25–27, which the Lucan Paul introduces by saying, "Well did the Holy Spirit speak through Isaiah the Prophet to your fathers." But it is not only prophecies from the Prophets that are fulfilled, but "prophecies" from elsewhere in Scripture, as well. Two different lines from the Psalms are cited in Acts 1:20 to explain the death of Judas; further, Ps 2:1–2 is taken, in Acts 4:25– 27, to be somehow prophetic of Jesus' end,[6] the Apostles repeating the words, "*ethnē* (Gentiles)," and, "*laoi* (peoples)," from the Psalm in their prayerful description about what happened to Jesus, apparently translat- ing "kings" and "rulers" in the Psalm into "Herod and Pontius Pilate," and revising the words, "at the same place against the Lord and against His Christ," in the Psalm to say that the Gentiles, people of Israel, Pilate, and Herod all came together "against [or: at] Your holy son Jesus whom You anointed *(echrisas)*."[7]

Even the Torah is prophetic.[8] It is hardly startling when Luke cites an obviously prophetic statement from the Torah (Deut 18:15–16: "The

---

[5] Cf. the study of Luke's use of Scripture by T. Holtz, *Untersuchungen über die alttestamentlichen Zitate bei Lukas* (TU 104; Berlin: Akademie, 1968). Holtz's primary interest was to establish the text used by Luke in his scriptural citations. Cf. further G. D. Kilpatrick, "Some Quotations in Acts," *Les Actes des Apôtres*, 81–97.

[6] Cf. M. Dibelius, "Herodes und Pilatus," *Botschaft und Geschichte. Gesammelte Aufsätze* (2 vols.; Tübingen: Mohr [Siebeck], 1953–56) 1. 289–91.

[7] The Lucan Stephen, in Acts 7, also cites quite a lot of Scripture, but the Scriptures are not quoted there in any prophetic sense.

[8] Holtz (*Alttestamentliche Zitate*, 61–130, 171–72) argues that Luke did not have access to a scroll of the Torah but had his Torah citations from a collection of proof texts. That may well be. Our concern here, however, is not to determine Luke's sources, but to understand Luke, himself. As A. T. Hanson (*The Living Ut- terances of God* [London: Darton, Longman and Todd, 1983] 79) says, "It would

Lord your god will raise up for you a prophet . . . like me") in Acts 3:22
to attest to Jesus' being a prophet—and perhaps to his being raised from
the dead, cf. v 21; but his other general statements in Luke 24:27, 44;
Acts 26:22; 28:23; and perhaps Acts 24:14 (where Luke places on Paul's
lips his own credo) about how the Law or Moses has been fulfilled, even
when no specific text is cited, show what he thinks.[9]

Of course, the Scripture may be used in other ways, as, for example,
when Luke establishes a few rules for the Gentile church (Luke 10:27;
Acts 15:29), or when he is at pains to show in Luke 2 how the youthful
Jesus and his family were faithful to Jewish requirements, or when he
buttresses his lengthy *Heilsgeschichte* in Acts 7 with frequent citations
from Scripture; but such examples do not help in defining Luke's *theology of Scripture*, for he would not say that the Scripture gives the rules
for Christian living. When Luke thinks of the Scripture in general, as a
unity, as the expression of the divine will, he says that it is prophetic.[10]
That he sometimes uses Scripture in other ways is irrelevant to that
general point.

What is it, then, that Luke thinks the Scripture has prophesied?

To a very great extent it is Jesus, especially his death and resurrection, and also the beginnings of Christianity.[11] This orientation is especially true in those places, like the ones to which we have already
alluded, where Luke does not quote any particular Scripture but refers
generally to its having been fulfilled. In addition to Jesus' explanation to

---

be unfair to suppose that [Luke] was not fully aware of the implications of what was
in his sources for the interpretation of scripture," on the assumption that Luke had
his scriptural quotations from Christian sources.

[9] The divine plan, in Luke–Acts, is prophesied not only in Scripture but also by
living prophets and by heavenly beings, as has been adequately emphasized by
C. H. Talbert, *Reading Luke. A Literary and Theological Commentary on the
Third Gospel* (New York: Crossroad, 1982) 234–40; cf. also Fitzmyer, *Luke*, 180.
Such prophetic themes in Luke-Acts, however, fall outside our current interest.

[10] That such an understanding of Scripture shows certain affinities with the understanding of Scripture found in the Dead Sea Scrolls has, of course, long been
recognized; cf. H. Braun, *Qumran und das Neue Testament* (2 vols.; Tübingen:
Mohr [Siebeck], 1966) 2. 301–25, where there is also a full bibliography. Of the
literature discussed there, cf. esp. K. Stendahl, *The School of St. Matthew* (2d ed.;
Philadelphia: Fortress, 1968) v–ix, 183–202. Cf. further W. H. Brownlee, "Biblical
Interpretation Among the Sectaries of the Dead Sea Scrolls," *BA* 14 (1951) 54–76;
idem, The Midrash Pesher of Habakkuk (SBLMS 24; Missoula: Scholars Press,
1979) 34–36; L. H. Silberman, "Unriddling the Riddle. A Study in the Structure
and Language of the Habakkuk Pesher," *RevQ* 3 (1961) 224–64; D. Patte, *Early
Jewish Hermeneutic in Palestine* (SBLDS 22; Missoula: SBL and Scholars Press,
1975), esp. pp. 299–308.

[11] Cf. esp. J. Dupont, "L'utilisation apologétique de l'Ancien Testament dans les
discours des Actes," *Etudes sur les Actes des Apôtres* (LD 45; Paris: Editions du
Cerf, 1967) 247–82, and *idem,* "L'interpretation des Psaumes dans les Actes des
Apôtres," ibid., 283–307.

his two companions on the Emmaus Road at the end of Luke 24, one may note, e.g., Luke 1:70–71, where Zacharias, in the Benedictus, affirms, "Thus He spoke through the mouth of His holy Prophets since ages ago, salvation from our enemies and from the hand of all those who hate us"— words which, to be sure, recall passages in the Psalms but do not actually quote them;[12] or Acts 3:18, where Peter claims that "God has thus carried out what He promised ahead of time, through the mouth of all the Prophets, His Christ would suffer." (Cf. further Acts 3:24; 10:43; 17:2–3; 18:28, 31; 26:22–23; 28:23.)

Further, of course, in addition to these general statements, Luke adduces numerous texts from the Prophets and the Psalms that "prove" the same things. Thus Jesus, at the outset of his public ministry (according to Luke)—as we have already noted—applies prophecies from Isaiah to himself (Luke 4:17–21). Again, the Ethiopian eunuch in Acts 8 is very conveniently reading from a passage in Isaiah pregnant with Christian interpretive possibilities (vv 32–33 = Isa 53:7–8) when Philip comes aboard, so that Philip is—so we are to understand—able to use that Scripture for the text of his following sermon (anoixas de ho Philippos to stoma autou kai arxamenos apo tēs graphēs tautēs euēggelisato autǭ ton Iēsoun. Peter's Pentecost sermon, of course, is also replete with citations of prophecies that have been fulfilled; for God "would not abandon [Jesus'] soul to Hell" (Acts 2:27 = Ps 16:10); and He said to him, "Sit on my right" (Acts 2:34 = Ps 110:1). A variation of this type of use of scriptural prophecy is Luke 13:35, where Jesus, himself, prophesies something to happen later and quotes Scripture in the process: "You will not see me until you say, 'Blessed is the one who comes in the name of the Lord'" (= Ps 118:26)—a prophecy that is then fulfilled in Luke 19:38, when the "multitude of disciples" (v 37) says exactly that in Jesus' presence as he enters Jerusalem.[13] There are, of course, other examples.

In addition to the significant events concerning Jesus and the early church, there are two other things that Luke thinks the Scripture has prophesied, and they go together. These two things are the rejection of the gospel by the Jews and its acceptance by the Gentiles.[14] That the

---

[12] Hanson (Living Utterances, 79) thinks that Luke means here that certain persons other than the Latter Prophets, like, e.g., Moses and David, are to be thought of as having been prophets. Luke doubtless subscribed to such a view, but his statement in Luke 1:70–71 is more an affirmation of a general view than it is an oblique reference to certain prophetic persons.

[13] W. C. Robinson, Jr. (Der Weg des Herrn [TF 36; Hamburg-Bergstedt: Herbert Reich · Evangelischer Verlag, 1964] 54) correctly calls attention to the fact that the prophecy is not entirely fulfilled, inasmuch as it is the disciples, not Jerusalem, who speak the words from the Psalm.

[14] On this point in general, cf. J. Dupont, "Le salut des gentils et la signification théologique du livre des Actes," NTS 6 (1959–60) 132–55; and S. G. Wilson, The Gentiles and the Gentile Mission in Luke-Acts (SNTSMS 23; Cambridge: University Press, 1973).

Gentiles are the intended objects of God's salvation is announced at the outset by John the Baptist: "All flesh will see the salvation of God" (Luke 3:6 = Isa 40:5); and the risen Jesus' charge to the Disciples in Acts 1:8 that they are to witness "to the end of the earth" is repeated by Paul in his first sermon in a scriptural quotation: "Thus the Lord commanded us: 'I have set you up as the light of the Gentiles, for you to become salvation to the end of the earth'" (Acts 13:47 = Isa 49:6)—so that we see clearly not only where Luke got the language of Acts 1:8, but what he meant by it.[15] For Luke's narrative, of course, the issue of the Gentile church reaches its critical decision point at the Apostolic Council, and here the Lucan James establishes its propriety by quoting Amos 9:12: ". . . so that the remainder of people may seek out the Lord, and all the Gentiles upon whom My name has been named" (Acts 15:17; "remainder of people" and "all the Gentiles" are, of course, a *parallelismus membrorum* and synonymous).

As far as Luke's narrative goes, the Gospel only hints at or prepares the way for what becomes so vivid in Acts—the rejection of the gospel by the Jews and its acceptance by the Gentiles; whereas, generally, what Jesus *says* in the Gospel about these issues points directly to the later development in Acts.[16] With regard to one scriptural prophecy, however, which Luke obviously thinks is important as prophesying both the rejection of the gospel by the Jews and its acceptance by the Gentiles, we have only an anticipatory and somewhat puzzling use in the Gospel, but then a clarified use in Acts, which latter use thus provides us an entré for understanding a part of Luke's Gospel that is somewhat puzzling. This scripture is Ps 118:22. The first time that Luke quotes it is at the conclusion of the parable of the Vineyard, Luke 20:9–16. Commentators have puzzled, quite understandably, over the identity of Luke's intended audience for this parable. Luke opens (v 9) by saying that Jesus directs the parable "at the people"; and it is then presumably they who respond to the conclusion that has pronounced the judgment that the vineyard will be given to other tenants, "Oh, no! *(mē genoito)*" (v 16). Then the Lucan Jesus quotes the Psalm (Luke 20:17): "The stone that the builders have rejected as unworthy, the same has become the cornerstone." Then Luke informs us (v 19) that "the Scribes and the Chief Priests . . . knew . . . that he told this parable at them." Further, they were unable to retaliate, because "they feared the people"—that is to say, because of

---

[15] One understands that we have to do with a command here, not with a prophecy; but Luke nevertheless finds a scriptural justification for the gospel's going to the Gentiles, as would have been the case had he cited the Scripture as prophecy rather than as command.

[16] I have demonstrated this in great detail elsewhere. The discrepancy between speech and narrative in Luke-Acts in this regard has been noted but inadequately explained by G. Lohfink, *Die Sammlung Israels* (SANT 39; Munich: Kösel, 1975) 44.

Jesus' popularity with "the people," who would presumably have prevented any retaliation. Well, then, who are the tenants who are to be replaced (as Luke understands the matter)? Are they "the Jews," who are to be replaced by the Gentiles,[17] or are they the Jerusalem priestly leadership, who are to be replaced by the Apostles?[18]

It is when we look at Luke's second use of this Scripture that we find our answer. In Acts 4, Peter (with John) has been arrested for the first time and is defending the Christian cause "in the Sanhedrin," as Luke would say (cf. Acts 5:27). He addresses himself first (Acts 4:8) to the "rulers of the people and elders," but then he includes the people, as well, by proposing, "Let it be known to you all and to all the people of Israel" (v 10) that the Apostles are only proclaiming God's promised salvation; and then he quotes—or, better, requotes Ps 118:22: "He is the stone that was set at nought by you the builders, which has become the cornerstone" (Acts 4:11). Surely here, however, there is no question about the intended recipients of this barb; it is "they all," which might, according to the verisimilitude of the narrative, be understood as only all the rulers and elders, except that Peter has made a point of adding "all the people of Israel" to his intended audience! The builders who rejected the building block are not merely the Jewish religious authorities (although they may have to bear the primary burden), but are "all the people of Israel," i.e., "the Jews."[19] "The Jews" have rejected Christ, who has then become the cornerstone not of a "renewed Israel," of "the redeemed within Israel,"[20] but of the church, which is Gentile.

Thus the parable becomes subject to explanation. Luke's primary meaning is that the Jews are to be replaced by the Gentiles, and so the parable is directed at "the people." But Luke has not yet reached the point in his narrative at which "the Jews" as a unit are shown to be

[17] A. Loisy, *L'Evangile selon Luc* (Paris: Nourry, 1924) 480.

[18] Talbert, *Reading Luke*, 189.

[19] E. Haenchen (*Die Apostelgeschichte* [MeyerK 3; 16th ed.; Göttingen: Vandenhoeck & Ruprecht, 1977] 215) however, understands the quotation to refer only to people generally; and then, if I understand him correctly, he restricts the application to the Sadducees (ibid., 221). Loisy (*Les Actes des Apôtres* [Paris: Nourry, 1920] 245) also refers to "the leaders of the people."

[20] Such an understanding of Luke's ecclesiology has been put forward especially by J. Jervell, *Luke and the People of God* (Minneapolis: Augsburg, 1972), esp. pp. 41–74, and by Lohfink, *Die Sammlung Israels*, esp. pp. 33–62. The position has been endorsed by Conzelmann—cf. most recently *Heiden—Juden—Christen* (BHT 62; Tübingen: Mohr [Siebeck], 1981) 239—and has been taken up by a great many other scholars, in North America probably by the vast majority; cf., e.g., only Fitzmyer, *Luke*, 188–91. One may wish to note the counter-arguments given by R. Maddox, *The Purpose of Luke-Acts* (FRLANT 126; Göttingen: Vandenhoeck & Ruprecht, 1982) 32–39.

[21] Unfortunately, this aspect of Lucan narrative development cannot be discussed further here. Cf. again above, n. 16.

opposed to the gospel,[21] and so he redirects Jesus' remarks at the end of the parable toward the limited group of "the Scribes and the Chief Priests"; but by his later use of the same scriptural prophecy we see what he intends the parable finally to mean: The Jews are out and the Gentiles in.

The matter is made clearer by the Lucan Paul's allusion to and use of Scripture in his first sermon. In Acts 13:27, Paul tells his audience that Jesus was put to death by "those living in Jerusalem and their rulers"— thus clearly broadening the guilty to include all the inhabitants of Jerusalem—because they were "ignorant of the voices of the Prophets read every Sabbath." Soon, in vv 40–41, he is cautioning his hearers not to fall into solidarity with their Jerusalemite kin: "Watch out lest there come upon you what is said in the Prophets: 'Behold, despisers, and wonder and disappear; for I am doing a work in your days—a work that you would not believe if someone explained it to you'" (= Hab 1:5). Is Paul's warning to the Antiochene Jews therefore not merely *pro forma?* Inasmuch as the Scripture has foretold that they (and all Jews) could not possibly understand, does not the Lucan Paul already know that they will inevitably concur with the Jerusalemite ignorance? Surely he does,[22] and therefore he can shortly quote, in v 47, the Isaiah Scripture about the light of the Gentiles, to which we have already referred. That quotation, we now need to emphasize, follows upon Paul's charging the Antiochene Jews with having "judg[ed] themselves not worthy of eternal life" (v 46).[23]

In some strange way, therefore—which Luke never adequately explains—those Jews who live in such far-flung places as Antioch of Pisidia and Corinth (Acts 18:6) fall under the same condemnation (in Luke's opinion) as do those in Jerusalem responsible for Jesus' execution, even though these Diaspora Jews could hardly have had anything to do with that execution. Their refusal of the gospel, however, is, in the Lucan theology, sufficient to warrant their condemnation and even destruction (Luke 19:27). A Diaspora Jew in Acts who rejects the gospel might as well have been in Jerusalem in the Gospel helping to get Jesus put to death. What is especially puzzling about this notion is that it applies only to Jews. Gentiles who reject the gospel are not so condemned. The reason that Luke can get away with such an unexplained and illogical notion is, it seems to me, that he finds it prophesied in Scripture. Inasmuch as the two-sided Jewish rejection, their rejection of the gospel and God's rejection of them, is prophesied in the Scripture, it needs no explanation; it is simply God's will and beyond human inquiry and conjecture.

---

[22] Cf. Loisy, *Les Actes des Apôtres,* 537.
[23] Cf. the discussion of Paul's Antioch sermon in Wilson, *Gentiles,* 222–24; cf. also Loisy, *Les Actes des Apôtres,* 541.

Luke-Acts almost says as much in its conclusion. The Lucan Paul, in Rome, presents the gospel to a representative group of Roman Jews and then throws Isa 6:9–10 at them (Acts 28:25–27):

> Go to this people and say,
> "With hearing you will hear, and you will not understand,
>   and, seeing, you will see, and you will not perceive;
> For the heart of this people has become dulled,
>   and with ears they have ill heard,
>   and their eyes they have closed,
>   lest they perceive with eyes
>   and with ears hear
> and understand in heart and turn about,
> and I will heal them."

Surely the Jews' rejection of and by God, as a people, is here foretold.[24] The result is therefore inevitable: "To the Gentiles has been sent this salvation of God; and *they* will listen" (Acts 28:28).[25] The Jews have no reply, for none is needed, as far as Luke is concerned. For him, the matter is settled; it is an open-and-shut case.

---

[24] D. R. A. Hare ("The Rejection of the Jews in the Synoptic Gospels and Acts," *AntiSemitism and the Foundations of Christianity* [ed. A. T. Davies; New York: Paulist, 1979] 37) interprets the scriptural quotation from the foregoing "schism" in the Roman Jewish congregation and concludes that the quoted Scripture is not intended to apply to all Jews. Such an interpretation, however, overlooks the climactic character of the quotation as well as the way in which this final scene in Acts and the opening scene of Jesus' ministry in Luke (Luke 4:16–30) bracket everything in between and place the bulk of Luke-Acts thus behind a minus sign—as W. Eltester ("Israel im lukanischen Werk und die Nazarethperikope," *Jesus in Nazareth* [by E. Grässer, et al.; BZNW 40; Berlin and New York: de Gruyter, 1972] 146–47) observes.

[25] That this is Luke's meaning has been seen by many authors. Especially to be noted are F. Overbeck in W. M. L. DeWette, *Kurze Erklärung der Apostelgeschichte* (4th ed. rev. by F. Overbeck; Leipzig: Hirzel, 1870) 474–80; Loisy, *Les Actes des Apôtres*, 932–39; Haenchen, "Judentum und Christentum in der Apostelgeschichte," *ZNW* 54 (1963) 183–86; and Wilson, *Gentiles*, 226–27. The discussion by Maddox, *The Purpose of Luke-Acts*, 42–46, is one of the finest on the subject. Cf. also my own study, "The Salvation of the Jews in Luke-Acts," *Luke-Acts: New Perspectives from the Society of Biblical Literature Seminar* (ed. C. H. Talbert; New York: Crossroad, 1984) 104–28. I cannot agree with Jervell (*The Unknown Paul* [Minneapolis: Augsburg, 1984] 135 and with R. C. Tannehill ("Israel in Luke-Acts: A Tragic Story," *JBL* 104 [1985] 69–85) that Luke views this inevitable rejection as a tragedy. Jervell's essay, "The Center of Scripture in Luke" (*Unknown Paul*, 122–37), has noted and accurately evaluated much of the evidence presented here. But Jervell takes the prophecies about the gospel's going from the Jews to the Gentiles to mean that "it is prophesied in Scripture that the salvation of the Gentiles will be linked to the destiny of Israel" (ibid., 134) and thus misunderstands Luke's intent.

THE VOYAGE OF DISCIPLESHIP:
NARRATIVE, CHREIA, AND CALL STORY

JAMES R. BUTTS
Le Moyne College
Syracuse, New York

1. *Bon Voyage*

Recently, A. Droge proposed a new and provocative thesis concerning the proper cultural and literary perspective from which to view the form and content of the call stories in the Synoptic gospels.[1] Much of what he suggests is convincing, and worthy of acceptance. There are, however, several inaccuracies to which attention must be brought. In addition, some aspects of his thesis are somewhat overstated and need slight modification. And finally, although he has certainly pointed future research on these stories in the proper direction, his thesis unnecessarily limits the horizons of that research.

2. *A Look Astern*

Few New Testament scholars have investigated either the form or the content of the call stories in the Synoptic tradition. And those who have done so were plagued with a certain myopia. It is either the Old Testament and Jewish traditions or it is the practices of Jesus himself which give the call story its remarkable form and character. Either call stories are all alike wherever they are found or there is no common typology at all. The choices presented by past scholarship are neglect and apologetic.

Droge intends his contribution to be a remedy for this scholarly squalor. He rightly chastises the early form critics and others[2] for giving call stories only passing consideration.[3] And he shows up for what they are

---

[1] A. Droge, "Call Stories in Greek Biographies and the Gospels," *SBL Seminar Papers, 1983* (ed. K. H. Richards; Chico, Ca.: Scholars, 1983) 245–57.

[2] R. Bultmann, *History of the Synoptic Tradition* (New York: Harper & Row, 1963) 28–29; M. Dibelius, *From Tradition to Gospel* (New York: Scribners, 1934) 44; E. Schweizer, *Lordship and Discipleship* (SBT 28; London: SCM, 1960) 11–20; W. Bieder, *Die Berufung im Neuen Testament* (AThANT 39; Zürich: Zwingli, 1961); M. Hengel, *The Charismatic Leader and His Followers* (New York: Crossroad, 1981) 19; and A. Schulz, *Nachfolgen und Nachahmen* (StANT 6; Munich: Kösel, 1962), all cited in Droge, "Call Stories," 246, nn. 7, 8, and 9.

[3] Droge, "Call Stories," 246.

the astigmatic tendencies of previous scholars to treat the call stories of
the Synoptic gospels solely in light of Jewish parallels or to treat them as
"an expression of [Jesus'] underivable 'messianic' authority."[4] It is the
inadequacy of these suggested paradigms that Droge intends to address.

One positive aspect of previous research, however, which Droge
highlights and sees no need to correct is the now long accepted observation that one of the distinguishing characteristics of call stories in the
Gospels "is that each is marked by the initiative of Jesus and the demand
for an immediate response."[5] It is, indeed, this feature which Droge calls
the "essential difference"[6] between the call stories in the Synoptic gospels and similar stories in Jewish material, including the Old Testament
and the Tannaitic literature. For example, although there are certainly
linguistic and structural similarities between Gospel call stories and
Elijah's call of Elisha, portrayed in 1 Kgs 19:19–21, this Old Testament
story differs from the Gospel narratives in that it allows Elisha to condition his following of Elijah on being granted the opportunity first to
"kiss [his] father and mother" (1 Kgs 19:20). As Droge rightly observes:

> It is just this kind of precondition that is explicitly rejected by
> Jesus in Lk 9:57–62. . . . The third saying, found only in Luke, is
> clearly reminiscent of the call of Elijah [sic]. But whereas Elijah
> permits his disciple to say farewell to his family, and even to offer
> a banquet for his friends, the call of Jesus permits no delay.[7]

3. *Charting a New Heading*

The thesis proffered by Droge can be summarized fairly under four
points. First, drawing on the work of several classics scholars,[8] Droge
thinks that in form and in content the Gospel call stories are of the same
ilk as the call stories of the Greek biographical tradition, exemplified best
by the traditions preserved in Diogenes Laertius. One example set forth
to support this first point is the story found in D. L. 2.48:

> Socrates encountered Xenophon in a narrow alley, and he
> stretched out his staff to bar the way, while he inquired where

[4] Hengel, *Charismatic Leader*, 87, cited in Droge, "Call Stories," 246, n. 9. As
examples of the dominance of Jewish parallels Droge cites Bultmann, *History*, 28
and Hengel, *Charismatic Leader*, 19 where he explicitly rules out the appropri-
ateness of analogies from Greek and Roman sources.
[5] Droge, "Call Stories," 245. Similar observations were made by A. Schlatter, *Der
Evangelist Matthäus*, 303, cited in Bultmann, *History*, 28, n. 1.
[6] Droge, "Call Stories," 250.
[7] Droge, "Call Stories," 250. For a critique of this discussion see section 6 below.
[8] O. Gigon, "Antike Erzählung über die Berufung zur Philosophie," *Museum
Helveticum* 3 (1946) 1–21; W. Schwer, "Beruf," *RAC* 2 (1954) 141–56; E. Norden,
"Antike Menschen im ringen von ihrer Berufsbestimmung," *Sitzungsberichte der
preussischen Akademie der Wissenschaften, Philosophisch-historische Klasse*
(Jahrgang 1932) XXXVII–LIII.

each kind of food was sold. When Xenophon had answered, Socrates asked another question, "Where do men become good and honorable?" But when Xenophon was puzzled, Socrates said, "Then follow me and learn." From that time on he was a disciple of Socrates.

Another example is the story about Zeno and Crates in D. L. 7.2–3:

> Zeno went up to Athens and sat down in a bookseller's shop, being then a man of thirty. As he was reading the second book of Xenophon's *Memorabilia,* he was so pleased that he inquired where men like Socrates were to be found. Just then Crates passed by and the bookseller pointed to him and said, "Follow that man." From that day on he became Crates' disciple.[9]

When these two accounts are compared with a Gospel call story, like Mark 1:16–18, certain similarities are apparent: they are chiefly anecdotal in nature; they portray an immediate, unconditional commitment of the disciple to the teacher; and this commitment entails a departure from previous life activities. In other words, the conditions and content of discipleship in the NT and non-NT call stories are understood in remarkably similar terms.

Second, these three formal and substantive commonalities are explained by Droge's rather daring suggestion that both the NT and non-NT call stories were modeled on the ancient rhetorical category of the *chreia,* and specifically those *chreiai* which are associated with the Cynic tradition of social critique and self-sufficiency. This traditional literary schema, that is, the *chreia,* which seems to have been a favorite vehicle for Cynic wit and wisdom, has provided both the formal and the substantive models for the construction of call stories wherever they are found.

Droge cites the following three texts as examples of *chreiai:*

> When someone inquired of Anaxagoras, "Have you no concern for your fatherland?" he replied, "I am greatly concerned with my fatherland," and pointed to the sky.[10]
>
> One day when Antisthenes was censured for keeping company with evil men, he replied, "Physicians attend to their patients without getting the fever themselves."[11]
>
> At Megara Diogenes saw the sheep protected by leather jackets, while the children went bare. "It's better," he said, "to be a Megarian's ram than his son."[12]

It is certainly true that the *chreia* was a popular subject of discussion in the handbooks authored by Hellenistic and Roman grammarians and

[9] Both stories are cited by Droge, "Call Stories," 251.
[10] D. L. 2.7
[11] D. L. 6.6
[12] D. L. 6.41

rhetoricians. It was used as an instructional exercise in proper and persuasive writing and speaking.[13] And there is no reason to doubt that the authors of the Gospels and the formulators of any specific segment of the Greek biographical tradition were familiar with the *chreia* and its use, especially in Cynic circles, as Droge himself suggests.[14]

The third point of the thesis is, in fact, that both the formal and substantive similarities between NT call stories and non-NT stories can best be explained by supposing that the gospel writers were exposed to the Cynic way with words and characters in their elementary education, as they learned to compose in Greek by working with *chreiai*. It is not, in other words, simply that the individual call stories of the NT and other Hellenistic biographies have been literarily modeled on *chreiai*. In addition to this formal relationship, the very understanding of discipleship as it is expressed in the call stories has been fundamentally and exclusively shaped by the gospel writers' Hellenistic rhetorical education, and specifically by their exposure to Cynic *chreia* traditions:

> The similarity, therefore, between the understanding of discipleship embodied in the gospel call stories and Cynicism is perhaps best explained in terms of Hellenistic rhetoric, rather than in terms of a common social ethos or a direct contact with Cynic philosophy.[15]

As examples which show this similarity of understanding Droge cites the following story from D. L. 6.36 about Diogenes the Cynic and the account in Luke 9:57–60.

---

[13] Droge, "Call Stories," 247–48 citing E. Ziebarth, *Aus der antiken Schule* (Bonn: Marcus und Weber, 1913) nos. 29 and 46; R. A. Pack, *The Greek and Latin Literary Texts from Greco-Roman Egypt* (Ann Arbor: University of Michigan, 1965) nos. 1985–96; F. H. Colson, "Quintilian I.9 and the 'Chreia' in Ancient Education," *Classical Review* 35 (1921) 150–54; H. I. Marrou, *A History of Education in Antiquity* (New York: Sheed and Ward, 1956) 156, 172, 174, 282; and S. F. Bonner, *Education in Ancient Rome* (Berkeley and Los Angeles: University of California, 1977) 253–54. See also now R. F. Hock and E. N. O'Neil, eds., *The Chreia in Ancient Rhetoric*. Volume I: *The Progymnasmata* (SBLTT 27; Atlanta: Scholars, 1986).

[14] Droge, "Call Stories," 248–49 citing in notes 19 and 20 M. Dibelius, *From Tradition,* 160; R. O. P. Taylor, *The Groundwork of the Gospels* (Oxford: Clarendon, 1946); R. M. Grant, *The Earliest Lives of Jesus* (New York: Harper & Row, 1961) 17–18 and 99–101; W. R. Farmer, "Notes on a Literary and Form-Critical Analysis of Some of the Synoptic Material Peculiar to Luke," *NTS* 8 (1961/62) 301–16; and V. K. Robbins, "Pronouncement Stories and Jesus' Blessing of the Children: A Rhetorical Approach," *SBL Seminar Papers, 1982* (Chico, Ca.: Scholars, 1982) 407–30, (now reprinted in *Semeia* 29 [1983] 43–74). See also James R. Butts, "The *Chreia* in the Synoptic Gospels," *BTB* 16 (1986) 132–38.

[15] Droge, "Call Stories," 257.

> Someone wanted to study philosophy under him. Diogenes gave him a fish to carry and commanded him to follow him. But the man threw it away out of shame and departed. Some time later Diogenes met him and laughed and said, "Our friendship was broken by a fish."
>
> As they were going along the road, a man said to him, "I will follow you wherever you go." And Jesus said to him, "Foxes have holes, and birds of the air have nests; but the Son of Man has nowhere to lay his head." To another he said, "Follow me." But he said, "Lord, let me first go and bury my father." But he said to him, "Leave the dead to bury their own dead; but as for you, go and proclaim the Kingdom of God."

Droge draws attention to the "decisive and paradoxical"[16] characterization of the act of becoming a disciple that these two stories embody:

> In each, an individual whose identity is unknown approaches a teacher seeking to become a disciple, and then fails to attain the goal of his quest because the cost of discipleship is too great. Although some might question the legitimacy of comparing Diogenes' requirement to "carry a fish" with Jesus' demand to "sell all," the difference is really one of degree and not kind. Both demands are radical in the sense that they require the prospective disciple to exercise complete disregard for social convention.[17]

It is not, however, that the gospel writers had direct contact with Cynic philosophy or philosophers. Nor is it that these call stories and their implicit theory of discipleship originated in a social and cultural matrix similar to that of the Cynic itinerant preachers. Rather, the explanation of this similarity in understanding, according to Droge, is that the gospel writers were exposed in their elementary education to Cynic *chreiai* and these then became both the formal and substantive model for the call stories in the Gospels.

This paradigmatic function of the *chreia* is even at work in those "call stories" which do not occur in exactly the same form as those already discussed. Droge thinks, for example, that the Lucan form of the call of the first disciples in Luke 5:1–11 and the story of "blind Bartimaeus" in Mark 10:46–52 are essentially call stories which have been expanded and elaborated with miracle story elements, although each of them has retained its original purpose and essential point of characterizing the requirements of following Jesus as a disciple. Droge's point is that this process of expansion and elaboration is also explained in the rhetoricians' discussion of the *chreia:*

[16] Droge, "Call Stories," 247.
[17] Droge, "Call Stories," 255.

> What is important to note is that in both Greek biography
> and the gospels these elaborations appear to be carried out in
> accordance with the prescriptions laid down by the rhetoricians
> regarding the elaboration *(ergasia)* of the *chreia*. In fact, the
> abbreviated style of the *chreia* tolerates many extensions without
> necessarily altering the form. The rhetoricians knew that in cer-
> tain situations *chreiai* could and should be expanded.[18]

Droge then cites from the *Progymnasmata* of Aelius Theon, a mid-first
century teacher of rhetoric in Alexandria, to show that various procedures were taught wherein the more concise form of the *chreia* was
manipulated into longer and more complicated forms.[19]

The main thrust of this third point in Droge's thesis, however, must
not be obscured. He is proposing that it is the Gospel writers' education
in the preliminary exercises in rhetoric (that is, the *progymnasmata*) that
best explains the similar understanding of discipleship that we see implied in the call stories of the NT and other Hellenistic biographies. This
proposal is quite venturesome, indeed, since it would entail a thorough
re-evaluation of the historical veracity of all that Synoptic material which
scholars like G. Theissen[20] and J. G. Gager[21] have used to delineate the
cultural milieu of early Palestinian Christianity. If Droge's thesis is sus-
tained, then this Synoptic material and its Cynic-like critique of cultural
conventions and its call to economic and social self-sufficiency could in
large part be a literary construction of a kind of golden age, an era of
perfection, uncorrupted by the concern for economic and social success,
a golden age modeled in form and in substance on material known only
from the stultifying confines of the school of rhetoric. And the ramifications of that possibility are staggering.

The fourth aspect of Droge's thesis concerns a typology of call stories
found in the Gospels and other Hellenistic biographies. There are,
according to his analysis, two types: the successful call story and the
unsuccessful call story. And each is characterized by specific and peculiar
literary developments and substantive understandings.

> In the *successful* call story the initiative comes from Jesus
> himself, whose call elicits an immediate and unconditional re-
> sponse on the part of the prospective disciple. Here the emphasis

---

[18] Droge, "Call Stories," 253.

[19] Droge, "Call Stories," 253 citing the *Progymnasmata* of Theon according to the
edition of L. Spengel, *Rhetores Graeci* (Leipzig: Teubner, 1852) 2:101–104.

[20] G. Theissen, *Sociology of Early Palestinian Christianity* (Philadelphia: Fortress,
1977) and "'Wir haben alles verlassen' (Mc. X 28): Nachfolge und soziale Ent-
wurzelung in der jüdisch-palästinischen Gesellschaft des 1. Jahrhunderts n. Ch.,"
NovT 19 (1977) 161–96.

[21] J. G. Gager, *Kingdom and Community: The Social World of Early Christianity*
(Englewood Cliffs: Prentice-Hall, 1975).

is on the miraculous nature of Jesus' call which abruptly detaches those who are called from their previous obligations. In the *unsuccessful* call story the prospective disciple approaches Jesus in an inappropriate fashion, and is summarily rebuffed by him. Here it is shown that following Jesus plunges the disciple into total lack of security, and requires a radical break with even the strongest of social conventions. Together, both types of call story stress that the act of becoming a disciple is a decisive, yet paradoxical, event.[22]

The call stories which Droge discusses are classified into these two types as follows:

Successful Call Stories	*Unsuccessful Call Stories*
Mark 1:16–18	Luke 9:57–62
Mark 1:19–20	Mark 10:17–22
D. L. 2.48	D. L. 6.36
D. L. 7.2–3	
Luke 5:1–11	
Mark 10:46–52	

The most significant difference between these two types concerns the source of the initiative to become a disciple. To paraphrase Droge: there is no such thing as successfully *volunteering* to follow Jesus or any other master teacher in the Greek biographical tradition.[23] A prior call, an immediate, unconditional response, and the willingness to sever all ties to convention are the necessary ingredients for a successful teacher-student concoction.

4. Corrections to the Course-Heading

Droge makes at least two important contributions to the venture of charting the waters of the call story. First, he brings into the currents the work of such scholars as Gigon, Norden, and Schwer[24] on the call story and discipleship in the Greek biographical tradition. Their work does, indeed, make it possible to see that there are some striking similarities between NT call stories and similar accounts in various Hellenistic biographical texts. Although their work is anywhere between 30 and 40 years old, it is obvious that the majority of NT scholars are unaware of it. The second important contribution is the fact that Droge's thesis joins and adds to the growing interest in Hellenistic rhetoric and education that has developed within the NT guild over recent years.[25] That interest

---

[22] Droge, "Call Stories," 257.
[23] Droge, "Call Stories," 246 and 254.
[24] See note 8 above.
[25] For a rather prominent example see, H. D. Betz, *Galatians: A Commmentary on*

is a fruitful development within the field and more scholars should gain an accurate and thorough knowledge of Hellenistic rhetoric in order to make the effort to analyze the NT and other Hellenistic literature from that perspective.

There are, however, several major weaknesses in Droge's thesis which unfortunately in the long run nearly outweigh its positive contributions.

First, although Droge continually implies that call stories are an important and common element in the Hellenistic biographical tradition, he actually discusses only three examples: the Socrates-Xenophon story, the Crates-Zeno account, and the Diogenes-fish tale. In addition, all these anecdotes come from only one source: Diogenes Laertius (2.48; 7.2–3; and 6.36 respectively). If there are "other examples,"[26] of such stories in the Hellenistic biographical tradition, then a simple listing in a note of the references to such stories would considerably strengthen the evidential base of the thesis, especially if those other examples appeared in some source other than Diogenes Laertius. Thus, Droge's argumentation fails to provide sufficient evidence.

Second, is it efficacious to rely primarily, if not exclusively, on post-NT sources to construct various historical and literary contexts for NT traditions and documents? Droge's thesis, as noted earlier, depends exclusively on Diogenes Laertius (199–250 CE) for actual instances of non-NT call stories. Diogenes Laertius was, of course, primarily a compiler and he did, indeed, use earlier sources. But even so, his material often comes to us at several removes from its original setting and perhaps even through several hands. Thus, the value of his information changes from passage to passage. But in all three of the examples of call stories which Droge cites from Diogenes Laertius, no previous authors are cited as sources from which Diogenes took these stories. Consequently, absolutely nothing can be said about the pre-Diogenean literary form or even substance of these accounts.

The difficulty faced by NT scholars who want to use Hellenistic biographies for NT interpretation is, of course, the relative dearth of such works stemming from the NT period itself. And although speaking of trajectories of traditions is in many instances an acceptable response to this difficulty, sometimes the use of sources is extremely fuzzy and loose. A disciplined sophistication in NT historical research that is subject to

---

Paul's Letter to the Churches in Galatia (Philadelphia: Fortress, 1979). See also V. K. Robbins, "Picking Up the Fragments: From Crossan's Analysis to Rhetorical Analysis," *Foundations and Facets Forum* 1, 2 (1985) 31–64; and most interestingly G. A. Kennedy, *New Testament Interpretation Through Rhetorical Criticism* (Chapel Hill and London: University of North Carolina, 1984).

[26] Droge, "Call Stories," 251.

[27] See note 22 above.

the control of a rigourous consideration of such pedantic questions as dates and sources is needed. Such an approach is missing from Droge's proposal and thus his use of evidence borders on the anachronistic.

Third, in spite of the apparent familiarity with Theon, Droge betrays an inaccurate and incomplete knowledge of the *chreia* discussions in the *progymnasmata*. There are four aspects of his treatment of this material that need correction and/or supplementation.

(1) It is true that in the original order of Theon's *Progymnasmata* the chapter on the *chreia* was placed first.[28] But to say that Theon "tells us that the *chreia* began the standard list of rhetorical *progymnasmata*"[29] tends to overstate the evidence in two ways: first, it implies that Theon in this place refers to a traditional order for these exercises, whereas actually all this text does is show that *Theon* is placing the *chreia* at the head of the list; and second, Droge's statement implies that there existed a standard list of *progymnasmata*, whereas actually there is no evidence to support such a statement. On one hand, we have no handbooks of *progymnasmata* prior to Theon, although they surely existed since Theon himself refers to them when he is trying to justify the fact that in several ways he departs from them.[30] Thus, in terms of his predecessors it is difficult to use Theon as any kind of standard. On the other hand, those handbooks which come after Theon, namely, Pseudo-Hermogenes[31] and Aphthonius[32] all agree that the *chreia* is *not* the first exercise. Rather, it is preceded by the fable and the narrative. Thus, to say that the position of the *chreia* in the curriculum of the first few centuries CE was "firmly fixed"[33] no doubt goes too far.

(2) Contrary to what Droge implies,[34] Theon does not include in his *Progymnasmata* a separate discussion of the *gnome* or maxim. It is not until Pseudo-Hermogenes and Aphthonius that a separate chapter on the

---

[28] On the question of the original order of the chapters in Theon see I. Lana, *I Progimnasmi di Elio Teone*. Volume Primo: *La Storia des Testo* (Torino: Universita di Torino, 1959) 156–72; and now most recently James R. Butts, *The Progymnasmata of Theon: A New Text with Translation and Commentary* (unpublished Ph. D. dissertation, Claremont Graduate School, 1986), forthcoming.

[29] Droge, "Call Stories," 248.

[30] See Theon I, 18–24 ([Butts] = 59, 18–25 [Spengel]).

[31] For the full text of Pseudo-Hermogenes' *Progymnasmata* see H. Rabe, *Hermogenes Opera* (Leipzig: Teubner, 1913) 1–27; and for an introduction, translation, and commentary on Pseudo-Hermogenes' chapter on the *chreia* see B. Mack and E. N. O'Neil, "The Chreia Discussion of Hermogenes of Tarsus," in *The Chreia in Ancient Rhetoric*, 155–81.

[32] For the full text of Aphthonius' *Progymnasmata* see H. Rabe, *Aphthonii Progymnasmata* (Leipzig: Teubner, 1926); and for an introduction, translation, and commentary on Aphthonius' chapter on the *chreia* see James R. Butts and R. F. Hock, "The Chreia Discussion of Aphthonius of Antioch," in *The Chreia in Ancient Rhetoric*, 211–34.

[33] Droge, "Call Stories," 248.

[34] Droge, "Call Stories," 248, note 17.

maxim appears in the *progymnasmata*. There are indeed numerous other differences between the content of Theon's handbook and those of his successors. For example, Pseudo-Hermogenes, Aphthonius, and Nicolaus of Myra[35] all have separate chapters discussing the procedures of refutation and confirmation. Theon, on the other hand, includes this discussion in his chapter of the narrative.[36] The result is, therefore, that it is not entirely accurate to say that there was a standard list of *progymnasmata*.

(3) Droge cites the Greek text of Theon's definition of the *chreia* in note 11 on page 247 and translates it on page 248 as follows: the *chreia* is "a concise and pointed account of something said or done, attributed to some particular person."[37] There are several problems involved here. Does the Greek phrase *met' eustochias* modify *apophasis hē praksis*, as Droge translates it, or does that phrase modify the participle *anapheromenē* and thus describe a quality of the attribution (namely, its aptness) rather than a quality of the statement or action (namely, their pointedness)? Judging by the syntactical placement of the prepositional phrase as well as the comparison of the definitions in the later handbooks, it is much more likely that the phrase functions adverbally in modification of the participle rather than adjectivally in modification of the two nouns.[38] Thus, a more accurate translation of Theon's definition of the *chreia* would be as follows: "A *chreia* is a concise statement or action which is attributed with aptness," etc.

Another problem with Droge's translation of Theon's definition of the *chreia* is his use of the word "account," for it implies that Theon's definition of the *chreia* says that the statement or action attributed to the character has a narrative framework of some sort. It is not just a statement or an action; it is an account of a statement or action. Actually, according to Theon's definition, understood correctly, a *chreia* does not need a narrative framework to be a *chreia*. It can be simply an attributed statement or action. In other words, Theon would consider the following to be a *chreia:* "Isocrates said 'The roots of education are bitter, but its fruits are sweet.'"

[35] For the full text of Nicolaus' *Progymnasmata* see J. Felten, *Nicolai Progymnasmata* (Leipzig: Teubner, 1913); and for an introduction, translation, and commentary on his *chreia* chapter see L. Grabbe and R. F. Hock, "The Chreia Discussion of Nicolaus of Myra," in *The Chreia in Ancient Rhetoric*, 237–69.

[36] For the fullest discussion of the proper placement of this material in Theon's *Progymnasmata* see James R. Butts, *The Progymnasmata of Theon*, forthcoming. Very helpful also is I. Lana, *I Progimnasmi*, 156–58.

[37] The Greek is as follows: *Chreia esti suntomos apophasis hē praksis met' eustochias anapheromenē eis ti hōrismenon prosōpon hē analoguon prosōpon.*

[38] For a full discussion of this rather pedantic issue see James R. Butts, *The Progymnasmata of Theon*, forthcoming.

Of course, based on the examples Theon uses in the rest of his chapter, statements or actions with a narrative framework attributed to a specified character are also *chreiai*, and admittedly those types of stories are more common and more important, especially when it comes to discussing the call stories. But a correct understanding of Theon's definition of the *chreia* and the recognition of the tension which exists between this definition and the materials used to illustrate it prevents the making of unsupportable distinctions among ancient literary categories, distinctions which in the long run do nothing more than obscure the reconstruction of the rhetorical tradition and its application to the NT. For example, Droge asserts that the *apophthegma* is distinct from the *chreia* because the *apophthegma* is "a terse, pointed saying of a particular person *without* a narrative framework."[39] Whether or not there is any difference between the *apophthegma* and the *chreia* as ancient literary categories is still open for debate. But one thing is certain: they do not differ in terms of the presence or absence of a narrative framework, as a correct understanding of Theon's definition of the *chreia* shows.

(4) On page 253 Droge states that the rhetorical exercise procedure which he is about to discuss is what the rhetoricians called the *ergasia* or elaboration.[40] Actually, the exercise which he discusses was called the *ekteinosis*, or expansion, and it occurs only in Theon. There was, indeed, an exercise procedure called *ergasia*, but it is not at all similar to Theon's *ekteinosis* exercise.[41] Consequently, Droge's statement that some of the Gospel call stories appear to have been lengthened "in accordance with the prescriptions laid down by the rhetoricians regarding the elaboration (*ergasia*) of the *chreia*"[42] either means that he is not aware of the difference between the exercise to which he refers (namely, the *ergasia*) and the exercise he actually discusses (namely, the *ekteinosis*); or it is simply an unintentional misstatement. If the latter, then perhaps what he meant to say was that this lengthening was carried out in accordance with the prescriptions laid down by Theon regarding the *ekteinosis*, or expansion of the *chreia*. But if that is what he meant, then his statement inaccurately implies that Theon lays down certain rules that are to govern the expansion. Actually, Theon does not explain at all the process of expansion. He simply does an expansion and leaves it to the reader to figure out what is involved. But Droge does not analyze Theon's expansion of the Epameinondas *chreia* and consequently makes no attempt to explicate precisely how Theon's expansion is a "good analogy"[43] to stories

---

[39] Droge, "Call Stores," 247, note 11.
[40] See notes 18 and 19 above.
[41] On the *ergasia* see Pseudo-Hermogenes 7, 10-8, 11 (Rabe) and Aphthonius 4, 12-6, 19 (Rabe).
[42] Droge, "Call Stories," 253 and see note 21 above.
[43] Droge, "Call Stories," 253.

in Mark and Luke. If such an analysis and explication had been undertaken, it would have become apparent that there are some striking
differences between Mark 10:46–52 and Luke 5:1–11, on one hand, and
Theon's Epameinondas expansion, on the other. Without going into all of
the details, the primary difference, which Droge himself mentions in
passing,[44] is that Mark and Luke have attempted to transform call stories
into miracle stories by adding a number of miracle story elements.
Theon's Epameinondas expansion has nothing in it which comes anywhere close to such an undertaking. Is the combination of a *chreia* and
another type of material the kind of procedure commonly undertaken
when one "expands" a *chreia*? This question should be investigated
before the claim is made that Mark and Luke in these two places are
expanding *chreiai*.[45]

A related problem has to do with the list of exercises approved by
Theon for use on the *chreia* which Droge quotes on page 253. This list
contains a series of technical rhetorical, literary, and grammatical terms,
the meanings of which Droge's translation either misses entirely or
obscures. For example, the second exercise, which Droge labels "varying," in Greek is called *klisis* and means, of course, the "inflexion" of a
chreia through the three grammatical numbers (that is, singular, plural,
and dual) and through the five grammatical cases. The translation "varying" obscures the technical meaning of the word. Or again: the seventh
and eighth exercises, which Droge labels to "construct" and "recon-
struct" respectively, are in Greek *anaskeuē* and *kataskeuē* which mean
respectively the "refutation" and "confirmation" of the *chreia* understood
as a thesis argued on the basis of commonplace rhetorical arguments, the
so-called *koinoi topoi*. Droge's translations entirely miss the point.

The fourth area in which Droge's thesis needs supplementation and
correction is his conclusion that the understanding of discipleship evidenced in the call stories in the NT and in the Cynic biographical
tradition has been exclusively shaped by the exposure of the writers to
chreiai from the Cynic tradition during their elementary education.[46]
Even if the *chreia* could be proved to be the controlling narrative
paradigm for the call stories,[47] the notion that the *chreia's* use in
Hellenistic education was the fundamental influence in the conceptualization of the conditions and content of following Jesus overstates
the case and is finally not supported by the evidence. On one hand, how
could it be proven that the gospel writers learned of the *chreia* in school?

---

[44] Droge, "Call Stories," 252.
[45] The question of what precisely is going on in Mark 10:46–52 and Luke 5:1–11 is
    addressed below in section 6.
[46] Droge, "Call Stories," 257; and see the discussion in section 3 above.
[47] See the discussion in section 6.

As the Tacitus text cited by Droge himself shows,[48] going to school was not necessary for learning the finer points of rhetorical practice:

> All these rules of the rhetoricians are common property and there is scarcely a bystander in the crowd who, if not fully instructed, has not at least been initiated into the rudiments of culture" (*Dialogus de oratoribus* 19).

On the other hand, this notion that the writers' Hellenistic educational experience is the sole factor responsible for the way they handle the call stories and discipleship is unnecessarily reductionistic. To dismiss the possibility of the influence of a common social ethos and put all the eggs in the basket of Hellenistic rhetoric weakens the overall thesis rather than strengthening it.

5. *Inventorying the Cargo*

In spite of the obvious similarities that do indeed exist among the various stories that Droge discusses, the fact is that there are also considerable differences which he fails to notice, much less examine at any length. And in several cases these divergences seriously undermine the tenability of his typology.[49]

The story in D. L. 7.2–3 about Zeno and Crates, for example, that Droge labels a "successful call story," is an anecdote that deals with how a person, Zeno, became a disciple of another person, Crates. And in this respect it is of the same ilk as the other stories labeled "successful call stories" by Droge. But in the Zeno-Crates story, Crates does not *call* Zeno to be his disciple. Rather, some anonymous bookseller in effect commissions Zeno to follow Crates *after Zeno makes a preliminary inquiry*. To name such a story a "call story," and thus class it alongside Mark 1:16–18 as the same type of account, seems to be a serious misnomer. A more accurate label would be something like "a discipleship quest story."

There is, however, more involved here than simply the question of an appropriate label. This story provides a glimpse of a different understanding of how a person can become a follower of another person. In the Zeno-Crates story the potential disciple is engaged in some appropriate preparatory endeavor. (Zeno is reading Xenophon's *Memorabilia*.) On that basis he seeks out some appropriate paradigmatic figure. (Zeno inquires where men like Socrates can be found.) In this type of "successful discipleship quest story" the potential disciple is the central character and the teacher does not figure at all prominently in it. Consequently, there is involved here a rather distinct conception of the process

---

[48] Droge, "Call Stories," 248, note 17.
[49] See the discussion in section 3 above.

of becoming attached to a teacher, a conception which does not revolve around the disruptive word of the teacher's call.

But before too much is made of this variation, it may be important to notice that this Zeno-Crates story is told by Diogenes Laertius in his chapter on Zeno and not in his discussion of Crates. Given that context it might seem reasonable that Zeno would be the central character and that Crates would be mentioned only in so far as necessary. In other words, in considering the dynamics of these small anecdotal units about becoming or gathering disciples, paying attention to the larger literary context may be just as important as a close analysis of the unit itself.

Droge's "unsuccessful call story" category also suffers from the problem of having a gap between the precise content of the stories in it and the meaning of the label. In fact, the accounts classed by Droge into this type (namely, Luke 9:57–62; Mark 10:17–22; and D. L. 6.36) are extremely variegated.

Take Luke 9:57–62 for example. In this text, as is quite well known, there are actually a series of encounters between Jesus and prospective followers. In the first encounter (In Luke 9:57–58) a man (Matthew says a scribe) declares his intention to follow Jesus, but is rebuked by Jesus with a statement that points out "the dangers the life of discipleship entails."[50] This story is more properly understood as an "unsuccessful discipleship quest story" since it embodies the same dynamics as the Zeno-Crates story but with the opposite result. (See the discussion at the beginning of this section.) The third encounter in Luke 9:61–62 is of the same type. These accounts depict a prospective disciple approaching a teacher in order to become a follower of that teacher and end with the would-be disciple being rebuffed by the teacher. There is, in other words, no initiative on the part of the teacher; that is to say, there is no call. Thus, to label these accounts "unsuccessful call stories" is to give to them a plot movement that is altogether absent from them. An "unsuccessful call story" would be an anecdote in which a teacher attempts to call someone to be a disciple and for some reason is unsuccessful in that attempt.[51] The story in Luke 9:59–60 is just such an anecdote:

> To another [Jesus] said, "Follow me." But he said, "Lord, let me first go and bury my father." But [Jesus] said to him, "Leave the dead to bury their own dead; but as for you, go and proclaim the Kingdom of God."

[50] Droge, "Call Stories," 254.

[51] Notice that this definition of the unsuccessful call story differs from the working definition of Droge. For Droge one of the distinguishing marks of the unsuccessful call story is the lack of a prior call by the teacher and instead the presence of an attempt to volunteer to become a disciple. A more accurate definition of the unsuccessful *call* story is to say that the teacher's attempt to call a person is unsuccessful.

Here Jesus attempts to call this man to be a disciple, but is unsuccessful. The man allows "the requirement of burying one's father, which was the most basic of all social and religious duties, [to] come between Jesus and his disciple."[52] Thus, Jesus is unsuccessful in his attempt to call this man to be his follower.

With respect to Mark 10:17–22 and D. L. 6.36, two stories which Droge also labels "unsuccessful call stories," it would be more accurate to admit that these two accounts are hybrids of the "unsuccessful call story" and the "unsuccessful discipleship quest story." In each one the teacher either implicitly or explicitly attempts to call someone to become a disciple. (See Mark 10:21 and the statement in D. L. 6.36 that Diogenes "commanded him to follow him.") But for various reasons that attempt meets resistance and ultimately fails. (See Mark 10:22 and the statement in D. L. 6.36 that the man "departed.") Therefore, these two accounts have the features of "unsuccessful call stories."

On the other hand, each of the anecdotes begins by depicting or referring to the fact that someone approaches the teacher seeking to become a disciple, although in the Marcan story this purpose of the rich man is not stated explicitly. (See Mark 10:17, 20 and the statement in D. L. 6.36 that "someone wanted to study philosophy under him.") Again, since the stories end with the prospective follower failing to attach himself to the teacher, they exhibit the primary characteristic of the "unsuccessful discipleship quest story." Consequently, the most accurate way to classify these two accounts is as hybrids, with the discipleship quest motif recognized as being most prominent.

There is involved here again a consequence that goes beyond the mere consideration of an approriate label. By treating such divergent stories under the same rubric, Droge obscures a rich and variegated congeries of ways to formulate the establishment and non-establishment of the teacher-disciple relationship. A typology which does justice to the multiplicity discovered in only these few stories would look something like the following:

Successful Call Stories	*Unsuccessful Call Stories*
Mark 1:16–18	Luke 9:59–60
Mark 1:19–20	
D. L. 2.48	
Luke 5:1–11	

Successful Discipleship Quests	*Unsuccessful Discipleship Quests*
D. L. 7.2–3	Luke 9:61–62
Mark 10:46–52	Luke 9:57–58

Hybrids
Unsuccessful Discipleship Quests/Unsuccessful Call Stories
Mark 10:17–22
D. L. 6.36

Consequently, the situation with regard to the variety of types of stories about calling to and questing for discipleship is recognized as the complex and rich tradition that it is. Before any final conclusions are drawn, however, a comprehensive search through the literature of the Hellenistic period must be undertaken. It is very dangerous to undertake the development of a typology, much less the task of analysis, on the basis of merely eight NT stories and three non-NT anecdotes.

6. *Beyond the Present Anchorage*

Droge's goal is to show "that, in the case of the gospel call stories, not only has a standard form been taken over (viz. the *chreia*) but also a specific content (viz. Cynic conceptions of discipleship)."[53] The similarity between the radical criticism of social convention embodied in some of the Gospel call and discipleship quest stories (for example, Luke 9:57–62) and the Cynic ideal of economic and social self-sufficiency can be taken as one of the givens of NT scholarship today.[54] Consequently, there is no quarrel with the second part of Droge's thesis. In fact, Droge himself provides enough evidence and argues the point sufficiently to carry it: in some call and discipleship quest stories following Jesus looks very much like living as a Cynic, and in all the NT texts "the act of becoming a disciple is a decisive, yet paradoxical, event,"[55] in which the call of Jesus permits no delay.

It is important, however, to recognize that such authoritative "calling" is not unknown in Jewish tradition. Droge himself refers to "some analogies in Jewish wisdom literature,"[56] and such stories as the commissioning of Saul in 1 Sam 11:5–7 also seem to incarnate a radical demand for immediate response similar to that found in the call stories of the Synoptic gospels. Although it is certainly an exaggeration, and is thus in essence incorrect, Hengel's statement that "in the last analysis only the call of the OT prophets by the God of Israel himself is a genuine analogy"[57] deserves further exploration. For example, perhaps Luke 9:61–62 is a midrashic reworking of 2 Kgs 19:19–21 in light of the classical OT prophetic tradition in which operates the authoritative call of Yahweh that cannot be delayed. The impetus for such a reworking could then be identified as familiarity with the radical demands of Cynic discipleship and the desire to portray Jesus as authoritative in a way that encompasses both of these important and socially relevant paradigms. The point is that future research must not fall victim to and continue the myopic and

---

[52] Droge, "Call Stories," 254.
[53] Droge, "Call Stories," 251.
[54] See, for example, G. Theissen, *Sociology of Early Palestinian Christianity.*
[55] Droge, "Call Stories," 257.
[56] Droge, "Call Stories," 250, n. 24.
[57] See M. Hengel, *Charismatic Leader*, 87.

astigmatic approaches of the past. Droge has performed the valuable task of openning the uncharted coast line of Hellenistic biographical traditions of calls to and quests for discipleship. This new two dimensional map must not be allowed to replace the old two dimensional map of the call story.

Droge fails, however, to show convincingly that call stories and discipleship quest stories are *chreiai*. In fact, he never actually argues the point, being content rather to assert the existence of "obvious" affinities between them. For example, he declares that the call story, rather than being an *apophthegma*, is "closer to the ancient rhetorical category of the *chreia*."[58] Then he goes on to adduce three *chreiai* from Diogenes Laertius, to discuss (incorrectly) the role of the *chreia* in Hellenistic education, and to cite Papias' description of Mark which he uses as a bridge to suggest that early Christians collected and created *chreiai* of Jesus.[59] In the next section of his article (pp. 249–51), Droge makes the point that OT call stories cannot explain the demand for immediate response so prevalent in the NT call stories (but see the discussion at the beginning of this section) and then sets forth the hypothesis that Greek call stories can account for this element. Next, two texts from Diogenes Laertius are cited (namely, the Socrates-Xenophon call story and the Zeno-Crates discipleship quest story) and these texts are then placed alongside Mark 1:16–18. Droge asserts at that point that "each story is cast in the form of a *chreia*."[60] What is obviously lacking is an analysis of these call and discipleship quest stories, detailing exactly how each of them has the form of a *chreia*.[61]

Although there are certainly some obvious elements shared by the story in Mark 1:16–18, the Socrates-Xenophon story, the Zeno-Crates account, and the standard *chreia*,[62] there are also some differences which, if noted, can provide enough clues for the proper understanding of the literary structure of these stories. For example, call stories and most discipleship quest stories (cf. Mark 1:16–18; D. L. 7.2–3; and Luke 5:1–11) have after the climactic saying a little note which indicates whether the prospective disciple has been successfully attached to the teacher. (N. B.: Mark 1:18; Mark 1:20; D. L. 2.48; 7.2–3; Mark 10:22; Mark 10:52; and Luke 5:11.) Does not the presence of this tag line

---

[58] Droge, "Call Stories," 247.

[59] Droge, "Call Stories," 247–49. See also James R. Butts, "The *Chreia* in the Synoptic Tradition."

[60] Droge, "Call Stories," 251.

[61] The kind of analysis which is called for is explempified by Charles J. Reedy, "Rhetorical Concerns and Argumentative Techniques in Matthean Pronouncement Stories, *SBL Seminar Papers, 1983*, 219–22.

[62] All these anecdotes share, for example, very brief narrative settings and pithy, poignant pronouncements.

distinguish call and discipleship quest stories from *chreiai* which *never* have material following the climactic statement or action? How can the presence of this last line be explained if the controlling literary paradigm is the *chreia*? It certainly is integral to the story and does not betray any of those telltale *aporiai* which NT scholars readily take as evidence of secondary redaction. A call story or a discipleship quest story would be seriously deformed without some indication of the success or failure of the call or quest.[63] But the *chreia* does not depend upon the narrational explication of the effect of its climactic statement or action. In fact, no *chreia* ever gives any indication how the climactic pronouncement or action effected the questioner or any other character in the story.

This difference at least raises a doubt about whether the *chreia* was the literary model upon which the call and quest stories were structured. In fact, the best explanation for this difference between call/quest stories and *chreiai* is that the story-telling model being employed in the call/quest stories is that of what the rhetors called the *diegesis* or *diegema*, (i.e., the *narrative*), which is itself the subject of another one of the chapters in the *progymnasmata*.[64]

The *narrative*, according to Theon, "is an explanatory account of incidents as they have occurred or as if they have occurred" (V, 2–3 Butts). And Theon discusses at great length the fact that when writing a *narrative* it is important to include the information that leads up to the central incident that is the subject of the *narrative, as well as those things which happened after this central incident*.[65] All three narrative moments are integral to the *narrative*. The *chreia*, on the other hand, even in an expanded form finds its completion in the climactic statement or action and does not need to mention what happened after the central, climactic event.

These two forms (that is, the *narrative* and the *chreia*) represent two distinct models of story-telling. And by noting only one seemingly innocuous difference between the form of the *chreia* and the form of the call/quest stories, it is possible to suggest that the *chreia* may not have provided the primary literary schema upon which the call/quest stories were modeled. Rather, the controlling literary paradigm seems to have been the *narrative*.

There are several other observations which point in the same direc-

---

[63] This observation is the most serious difficulty involved in setting the anecdotes contained in Luke 9:57–62 alongside such texts as Mark 1:16–18. The encounters in Luke 9 do not give any explicit information about the success or failure of the calls to and quests for discipleship which are depicted there. Their unsuccessful outcome must be implied from the context.

[64] See for example Theon chapter V (Butts); Hermogenes chapter 2 (Rabe); and Aphthonius chapter 2 (Rabe).

[65] See Theon V, 239-70 (Butts = 86, 7-87, 12 Spengel).

tion. For example, in the Socrates-Xenophon story in D. L. 2.48 there is at least an allusion to the typical Socratic chain-questioning which ends with Socrates' question addressed to Xenophon about good and honorable men, a question which leads to Xenophon's puzzlement and eventually to his call to follow Socrates. If this story had been modeled on the *chreia* form, it would have been Xenophon who asked Socrates about where to find good and honorable men, since that would have set the stage for some climactic pronouncement from Socrates, such as "Follow me and learn."

Another example comes from the Zeno-Crates story in D. L. 7.2–3. It is very doubtful that this anecdote would have been recognized as a *chreia* by Hellenistic authors since Crates, who is the paradigmatic figure here, should utter the climactic statement if this story were following the model of the *chreia*. Actually, Crates neither says nor does anything and figures only peripherally in the story. Such a role is permissable when telling a *narrative*, but never so when recounting a *chreia*.

Therefore, the call stories of the Synoptic gospels and other Hellenistic biographies are most accurately understood to be what the rhetors called *narratives*. As *narratives*, the call/quest stories contain the required three-part development of the plot line (that is, telling what happened before, during, and after the central, climactic event) and they exhibit the relatively free manipulation of characters allowed in *narratives* (that is, the paradigmatic figure need not always be the central character). Theon and his cohorts would have easily recognized such biographical call/quest stories as *narratives*.

It is also very likely that the form of Mark 10:46–52 and Luke 5:1–11 is controlled, not by the *expansion* of *chreiai*, as Droge argues (see section 4 above), but rather by another rhetorical procedure applied by the teachers of rhetoric to the *narrative*. This procedure Theon calls *sumplekein*, "to combine," and defines it as follows: "To combine a narrative with a narrative is when we attempt to narrate two or even more narratives at the same time" (V, 427–428 Butts).[66] Theon also cites for us two examples from the *Panegyricus* of Isocrates: paragraphs 54ff. and 68ff. A little earlier in his *Progymnasmata* Theon classifies *narratives* into two types: the *pragmatikē diēgēsis* and the *mythikē diēgēsis;* that is, the *factual narrative* and the *mythical narrative*, respectively. The latter category refers to stories that are judged by various criteria to be "false according to nature," as one of the later commentators on Theon put it.[67]

---

[66] The Greek is: *Diēgēsis de diēgēsei sumplekein estin hotan duo diēgēseis hē kai pleious hama diēgeisthai epicheiromen.* See Theon V, 427–28 ([Butts] = 92, 24–25 [Spengel]).

[67] John of Sardes 16, 23–24. The Greek is: *kai mythika men legetai ta kata phusin onta pseudē.* For the critical text of Sardes see H. Rabe, *Ioannes Sardianus— Commentarium in Aphthonium* (Leipzig: Teubner, 1928).

Such stories listed by Theon as belonging to this category include the old
Lydian legend about the ring which gave to Gyges the power of invis-
ibility and through which he gained his kingdom (Plato, *Rep.* 359D–
360A), the myth about the birth of Love from the union of Resource and
Poverty (Plato, *Smp.* 203B); the legend of Er's journey to and return from
"the world beyond" (Plato, *Rep.* 614A–621B); and the story about
Seilenos (Theopompus, *Philip* VIII). These *mythical narratives* are those
"told by the poets and historians about gods and heroes" (Theon, V, 506–
507 Butts = 95, 4–5 [Spengel]) and would in all likelihood include those
accounts in the Synoptic tradition commonly identified as miracle stories, although none of the examples listed by Theon are technically
considered such.

Even though this thesis would have to be tested by a search through
the contemporaneous literatures, it seems altogether likely that the
longer call story in Luke 5:1–11 and the discipleship quest story in Mark
10:46–52 are examples of the combination of two types of *narratives*. In
Luke 5:1–11 two call stories (taken from Mark 1:16–20), which would be
pragmatikai narratives, are combined with a miracle story (similar to the
later variant in John 21:1–14[68]), which would be a *mythikē narrative*. In
Mark 10:46–52 a *mythikē narrative* (that is, a miracle story) has had layed
over it several elements characteristic of the successful discipleship quest
story (for example, the initiative shown by the prospective disciple in vv
47, 48, 51 and the concluding note in v 52 on the success of the quest).
The discipleship quest story is typologically a *pragmatikē narrative*.[69]

A thorough and accurate knowledge of ancient rhetoric can serve
quite well the endeavor to understand the formation of the literary
deposits of early Christianity. In particular, the call/quest stories of the
Gospels and other Hellenistic biographies can be perceived in their

---

[68] See Bultmann, *History of Synoptic Tradition,* 217–18, 230, 304.

[69] To classify a discipleship quest story as a *pragmatikē narrative*, (that is, a "factual
narrative") does not imply anything about its historical veracity. The problem is
one of translation. "Factual narratives" actually gives an incorrect impression;
namely, that the most important aspect of these narratives is that they actually
happened, whereas it is more accurate to say that the most important aspect is that
they are told as having occurred strictly on the plane of history, as can be seen
from the texts Theon cites as examples of this type of narrative, texts which clearly
include numerous legendary elements: the story of Cylon's attempt to overthrow
the government of Athens, and his resulting arrest and execution (Hdt V. 71 and
Thuc I.126); the story of the founding of Amphilocian Argos (Thuc II.68); the story
of Cleobis and Biton (Hdt I.31); the story related by Demosthenes about
Aeschines' encountering some Olynthian captives (De F. Leg. 305–06); and the
now lost story of Daedalus' journey to Sicily (Ephorus, *Hist* VII and Philistus, *Hist*
I). English seems to lack a word which describes accurately all these stories as
pragmatikē. Nevertheless, Bultmann's observation that such stories as Mark 1:16–
20 are "ideal scenes" (*History of the Synoptic Tradition,* 28) is just as accurate in
reference to a *pragmatikē narrative* like Mark 10:46–52.

proper literary and social matrices. They exhibit a content which springs from a social context similar in essence to that radical Cynic imagination which was preserved in abundance by various authors in the form of *chreiai*. And they are structured literarily on that story-telling paradigm which the rhetors called the *diēgēsis*.

OBDURACY AND THE LORD'S SERVANT: SOME OBSERVATIONS ON THE USE OF THE OLD TESTAMENT IN THE FOURTH GOSPEL

CRAIG A. EVANS
Trinity Western University
Langley, British Columbia

Introduction

In recent years there has been an increase of interest in the question of how the Jewish scriptures were understood and employed in Johannine tradition. The purpose of this study is to review some of the more significant trends in scholarship and to explore the possibility of the need for a reassessment of John and the Old Testament in general and, more specifically, to explore the possible need to reassess our understanding of the extent to which Isaiah's Servant Songs may have influenced the fourth gospel. The study is divided into three parts. The first part briefly looks at the broader question of John and the Old Testament, particularly with reference to his quotation formulas. The second part reviews the prominence of Isaiah in the gospel, while the third part examines the specific theme of obduracy and the Lord's Servant.

I. The Fourth Gospel and the Old Testament

More than 60 years ago A. Faure thought that the various quotation formulas in the fourth gospel provided clues as to the existence and extent of various written sources utilized by the evangelist in composing his gospel.[1] In response to Faure's these F. Smend argued that the quotation formulas reveal neither the presence nor the parameters of literary sources in John.[2] Although the quest for discovering written sources underlying the fourth gospel has gone on virtually unabated,[3]

---

[1] A. Faure, "Die alttestamentlichen Zitate im 4. Evangelium und die Quellenscheidungshypothese," ZNW 21 (1922) 99–121.

[2] F. Smend, "Die Behandlung alttestamentlicher Zitate als Ausgangspunkt der Quellenscheidung im 4. Evangelium," ZNW 24 (1925) 147–150.

[3] R. Bultmann (*The Gospel of John: A Commentary* [Philadelphia: Westminster, 1971]) believed that he had discovered three written sources underlying John: (1) a "signs" source, (2) a gnostic discourse source, and (3) a passion source. The following scholars accept only the "signs" source: E. Schweizer, *Ego Eimi* (Göttingen: Vandenhoeck & Ruprecht, 1965) and W. Nicol, *The Semeia in the Fourth*

insufficient attention has been paid to the Johannine quotation formulas.[4]

However, the quotations themselves have not been ignored. About 20 years ago E. Freed argued that the fourth evangelist's quotations are not derived directly from any one of the various Old Testament versions available in the first century, but are derived secondarily from the Synoptic gospels.[5] Freed's conclusion is problematic, for the question of John's relationship to the Synoptics is far from settled.[6] Freed's approach also leaves the interpreter wondering to what extent the fourth evangelist was capable of independent and original usage of the Old Testament. Surely there is more to the presence of the Old Testament in the fourth

---

Gospel: Tradition and Redaction (NovTSup 32; Leiden: Brill, 1972). R. T. Fortna (*The Gospel of Signs: A Reconstruction of the Narrative Source Underlying the Fourth Gospel* [SNTSMS 11; Cambridge: University Press, 1970]) attempted to show that the "signs" source was really a "signs gospel" that included a passion account as well as several signs. Fortna's thesis has been challenged by several scholars who doubt that John's "signs" source ever included a passion account. See J. M. Robinson, "The Johannine Trajectory," in *Trajectories through Early Christianity* (with H. Koester; Philadelphia: Fortress, 1971) 232–268; *idem*, review of Fortna (*Gospel of Signs*) in *JAAR* 39 (1971) 339–348; and reviews by M. Rissi, *Interp* 25 (1971) 372–373 and R. Kysar, *Perspective* 11 (1970) 334–336. Though not in reference to Fortna, Schweizer (p. iv) expresses doubt that there were any sources beyond a signs source underlying the first half of the gospel.

[4] See N. J. Young, "Bultmann's View of the Old Testament," *SJT* 19 (1966) 269–279.

[5] E. Freed, *Old Testament Quotations in the Gospel of John* (Leiden: Brill, 1965).

[6] Most of the attention has focussed recently on John's relationship to the Gospel of Mark. Currently there are three basic positions: (1) John knew and used Mark as a literary source, a position advocated by J. R. Donahue, *Are You the Christ? The Trial Narrative in the Gospel of Mark* (SBLDS 10; Missoula: Scholars, 1973) 58–63 and N. Perrin, *The New Testament: An Introduction* (New York: Harcourt, Brace, Jovanovich, 1974) 229; B. de Solage (*Jean et les Synoptiques* [Leiden: Brill, 1979]) has attempted to argue that John knew all three Synoptics, but did not utilize them as sources. (2) John and Mark utilized a common source, a position supported by A. B. Kolenkow, "Healing Controversy as a Tie between Miracle and Passion Material for a Proto-Gospel," *JBL* 95 (1976) 623–638 and R. T. Fortna, "Jesus and Peter at the High Priest's House: A Test Case for the Question of the Relation between Mark's and John's Gospels," *NTS* 24 (1978) 371–383. (3) John and Mark are literarily independent, a position supported by Bultmann and Robinson ("Johannine Trajectory," 241, 266–268) and recently by this writer in "'Peter Warming Himself': The Problem of an Editorial 'Seam'," *JBL* 101 (1982) 245–249. See also the studies by D. M. Smith, "John 12:12ff. and the Question of John's Use of the Synoptics," *JBL* 82 (1963) 58–64; "The Sources of the Gospel of John: An Assessment of the Present State of the Problem," *NTS* 10 (1964) 336–351; "John and the Synoptics: Some Dimensions of the Problem," *NTS* 26 (1980) 425–444; and "John and the Synoptics," *Bib* 63 (1982) 102–113. Many of these studies have been reprinted in D. M. Smith, *Johannine Christianity: Essays on Its Setting, Sources, and Theology* (Columbia: University of South Carolina, 1984). Smith finds no compelling evidence to suggest that John was dependent upon Mark, but he does not rule out the possibility that the fourth evangelist may have been aware of the Synoptics.

gospel than the proposal that it was derived secondarily from the Synoptics. More recently G. Reim has argued that except for the three quotations from Psalm 69 (cf. John 12:17; 15:25; 19:28) the fourth evangelist acquired all of his Old Testament texts from his various written sources.[7] Unfortunately, his thesis is based upon a rather complicated source theory which has gained little acceptance.[8] Reim's hypothesis is open to the same criticism as in the case of Freed. John's use of the Old Testament appears to point to more creativity and individuality than that allowed by a theory that sees the evangelist limited to the Old Testament as it happens to appear in his written sources. Of course, Freed and Reim do understand the fourth evangelist as exercising some skill in selecting and editing these sources containing Old Testament references. Moreover, in recent work Reim has tried to show to what extent targumic-like traditions have found their way into the fourth gospel.[9] His studies should help awaken further interest in the question of the Old Testament in John, a subject that became somewhat dormant in the wake of Bultmann's influential work.

D. M. Smith has recently produced a study which has brought the question of Johannine quotations and Old Testament usage back into a more promising light.[10] His study seems to relate better to the structure and theology of the gospel as a literary whole. For heuristic purposes let us follow C. H. Dodd and say that the fourth gospel seems to consist of two major divisions, what Dodd called the "Book of Signs" (chaps. 2–11) and the "Book of the Passion" (chaps. 13–20).[11] The chapter that ties together these two halves, both structurally and theologically, is chapter 12. This chapter provides a theological review of the public ministry of signs and notes that Jesus' ministry resulted, for the most part, in unacceptance and unbelief.[12] Structurally, chapter 12 ties together the public "signs" ministry and passion week. Theologically, the chapter tries to explain how a messianic claimant who performs one messianic sign after another finds himself rejected and crucified. It is in view of these observations that others have made that Smith has made an intriguing case for viewing John 12:37–40 (and possibly v 41) as "a primitive transi-

[7] G. Reim, *Studien zum alttestamentlichen Hintergrund des Johannesevangelium* (SNTSMS 22; Cambridge: University Press, 1974) 94–95.

[8] See the negative reviews of B. Lindars, *JTS* 26 (1975) 165–167 and R. E. Brown, *TS* 35 (1974) 558–561.

[9] See G. Reim, "Targum und Johannesevangelium," *BZ* 27 (1983) 1–13.

[10] D. M. Smith, "The Setting and Shape of a Johannine Narrative Source," *JBL* 95 (1976) 231–241 (*Johannine Christianity*, 80–93).

[11] These are the headings of C. H. Dodd, *The Interpretation of the Fourth Gospel* (Cambridge: University Press, 1953) 289.

[12] See G. MacRae, "The Fourth Gospel and *Religionsgeschichte*," *CBQ* 32 (1970) 20–21.

tion" linking the seemingly contradictory christologies expressed in the two parts of the gospel.[13] Smith believes that this transitional unit was "part of John's larger source" which may be regarded as some sort of proto-gospel consisting of miracles and a passion account.[14] Smith notes with approval the conclusions of J. L. Martyn, W. Nicol, and R. T. Fortna who see the fourth gospel against the background of Jewish Christian and Jewish non-Christian debate and polemic within the context of the synagogue.[15] Smith has argued that any missionary tractate designed to convince Jews that Jesus was the Messiah would run into difficulties if a satisfactory explanation of Jesus' rejection and death was not offered. Contrary to a Hellenistic setting where the proclamation of the resurrection itself would be adequate explanation and justification (as in the case of the Pauline kerygma), there would have to be some specific explanation for the rejection.[16] Smith has offered at least two apologetic points that such missionary propaganda would have to make in order to convert Jews and answer Jewish criticisms.[17] First, the crucifixion would have to be explained. This need is met by the inclusion of a passion account. Secondly, an Old Testament scriptural apologetic would have to be provided in order to justify the passion itself. This apologetic, Smith believes, is primarily found in the transition that he has identified (12:37–40[41]) which, if his hypothesis is correct, the evangelist has bolstered by the addition of a half dozen or so Old Testament testimonia. Smith concludes that such a combination of materials (i.e., miracles and passion) along with adequate scriptural support would be required of Christians addressing a Jewish audience.[18]

Although Smith's appeal to a proto-gospel source containing the transitional unit of 12:37–40(41) is debatable, his understanding of the theological rationale for the unit is not without merit. Here, at last, is a study in which the fourth evangelist's, or at the very least his tradition's, use of the Old Testament is viewed as having significant theological and structural function, rather than being viewed as scarcely more than clues pointing to the presence of hypothesized sources.

---

[13] Smith, "Setting and Shape," 239.

[14] Smith, "Setting and Shape," 240. Smith has developed an intriguing hypothesis, but I wonder if it is necessary, or even possible, to resort to a proto-gospel source, the existence and extent of which are difficult to prove, for Fortna's reconstruction, which included parts of John 12 and a passion account, has not escaped serious criticism (see note 3 above).

[15] Smith, "Setting and Shape," 234–238. He cites J. L. Martyn, *History and Theology in the Fourth Gospel* (New York: Harper & Row, 1968). Similar backgrounds are assumed by Fortna and Nicol (see note 3 above).

[16] Smith, "Setting and Shape," 236

[17] Smith, "Setting and Shape," 236–238.

[18] Smith, "Setting and Shape," 240–241.

It would be useful to view the quotation formulas together. The Old Testament quotation formulas as they appear in John are as follows (with the Old Testament reference given in parentheses).[19]

1:23   *ephē* (Isa 40:3)
2:17   *hoti gegrammenon* (Ps 69:9)
6:31   *kathōs estin gegrammenon* (Ps 78:24)
6:45   *estin gegrammenon en tois prohētais* (Isa 54:13)
7:42   *hē graphē eipen hoti* (2 Sam 7:12; Mic 5:2)
10:34 *estin gegrammenon en tō nomō hymōn hoti* (Ps 82:6)
12:14 *kathōs estin gegrammenon* (Zech 9:9)
12:38 *ho logos Esaiou tou prophētou plērōthē hon eipen* (Isa
      53:1)
12:39 *palin eipen Esaias* (Isa 6:10)
13:18 *hē graphē plērōthē* (Ps 41:9)
15:25 *hina plērōthē ho logos en tō nomō autō gegrammenos
      hoti* (Ps 35:19)
19:24 *hina hē graphē plērōthē hē legousa* (Ps 22:18)
19:28 *hina teleiōthē* (Ps 22:15)
19:36 *hina hē graphē plērōthē* (Exod 12:46; Num 9:12; Ps
      34:20)
19:37 *kai palin hetera graphē legei* (Zech 12:10)

Two other Old Testament texts are cited, but without formula in 1:51 (Gen 28:12) and 12:13 (Ps 118:25–26). Three other instances should be mentioned where a formula is given, but no Old Testament quotation is actually cited: 17:12, *hina hē graphē plērōthē* (no citation); 18:32, *hina ho logos tou Iēsou plērōthē hon eipen* (reference seems to be to John 3:14; 8:28; 12:33); 18:9, *hina plērōthē ho logos hon epien* (reference seems to be to John 6:39). Some of these quotations are given as editorial comments of the evangelist (e.g., 2:17; 12:14–15, 38–40; 19:28, 36–37), while others are spoken by Jesus (e.g., 6:45; 10:34; 13:18; 15:25), or by other characters in the gospel (e.g., 1:23; 6:31; 7:42). Of Old Testament personalities Isaiah is mentioned by name three times (1:23; 12:38, 39). The name of Moses occurs about a dozen times and only in chapters 1–9. Usually reference to "Moses" is to be understood as reference to the Pentateuch.

The most interesting feature to observe is the regularity of the *hina plērōthē* formula from 12:38 onward through the passion, at a place where Smith sees an important transition taking place. An exception would be the *hina teleiōthē* formula (19:28), which R. Bultmann suspected may have belonged to an earlier written source[20] and, in any

[19] See C. A. Evans, "On the Quotation Formulas in the Fourth Gospel," *BZ* 26 (1982) 79–83.
[20] Strictly speaking, the quotations of Isa 6:10 (John 12:40) and Zech 12:10 (John

event, is virtually identical in meaning to the *hina plērōthē* formula. In John 1:23–12:15 there are nine quotations, seven with introductory formulas, and not one instance of the verb *plēroun* or equivalent. In the second half of the gospel (12:38–19:37) there are eleven quotation formulas, of which eight actually introduce Old Testament quotations and three others which introduce previous remarks of Jesus, and, with one exception, all use the verb *plēroun*. Although these various quotation formulas probably do not point to source(s) in John, they may very well provide some important structural and theological clues for the interpretation of the fourth gospel. We shall return to this question in the third part of the paper.

Other recent studies in the fourth gospel have detected the presence of midrash. The first and perhaps best known of such work is that of P. Borgen who sees John 6:31–58 as a midrash on Ps 78:24 and the manna tradition.[21] Moreover, J. Dahms and H. Lausberg have argued that the Johannine logos doctrine involving God's word being sent into the world and then returning to heaven has been greatly informed by Isa 55:10–11.[22] A. Hanson has recently provided a compelling case for understanding that a midrash on Exodus 34 (where Moses "sees" God) underlies the concluding section of the Johannine Prologue (1:14–18).[23] Finally, in a recent study Reim has tried to show that underlying the Johannine concept of Jesus as God could very well be a midrash on Psalm 45, possibly as it circulated in emerging targumic tradition.[24]

II. *Isaiah in the Fourth Gospel: Some General Observations*

Nearly 30 years ago F. Young published a study in which he showed to what a significant extent the fourth gospel was indebted to the Book of

---

19:37) are also exceptions in that *hina plērōthē* does not immediately precede them. But in view of the close relationship and proximity of these texts with the ones cited immediately before them (in John 12:38 and 19:36, respectively), the introductory formula of the lead texts is surely meant to be applied to the subsequent quotations. This understanding is supported by the presence of *palin*, which links the second quotations to the first ones.

[21] P. Borgen, "Observations on the Midrashic Character of John 6," ZNW 54 (1963) 232–240; idem, *Bread from Heaven: An Exegetical Study of the Concept of Manna in the Gospel of John and the Writings of Philo* (NovTSup 10; Leiden: Brill, 1965).

[22] J. V. Dahms, "Isaiah 55:11 and the Gospel of John," *EvQ* 53 (1981) 78–88; H. Lausberg, "Jesaja 55, 10–11 im Evangelium nach Johannes," in *Minuscule Philologica* (Nachrichten der Akademie der Wissenschaften im Göttingen 7; Göttingen: Vandenhoeck & Ruprecht, 1979) 131–144.

[23] A. T. Hanson, *The New Testament Interpretation of Scripture* (London: SPCK, 1980) 97–109.

[24] G. Reim, "Jesus as God in the Fourth Gospel: The Old Testament Background," *NTS* 30 (1984) 158–160. He also suspects that a midrash on Isa 42:6 underlies John 9; see Reim, "John 9—Tradition und zeitgenossische messianische Diskussion," *BZ* 22 (1978) 245–253, esp. 250; *idem*, "Johannesevangelium und Synagogengottesdienst—eine Beobachtung," *BZ* 27 (1983) 101.

Isaiah (especially Second Isaiah) and various legends about the eighth-century prophet.[25] Young observes that certain Johannine concepts such as "making known the name of God" or referring to God as the "true God" are typical expressions found in Second Isaiah.[26] Of importance also is the deutero-Isaian theme of having all things "announced" (anag-gelein), which seems to be an element of major interest in later specula-tions about the nature of the prophet's vision, and also which seems to be an important theme in the fourth gospel as well.[27] Perhaps the most convincing part of his study is where he shows that the miracle at the pool of Siloam is replete with Isaian and Isaiah-related legendary tradi-tions.[28] More recently, studies by M. Tenney and H. Songar, as well as the commentaries of R. E. Brown, B. Lindars, and L. Morris, have all expressed an awareness of the significance of Isaiah for the fourth gos-pel.[29]

III. *The Fourth Gospel's Use of Isaiah: The Obduracy Motif and the Lord's Servant*

A. The Obduracy Motif

Throughout the fourth gospel Jesus is rejected and opposed. This theme is clearly expressed in the Prologue: "He came to his own things, and his own people did not receive him" (1:11). Despite a promising beginning, marked by Nathanael's confession, "Rabbi, you are the Son of God; you are the King of Israel" (1:49), the first sign at Cana of Galilee (2:1–11), and the cleansing of the Temple (2:13–22), which provoked skepticism, but apparently no opposition, the section closes on the ominous note: "Many believed in his name when they saw the signs which he did; but Jesus did not trust himself to them, because he knew what was in man and needed no one to bear witness of man; for he himself knew what was in man" (2:23–25). This passage clearly anticipates the summarizing statement found at the conclusion of the ministry of signs: "Though he had done so many signs before them, yet they did not believe in him" (12:37).

[25] F. W. Young, "A Study of the Relation of Isaiah to the Fourth Gospel," *ZNW* 46 (1955) 215–233.

[26] F. W. Young, 222–224.

[27] F. W. Young, 224–226.

[28] F. W. Young, 220–221.

[29] M. C. Tenney, "The Old Testament and the Fourth Gospel," *BibSac* 120 (1963) 300–308; H. S. Songer, "Isaiah and the New Testament," *RevExp* 65 (1968) 459–470; R. E. Brown, *The Gospel according to John* (AB 29 and 29A; Garden City: Doubleday, 1966 and 1970); B. Lindars, *The Gospel of John* (NCB; London: Oliphants, 1972); L. Morris, *The Gospel according to John* (NIC; Grand Rapids: Eerdmans, 1971).

The rejection theme reaches its climax in the unit (12:37–40[41]) which Smith has isolated as a primitive transitional unit. In the citation of Isa 53:1 and 6:10 the evangelist (or the tradition before him) has explained Jesus' rejection in terms of obduracy, a motif which is found elsewhere in the New Testament (e.g., Mark 4:11–12 par.; Acts 13:38–52; 28:23–28; Rom 11:7–10).[30] That the evangelist seems to be saying that it was God's will that few believe in Jesus because of hardened hearts seems to be unavoidable.[31]

It is significant to note that these two Isaian quotations are the first quotations in the series of quotations to be introduced by the *hina plērōthē* formula. The previous quotations are introduced by a variety of formulas, such as *kathōs estin gegrammenon*. In a previous study I have argued that the earlier quotation formulas and the quotations themselves are meant to illustrate the fact (or claim) that various details in the public ministry of Jesus are viewed in terms of correspondence to certain Old Testament passages (i.e., "just as it is written"), whereas details in the passion are regarded as accomplished in order to fulfill scripture (i.e., "in order that it be fulfilled").[32] It would appear that the evangelist's quotation formulas reflect the theological and structural shift from the public ministry of signs to the passion. Whereas the signs in the first half of the gospel are meant to prove that Jesus is the Messiah, the Old Testament testimonia in the second half are meant to prove more specifically that the disgrace of the crucifixion, a controversial item in any dialogue with Jews, was Jesus' very purpose and work and, indeed, was his hour of glorification and return to his Father in heaven.

But in citing these Isaiah texts in the manner in which he has, does the evangelist wish only to appeal to the obduracy motif for his apologetic or does he have in mind a much wider and more positive application? Is it possible, or perhaps even probable, that these texts are meant not only to explain why Jesus was rejected, but also to identify Jesus in terms of the Servant of the Lord? To this question we shall now turn.

B. The Servant of the Lord

For years it has been assumed that New Testament writers understood Jesus in terms of the "Servant of the Lord" passages in Second Isaiah (42:1–9; 49:1–13; 50:4–9; 52:13–53:12). J. Jeremias' contribution to

---

[30] See C. A. Evans, *Isaiah 6:9–10 in Early Jewish and Christian Interpretation* (unpublished dissertation; Claremont: Claremont Graduate School, 1983).

[31] See C. A. Evans, "The Function of Isaiah 6:9–10 in Mark and John," *NovT* 24 (1982) 124–138, esp. 136–137; *idem*, "The Hermeneutics of Mark and John: On the Theology of the Canonical 'Gospel,'" *Bib* 64 (1983) 153–172, esp. 162–164. See also F. Watson, "The Social Function of Mark's Secrecy Theme," *JSNT* 24 (1985) 49–69, esp. 62–63.

[32] See Evans, "On the Quotation Formulas," 82–83.

TDNT is classic.[33] O. Cullmann devotes an entire chapter in his
Christology of the New Testament to Jesus as the Servant of the Lord.[34]
However, the appearance of M. D. Hooker's little book, *Jesus and the
Servant*, in 1959 was a bomb shell in which she called into question the
assumption that Second Isaiah's Servant Songs had had significant influ-
ence on early christology.[35] In large measure her thesis still stands.[36]

In her discussion of the Servant theme in John, Hooker summarizes
the potential evidence of the presence of such a theme as follows: (1) the
Baptist's declaration: "Behold, the lamb of God who takes away the sin of
the world" (1:29; cf. 1:36); (2) the lifting up sayings (3:14; 8:28; 12:32); and
(3) the quotation of Isa 53:1 (12:38).[37] With reference to the first point
Hooker notes that the Servant in Isa 53:7 is likened to "a lamb" (anar-
throus) and is not actually called a lamb or "the lamb" (*ho amnos*) as John
has it. She rejects the suggestion that is made from time to time that
underlying the Baptist's word for lamb is the Aramic word *tly*, which is
equivalent to the Greek word *pais*, which came to be confused (acciden-
tally or deliberately) with the Hebrew word for lamb, *tlḥ*.[38] The possibility does appear remote when it is noted that the LXX never
translates *tlḥ* with *amnos*, nor are there examples of *tly* being used for
ʿbd.[39] She is willing to concede, however, that whereas the original idea
(especially in connection to the Baptist) was that of the messianic lamb of
apocalyptic, it had probably come to be understood as "a reference to the
Paschal lamb, with which the lamb of Isa. 53, through the influence of
the Christian eucharist, had become fused."[40]

With respect to the lifting up sayings she notes that *hypsoun* occurs
in Old Testament passages other than Isa 52:13, in which the word *doxa*

[33] J. Jeremias, *TDNT* 5.677–717.
[34] O. Cullmann, *The Christology of the New Testament* (Philadelphia: Westminster, 1959) 51–82.
[35] M. D. Hooker, *Jesus and the Servant: The Influence of the Servant Concept of Deutero-Isaiah in the New Testament* (London: SPCK, 1959).
[36] See the recent study of D. L. Jones, "The Title 'Servant' in Luke-Acts," *Luke-Acts: New Perspectives from the Society of Biblical Literature Seminar* (ed. C. H. Talbert; New York: Cross Road, 1984) 148–165, esp. 158. For a defense of the view that the Servant concept had a significant influence upon early christology see R. T. France, *Jesus and the Old Testament: His Application of Old Testament Passages to Himself and His Mission* (London: Tyndale, 1971) 110–135.
[37] Hooker, 103.
[38] So Jeremias, *TDNT* 5.702, 1.339; and W. H. Brownlee, "Whence the Gospel according to John?" *John and Qumran* (ed. J. H. Charlesworth; London: Geoffrey Chapman, 1972) 166–194, esp. 177–178. Other scholars favoring this view would include C. F. Burney, O. Cullmann, M.-E. Boismard, I. de la Potterie, and B. Reicke.
[39] C. H. Dodd, *Interpretation*, 235–236; Hooker, 104; Brown, 1.61; C. K. Barrett, "The Lamb of God," *NTS* 1 (1955) 210–218.
[40] Hooker, 104.

also occurs frequently (e.g., Pss 3:3; 22; 28; 30; 50:15; 21:1–6), though she concedes that the evangelist may have had the Isaian reference in mind. Her main point seems to be that the conceptions of *hypsoun* in Isaiah and John are different: "Whereas in Deutero-Isaiah the Servant is glorified by his restoration, and Yahweh by the Return of Israel, in John both the Father and the Son are glorified already at the crucifixion."[41] However, one may wonder if Hooker's summary of the meaning of *hypsoun* in Isa 52:13 is not in fact descriptive of the fourth evangelist's descent/ascent schema in which Jesus, when lifted up on the cross, is in fact restored to the Father.[42] The gathering of the sheep (John 10:14–16) may in fact reflect the idea of Yahweh's glorification by the return or regathering of Israel (i.e., a true Israel composed of both Jews and Gentiles; see John 10:16, "I have other sheep not of this fold"). That both the Father and the Son are to be "glorified" is a Johannine idea (cf. 13:31–32). Ironically, what Hooker sees as a contrast between Isaiah's and John's understanding of *hypsoun* may in fact represent a succinct statement of their close theological affinity. But more of this will have to be made on another occasion.

With respect to the quotation of Isa 53:1, Hooker notes that the Old Testament verse refers not to Jesus' death and resurrection (themes possibly derived from the whole of the Servant Song), but to "the failure of Jews to believe the signs which had been performed by Jesus."[43] "The passage appears to have been used simply as an Old Testament proof-text of the incurable obduracy of Israel."[44] This conclusion was held by Bultmann and has been repeated more recently by R. Schnackenburg.[45]

It would appear that Hooker's study does not close the door decisively on the possibility of seeing the Isaian Servant motif underlying Johannine theology. With reference to the Lamb of God saying she is willing to concede an association with Isa 53:7, and in the case of the lifting up sayings there may be closer parallels between Second Isaiah and John than she has realized. With reference to her third point, namely that Isa 53:1 in John refers not to the report of the Servant's exaltation, but refers to Jewish unbelief in Jesus despite his signs, there are other relevant items to be considered.

First of all, the relationship between the two Isaian texts involves more than the idea of obduracy. As an instance of what is probably the exegetical principle of *gezera šawa* ("equivalence of expression") the

---

[41] Hooker, 106.
[42] See G. C. Nicholson, *Death as Departure: The Johannine Descent-Ascent Schema* (SBLDS 63; Chico: Scholars, 1983).
[43] Hooker, 106.
[44] Hooker, 106.
[45] R. Schnackenburg, *The Gospel according to St. John* (New York: Seabury, 1980) 2.413–414.

evangelist has intentionally linked these two Old Testament texts.[46] The obvious evidence for such a linkage is in the fact that the two quotations are found side by side in the gospel, are connected by *palin*, and are introduced by only one quotation formula. As already noted, there is a thematic linkage in that both Isaian texts speak of obduracy. However, when the fuller contexts of both texts are studies (i.e., 6:1–13 and 52:13–53:12) another theme becomes apparent, one that figures prominently in the fourth gospel. Compare the following excerpts from Isaiah:

6:1	I saw the Lord sitting upon a throne, high [*rwm*] and lifted up [*nś*]
6:3	the whole earth is full of his glory [*kbwd*]
6:5	my eyes have seen the king [*mlk*]
6:7	your guilt is taken away, and your sin [*ḥṭ*] forgiven
6:9	Hear and hear [*šmʿ*], but do not understand [*byn*]; See and see [*rʾh*], but do not perceive [*ydʿ*].
52:13	He shall be exalted [*rwm*] and lifted up [*nś*]
52:15	Kings [*mlk*] shall. . .see [*rʾh*] and that which they have not heard [*šmʿ*] they shall understand [*byn*].
53:12	He bore the sin [*ḥṭ*] of many

In the Hebrew of Isa 6:3 *kbwd* does not parallel any item in 52:13–53:12. But in the LXX there is the cognate parallel between 6:3 *(doxa)* and 52:13 *(doxazein)*. The fact that the fourth evangelist appears to follow Hebrew, Greek, and Aramaic traditions as he quotes scripture makes the above Hebrew parallels not unimportant. Besides the aforementioned theme of obduracy, there are present several points of contact between these two Isaian passages. What is probably the most important of these parallels is the theme of exaltation and glorification (so esp. the LXX). These parallels occur at the head of each passage and so according to

---

[46] S. Lieberman (*Hellenism in Jewish Palestine* [Texts and Studies of the Jewish Theological Seminary of America 18; New York: JTSA, 1950] 57–62) has argued that one of Hillel's seven rules by which Torah was to be interpreted appears to be identical to a philological method practiced at Alexandria. In the Halakah it is referred to as *gzrh šwh*, and in Greek as *dis legomena*. Lieberman concludes that this rule is actually derived from a technical term employed by the Greek rhetors and accordingly should be translated *sygkrisis pros ison* ("a comparison with the equal"). Hence, *gezera šawa* is interpretation based upon similarity of language in two passages. That this hermeneutical principle was in academic circles wider than those of the Rabbis makes even more plausible the suggestion that the fourth evangelist consciously developed such an exegesis. One of the theses of Freed (*Old Testament Quotations*) is that the fourth evangelist was thoroughly conversant with principles of Jewish interpretation. Brownlee ("Ezekiel," *ISBE* 2.259) has found evidence of this rabbinic method of exegesis in the revising of Ezekiel. G. Brooke (*Exegesis at Qumran: 4QFlorilegium in its Jewish Context* [JSOTSup 29; Sheffield: JSOT, 1985] 166, 279, 294, 297–298, 306–308) has found the method practiced at Qumran.

Jewish convention would in all probability be remembered as descriptive of the passages as wholes. In view of these similarities, the proposal that such an exegetical linkage underlies these two quotations in John is quite plausible.

The recurring Johannine themes of "lifting up" and "glorification" would provide at least a small measure of support to the suggestion that the fourth evangelist linked these passages, not simply because both describe obduracy, but because both relate in a significant way to the evangelist's christology. In the case of Isa 6:10 this seems obvious because of the evangelist's subsequent comment: "Isaiah said these things because [or when] he saw his glory, and spoke concerning him" (12:41).[47] It is likely that the evangelist is saying that when the prophet Isaiah saw the glory of the Lord he actually saw Christ himself. The idea of looking ahead to a future messianic event would accord well with what has been observed about the legendary speculations regarding what Isaiah saw in his vision.[48] But when the evangelist says, "and spoke concerning him," what speech does he have in mind? It is tempting to entertain the possibility, in view of the linkage of the two Isaian texts, that the evangelist may in fact have had the Servant Song in mind. However, such a suggestion must remain quite tentative, or at least until further evidence is put forth. In Isa 6:5 the prophet exclaims: "I have seen the King, the Lord of hosts." The fourth evangelist also calls Jesus "king" (cf. 1:49; 12:13) and so the evangelist may have no more in mind than Isaiah's exclamation. Or, perhaps better, he has in mind a reading that conforms to what is found in Targum Jonathan: "My eyes have seen the glory of the shekinah of the King of ages, the Lord of hosts." Perhaps this is what the evangelist supposed Isaiah said because (or when) he saw God's glory, namely, Christ.

But can more substantial evidence be offered that would support the contention that John's portrayal of Jesus is in fact significantly influenced by the Servant Songs? The tentative hypothesis of this study is that John 12:1–43 is, at least in part, a midrash on Isa 52:7–53:12. Evidence for the presence of such a midrash, as in most cases, is cumulative. Some of the evidence may appear strong, while some may appear coincidental.

(1) The idea that Jesus was to be "glorified" (*doxazein;* 12:16, 23) could owe its origin to the LXX's use of this verb in the opening line of the Servant Song (Isa 52:13). *Doxazein* is distinctive to the Greek version

---

[47] *Tg. Jon.* Isa 6:1 reads: "I saw the glory of the Lord" (cf. 6:5).

[48] F. W. Young, 216–218 (see Sir 48:22–25). It is interesting to note that Jerome took the liberty of translating one of the Hebrew infinitives in Isa 6:9 as *visionem,* i.e., "and see the vision." Perhaps he took advantage of such Jewish speculation regarding Isaiah's vision of future things and christianized the text (with John 12:41 in mind); see my study, "Jerome's Translation of Isaiah 6:9–10," *VC* 38 (1984) 202–204.

and may suggest that the evangelist either derived the word from the Isaian passage or at least intends his readers to see the connection. (2) The "lifting up" idea in both Isaiah (52:13) and John (12:32–34) is expressed by the verb *hypsoun*. In both Greek and Hebrew the double meanings of (literal) elevation and (figurative) exaltation are possible connotations. Just as the Servant is to be lifted up and glorified, so Jesus is to be lifted up (both literally and figuratively) and glorified. It is interesting to note that both occurrences of *doxazein* (vv 16, 23) and both occurrences of *hypsoun* (vv 32, 34) are in the form of aorist passives, possibly suggesting that what was regarded by Isaiah as a future event (LXX: future passives) has now, in the understanding of the fourth evangelist, been fulfilled with the arrival of Jesus' "hour." It is in this connection that for the first time Jesus is able to declare: "The hour has come" (12:33).

(3) Jesus' rejection, despite his signs, is explained in terms of quotations from the two Isaian passages (i.e., Isa 53:1 and 6:10) in John 12:37–43. Just as Isaiah's message was doomed to fall upon deaf ears and blind eyes, so too would the Christian proclamation be received by the Jewish people. Despite the vision of Christ's glory (i.e., Isa 6:1–5; cf. John 12:41), Isaiah prophesies an obdurate response (cf. Isa. 53:1; 6:9–10).

(4) Elsewhere I have suggested that the voice from heaven (John 12:28: "'Father, glorify your name.' A voice came from heaven: 'I have glorified [it] and I shall glorify [it] again.'") may be an allusion to Isa 52:6, where God is understood as speaking (LXX): "For this reason my people will know my name in that day, that I am the one who speaks."[49] Three items may be noted: (a) The phrase *en tē hēmera ekeinē* is remarkably similar to the Johannine usage of "hour" (cf. 2:4; 4:21, 23; 5:25, 28; 7:30; 8:20; 12:23, 27; 13:1; 16:2, 4, 25, 32; 17:1). (b) The concern with knowing or recognizing *(ginōskein)* the Lord's name *(onoma)* is typically Johannine (cf. 17:26: *egnōrisa autois to onoma sou*).[50] (c) The expression, *egō eimi autos ho lalōn*, is remarkably similar to John 4:26, where Jesus says: *egō eimi, ho lalōn soi*. It is possible that the voice from heaven is meant to be understood along the lines of the *bath gol* (lit. "daugter of sound," i.e, "echo") of rabbinic literature, in which such a heavenly voice is understood as a sort of confirmation.[51] However, it should be noted that Isa 52:6 falls outside of the 52:7–53:12 passage, and so further discussion is warranted. At 52:7 the MT has a samekh for "Seder," indicating the

---

[49] C. A. Evans, "The Voice from Heaven: A Note on John 12:28," *CBQ* 43 (1981) 405–408.

[50] See F. W. Young, 222–224. The expression, "in that day," is found in the context of asking in Jesus' "name" (cf. 16:26).

[51] Cf. *b. Sanh.* 11a; Barrett, *The Gospel according to St. John* (second edition; Philadelphia: Westminster, 1978) 425.

beginning of a new section of scriptural reading. 1QIsaiah[a] has a "hat" at this same point. Although of uncertain meaning, it is likely that it indicates that 52:7 begins a new section. There is a minor paragraphing between 52:10 and 11, a major one between 52:12 and 13, another paragraphing between 52:15 and 53:1, at which point there is a marginal line drawn. This last feature may indicate that the larger unit of 52:7–15 functions as an introductory paragraph to chapter 53.[52] Thus, it seems clear that Isa 52:6 in the Hebrew tradition was viewed as belonging to the preceding section. However, there is no such paragraphing in the LXX. Moreover, 52:6 and 7 appear to be syntactically linked.[53] It is from the LXX, we should remember, that the 53:1 quotation is derived. In view of this observation the paragraphing of the Hebrew tradition does not prohibit the suggestion that the heavenly voice of John 12:28 may be an allusion to Isa 52:6. There is also the possibility that another Servant Song may be in the background. In LXX Isa 49:3 we read: "He said to me, 'You are my servant [*doulos*], Israel, and in [or among] you I shall be glorified [*doxasthēsomai*]." If the evangelist does have this text (or other texts) in mind then it is likely that he understands Jesus as the Servant through whose glorification God himself will be glorified, and whose people will come to know God's name.

(5) W. H. Brownlee has argued that the term *msḥt* in MT Isa 52:14 is ambiguous and may mean either "marring" or "anointing."[54] He is convinced that antiquity must be granted to this reading. He believes that the copyist of 1QIsaiah[a] exploited the ambiguous term rendering the text thus: "As many were astonished at you, so I anointed his face more than any man, and his body more than the sons of men."[55] The Targum, of course, presents Isa 52:13–53:12 in an overtly messianic manner (cf. 52:13, "Behold, my Servant, the Messiah"; cf. 53:10), although how early this interpretation can be assigned is problematic.[56] If such an anointing

---

[52] 1QIsaiah[b] is not preserved at 52:7, but 52:8–54:6 is sufficiently preserved to indicate a minor paragraphing between 52:10 and 11, and one continuous paragraph from 52:11–53:12. Since the paragraphing at 52:11 is minor (a space within a line, rather than an incomplete line), in all likelihood 52:7–53:12 makes up a major unit in 1QIsaiah[a]. 11QMelchizedek interprets the "herald of glad tidings" of Isa 52:7 as "the anointed of the Spirit" (which is doubtlessly an allusion to Isa 61:1).

[53] In the LXX vv 6–8 appear to make up one sentence.

[54] W. H. Brownlee, *The Meaning of the Qumrân Scrolls for the Bible, with Special Attention to the Book of Isaiah* (New York: Oxford University, 1964) 204–215. Both *šḥt* ("mar") and *mšḥ* ("Anoint") could have been seen in *mšḥt* (cf. Dan 9:26).

[55] Brownlee, 215.

[56] See B. D. Chilton, *The Glory of Israel: The Theology and Provenience of the Isaiah Targum* (JSOTSup 23; Sheffield: JSOT, 1983) 91–96. Chilton concludes that the portrait of the Servant as a victorious Messiah arose prior to Bar Kokhba (132–135 c.e.). See S. H. Levey, *The Messiah: An Aramaic Interpretation. The Messianic Exegesis of the Targum* (Monographs of the Hebrew Union College 2;

interpretation was known to the evangelist (and this gospel's relationship to Qumran is a matter of scholarly interest), then he may have intended his readers to see a correspondence between the Servant's anointing and the anointing of Jesus at Bethany (12:1–8). (6) A related item is Mary's anointing of Jesus' feet, an action which may be intended to recall Isa 52:7: "How beautiful upon the mountains are the feet of him who brings good tidings, who publishes peace, who brings tidings of good, who publishes salvation, who says to Zion, 'Your God reigns.'" This verse contains a few vocabulary items found in the fourth gospel (e.g., "peace," "salvation," "good tidings"). The verb *euaggelizesthai* is found in the eschatologically understood Isa 61:1 passage: "The Spirit of the Lord is upon me, because the Lord has anointed me to bring good tidings . . ." (vv 1ff.) Among the (Messianic) tasks mentioned in this passage is the giving of the "oil of gladness" to "those who mourn in Zion" (61:3).[57] Finally, it might be pointed out that anointing was also an aspect of grooming and beauty. In Matt 6:16–18 a gloomy face and a neglected appearance stand in sharp contrast to an anointed head and washed face. Note also the example of Ruth whose mother-in-law told her to wash, anoint herself, and put on her best clothing in a bid to captivate the heart of Boaz (Ruth 3:3).[58]

Finally, a few more possible allusions are worthy of passing notice. (7) The crowd which went out *(exēlthon)* of Jerusalem to greet Jesus (12:12–13) may fulfill the exhortation in Isa 52:11 to go out *(exelthate)* of Jerusalem. Isa 52:11 also tells its readers to "touch nothing unclean," but to "purify" themselves, an idea which suits the Johannine Passover *(hē heortē)* context very well, since on such an occasion there would be a concern for ritual purity (see 18:28). (8) The jubilant shouting of the people (John 12:13) could be viewed as a fulfillment of Isa 52:8–9. The return of the Lord to Zion, as described in Isaiah, could be seen as fulfilled in the return of Jesus to Jerusalem which he has previously visited. When the people see Jesus they see the Lord (cf. John 12:45, "the one who sees me sees the one [i.e., the Lord] who sent me"). The presence of Ps 118:25–26 is no doubt traditional, and against the Isaian background it is enriched. (9) Hailing the approaching Jesus as "king" (see John 12:13, where "king of Israel" is added to the Psalm 118 citation,

---

Cincinnati: Hebrew Union College, 1974) 67. Levey (p. 70) finds "messianic implications" in the LXX, Vulgage, and Peshitta.

[57] The "mountains" of Isa 52:7 are probably not paralleled in John, unless one wishes to suggest the Mount of Olives where Bethany is situated (cf. John 12:1).

[58] Psalm 45, interpreted messianically in early Jewish and Christian tradition, describes the king as beautiful (vv 2–3, 8, 11, 12b–14). Heb 1:8–9 applies vv 6–7 to Jesus, while *Pal. Tg.* Gen. 49:8, influenced by Psalm 45, reads: "How beauteous is the King Meshiha, who is to arise from the house of Jehuda!" (cf. Reim, "Jesus as God," 160, n. 8).

and 12:14 where Zech 9:9 is quoted) correlates with Isa 52:7 which announces to Zion: "Your God is King!"[59] The LXX uses the future, *basileusei* ("He will be king," or "He will reign"), which lends the passage more readily to the idea of fulfillment. (10) When the Greeks or foreign Jews *(Hellēnes)*, who have come to worship at the feast, request to see Jesus (John 12:20–21) Isa 52:10 may here be echoed: "The Lord has bared his holy arm in the sight of all nations; that all the ends of the earth may see [LXX: "will see"] the salvation of our God." (11) With reference to the final line of Isa 52:10 we should recall that Jesus' very name, in its full Hebrew form, means "Yahweh saves." Thus, it is possible that the fourth evangelist would have us understand the Greeks' desire to see Jesus as the fulfillment of the promise that all people would someday see God's salvation.

There are at least two allusions outside of John 12 which may reflect Isaiah 53. These consist of the previously mentioned reference to the "lamb of God who takes away the sin of the world," which may refer to the lamb simile (53:7) and the idea of bearing sin (53:10–12); while the promise to raise up the "Temple" *(naos)*, which Jesus' opponents misunderstand, may reflect the tradition of the Messiah either cleansing or rebuilding the Temple, a tradition found in *Tg. Jon.* Isa 53:5. With reference to this last point it is admitted that the targumic tradition is of uncertain date. However, it is likely that it refers to the destruction of the second Temple and so may possibly have become part of the targumic tradition prior to the writing of the fourth gospel. The fact that it came to be added to this Isaiah passage may suggest that at an earlier stage in Jewish tradition the Temple cleansing (or rebuilding) motif had become understood as part of the Messiah's (or Servant's?) task.

Conclusion

If the evidence put forward in this study is convincing and compels us to understand John 12:1–43 as a midrash on Isa 52:7–53:12, then it will become necessary for us to reconsider the extent and nature of the influence that the Servant Songs may have had on Johannine christology.

---

[59] The MT reads *mlk*, "is king" or "reigns."

TRADITIONS IN THE PASTORAL EPISTLES

E. EARLE ELLIS

Southwestern Baptist Theological Seminary
Fort Worth, Texas

The presence of traditional Pauline motifs in the Pastoral epistles is widely accepted by those who assign the letters to a later generation[1] as well as by those who consider them to have been written by or under the eye of the Apostle.[2] A few preformed traditions (in addition to Old Testament quotations) have also long been recognized, particularly the confession at 1 Tim 3:16[3] and "the faithful Word" (pistos ho logos) sayings.[4] They also may be indicated in other passages that are accompanied by formulas or that are set apart from their context in other ways. Such traditions are the concern of the present essay and, although they have received little attention, they appear to be quite extensive.

The following remarks will (1) offer certain criteria by which one may recognize preformed traditions and then (2) attempt to identify and classify a number of them. In conclusion, it will briefly (3) assess the significance of these phenomena for placing the Pastoral epistles in the history of the early Christian mission.

---

[1] E.g., Trummer, Die Paulustradition der Pastoralbriefen (Frankfurt: Lang, 1978); cf. M. Dibelius and H. Conzelmann, The Pastoral Epistles (Philadelphia: Fortress, 1955) 8ff. (GT: 7ff.).

[2] E.g., D. Guthrie, The Pastoral Epistles (London: Tyndale, 1957) 39; J. Jeremias, Die Briefe an Timotheus und Titus (Göttingen: Vandenhoeck & Ruprecht, 1947) 5f.; J. N. D. Kelly, The Pastoral Epistles (London: A & C Black, 1963) 16–21; A. Schlatter, Die Kirche der Griechen (Stuttgart: Calwert, 2 1958 [1936]) 14ff.

[3] E.g., W. G. Conybeare and J. S. Howson, The Life and Epistles of Paul (London: Longmann, Green: 3/873 [1852]) 752n.; J. E. Huther, Timothy and Titus (New York: Funk & Wagnalls, 1885 [4 1875]) 130.

[4] Conybeare and Howson (note 3), 752n.; H. Alford, The Greek Testament (4 vols.; London: Rivingtons, 2 1857) 3.364 (on 2 Tim 2:11). The formula appears specifically at 1 Tim 1:15; 3:1a; 4:9; 2 Tim 2:11; Tit 3:8. See also 1 Tim 4:6; Tit 1:9; Rev 21:5; 22:6. Similar: 1 Cor 1:9; 10:13; 2 Thess 3:3. Cf. G. W. Knight III, The Faithful Sayings in the Pastoral Letters (Kampen: Kok; Nutley, NJ: Presbyterian and Reformed, 1968).

I

A number of more or less obvious criteria must be satisfied before one can identify a passage as a cited and traditioned piece. Fairly clear indicators are (1) a formula that elsewhere introduces or concludes quoted material and (2) the self-contained and independent character of the passage vis-a-vis its context. Also significant are (3) a vocabulary with a relatively large number of *hapax legomena* and an idiom, style or theological viewpoint that differ markedly both from the rest of the letter and from other writings by the same author, and (4) a strikingly similar piece in another writing where no direct literary dependence is probable. Of course, not all of these criteria will usually be present and those that are may be evaluated differently. Peculiar vocabulary and idiom, for example, may not alone be very significant since an author's vocabulary will change in the course of time and in accordance with the subject matter addressed and the amanuensis employed. Also, not every quotation will necessarily be a transmitted tradition, for example, the citation of the pagan prophet at Titus 1:12; and quotations that are traditional may be paraphrased or reworked or interpolated by the author or his amanuensis. While subjective factors will always enter into one's identification of a preformed and traditioned pericope, the above criteria will, it is hoped, provide guidelines for measuring the probabilities.

II

Passages in the Pastorals that fall to be considered as preformed traditions represent a variety of topics and several literary patterns. Topically, they may include doxologies,[5] a vice list,[6] congregational regulations,[7] prophecies,[8] confessions[9] and admonitions.[10] Among the literary forms to be discerned are implicit and explicit midrash, that is, commentary on Old Testament texts,[11] and hymns.[12] It is not unlikely

[5] 1 Tim 1:17; 6:15f.
[6] 1 Tim 1:9f.
[7] 1 Tim 2:11–3:1a or 2:13–3:1a (wives) and 1 Tim 3:2–13; Titus 1:7ff. (overseers and ministers).
[8] 1 Tim 4:1–5.
[9] 1 Tim 1:15; 2:5f.; 3:16; 2 Tim 1:9f.; Titus 3:3–7.
[10] 1 Tim 6:7f., 11f.; 2 Tim 2:11ff.; Titus 2:11–14.
[11] 1 Tim 1:9f.; 2:11–15; 5:17f.; 2 Tim 2:19f.; Titus 3:3–7. On the distinction between explicit and implicit midrash cf. E. E. Ellis, *Prophecy and Hermeneutic* (Tübingen: Mohr; Grand Rapids: Eerdmans, 1978) 188–197. Titus 3:4–7 combines (implicit) midrash and a hymnic form, both of which are characteristic of early Christian prophetic writing. Cf. D. E. Aune, "The Odes of Solomon and Early Christian Prophecy," *NTS* 28 (1983) 453ff. ("the prophetic hymn"); K. P. Jörns, *Das hymnische Evangelium . . . in der Johannesoffenbarung* (Gütersloh: Mohn

that a number of passages not to be considered here, for example, certain congregational and social regulations,[13] also rest on traditioned material since the topics appear elsewhere in the Pastorals and/or in other Pauline letters as preformed traditions.[14]

Repeated formulas in the Pastorals that appear to signal the citation of traditional pieces include "faithful is the Word" *(pistos ho logos)*, 'knowing this that' *(touto ginōskein/idein hoti)* and "these things *(tauta)* teach," ". . . command," ". . . exhort," ". . . observe," ". . . place." They often introduce or conclude passages that read like set pieces and that can be distinguished from their context by other criteria mentioned above.

The formula, "faithful is the Word," is found in five passages, introducing the saying at 1 Tim 1:15, 2 Tim 2:11 and probably at 1 Tim 4:9[15] and concluding it at Titus 3:8 and probably at 1 Tim 3:1a.[16] It is clearly a formula of quotation in some instances and, since it used similarly throughout the Pastorals, it should be so regarded whether it introduces or concludes the saying.[17] The phrase is found in Jewish[18] and Greco-

---

1971); Ellis, *Prophecy and Hermeneutic,* 147–237 *et passim* ("prophecy as exegesis"). The affinities with Pauline idiom and themes elsewhere (cf. Rom 3:24; 5:5; 11:22; 12:2; 1 Cor 6:11) invites the conclusion that Paul himself created this "faithful saying" (Tit 3:8) prior to its use here. However, since no such sayings occur in Paul's letters outside the Pastorals, it may be argued that some faithful sayings represent the (reworked) traditioned material of others. Cf. Kelly (note 2), 161f., 254 *et passim.*

[12] 1 Tim 2:5f.; 3:16; 6:11f., 15f.; 2 Tim 1:9f.; 2:11ff.; Tit 2:11–14; 3:4–7.

[13] 1 Tim 2:1f., 9f.; 6:17ff.; Titus 3:1f., 10f.; 2 Tim 2:24ff.

[14] For example, 1 Tim 2:11–3:1a; 3:1b–13 (see below); I Cor 11:3–16; 14:34f. (congregational regulations); Rom 13:1–7; 1 Pet 2:13–17 (societal rules); Col 3:18–4:1 (household regulations); cf. G. E. Cannon, *The Use of Traditional Materials in Colossians* (Macon, GA: Mercer University, 1983) 111–121, 129; E. E. Ellis, *The Formation of the New Testament Writings,* forthcoming.

[15] The question is difficult and the commentators divided as to whether the formula at 1 Tim 4:9 introduces or concludes the "faithful saying." Favoring an *introductory* formula are a style and subject matter similar to 1 Tim 1:15 and the fact that the following phrase, *eis touto gar,* introduces or is a part of a cited tradition at 1 Pet 2:21; cf. 4:6; Rom 14:9; 1 Jn 3:8. Cf. also the punctuation of E. Nestle-K. Aland, *Novum Testamentum Graece* (Stuttgart: Bibelstiftung, 261979); Guthrie (note 2), 95f. On the other hand this same phrase, *eis touto gar,* is found at 2 Cor 2:9, and other significant vocabulary in 1 Tim 4:10 is Pauline idiom (cf. Schlatter, note 2, 126); but this is hardly decisive.

[16] So, Nestle-Aland (note 17); Schlatter (note 2), 94f.

[17] *Pace* Dibelius-Conzelmann (note 1), 28 (GT: 23). The *legei kyrios* formula often concludes the cited Old Testament passage (cf. Rom 12:19; 1 Cor 14:11; 2 Cor 6:18; Heb 10:30a; similar: Acts 7:49; 15:17), and more generally used formulas in the New Testament also conclude the quotation once or twice (John 1:23; Rom 2:24; similar: John 12:41). This location of the formula appears to be a matter of style, perhaps originating in oral speech or in written matter intended for oral reading.

Roman writings,[19] not as a formula, however, but in the sense of "the report is credible." The closest parallel outside the New Testament that I am aware of is the formulaic phrase in Qumran's apocalyptic Book of Mysteries (1Q27 1:8):

> Certain is the Word *(nkwn dbr)* to come to pass
> And true the prediction *(w'mt hmš')*.

Even closer are the words of the *angelus interpres* at Rev 22:6 (cf. 21:5) which, like the formulas at 1 Tim 3:1a and Titus 3:8, conclude John's recording of his visions:

> These words are faithful *(hoi logoi pistoi)* and true.

There are indications in the Pastorals also that the phrase may be associated with the teaching of prophets.[20] The cited tradition at I Tim 4:1–5 (see below), which is introduced with the formula for prophecy, "the Spirit says," is concluded by Paul's admonition to Timothy:

> If you place these things *(tauta)* before the brothers
> You will be a good servant of Jesus Christ
> Nourished on the words of faith *(tois logois tēs pisteōs)* . . .
> And of the good teaching which you have followed
>
> 1 Tim 4:6

The faithful saying in 2 Tim 2:11–13 is concluded (2:14) in a similar manner. More broadly, the summarized tradition[21] on the qualifications of the elder (= bishop) at Titus 1:6–9 includes the requirement that he must "hold to the faithful Word *[pistou logou]* as taught in order that he also may be able by sound teaching to exhort and to convict those who speak against it."[21]

The faithful sayings, including the formulas, total 188 words[22] in the

---

[18] For example, Josephus, *Ant.* 16.100; 19.132 (= 16.4.2; 19.1.16).

[19] For example, Dio Chrysostom, *Discourses* 45, 3. Further, see J. Wettstein, *Novum Testamentum Graecum* (2 vols.; Graz: Akademische, 1962 [1752]) 2.319.

[20] Cf. also Sir 46:15 AC: *en rhēmasin autou pistos = bdbrw b'mn* (re Samuel); 48:22 (re Isaiah).

[21] Cf., on Tit 1:7–9, Dibelius-Conzelmann (note 1), 132 (GT: 99f.). The "faithful Word" formula governed teaching that was given and received as prophetic proclamation and, on the analogy of Sirach's (46:15; 48:22) application of it to the prophetic word of Samuel and Isaiah, it had a "word of God" status in the Pauline (and Johannine) communities (cf. 1 Thess 2:13). The "word" was not the saying as such but the word of God embodied and expressed in it and it could, therefore, be imposed on those with teaching ministries in the community as well as on their hearers. To make this clear, I have capitalized it.

[22] In the word-count from Nestle-Aland (note 15) I include the words that may be a reworking or elaboration of the received pericope but omit those (e.g., 1 Tim 1:15c; 2:12) that appear to be the author's parenthetical insertions, perhaps into

following 16 verses: 1 Tim 1:15; 2:11–3:1a;[23] 4:9f.;[24] 2 Tim 2:11ff.; Tit 3:3–8a.[25] Topically, they focus on soteriological themes and usually take the form of confessional statements.[26] Both their themes and vocabulary are generally Pauline with only 13 words (seven of them in Tit 3:3–5) that do not occur in the Pauline corpus outside the Pastorals. The formula and a few idioms also do not appear elsewhere in Paul although the phrase in 1 Cor 10:13 is close: *pistos ho theos*.[27] As a formula, "faithful is the Word," apparently had its origin in apocalyptic prophets of the Essene-Qumran community (1Q27 1:8), was employed similarly by prophets of the Johannine circle (Rev 22:6), and probably would have come within the purview of Paul and his co-workers either during Paul's Caesarean or his first Roman imprisonment. Its absence from the other ten letters of the Pauline corpus argues against an earlier usage, but it would be quite at home in Caesarea and Rome since both had a teaching cadre from the mission based on Jerusalem,[28] a church that itself had contact with and converts from the Qumran community.[29]

---

the amanuensis' final draft. In the tabulation of words peculiar to the Pastorals I use, with a few variations, P. N. Harrison, *The Problem of the Pastoral Epistles* (Oxford: Oxford University, 1921) 185–200 (Appendix IV) and R. Morgenthaler, *Statistik des neutestamentlichen Wortschatzes* (Zürich: Gotthelf, 1958).

[23] See above, note 16. Cf. E. E. Ellis, "The Silenced Wives of Corinth (1 Cor 14:34–5)," *New Testament Textual Criticism* (ed. E. J. Epp; Oxford: Clarendon, 1981) 214ff.

[24] See above, note 15.

[25] So, Dibelius-Conzelmann (note 1), 28 (GT: 24). The faithful saying may include only Tit 3:4–8a, but against this is the shift to the first person plural at 3:3 and the necessity of 3:3 as the counterpoint to 3:4–7. The counterpoint pattern is typically Pauline (cf. Rom 3:23f.; 16:17f., 23; 7:23ff.; 11:30f.; Eph 2:3f., 11ff.; Col 1:21f.; 1 Tim 1:13f.), but it is also found elsewhere (2 *Clem.* 1:6ff.).

[26] 1 Tim. 2:11–3:1a is an exception, but it may include a soteriological aspect, depending on the interpretation of 2:15.

[27] Cf. also 1 Cor 1:9; 2 Cor 1:18; 1 Thess 5:24; 2 Thess 3:3. Expressions not found in the other ten Pauline letters include 'our Savior God' (Tit 3:4; cf. 1 Tim 4:10) and "Christ came" (1 Tim 1:15; contrast Rom 8:3; Gal 4:4).

[28] Re Caesarea: Acts 6:5; 8:40; 11:1–18; 21:8f. (Philip). Re Rome: The evidence is less direct but may be inferred from the presence of ritually strict "Hebraist" believers (Rom 14:1–13), including opponents of a "judaizing" type (16:17f; cf. Ellis, note 11, 102–109, 116–128). Cf. also Acts 2:10; Rom 16:13 with Mark 15:21; F. F. Bruce, *New Testament History* (Garden City, NY: Doubleday, 1972) 395. Further, see F. J. A. Hort, *Prolegomena to St. Paul's Epistles to the Romans and the Ephesians* (London: Macmillan, 1895), 7–18; L. W. Barnard, *Studies in Church History and Patristics* (Thessaloniki: Patriarchal Institute, 1978), 150–154. The fictional story in the (third-century?) Clementine literature (*Recognitions* 1, 9; cf. *Homilies* 1, 7) that Barnabas brought Christianity to Rome has no evident historical basis.

[29] Cf. Acts 4:32; 6:1, 7; M. Black, *The Scrolls and Christian Origins* (London: Nelson, 1961) 75–88; R. Riesner, "Essener und Urkirche in Jerusalem," *Bibel und*

Judging from the themes and concept-words, Paul is the most likely candidate as the formulator of the "faithful Word" sayings with the exception of 1 Tim 2:11–3:1a and possibly Titus 3:3–8. Titus 3 includes an implicit midrash on Joel 2:28f. (= 3:1f.), understood as fulfilled at Pentecost, and 1 Tim 2:11–3:1a is based on or a variation of a tradition which appears in 1 Cor 14:34f. and, as that passage shows (14:33b), is common to Pauline and other circles.

III

A second formula that sometimes[30] appears to introduce cited material is "knowing (this) that" or "know this that." The first, participial, phrase appears elsewhere as a formula introducing a paraphrastic quotation of an Old Testament text (Acts 2:30), a summary of a traditional piece (Rom 6:6)[31] and perhaps a citation of a hymn-like fragment (Rom 6:9f.);[32] the same formulaic usage may also be present at Jas 1:3, 2 Pet 1:20; 3:3 and at 2 Cor 1:7, which like Rom 6:8 has similarities with the faithful saying at 2 Tim 2:11f.[33] It is clearest at Acts 2:30 and at Eph 5:5 where it introduces a cited judgment on certain vices:[34]

> For certain knowing this *[touto ginōskontes hoti]*, "No fornicator or an impure or a covetous person (who is an idolator) has any inheritance in the kingdom of God."

In the Pastorals the participial formula *(eidōs touto hoti)* appears at I Tim 1:9 where it introduces a midrashic rendering of the fifth through the

---

Kirche 40 (1985) 64–76. Interestingly, the idiom, "God our (my) Savior," appears elsewhere in early Christian writings only at Luke 1:47 and Jude 25, passages which have their origin in Jerusalem traditions (cf. E. E. Ellis, *The Gospel of Luke* [Grand Rapids: Eerdmans, 4 1983] 29, 67; *idem* [note 11], 226–236).

[30] Of course, these phrases are also found without any apparent formulaic significance: 2 Cor 4:14; Gal 2:16; Col 3:24; 1 Thess 1:4f. *(eidotes hoti)*; 2 Tim 2:23; Titus 3:11, Phlm 21 *(eidōs hoti)*. At Jas 1:3; 2 Pet 1:20; 3:3 they may possibly be formulas, introducing cited traditions. In Gal 3:7 *ginōskete hoti* introduces the interpretation of a cited text.

[31] Cf. E. Käsemann, *Romans* (Grand Rapids: Erdmans, 1980) 169 (GT: 161): "Paul is interpreting in his own mode of expression *(Ausdrucksweise)* the tradition used by him." Polycarp *(Phil.* 4:1) cites 1 Tim 6:7 almost verbatim, using the formula, *eidotes oun hoti*.

[32] If the words, *christos* and *ephapax* in Rom 6:9f. are editorial, the rest is conformable to a distinct and balanced rhythm.

[33] Both Rom 6:8 and 2 Cor 1:7 have the same suffering/redemption pattern as 2 Tim 2:11f.

[34] The cited tradition, known to the recipients, reinforces and illustrates the gravity of Paul's admonition in Eph 5:3. The same kind of traditioned material is introduced at 1 Cor 6:9f. with the formula, "Do you not know that" *(ouk oidate hoti)*.

ninth commandments of the Decalogue, a pericope (1:9–10a) of 23 words including eight that do not appear in the Pauline corpus outside the Pastorals.[35]

The imperatival phrase at 2 Tim 3:1, "know this that" *(touto ginōske hoti)*, is unusual but nonetheless has all the marks of an introductory formula for a cited tradition.[36] The substance of the tradition appears to be an apostolic prophecy, which is cited as such in Jude 18 *(elegon hoti)* and which is also quoted at 2 Pet 3:3 *(touto ginōskontes hoti)*. The form of the prophecy cited in 2 Tim 3:1–5b has been elaborated to incorporate an extensive vice list, and its conclusion is signaled by the shift to an imperative at 3:5c. Thus understood, it is a passage of 40 words, including 18 words not found in the Pauline corpus outside the Pastorals and seven words found nowhere else in the New Testament. Together the traditions introduced by this formula include 63 words.

IV

A third formula, "these things *[tauta]* teach," ". . . command," ". . . exhort," ". . . guard," ". . . place," occurs at the conclusion of a number of preformed pieces. The formulaic usage of this kind of imperative is clearest at 1 Tim 4:6, 1 Tim 4:11 and 2 Tim 2:14, where the phrase stands at the conclusion of pericopes that have all the earmarks of traditioned material. 1 Tim 4:11 and 2 Tim 2:14 follow faithful sayings which, as we have seen above, are cited traditions.[37] 1 Tim 4:6 concludes an (elaborated) oracle (4:1–5) introduced by the formula, "the Spirit says," a phrase occasionally used elsewhere for the citation of a prophecy or a prophetic writing.[38]

There is also a high probability that the phrase at 1 Tim 6:2 and at Titus 2:15 looks back to previously cited traditions which are, however, less explicitly quoted and therefore less easy to identify. At 1 Tim 6:2 it may refer only to the immediately preceeding household rule (6:1–2), which was a traditioned motif in the Pauline mission-circle[39] or, more

---

[35] In other Pauline letters the act rather than the offender is often named (e.g., *anomia/anomos*) or a different synonym is preferred (e.g., *ataktos/anypotaktos*). For a comparison of terms in vice lists cf. S. Wibbing, *Die Tugend- und Lasterkataloge im Neuen Testament* (Berlin: Töpelmann, 1959) 87f.

[36] A similar imperative, "be not unaware of this that" *(touto mē Lanthanetō hoti)*, introduces a (preformed) midrash at 2 Pet 3:8–13.

[37] The command is reiterated in 1 Tim 4:15f., "Consider these things and devote yourself to them," where the things are identified with "teaching" which one is to "abide in" *(eipmenein)*.

[38] E.g. 2 Sam 23:2; Acts 21:11; Heb 3:7; Rev 14:13; 22:17; *1 Clem.* 13:1; Justin, *I Apol.* 39:1; cf. Acts 20:23; 28:25; Rev 2:7 *et passim*; *1 Clem.* 16:2f. A similar prophecy is cited in Jude 17f. as a prediction of the apostles of Christ. Cf. 2 Pet 3:2ff.

[39] Eph 5:21–6:9; Col 3:18–4:1. Cf. Cannon (note 14), 95–131, and the literature cited.

E. Earle Ellis

244

likely, to additional congregational regulations in 1 Timothy 5 concerning widows and elders[40] and, perhaps, to earlier items as well.[41]

At Titus 2:15 the phrase, "these things speak," and the similar imperative at 2:1 appear to bracket the regulations given in 2:2–14 that, like traditioned materials elsewhere, are identified as "the sound teaching" (*tē hygiainousē didaskalia*)[42] and that consist of (summarized) household and congregational regulations (2:2–10) and a confessional hymn (2:11–14). Admittedly, in 1 Tim 6:2 and Titus 2:15 the phrase refers not to explicit quotations but to reworked and summarized traditional materials which may, nonetheless, be counted among the traditions transmitted by the Pastoral epistles.

A third type of *tauta* phrase, with an indicative rather than an imperative, appears at 1 Tim 3:14 and, like Titus 2, it relates to the preceeding congregational regulations (1 Tim 2:1f., 8–15; 3:1b–13), as the following subordinate clause makes clear:

> These things I write . . . in order that you might know how people ought to behave themselves in God's household.[43]

Among these regulations the citation of preformed material seems fairly clear in the case of the faithful saying (1 Tim 2: 11–3:1a), discussed above, and in the qualifications for bishops and ministers (3:1b–13).[44]

1 Tim 3:1b–13 is not introduced by a customary formula of citation, but the conditional sentence at 3:1b may serve in that capacity.[45] And the passage has other features indicating that it is quoted material even if, like some of Paul's Old Testament citations, it is reworked and modified: (1) Like cited traditions elsewhere, the passage is concluded by and forms the immediate referent of the *tauta* formula. (2) Standing between the faithful saying (2:11–3:1a) and the *tauta* phrase (3:14), it is independent of its context, a feature that is to be interpreted as a sign not of its

[40] 1 Tim 5:3, 5f., 9f., 17–20. The *tauta* at 1 Tim 5:7; 5:21; 6:11 also may be formulaic.
[41] A more general reference is indicated by the close connection between the *tauta* (1 Tim 6:2) and the "sound words" and "teachings conforming to godliness" (6:3). Kelly (note 2, 133) thinks that *tauta* "probably cover all the subjects treated and the instructions given in the letter."
[42] Titus 2:1; cf. 1:9 (where 'sound teaching' is identified or closely associated with the "faithful Word"); 1 Tim 1:10; 6:2f.; 2 Tim 1:13f.; 4:3. See note 41; cf. Kelly (note 2), 247; J. H. Bernard, *The Pastoral Epistles* (Grand Rapids: Baker, 1980 [1899]) 92, 174.
[43] Cf. Bernard (note 42), 60f.
[44] On *diakonos* in Pauline usage Cf. Ellis (note 11), 7–13. The two types of ministries are coupled in Phil 1:1 as well as in the Apostolic Fathers, e.g., in *Did.* 15:1; *1 Clem.* 42:4 and, somewhat differently, in Ign. *Magn.* 2:1; 6:1; 13:1; *Trall.* 3:1; 7:2; *Phld.*, Incipit; 4:1; 7:1; *Smyrn.* 8:1 *et passim*.
[45] A similar kind of conditional sentence stands before a traditioned piece at 1 Tim 1:8 and probably at 1 Tim 5:4.

later interpolation (Harnack) but of its pre-existing traditional character.[46] (3) The close affinities-with-variations of this passage with Tit 1:6–9 precludes a direct dependence and is best explained "if we assume that in both passages Paul is borrowing from a conventional list" (Kelly).[47] Since Titus 1:7–9 is also an independent piece with rough connections to its context, it too should be regarded as preformed material.[48]

The key to the periodic *tauta* formulas in the Pastoral epistles seems to be found at 1 Tim 1:18, 6:2 and 6:20.[49] At 1 Tim 1:18 Paul's instruction *(paraggelia)* basically means the whole letter, and his entrusting or depositing *(paratithesthai)* it with Timothy identifies its content as transmitted tradition. This identification is confirmed by some of the verbs found in passages governed by the *tauta* formula, especially *didaskein* ("teach"), *(hypo) mimnēskein* ("remember"), *paratithesthai* ("entrust") and *phylassein* ("guard"), terms which were of long usage in Judaism for the preservation, transmission and interpretation of religious tradition.[50] It is perhaps most pointed in 1 Tim 6:20, "Guard the entrusted deposit" *(tēn parathēkēn phylaxon)*, which primarily refers to traditions transmitted in the letter.[51] The same conception governs 2 Timothy, as may be seen in 2 Tim 1:13f.; 2:2, although the *tauta* (2:2) here seems to refer to the content of a chain of oral tradition similar to that implied in 1 Cor 4:17. While it is not so comprehensively stated in Titus, it may be inferred from Titus 2:1, 15; 3:8.

Summing up, the preformed traditions governed by (or in Tit 1:7–9 associated with) the *tauta* formula total some 631 words in the following 46 verses: 1 Tim 3:1b–13; 4:1–5, 9f.; 5:5f., 9f., 17–20; 6:1–2; 2 Tim 2:11–13; Titus 1:7–9;[52] 2:2–14. If one eliminates the two faithful sayings (1 Tim

---

[46] A. Harnack (*Geschichte der altchristlichen Literatur bis Eusebius* [2 parts in 4 vols.; Leipzig: Zentralantiquariat, 1958 (1893–1904)], 2 [*Chronologie*] 1.482) recognized 1 Tim 3:1–13, Titus 1:7–9, and related pieces in 1 Timothy 5 to be independent of their context and considered them to be later interpolations taken from a "book of church order" *(Kirchenordnung)*. Cf. also A. Harnack, *The Constitution and Law of the Church* (London: Williams & Norgate, 1910) 68; Dibelius-Conzelmann (note 1), 56 (GT: 46).

[47] Kelly (note 2), 231. For a convenient comparison of the terms in 1 Tim 3:1–7 and Titus 1:7–9 cf. Dibelius-Conzelmann (note 1), 133 (GT: 100).

[48] So, Harnack, *Geschichte* (note 46).

[49] Cf. Dibelius-Conzelmann (note 1), 32 (GT: 27); See above, note 41.

[50] See *TDNT* 2.137, 145–148, cf. 163f. (Rengstorf); 4.677f. (Michel); 8.163f. (Maurer);

[51] A few manuscripts have *parakatathēkē* at 1 Tim 6:20. Cf. 1 Tim 5:21. For a significant parallel illustrating the Jewish background of the terminology and conception cf. Philo, *Quod det. pot.* 65–68 = 19 *(phylakē, parakatathēkē)*. For Clement (*Stromateis* 6.15) "the entrusted deposit [*parathēkē*] . . . is the understanding and discipline of sacred tradition [*paradoseōs*]."

[52] Titus 1:7–9 is not governed by a formulaic *tauta* but is included here because of its relationship to 1 Tim 3:1b–13; probably Titus 1:6 is from the same tradition.

4:9–10; 2 Tim 2:11–13), which have been tabulated above, these traditions total 579 words, including 94 words not found in the Pauline corpus
outside the Pastorals.

V

In addition to the pericopes discussed above, a number of other
miscellaneous passages are also most likely preformed material. Fore-
most among them are hymnic-type confessions (1 Tim 2:5f.; 3:16; 2 Tim
1:9f.),[53] a doxology (1 Tim 1:17), a citation of a pagan prophet (Titus
1:12b), admonitory (1 Tim 6:7f., 10a)[54] and other sayings (2 Tim 1:7).[55]

1 Tim 6:11–20 presents something of a puzzle. It bears some marks of
an inserted piece[56] but is not itself a unity, at least at first impression,
apparently consisting of a commissioning charge (6:11–14)[57] concluded
by a doxology (6:15f.). Perhaps a combined tradition, a "charge +

---

[53] On the problem with this classification see E. Norden, *Die antike Kunstprosa* (2
vols., Stuttgart: Teubner, 1958 [²1909]) 2.852ff.

[54] The *tauta* at 1 Tim 6:11 may be formulaic, and the substance of 1 Tim 6:7f., 10a is
found elsewhere as maxims. On 1 Tim 6:7f. cf. Eccl 5:15; Philo, *spec. leg.* I, 294f.:
". . . you who brought *eisēnochota*) nothing into the world. . . ." *Pace* Dibelius-
Conzelmann (note 1, 85; GT: 65f.) Polycarp in *Phil.* 4:1 cites I Tim 6:7f. and not a
common tradition since an illusion to 1 Tim 6:10 appears in the same verse. But it
remains probable that 1 Tim 6:7f., 10 are quotations of ethical maxims introduced
by *gar* (cf. Rom 10:13; 13:9; 1 Cor 2:16; 10:26; 15:27). Cf. Bernard (note 2), 95f.;
Simpson, E. K. *The Pastoral Epistles* (London: Tyndale, 1954) 85f.

[55] Note the introductory formula *gar* and the shift to the aorist tense and the first-
person plural. The verse may be a variant form of the thought expressed in Rom
8:15, as Dibelius-Conzelmann (note 7, 98; GT: 73) think, but it cannot for that
reason be regarded as a post-Pauline imitation.

[56] (1) The phrase *su de* (1 Tim 6:11) introduces cited traditions at Titus 2:1 (see
above). (2) The designation, "man of God," contrasts with the personal address,
"Timothy" (6:20), and suggests a more general reference. (3) 1 Tim 6:11–16
interrupts an admonition concerning the danger of riches (6:6–10) which is picked
up again at 6:17.

[57] So, J. Jeremias (note 2), 37; O. Michel in *TDNT* 5.216; E. Käsemann, "Das
Formular einer neutestamentlichen Ordinationsparänese," *Neutestamentlichen
Studien* (ed. W. Eltester; Berlin: Töpelmann, 1954) 261–268. Cf. Acts 13:1–3; 20:
18–35; 1 Tim 1:18; 4:14. Favoring a commissioning charge (rather than an admonition at baptism or before arrest and/or martyrdom) is the address, "man of God," a
name for the Old Testament prophet (e.g., Deut 33:1; 1 Sam 9:6f.; 1 Kgs 12:22;
17:18; Philo, *de mut.* 24ff. = 3; *de gig.* 61 = 13 end; 2 Pet 1:21 A) and, in the
Pastorals, for the pneumatic or Christian prophet. In 2 Tim 3:17 the "man of God"
is described as (ideally) *artios* = *teleios* (cf. J. H. Moulton and G. Milligan, *The
Vocabulary of the Greek Testament* [Grand Rapids: Eerdmans, 1950] 80), a term
that Paul associates with the pneumatic or Christian prophet (1 Cor 2:6–16; 3:1;
14:37; cf. Ellis, note 11, 45–62). Although the phrase, "man of God," could be

doxology," has been inserted, but more likely a traditioned commission-form is followed by a traditional doxology that concludes the amanuensis' drafted form of the letter and to which Paul added, as was his custom, a closing word in his own hand (6:17–20).[58] In either case 1 Tim 6:11–16 seems to be (reworked) traditional material consisting of 107 words, including eight words not found in the Pauline corpus outside the Pastorals.

Two other passages are less clear but have, I think, a fair probability of being preformed pieces, the midrash at 2 Tim 2:19–21 and a traditional maxim at Titus 1:15a. These verses together with the preceeding miscellaneous passages total 337 words, including 23 not found in the Pauline corpus outside the Pastorals.

The passages in the Pastoral epistles which have been examined above and found to be preformed traditions are as follows:

I Timothy	Titus	2 Timothy
1:9–10a	1:7–9	1:7
1:15	1:12b	1:9f.
2:5f.	1:15a	2:11–13
2:11–3:1a	2:2–14	2:19–21
3:1b–13	3:3–8a	3:1–5
3:16		
4:1–5		
4:9f.		
5:5f., 9f., 17–20		
6:1f.		
6:7f., 10a		
6:11–16		

The passages identified by certain formulas (about 70%: 833 words with 134 Pauline hapaxes) together with the miscellaneous passages (about 30%: 337 words with 23 Pauline hapaxes) total 1170 words, including 157 not found in the Pauline letters outside the Pastorals. These preformed traditions make up about 41% of 1 Timothy (659 words), 16% of 1 Timothy (202 words) and 46% of Titus (309 words), and contain about 35% of the words in the Pastorals, including repetitions, not found in

---

used more broadly (*Ep. Arist.* 140; cf. *Sentences of Sextus* 2f.; J. Jeremias in *TDNT* 1.364f.), in the Pastorals it very likely refers to a pneumatic and his prophetic teaching-task in the community. Käsemann (p. 268) is, therefore, quite justified in understanding "man of God" as a variation of *pneumatikos*.

[58] Cf. Jeremias (note 2), 37; Rom 16:25ff.; 1 Cor 16:21ff.; 2 Cor 13:11–14; Gal 6:11–18; Eph 6:21–24; Phil 4:21ff.; Col 4:18; 1 Thess 5:25–28; 2 Thess 3:17f.; 2 Tim 4:19–22; ? Titus 3:12–15.

other Pauline letters.[59] A more intensive study could, I think, identify a number of other passages that consist of or rest upon preformed material.

Preformed traditions in the Pastorals have important implications both for the question of their authenticity and for the related question of their process of composition vis-a-vis that of other Pauline letters.[60]

VII

The authorship of the Pastoral epistles has now been in dispute for almost two centuries[61] and two schools of thought, which we may for convenience label the Baur-Holtzmann[62] and the Lightfoot-Roller traditions,[63] have posed the principal alternatives. One strength of the Baur-Holtzmann pseudepigraphal tradition was thought to be the post-Pauline developments in early Christianity that were present in the Pastorals. However, on examination these "developments" are found only in historical reconstructions in which *inter alia* the post-Pauline origin of the Pastorals was assumed to have been established. Thus, in a circular kind of reasoning, the assumption was integral to the reconstruction which was then used to give historical support to the assumption.

In the present century Baur-Holtzmann has drawn its persuasive power primarily from another factor, the patent differences between the Pastorals and other Pauline literature in vocabulary, idiom and theological expression. Even after other arguments lost much of their force,[64]

---

[59] Harrison (note 22, 137) counts 437 words, including repetitions, "found in the Pastorals, but not in the ten Paulines."

[60] While it cannot be detailed here, preformed traditions, reworked or inserted *en bloc*, make up a considerable portion of most of Paul's letters. In 1 Corinthians, for example, they constitute in my judgment at least 15% of the letter: 1 Cor 2:6–16; 3:16; 6:15, 19; 7:10f.; 8:6; 9:14; 10:1–13, 16; 11: 3–16, 23; 12:4–11; 13:1–13; 14:34f.; 15:3–7, 51. In this respect the Pastorals, although they represent a more intensive utilization of traditional materials, are quite Pauline in their method of composition. Cf. E. E. Ellis, "Traditions in I Corinthians," *NTS* 32 (1986) 481–502.

[61] E. Evanson, *The Dissonance of the Four Generally Received Evangelists* (Ipswich UK: George Jermyn, 1792) 267ff. (re Titus); F. D. E. Schleiermacher, "Über den sogenannten ersten Brief des Paulus an den Timotheos," *Sämtliche Werke* (32 vols.; Berlin: G. Reimer, 1835–1862) 1.2 (1836), 221ff., cited in W. G. Kümmel, *The New Testament: The History of the Investigations of Its problems* (Nashville: Abingdon, 1972) 84 (GT: 100).

[62] F. C. Baur, *Die sogenannten Pastoralbriefe* (Tübingen: J. G. Gotta'schen, 1835); H. J. Holtzmann, *Die Pastoralbriefe* (Leipzig: Wilhelm Engelmann, 1880), which provides the definitive case for the pseudepigraphal theory.

[63] J. B. Lightfoot, "The Date of the Pastoral Epistles" (1862, 1865), *Biblical Essays* (London: Macmillan, 1893) 399–418; O. Roller, *Das Formular der paulinischen Briefe* (Stuttgart: Kohlhammer, 1933) 92–99 *et passim*.

[64] For a brief summary of Holtzmann's five points against authenticity and subse-

these peculiarities have continued in the minds of many to be a decisive objection to Pauline authorship. Even when the Pastorals express the same thought as another Pauline letter, they often use different terminology[65] and they lack many word-groups that are common to the other letters.[66] On the other hand a primary weakness of the Baur-Holtzmann tradition, which was early noticed by A. Harnack,[67] was the equally clear and deeply embedded Pauline characteristics of the letters.[68] Harnack concluded that "Pauline letters (or letter-fragments?) from AD 59–64 underlie the Pastoral letters." They were reworked about the turn of the second century and a number of pericopes interpolated at a still later date.[69]

The Lightfoot-Roller tradition, alternatively, made its case for authenticity on the basis of the letters' own claim to be from Paul, their many Pauline characteristics and their early and virtually undisputed attestation in a church that, in its more astute circles, was alert and well practiced in spotting imitations of apostolic writings.[70] It attributed their peculiarities of style, idiom, and theme to their composition in the post-Acts 28 period of Paul's mission (c. AD 63–68) and, in the case of Roller,

---

quent responses to them cf. E. E. Ellis, *Paul and His Recent Interpreters* (Grand Rapids: Eerdmans, [5]1979) 49–57.

[65] E.g., *parousia/epiphaneia*. More broadly, see Dibelius' discussion of "the soteriological terminology of Titus 2:11–14 and 3:4–7" in Dibelius-Conzelmann (note 1), 4, 143–146. (GT: 3, 108ff.).

[66] E.g., *apokalyptein, energein, kaukasthai, perisseuein hypakouein, phronein*.

[67] Harnack, *Geschichte* (note 46), 2.1.480–485. Cf. also C. H. Dodd, *According to the Scriptures* (London: Nisbet, 1953) 30: "even if certain of the writings contained in [the Pauline corpus] may not be from the hand of the apostle, they all depend largely on him."

[68] Harnack, *Geschichte* (note 46), 2.1.484f. His work was cited by P. N. Harrison (note 22, x, 184) and may have sparked that scholar's thoroughly worked out "fragment hypothesis." For other early advocates of a fragment hypothesis cf. Bernard (note 42, xliv), who also notes its fatal weakness: "[It] has not a shred of external evidence in its favor."

[69] Chiefly on church order. In this respect Harnack was apparently influenced by (even while he criticized) R. Sohm's mistaken scheme of development. But he later modified his views: A. Harnack, "*Kopos*," ZNW 27 (1928) 1–10; cf. Ellis (note 11), 7n. Cf. Harnack, *Constitution* (note 46), 9.66ff., 175–204, 204–258.

[70] Tertullian (*Adv. Marcion* 5.21) mentions the heretic Marcion's exclusion of the Pastorals from his canon but may hint that the alleged reason was that they were Paul's letters to individuals rather than to churches. Jerome (*Preface to his Commentary on Titus*) gives no reasons for the rejection of 1 and 2 Timothy by Tatian and of Titus by Marcion and Basilides (J. P. Migne, *Patrologiae Cursus Completus: Series Latina* [Vol. 26; Paris: Garnier, 1884] 589f.). Whether the lost ending of the Chester Beatty codex (**p46**) contained the Pastorals, and if not why not, is an unanswerable question, as Jeremias (note 2, 3f.) pointed out. Cf. also Guthrie (note 2), 14.

to the greater influence of a different amanuensis—plausibly suggested to
be Luke[71]—on their style and idiom.[72]

   The role of the amanuensis, together with other factors, seems to
answer adequately the literary-critical objections to Pauline authorship.[73]
While it has been illuminated by the magisterial work of Otto Roller, by
A. N. Sherwin-White's commentary on *The Letters of Pliny* and, for
nonepistolary literature, by H. St. J. Thackeray's study of Josephus,[74] it
remains nevertheless a subject on which much work still needs to be
done. If the arguments of the present paper are correct, however, the
role of the amanuensis may be less important than the effect of non-
Pauline preformed traditions on the literary expression and formation of
the letters. As was mentioned above,[75] Paul's use of traditions from his
and other apostolic circles was characteristic of his major letters and is to
be counted as a Pauline trait in the Pastorals even though it occurs there
in much greater abundance.

   The assumption of nineteenth-century scholarship, apparently without exception, was that Paul either penned his own letters or dictated
them verbatim. It provided the literary grounds for Baur-Holtzmann,
using certain letters as a touchstone, to test and reject the Pauline
authorship of the Pastorals and other letters by such internal criteria as
style, idiom and theological expression. In the light of the influence of
the amanuensis and of non-Pauline traditions, however, this assumption
can now be seen to have been mistaken. Consequently, internal criteria

---

[71] See 2 Tim 4:11. Cf. A. Strobel, "Schreiben des Lukas? Zum sprachlichen Problem
   der Pastoralbriefe," *NTS* 15 (1968–69) 191–210; C. F. D. Moule, "The Problem of
   the Pastoral Epistles: A Reappraisal," *BJRL* 47 (1964–65) 430–452, 434: . . .
   "Luke wrote all three Pastoral epistles. But he wrote them during Paul's lifetime,
   at Paul's behest, and, in part (but only in part), at Paul's dictation." Somewhat
   differently: S. G. Wilson, *Luke and the Pastoral Epistles* (London: S. P. C. K.,
   1979); J. D. Quinn, "The Last Volume of Luke," *Perspectives on Luke-Acts* (ed.
   C. H. Talbert; Danville, VA: Association of Baptist Professors of Religion, 1978)
   62–65.
[72] Roller (note 63), 148, who was anticipated in this respect by Bernard (note 42), xli,
   xlv.
[73] So my teacher, J. Jeremias, long ago presuaded me. Cf. Ellis (note 64), 54f., and
   R.N. Longenecker, "Ancient Amanuenses and the Pauline Epistles," *New Dimensions in New Testament Study* (Grand Rapids: Zondervan, 1974) 281–297, for
   other factors affecting statistical analysis. The logarithmic approach of K. Grayson
   and G. Herdan ("The Authorship of the Pastorals," *NTS* 6 [1959–60] 1–15), if I
   follow it correctly, also does not escape the limitations of other forms of literary
   statistical analysis.
[74] Roller (note 63); A.N. Sherwin-White, *The Letters of Pliny* (Oxford: Clarendon,
   1966) 536–546; H. St. J. Thackeray, *Josephus the Man and the Historian* (New
   York: Jewish Institute of Religion, 1929) 100–124; *idem.*, *Josephus* (*LCL;* 9 vols.,
   London: Heinemann, 1926–1965) 1.15; 2.13–19; 4.14–17.
[75] See above, note 60.

can no longer be used in any precise manner to determine the authorship of letters ascribed to Paul since in his letters, as in other ancient literature, authorship itself was a more complex phenomenon than scholars of the nineteenth and early twentieth century suspected. Ironically, it is literary criticism that now makes apparent the fallacy of the viewpoint that made its case above all on literary criticism. The Baur-Holtzmann tradition, like others with strong vested interests, will probably continue, but it is difficult to see on what basis it will rest, apart from the clouds of scholarly imagination. In any case, if the arguments above are credible, the critical enterprise lies in a different direction.

VIII

The release of Paul from his first Roman imprisonment is, as Harnack put it, "a certain fact of history" (gesicherte Tatsache)[76] and his journey to Spain historically probable.[77] The most important, and to my mind decisive, evidence is that of Clement of Rome, a younger contemporary of Paul, who within a few years (AD 70) or at most three decades (c. AD 95) of the Apostle's death wrote that Paul became "a preacher both in the East and in the West" and reached "the extreme limits of the West" (to terma tēs duseōs).[78] In roughly contemporary Roman writings "the West" geographically seems to refer mostly to Spain and sometimes to Gaul or Britain but never, as far as I am aware, to Rome.[79] Nor can to terma tēs duseōs be weakened to mean Rome as Paul's "western goal" since the

[76] Harnack, Geschichte (note 46), 2.1.240n. He gives three grounds: (1) 1 Clem. 5:6f., (2) the time gap between the end of Acts and the year of Paul's death and (3) the impossibility of fitting the undeniably genuine elements in the Pastorals into a prior period of Paul's ministry.

[77] A Harnack, The Mission and Expansion of Christianity in the First Three Centuries (2 vols.; New York: Putnam, ²1908) 2.94n.; J. Lebreton and J. Zeiller, A History of the Early Church (4 vols.; New York: Collier, 1962) 1.283f.; Lightfoot (note 79); T. Zahn, Introduction to the New Testament (3 vols.; Grand Rapids: Kregel, 1963 [1909]) 2.60–67; cf. J. Weiss, The History of Primitive Christianity (2 vols.; New York: Wilson-Erikson, 1937) 1.390ff. Otherwise: A. Schlatter, The Church in the New Testament (London: S.P.C.K., 1955 [1936]) 220, 236 (GT: 259, 279f.).

[78] 1 Clem. 5:6f. cf. Acts of Peter (Vercelli) 1:1, 3; Muratorian Canon. For the earlier and in my (tentative) judgment more probable dating of 1 Clement cf. the Bampton Lectures of G. Edmundson, The Church in Rome in the First Century (London: Longmans, Green, 1913) 188–205; J. A. T. Robinson, Redating the New Testament (London: SCM; Philadelphia: Westminster, 1976) 313–334. Clement's listing of Paul's feats of ministry does not suggest that Paul's preaching in "the West" or his going to "the extreme limits of the West" immediately preceded his martyrdom.

[79] Josephus (Against Apion 1.67), for example, speaks in this way. Cf. also Tacitus, Histories 4.3; Strabo, Geography 1.1.8; 1.2.1; 1.4.6; 2.1.1; 2.4.4; 3.1.2; otherwise:

clearly makes Spain his western goal.[80] A post-Acts 28 ministry of Paul provides the most probable and perhaps the only convincing historical occasion for his authoring of the Pastorals,[81] and it also enables the historian to explain best the internal peculiarities of these letters, that is, their different terminology, their variation of scene and theme and their evidence for a different and more influential amanuensis.

Paul pursued his ministry from a number of bases of operation—Antioch, Ephesus, (Caesarea) and Rome. At Rome, and perhaps already at Caesarea, he apparently found traditions, especially some with a soteriological and church-order idiom and emphasis reminiscent of the Jerusalem church,[82] which he incorporated into his letters to Timothy and Titus. To discover why he did so requires that one consider, with some historical imagination, both the church problems presented in the Pastorals and the probable setting of the post-Acts 28 ministry of Paul.

After his release from imprisonment in Rome (and a visit to the Aegean area?), Paul completed his intended mission to Spain but, receiving grave news about his churches around the Aegean, he soon returned to Greece. Although his churches have multiplied, they have been increasingly buffeted by false teachers, suffered from defections, and some are near a state of collapse.[83] He cannot address a letter to each of the many congregations and send a colleague to explain and apply it as he did earlier.[84] Instead, he sends letters, or better, virtual manuals of traditions and commentary,[85] to co-workers who will in turn convey the

---

2.4.3. Cf. Harnack, *Geschichte* (note 46), 2.1.240n: *to terma tēs duseōs* could not in a Roman writing refer to Rome. Similarly, J. B. Lightfoot, *The Apostolic Fathers* (3 vols. in 5; London: Macmillan, 1890) 1.2.30f. The tendency of some modern writers to identify "the West" with Rome may be due to their reading the texts from a post-Constantinian perspective.

[80] Rom 15:24. Cf. *1 Clem.* 35:5f.; 33:1 with Rom 1:28–32; 6:1; D. Hagner, *The Use of the Old and New Testaments in Clement of Rome* (Leiden: Brill, 1973) 214–220. Greco-Roman writers use very similar expressions for the region around Gades (= Cadiz), Spain (e.g. Philostratus, *Life of Apollonius* 5, 4; Strabo, *Geography* 2.4.3; 2.5.14; 3.1.4; 3.5.5; Diodorus Siculus, *History* 25.10.1; Pliny, *Natural History* 3.1.3; Livy 21.43.13; 23.5.11).

[81] So, *inter alios*, Kelly (note 2), 6–10, 34ff.; Bernard (note 42), xxi–xxxiv; Zahn (note 77), 2.35–38, 49–52, 54–67. Otherwise: B. Reicke, "Chronologie der Pastoralbriefe," *TLZ* 101 (1976) 81–94, who places 1 Timothy and Titus at the end of the Aegean mission and 2 Timothy at Caesarea; similarly, Robinson (note 78), 67–84.

[82] See above, notes 28 and 29.

[83] 1 Tim 1:3–7, 18ff.; 4:1–3; 6:20; 2 Tim 1:15–18; 2:17f.; 3:1–9; 4:3f., 10, 14f.; Titus 1:10–16; 3:9ff. Titus 1:5 refers not to evangelization but to the reorganization of churches that had been ravaged by an opposing mission.

[84] 1 Cor 4:17; 2 Cor 7:6, 12f.; Eph 6:21; Col 4:7f.; Phil 2:25.

[85] W. H. Brownlee (*The Meaning of the Qumrân Scrolls for the Bible* [New York:

Apostle's instructions to the various congregations. By this means Paul can give his personal communications to Timothy and Titus and at the same time provide them with an apostolic authorization for their teachings. Thus understood, the Pastoral letters not only meet a problem of certain churches of the mid-sixties but also provide a paradigm by which Pauline and other apostolic writings became a *vade mecum* for a succession of Christian teachers, even to the present day.

Professor William Brownlee recognized the manual-like characteristics of the Pastoral epistles and, some two decades ago, perceptively called attention to their genre-affinities with Qumran's Manual of Discipline.[86] It is particularly appropriate, then, to dedicate this essay to his memory.

Oxford, 1964] 150) rightly called attention to the genre-affinities of the Pastorals with Qumran's Manual of Discipline.
[86] See above, note 85.

INDEX TO ANCIENT WRITINGS

A. OLD TESTAMENT

B. OLD TESTAMENT APOCRYPHA AND PSEUDEPIGRAPHA

D. QUMRAN

INDEX TO MODERN AUTHORS